Gilligan Unbound

Pop Culture in the Age of Globalization

PAUL A. CANTOR

ROWMAN & LITTLEFIELD PUBLISHERS, INC.
Lanham • Boulder • New York • Oxford

ROWMAN & LITTLEFIELD PUBLISHERS, INC.

Published in the United States of America
by Rowman & Littlefield Publishers, Inc.
A wholly owned subsidary of The Rowman & Littlefield Publishing Group, Inc.
4501 Forbes Boulevard, Suite 200, Lanham, Maryland 20706
www.rowmanlittlefield.com

PO Box 317
Oxford
OX2 9RU, UK

British Library Cataloguing in Publication Information Available

The hardcover edition of this book was cataloged by the Library of Congress as follows:

Cantor, Paul A. (Paul Arthur), 1945–
    Gilligan unbound : pop culture in the age of globalization / Paul A. Cantor.
      p. cm.
    Includes bibliographical references and index.
    Contents: "The courage of the fearless crew": Gilligan's island and the
    Americanization of the globe—Shakespeare in the original Klingon : Star trek and the
    end of history—Simpson Agonistes : atomistic politics, the nuclear family, and the
    globalization of Springfield—Mainstreaming paranoia : The X-files and the
    delegitimation of the nation-state.
    1. Television programs—United States. 2. Television broadcasting—Political
    aspects—United States. 3. Popular culture—United States—History—20th century.
    I. Title.

    PN1992.3.U5 C29 2001
    302.23 '45 '0973—dc21   2001019918

    ISBN 0-7425-0778-5 (cloth : alk. paper) — 0-7425-0779-3 (pbk. : alk. paper)

Printed in the United States of America

 The paper used in this publication meets the minimum requirements of American
National Standard for Information Sciences—Permanence of Paper for Printed Library
Materials, ANSI/NISO Z39.48-1992.

IN MEMORY OF MY DEVOTED VCR, SONY SLV-420

July 20, 1994–December 29, 2000

Without which this book could not have been written

Tragically, within three months of the completion of this manuscript,
the gallant machine passed away while attempting to record
eighteen hours of a *Star Trek* marathon on the Sci-Fi Channel

Contents

Introduction

In the late 1980s, I started giving public lectures on popular culture, dealing with such topics as *Star Trek* and *Gilligan's Island*. I did my best to make sense out of these television shows for my audiences, drawing upon the analytic skills I had developed during years of studying literature. But I have to admit that originally I chose these topics basically for the fun of it—as a relief from my normal academic routine. I never expected that I would eventually write a book on the subject. And yet the way people responded to my work on popular culture gradually convinced me that I was not wasting my time. It was clear from the reaction to my lectures and especially from the question-and-answer sessions afterward that intelligent and well-educated people are genuinely interested in hearing shows such as *The Simpsons* and *The X-Files* analyzed in a serious academic manner. This impression was confirmed when I began publishing versions of the lectures. In a miniature example of the globalization I write about in this book, I received comments, particularly on my *Simpsons* essays, from all around the world (usually via e-mail), and even requests to reprint them in both Australia and the United Kingdom. I was particularly struck by the enthusiastic response I got from college students to my observations about popular culture. When I gave a talk on *The Simpsons* at my own institution, the University of Virginia, I found that the students could hardly wait to join in the discussion. And I was impressed by the seriousness and insightfulness of their comments on the way the show provides an image of the American nuclear family. Above all, I noticed that when they spoke about the show, they could refer to individual episodes in detail and expect their classmates to know what they were talking about. For good or ill, television seems to be providing students today with whatever common culture they possess.

Thus I eventually became persuaded that it would be worth the effort to put together a book out of my studies of popular culture. I was originally planning on just a collection of essays, but as I thought about the project, a pattern began to emerge that seemed to offer a way of integrating the essays into a larger argument.[1] Generally, I was concerned with the social and political content of individual television shows and especially the ways in which they reflect the democratic ideology of America. I had approached *Star Trek*, for example, in light of the debate about the end of history—whether the collapse of the Soviet Union and the West's victory in the Cold War really amount to the worldwide triumph of liberal democracy. As I surveyed my material, I noticed that the shows I was interested in seemed to fall into two categories or even historical phases. The shows from the 1960s, especially *Gilligan's Island* and *Star Trek*, seemed to represent a sort of national era in television, embodying a fundamental faith in American liberal democracy and a willingness to project it as a universal ideal. Each in its own way portrays America as the democratic center of the universe, with its power radiating out to any random point on the planet in *Gilligan's Island* and to all points in the galaxy in *Star Trek*. By contrast, the shows from the 1990s I had been discussing, especially *The Simpsons* and *The X-Files*, seemed to represent a sort of global era in television, portraying in one way or another a decentering of America. They display a certain skepticism and even cynicism about American government and more generally an unwillingness to buy into the traditional ideology of the nation-state. Rather than portraying the Americanization of the globe, the later shows tend to portray the globalization of America. In *The Simpsons* and *The X-Files* the American nation-state has somehow been displaced from the center of its citizens' lives, and they end up concerned with issues that are at once more local and more global.

I decided to see how far I could go organizing my material this way, and indeed as I thought about it, the differences between the television shows from the 1960s I had analyzed and those from the 1990s seemed to reflect broader historical trends, thus confirming my sense that popular culture offers us a window into ideological developments in America. I began to realize that both *Gilligan's Island* and *Star Trek* are products of the Cold War atmosphere of the 1960s, whereas both *The Simpsons* and *The X-Files* are distinctly post–Cold War phenomena. Indeed, each of these series seems to be rooted in its own particular historical moment. In *Gilligan's Island* and *Star Trek*, as products of the 1960s, World War II is close enough to be a living historical memory, and in both series it is still helping Americans form their sense of their place in the world and encouraging them to think of themselves as the true champions of freedom and democracy. In *Gilligan's Island*, the Skipper recalls his World War II exploits as if they had happened the day before and a Japanese soldier who does not even know the war is over turns up in a couple of episodes. In *Star Trek*, the very name of the starship *Enterprise* of course conjures up memories of World War II. As for the Cold War atmosphere in these series, it is signaled by the way they both dwell upon one of the ideological focal points of the conflict between the United States and the Soviet Union—the space race. It is surprising how many episodes of *Gilligan's Island* deal with astronauts, cosmonauts, space capsules, and ICBMs—until one remembers that the series was created virtually in the wake of the 1962 Cuban Missile Crisis. *Star Trek* was in a sense simply the 1960s space race projected onto a galactic plane, and the show ended up providing a sort of ongoing TV commercial for NASA and the Apollo Program.

The *Simpsons* and *The X-Files* are obviously products of a later period in American history. In *The Simpsons* World War II has become a dim and distant memory, meaningful only to the oldest characters in the series, such as Grandpa Abe Simpson and the decrepit Mr. Burns. *The X-Files* frequently harks back to World War II, but only to reinterpret it, or at least its outcome. The show keeps suggesting that the U.S. military ended up collaborating with their German and Japanese enemies after the war, thus undermining America's moral credibility. As for the space race, both *The Simpsons* and *The X-Files* treat it cynically, portraying NASA as more concerned with its TV ratings and its budget than with its scientific mission. The debunking of NASA in the two series from the 1990s is symptomatic of an ideological shift brought about at least in part by the end of the Cold War. *Gilligan's Island* and *Star Trek* were energized by the clear-cut ideological polarities of the U.S.-U.S.S.R. conflict, which in many respects was at its height in the 1960s. Both shows portrayed Americans as standing for good because they thought of Russians, and other foreigners with their undemocratic and un-American ways, as standing for evil. In *The Simpsons* and *The X-Files*, by contrast, with the threat from the Soviet Union, and indeed from all foreign enemies, seemingly removed by the end of the Cold War, the hold of the American national government on its citizens is weakened and it becomes more difficult to maintain a clear sense of national purpose. The later shows are less likely to embrace American institutions uncritically because they no longer portray the American way of life as threatened by foreign alternatives.

As we will see, on a whole series of such issues *Gilligan's Island* and *Star Trek* stand on one side of a historical divide, with *The Simpsons* and *The X-Files* on the other. The differences between the two sets of series can even be related to the history of television itself. In the 1960s, the three national networks—CBS, NBC, and ABC—dominated American television. It was the time when they achieved their highest overall share of the TV audience and also when they assumed control of programming, basically determining what the American public got to see. It seems no accident, then, that in an era dominated by the national networks, American television should have been largely national in its outlook. Trying to appeal to as wide a national audience as possible, the networks had an interest in encouraging shows that reflected the ideology of the American nation-state.

By the 1990s, the structure of the American TV industry had changed radically, in ways that significantly reduced the power of the national networks and launched television on its way to becoming a truly global medium. In the 1980s and 1990s, as a result of the growing availability of all sorts of new ways to deliver TV programming—cable, satellite transmission, VCRs, and so on—Americans experienced a broadening of their television horizons. The traditional national networks saw their share of the audience eroded, and more significantly, they lost their ability to control trends in programming. They often found themselves outmaneuvered by upstart networks such as Fox (which gave us both *The Simpsons* and *The X-Files*) or the new forces in cable TV, such as HBO and Showtime. Would-be television producers now could get their shows before the public without having to go through a small set of network executives in charge of programming. Of course CBS, NBC, and ABC did not simply disappear from the scene and in fact remained major players in the television industry in the 1990s, but often only by joining forces with the new players in cable and other modes of TV production and transmission. The result was that TV programming began to open up in the 1980s and became simultaneously more local and more global in its perspective, as a national outlook no longer dominated television. Local stations, such as WGN in Chicago and WTBS in Atlanta, used satellite technology to become "superstations," broadcasting all across the country and thereby bypassing the traditional networks. Perhaps the most significant television development in the 1980s was the emergence of CNN, the international news channel, which became, in effect, the first truly global TV network. With such a major restructuring of the television industry, and such a broadening of the potential for participating in it, it is not surprising that the content of TV programming changed as well. Indeed, in the terms of one of the most famous analysts of television, Marshall McLuhan, one would expect changes in the TV "medium" to produce changes in its "message."

I am of course by no means the first to note these developments in American television. It has become commonplace to talk about a revolution in the TV industry in the 1980s and 1990s, for example, the shift from "broadcasting" to "narrowcasting" in the way sponsors target their audiences. But I am interested in taking this kind of analysis a step further and looking at changes not just in broad programming trends but in the content of specific shows that can be correlated with the larger revolution in television. Television has clearly become one of the major forces behind globalization in the world today. I want, therefore, to analyze how globalization has itself become a theme in specific television programs, and especially how they express changing attitudes toward the process. The de-emphasis and devaluation of national politics in *The Simpsons* and *The X-Files* somehow reflect a new attitude toward globalization in the 1990s. In short, what unites the shows I have chosen to focus on in this book is the theme of globalization; what divides *Gilligan's Island* and *Star Trek* from *The Simpsons* and *The X-Files* is, broadly speaking, the fact that in the earlier shows globalization is something that America does to the rest of the world; in the later shows globalization is something that is happening to America itself. In order to explore the significance of these changes in American popular culture, I have divided this book into two parts: one dealing with the 1960s and what I am calling the "era of national television," and one dealing with the 1990s and what I am calling the "era of global television." For each era, I have chosen to analyze in detail two representative programs, one comic and one serious. I think that my argument is strengthened by the fact that the trends I discuss cut across the distinction between comic and serious programming.

There are dangers in organizing the book this way, and I am the first to recognize them. I am risking giving an overly schematic and perhaps even reductive view of the developments I am analyzing, but I am willing to run that risk for heuristic purposes—to bring out the contrasts as sharply as possible. I grant that these distinctions are not absolute. One could, for example, find "global" shows in what I am calling the era of national television and "national" shows in the global era. The brilliant British TV series *The Prisoner* was produced in the late

1960s, and yet in many ways it anticipates *The X-Files* in its unnerving portrait of a shadowy government conspiracy that cuts across national lines and that makes it impossible to tell the good guys from the bad guys on the international scene.[2] And one can certainly find good old American patriotism alive and well in many television shows in the 1990s, including at times *The Simpsons* itself. But I would not regard my argument as invalidated by isolated counterexamples. I am dealing with a broad but not a universal and uniform development in this book—it is in the nature of popular culture that it never moves as a whole, with every single TV program advancing in lockstep according to some master plan. That is why I am quite ready to grant exceptions to the pattern I outline, and indeed I qualify my argument at many points when I get down to discussing the four series in detail.

All I am claiming is that, once the necessary qualifications have been made, we can still observe a significant shift in the ideological content of American television between the 1960s and the 1990s, and the two pairs of shows I have chosen by and large reflect this change and in that sense can justifiably stand for their respective decades. It is at least reasonable, though no doubt debatable, to argue that *The Simpsons* and *The X-Files* are the television shows that defined the 1990s. As for *Gilligan's Island* and *Star Trek*, although they were not the most popular shows of their day and were both abruptly canceled by network executives, in their afterlife in syndication, they have become among the most watched programs of the 1960s, and certainly two of the series audiences look back to when they think about the era. I admit that there is something ultimately arbitrary about my choice to concentrate on these particular shows—it is no doubt the result of certain contingent facts, some of them no more significant in the grand scheme of things than individual speaking engagements I once received. I am not claiming that the process I am charting in this book has to be analyzed in terms of just these four shows, and no others. Indeed, in writing this kind of book, one must inevitably make difficult choices about what to include and what to exclude. I realize that dealing with other programs could have helped me fill out the story I am telling, perhaps in important ways, while writing about still other programs might have led me down different paths. In the end, I decided to concentrate on fewer programs in order to be able to analyze them in depth, since one of my aims is to document how complex a phenomenon a long-running television show can be. I am by profession not a television historian but a literary critic, and whatever talents I have lie in the direction of interpreting plots and not chronicling masses of fact. What fundamentally interests me in this material is what the different programs have to say about globalization, which upon closer examination I find to be at times quite subtle and provocative. Ultimately I view this book as a contribution to our understanding of globalization, and if my choice to analyze these particular series has helped illuminate that issue, I believe that it is justified.

◆

I will now outline the developments I trace in this book and suggest in advance how its chapters cohere. I begin with *Gilligan's Island* as an example of how television in the 1960s reflected the ideology of the American nation-state. The show's premise was that a group of representative Americans could be dropped anywhere on the planet and they would *rule*. With a kind of pioneer spirit, they would re-create America in one of the blank spaces on the world map. The show embodied a naive faith in America's power and its goodness, and especially in the ability of the country's economic, scientific, and military might to prevail in any corner of the globe. In *Gilligan's Island*, we will see what globalization originally meant to Americans—the Americanization of the globe. Whatever happened on the island—whether the native inhabitants returned or foreign forces "invaded"—the spirit of Gilligan always triumphed in the end, and in his very ordinariness and his refusal to claim to be better than his fellow castaways, Gilligan provided the image of democratic man par excellence.

If *Gilligan's Island* globalized American democracy, *Star Trek* set out to galacticize it. Whatever the stated goals of the mission of the starship *Enterprise* may have been, its real task was to make the universe safe for democracy. Cutting a broad path through interstellar space, its crew left a trail of total destruction among the aristocracies and theocracies they encountered. Indeed despite the famous Prime Directive and its prohibition against interfering in other planets' affairs, *Star Trek* portrayed Captain Kirk and his crew attempting again and again to remake any planetary regime they found on the model of 1960s America and its liberalism. Even more than *Gilligan's Island*, the show captured the New Frontier spirit of John Fitzgerald Kennedy's America. In its expansive movement—"to boldly go where no man has gone before"—*Star Trek* expressed America's self-confidence in the 1960s. In particular, in its team of Captain Kirk and Mr. Spock reshaping life on planets throughout the galaxy, the show mirrored the faith of 1960s American liberals that a central government and a scientific elite could solve all problems and make the world a better place to live, even for people who resented and resisted this interference.

The *Star Trek* chapter is the one place in this book where I make a sustained excursion outside the realm of television. My discussion of the film *Star Trek VI* seemed justified, since the *Star Trek* movies obviously grew out of the original TV series and in many respects carry on its spirit. Nevertheless, this movie marks a turn in the ideology of *Star Trek* and thus is very important to my overall argument. The TV series was a product of the Cold War; *Star Trek VI* in effect deals with the end of the Cold War and what has come to be known as the end of history. I show that the movie develops and deepens doubts about the universal validity of American democratic principles that had already begun to surface in the TV series, largely provoked by distaste for the Vietnam War. I relate the multiculturalist rhetoric of *Star Trek VI* and its postmodern feel as a movie to its place at the end of history. *Star Trek VI* helps highlight how crucial the Cold War was to sustaining the kind of nationalist ideology I analyze in television in the 1960s. The movie thus provides a bridge to the second part of the book, where I analyze the global era of television, the period in the 1990s when the end of the Cold War freed television programs to question the centrality of the nation-state in American life.

In turning to *The Simpsons* and *The X-Files*, I will show how both shows grow out of a disenchantment and a disillusionment with national government and in particular with the idea that political elites can run people's lives better than they themselves can. *The Simpsons* takes a cynical view of all government and especially of government remote from the people. The show portrays the citizens of Springfield, USA, as largely unconcerned and unimpressed with what happens in Washington, D.C. Indeed *The Simpsons* marks a return to the importance of the nuclear family on television, as well as of the local institutions that support it, such as churches and neighborhood schools. In general the show celebrates the spirit of small-town America. To be sure, this is partly the product of a mood of postmodern nostalgia for the early days of TV sitcoms such as *Father Knows Best*, but it also is the result of a reaction against decades of interference by the national government in local communities. As we will see, among the biggest "villains" in *The Simpsons* are the FBI and the IRS.

While *The Simpsons* celebrates the local, it also shows the new importance of the global in the lives of its characters. In marked contrast to *Gilligan's Island*, which portrays the Americanization of the globe, *The Simpsons* chronicles the globalization of Springfield. For an Amer-

ican small town, it is pictured as remarkably open to foreign influences. Resident aliens play an important role in the community, above
all the Hindu who runs the local convenience store, Apu Nahasapeemapetilon. (I would like to see Jim Anderson of *Father Knows Best*
pronounce that.) *The Simpsons* sometimes dwells on the tension between the local and the global (especially when the volatile issue of
limiting immigration comes up), but overall in the series the combination of localizing and globalizing forces in Springfield means that the
nation-state tends to get crowded out of the lives of its citizens. In the
post–Cold War atmosphere of *The Simpsons*, the national government
seems much less necessary to protect its citizens from foreign enemies
and hence cannot make as great a claim on their allegiance as it did in
earlier decades.

    The X-Files goes further than *The Simpsons* in undermining the ide-
ology of the nation-state, and not just because it gives a much darker
portrait of the FBI and not just because it shows "aliens" playing an
even more powerful role in contemporary America. The series repeatedly suggests that presidents and congressmen are mere figureheads.
Americans may think that these prominent national figures control
their destiny, but according to *The X-Files*, it is mysterious forces behind
the scenes who are really calling the shots, and they do not do so in the
name of America. The show's central image for globalization is a shadowy conspiracy between a band of invading aliens and a syndicate of
businessmen, government officials, and scientists whose allegiances
cut across and indeed go against national loyalties. Thus *The X-Files* reverses the movement of *Star Trek*. In the earlier series, America is on the
move, expanding outward and spreading its influence throughout the
galaxy. Wherever the crew of the *Enterprise* turn, they in effect invade
and transform one alien planet after another. The movement in *The X-
Files* is by contrast inward, and the sphere of American control seems
to be collapsing, or at least is shrinking. In *The X-Files* America itself is
being invaded by aliens, and the country seems hard-pressed to ward
off their influence and preserve its integrity as a nation.

    To be sure, *The X-Files* did not invent the theme of alien invasion,
which can be traced back to the very beginnings of science fiction in
H. G. Wells's *The War of the Worlds*. The image of America being invaded by aliens from outer space was a mainstay of science fiction
movies in the 1950s. But these alien invasion plots generally had an
inflection very different from that of *The X-Files*. In retrospect, it is
now clear that the alien invasion motif in 1950s science fiction movies
reflected the Cold War atmosphere of the period. The extraterrestrial

invaders were stand-ins for America's foreign enemies right here on Earth, and especially the totalitarian forces on the other side of the Iron Curtain. That is why the extraterrestrials were usually portrayed in the 1950s as soulless, godless automata—exactly America's nightmare image of its communist opponents at the time. The invaders were presented as scheming to take away the freedom of Americans and impose an alien totalitarian regime on them. In short, in the alien science fiction plots of the 1950s, it was usually a clear-cut case of "us" versus "them." The ideological battle lines were sharply drawn, as America's love of freedom was set against the aliens' tyrannical ambitions. The plots of these movies usually worked out so that heroic Americans frustrated the sinister efforts of aliens to defeat them in open combat or to infiltrate their ranks and conquer the United States from within. From time to time in these movies, an American might treacherously or, more often, misguidedly work with the aliens, but such actions failed to sway the tide in favor of the extraterrestrial invaders and were usually punished horribly in the end. Thus the alien invasion stories of the 1950s actually worked to support the ideology of the American nation-state, portraying its enemies as evil and ultimately doomed to defeat.

By contrast, the point of the alien invasion plot in *The X-Files* is to blur the line between America and its enemies, indeed to leave all ideological divisions muddy and unclear. The aliens have powerful allies within the U.S. government working on their behalf. At the same time, U.S. officials have formed alliances either for or against the aliens with their counterparts in other nations on Earth, some of them traditionally thought of as America's enemies (for example, the show at various times suggests links between the American military and either German or Japanese or Russian scientists). To complicate matters further, *The X-Files* goes on to portray the aliens themselves as divided into two factions, working at cross-purposes and seeking to destroy each other. In sum, *The X-Files* creates an image of the world that is the very opposite of the simple bipolarity characteristic of the Cold War mentality. The show reflects the ideological uncertainty and confusion of the post–Cold War era in the way it continually leaves its audience wondering if they can tell the good guys from the bad guys anymore. By questioning whether it is still meaningful to speak of distinct sides in the world, *The X-Files* fundamentally calls into question traditional nation-state ideology.

I suppose it is fair to say that in one respect *The X-Files* is clear—at least it calls upon us to root for the human race. But in its terms, that does not mean to root for America. In contrast to the alien invasion movies of the 1950s, *The X-Files* pointedly refuses to identify the cause of the United States with the cause of humanity, and it continually implies that the nation-state is no longer the most important or the most meaningful unit for dealing with human problems. The show makes us care about the fate of its various heroic figures, above all special agents Mulder and Scully, but we never have the sense that their personal survival depends on the survival of particular American political institutions, such as Congress or the presidency.

As if to remind us of the glory days of nation-state ideology in American popular culture, in 1996 Hollywood served up a thinly disguised remake of *The War of the Worlds* in a film called *Independence Day*, which went on to become the blockbuster hit of the summer. In this movie America does lead the nations of the world against invaders from another planet, and indeed the American president must get personally involved in order to ensure the survival of the human race. The popularity of this film suggests that old-fashioned patriotism still has its appeal in American popular culture, and I am the first to admit that. But *Independence Day* did have a distinctly recycled feel to it and came across as a throwback to the invasion movies of the 1950s. As for a comment on this film from the makers of the TV series—at one point in the 1998 *X-Files* movie, Agent Mulder urinates on a fading poster for *Independence Day* in a particularly sleazy back alley. Envy of the box office success of the earlier film may of course have fueled this cinematic gesture, but I cannot help thinking that it was just another way for *The X-Files* to signal its departure from the old-style nationalist ideology of the Cold War era and its "invaders from outer space" movies. I have devoted what may seem to be a disproportionate amount of space to *The X-Files* in this book because it strikes me as illustrating most fully the turn away from the ideology of the nation-state that I wish to document in American popular culture. The series seems to me to offer the most coherent, thoroughgoing, and far-reaching response on American television to the changed geopolitical conditions in the world at the end of the twentieth century. Above all, *The X-Files* seems to me to delve seriously into many of the problematic aspects of the globalization that is the defining event of our day. I realize that this is a lot to claim for a show that often seems to present us with little more than fat-sucking vampires, fake alien autopsies, and endless cell phone conversations between its hero and heroine, but I hope to make my case for the seriousness of *The X-Files* in later pages.

◆

Finally, I should say a few words to introduce the central concept of this book—globalization. Anyone who has been greeted by the sight of a McDonald's on the streets of Beijing or has admired a Chicago Bulls T-shirt on an Aborigine in the Australian outback is familiar with globalization. It tells us something that it is only necessary to see such images on television in order to appreciate the force of globalization in the world today. But in all its theoretical ramifications, the idea can become quite complex and controversial. Globalization is at once an economic, a political, a social, and a cultural process, to name only the most important ways in which the phenomenon manifests itself.[3] For the purposes of this book, I am most interested in the aspect of globalization that has come to be known as "the end of the nation-state." Even more than the related phrase "the end of history," this term has proven to be better at generating controversy than at accurately describing the phenomenon it purports to name. When theorists such as Kenichi Ohmae or Jean-Marie Guéhenno talk about "the end of the nation-state,"[4] they do not mean that one day in the near future we will wake up and find that every national political unit from Afghanistan to Zaire has suddenly dropped off the face of the earth. The phrase "the end of the nation-state" is not quite as apocalyptic as it sounds. In fact, it refers more to a process than an end result, and more to a complex reordering of priorities and hierarchies in the contemporary world than a simple replacement of one form of order by another. Even the most committed theorists of the end of the nation-state expect that entities such as France, Germany, and the United States will be with us for a long time. It is just that these theorists believe that, as units of communal organization, these entities have lost their centrality in human life and will continue to see their power and control over their citizens erode over time. All over the world, national units of organization are being challenged and to some extent displaced by more local and more global units.

Perhaps the best way to get at what is meant by "the end of the nation-state" is to look at the economic aspects of the phenomenon. For much of the twentieth century, national governments sought to dictate policy to the economic actors under their jurisdiction and control. This was especially true for nations that embraced various forms of economic central planning, whether of the right (fascism, national socialism) or of the left (Soviet or Chinese communism). But even in countries that claimed to embrace capitalism, markets were only relatively free, and national governments used their control over interest rates, monetary and tax policy, and other forms of regulation to manipulate their economies. The collapse of communism at the end of the 1980s did more than anything else to discredit the model of the command economy, but throughout roughly the last quarter of the twentieth century a number of forces conspired to weaken the power of government economic regulation and strengthen the power of free markets. Unheralded though it may have been, perhaps the most significant economic development in the last three decades of the twentieth century was the increasingly free flow of capital on international financial markets. The fact that governments around the world were gradually forced to abandon foreign exchange controls and other impediments to the free flow of capital was itself a sign of the growing power of markets to impose their economic discipline on nation-states. But once the globalization of financial markets took shape, national governments really saw their power to dictate terms to their economies diminished. Governments that pursued monetary or fiscal policies deemed unacceptable by international financial markets quickly saw their economies drained of capital. In a process that seems to have occurred largely below the radar screens of politicians worldwide, the long-standing relation between politics and economics was reversed. Instead of governments dictating terms to financial markets, financial markets began to dictate terms to government.

Of course this development did not involve a complete turn-around and really should more properly be described as a shift in the balance of power between national governments and financial markets. To the hapless businessman hauled into court, a government regulator can still look like the proverbial 900-pound gorilla. But power is always relative, and the point that economic theorists of the end of the nation-state make is that back in the 1940s or 1950s, that gorilla would have seemed more like 2000 pounds. However much power nation-states retain to regulate their economies (and in some areas, such as environmental concerns, their power has actually increased), on the whole government economic intervention was once greater and shows signs of diminishing further in the future (think of the trend from nationalization to privatization that swept Europe beginning in the 1980s under Margaret Thatcher's leadership). Moreover, as Ohmae points out, the nation-state is increasingly unable to present itself as the logical unit of economic organization. The development of smaller units, such as foreign investment zones in China, or larger units, such as NAFTA or the EU, is one of the most important signs that the economic hegemony of the nation-state is weakening. The fact that regional economic communities such as the EU have posed serious questions of national sovereignty for their member countries is the best indicator of how great a threat regional integration and economic globalization really are to the long-term viability of nation-states as units of communal organization.

As much as I am fascinated by the subject, this is not a book on economics, and I can give only the most superficial overview of the extremely complex issue of economic globalization. By way of introduction, I merely wish to point out that the realm of economics helps make clear how equivocal a development globalization appears to be. The global integration of financial markets has had an extraordinarily beneficial effect in rationalizing the investment of capital around the world, helping to put an end to inefficiencies and malinvestments caused by misguided government efforts to manage economic life and especially attempts to promote one industry at the expense of others. But this very process has seemed threatening to many, especially the vested interests on whose behalf governments intervened in the first place with their subsidies and economic protectionism. Thus for all the benefits of economic globalization, the phenomenon has generated great anxiety in many quarters. Complaints about losing jobs to foreigners still receive sympathetic ears in most national political arenas. As we will see, these ambivalent responses to globalization are evident in both *The Simpsons* and *The X-Files*, often involving the economic issues we have been discussing. In general, *The Simpsons* tends to look at the "bright" side of globalization and *The X-Files* at the "dark" side, but both shows end up suggesting what a complex phenomenon it truly is. Above all, *The X-Files* conveys a sense of how unnerving and even uncanny the process feels to many people—especially in the way it defies conventional expectations about the future—precisely because people remain captive of the ideology of the nation-state and, hence, have a hard time thinking outside its categories.

This is an important point. One reason I have been drawn to the issue of the end of the nation-state is that it cuts across traditional ideological polarities and thus promises to open up new paths of speculation. The intellectual left and right are both attracted to certain aspects of globalization, but neither is completely comfortable with the results. The left has always had its doubts about nationalist ideology and, to put it delicately, has not always viewed the United States as playing a positive role in world affairs. Thus the left has tended to embrace the internationalism and cosmopolitanism of globalization and looked favorably on the process when seen as a means to its cherished goal of world government. But almost by definition, the left has never felt comfortable with free markets, and thus insofar as economic globalization has limited the ability of governments to interfere in economic activity, it has been perceived by the left as a threat. It is this very aspect of globalization that has, on the other hand, made it attractive to the intellectual right, which generally welcomes anything that weakens the power of governments to interfere with the free flow of economic activity. But given its generally patriotic impulses, the right has tended to feel uncomfortable with the ways in which globalization undermines national sovereignty. The complexities of globalization as an issue— and especially the many ways it refuses to fit into standard ideological categories (which were, after all, largely framed in the context of the traditional nation-state)—explain the peculiar alliances that the issue often provokes. Globalization indeed makes strange bedfellows. The far left and the far right have sometimes united in their opposition to the World Trade Organization—the former because they view it as a device for exploiting Third World populations, the latter because they view it as a device for hiding new levels of government economic regulation behind a false banner of free trade.

For readers impatient for me to get to *Gilligan's Island*, let me reassure them that this book will not be about the WTO, GATT, NAFTA, or the EU. I am just preliminarily trying to suggest why I think that the question of globalization, and especially the concept of the end of the nation-state, is so important and so fascinating. This issue gives us a chance to step outside of categories that have long held sway over our thinking and thus offers an opportunity to move beyond ideological impasses that have seemed inescapable. For, in effect, introducing me to the issue of the end of the nation-state, I am grateful to American popular culture, although I doubt that even the producers of *The X-Files* had any idea that they were performing this service for me. I hope that this book will in its own way make a contribution to the "end of the nation-state" debate. I ask my readers to be prepared for some intellectual surprises in entering this new territory in American popular culture, and above all, I urge them to maintain an open mind and try to keep their standard ideological reflexes in check.

That is what I have tried to do in approaching this material, and accordingly I have often been surprised myself by what I have found in the shows I studied. Like many people, I normally think of the American entertainment industry as dominated by left-wing views, and *The Simpsons* and *The X-Files* have often struck their critics as among the more left-wing of Hollywood productions. I certainly document tendencies in both series that would place them toward the left of the political spectrum. But since the issue of the end of the nation-state cuts across conventional ideological polarities, I would argue that those on the intellectual right have much to learn from these two series, even if they are initially put off by what seem to be standard left-wing gestures in both shows. I have genuinely tried to suspend my own ideological views and biases in approaching the shows I study in this book and indeed they have led me in directions I never anticipated. For the record, I do not endorse the ideological positions taken by any of the series I discuss in this book. In fact the show I most admire intellectually, *The X-Files*, is precisely the one whose political position I sometimes find positively repellant. But as I have said, I have tried not to let my personal views interfere with my understanding and appreciation of the four shows I have chosen to discuss. I have worked hard to give as fair and accurate an exposition as I can of what I take to be the view of the world developed in each series. But again, such exposition should not be mistaken for endorsement. The fact that I find a show interesting does not mean that I agree with its politics.

If I had to give a concise statement of my own view of the issues I explore in this book, I would say that I think that globalization, especially the world integration of financial markets, is on the whole a positive development, and indeed nothing more or less than the extension on an international scale of the very principle of modern civilization—the division of labor. That this is not the view developed in any of the TV series I discuss I readily admit, but that does not make them any less intriguing to me. In fact, precisely because I look upon globalization as a positive development, I value attempts to suggest the negative aspects of the process. In general, I have welcomed the opportunity working on this book has offered me to enter into a dialogue with American popular culture about globalization—a development I have come to regard as the most pressing issue of our day. I hope that my readers will share a similar sense of discovery as I try to lead them along the paths of intellectual exploration I myself have pursued.

I regard this book as an experiment—to see what happens if we provisionally drop our intellectual prejudices against television and try to learn from it, particularly from some of its more sophisticated specimens, such as *The Simpsons* and *The X-Files*. In particular I want to explore the potential richness of the long-running TV series as an artistic medium. To be sure, this medium has its obvious pitfalls and defects—grinding out episodes week after week, year after year can

exacerbate a troubling tendency toward artistic inconsistency in television. But at the same time, when a series is done well, and particularly when some kind of creative visionary remains at the helm, it offers an opportunity to develop a whole imaginative world, rich in
detail and perhaps even deep in significance. And if we are interested
in the cultural reflections and ramifications of globalization, then we
have reasons to turn to television. We can of course find globalization
as an issue in more conventional areas of academic study—in the contemporary novel, for example, and particularly in such authors as Don
DeLillo and Salman Rushdie.[5] But given the central role of television
in the globalizing process, there is a certain logic in turning to television shows themselves if we want to find out something about contemporary attitudes toward globalization. Some may find it absurd
that I invoke the names of Plato, Rousseau, Hegel, and Nietzsche in
the course of discussing a bunch of TV shows. But if—as is often
claimed—these great thinkers really do deal with perennial issues,
then the problems they explore ought to be manifest even in the television programs of our day—precisely to the extent that they mirror
the problematic character of contemporary life. Indeed since our reality is now partly constituted by television, popular culture may well
offer us one of our best entry points into understanding our world. I
think that, were Nietzsche alive today, he would understand what I
mean when I say that if we want to see the end of history (and what
he called "the last man"), we might well begin by turning on our televisions. We may not always like what we see there—this tends to happen with mirrors—but we can still learn from it.

Acknowledgments

Over the years many people have aided and abetted me in this fugitive project. Pride of place must go to James Pontuso, who invited me to give my first public lecture on popular culture at Hampden-Sydney College in 1988 and kept asking me to return for encores in later years. He also joined me in several panels on popular culture at the Annual Meeting of the American Political Science Association. Sponsored by the Politics and Literature section of the APSA, these occasions gave me a further opportunity to develop and test my ideas in a public forum. I wish especially to thank Peter Lawler and Joseph Knippenberg, who organized some of the panels and arranged for publication of earlier versions of some of these essays. Tracy Strong had the courage to publish the first version of my *Simpsons* essay in the last issue he edited of *Political Theory*. As someone who has always relied on the kindness of strangers when it comes to editors, I would also like to thank the following for encouraging my work on popular culture: Scott Walter, Jeff Tucker, Nick Gillespie, John Podhoretz, Jody Bottum, and Bill Kristol.

Among the friends who have contributed to this book, I owe a particular debt of gratitude to Jack Jackson, who first got me interested in *The X-Files*. I watched the show occasionally in its premiere season, but, quite honestly, thought it silly and found the lack of closure in its plots not at all to my taste. The Reverend Jackson, who must be the only Methodist minister who builds sermons around the adventures of Mulder and Scully, is a convincing speaker and managed to talk me into giving *The X-Files* a second chance. After watching a few episodes carefully, I got over my initial negative reaction and began to realize why my friend was drawn to it—and not just because it deals on a weekly basis, just as he does, with the issue of faith in an age of doubt.

Michael Valdez Moses began as my student but soon became my teacher when it comes to popular culture. I know no one who is better at "reading" a movie or a television episode on the spot, and his interpretive talents have proved invaluable to me, especially in making sense out of some of the murkier moments in *The X-Files*. He helped me develop some of my basic ideas about the series and has also read and commented on the manuscript of this book.

In writing a book on globalization, I have been fortunate in being able to draw upon the experience of an international businessman par excellence, my friend Bob Krupp. While other people simply write about globalization, he has been doing it for the past twenty-five years or so, first as a pioneer in U.S. investment banking activities in the Eurodollar market and later, among other positions, as chief financial officer of a multinational petrochemical engineering firm. In retrospect, I now realize that he was teaching me about globalization before most people were even using the term.

With television as my subject, I cannot fail to mention my brother, Donald Ochacher. From the early days of Ernie Kovacs to the present, we have always shared our television experiences, and since he is eight years older, he was the one who first introduced me to the joys of talking critically about TV shows.

For information on *The Simpsons* in Canada, and help with vital research on donuts, I want to thank Lorraine Clark and Don Kjelmyr. Others with whom I have discussed *The X-Files* in particular and television in general over the years, or who have commented on various sections of this book, include Neil Arditi, Gordon Braden, Steve Cox, Jonathan Flatley, Peter Henry, Elizabeth Hull, Eric Lott, Harvey Mansfield, Paul Outka, Tom Peyser, Eric Susser, and Carey McWilliams. For help in preparing the manuscript, I thank Rebecca Kroeger. Finally, it has been a pleasure working with Steve Wrinn, Mary Carpenter, and Lynn Weber at Rowman & Littlefield, and I want to thank them for all they have done to make this book possible.

Notes on Method

♦

As a professor, I am expected to give an account of my methods. My general readers, who are mainly interested in what I have to say and not in how I am going about saying it, may feel free to skip this section. My academic readers will probably conclude that I am epistemologically naive no matter what I say. Now that nobody is reading, I feel ready to proceed.

Writing about four successful television series is a daunting task. *Gilligan's Island* consists of 98 episodes, the original *Star Trek* amounted to 79 episodes, *The Simpsons* passed its milestone 250th episode in the fall of 2000, and *The X-Files* has reached well over 150 episodes already. For the record, I believe that I have seen just about every episode of all four series at least once. Over the years I have taped most of *The Simpsons* and *The X-Files*; for the purposes of this book, I taped a significant number of episodes of *Gilligan's Island* and *Star Trek* (both shows are still widely available in syndication). Thus I was able to review the episodes I discuss at length carefully before writing about them. All quotations from the four series are based on transcriptions I made myself; wherever possible I checked them against transcripts available in various forms, particularly in the many guidebooks published about these series. I have tried hard to ensure the accuracy of the quotations, but I beg forgiveness if I have made an occasional error.

Given the large body of primary material I am dealing with, I have had to be highly selective in which episodes I discuss. I thus apologize in advance to anyone whose favorite moments in a given series I have neglected. To be honest, I omitted many of my own favorite episodes in order to keep focused on my specific thematic concerns. I am sure that readers who are even more familiar with these shows than I am will be able to point out important episodes relevant to my argument that I have omitted; they probably will also be able to identify episodes that may contradict points I have made, or at least appear to be in tension with them. For reasons that I will turn to shortly, long-running television series are not the most artistically consistent products of the human imagination. Thus, in my defense, I can only say that I have tried to deal with representative episodes, and I believe that I have remained true to the underlying spirit of each of the series I discuss. I have sought to document all my claims as thoroughly as possible, but at some point I realized that this book would become unmanageably long if I cited all the evidence I had at my disposal.

The background material available on the four series I discuss is also vast, and I cannot claim to have mastered it. To the extent possible, I have made use of the kind of tell-all books that participants in television series often get around to writing. This kind of "behind the scenes" information, together with what is available in fan magazines and entertainment industry journals, has often been quite helpful to me, especially in sorting out the intentions of the creators of these four shows. I understand the need to be skeptical about what often amounts to little more than press agent releases and have generally checked any one source against others. This book of course is not an attempt to write a history of these four television shows. Nevertheless, I have tried to enrich my argument with as much anecdotal material as possible.

While struggling with the mass of primary material, as well as all the background material, I must confess that I have largely neglected the academic scholarship that has accumulated over the years about each of these programs, and television in general. This scholarship is often of high quality, and I have at times found it helpful, for example, an issue of the science fiction journal *Extrapolations* devoted to *Star Trek* or a collection of essays called *"Deny All Knowledge": Reading The X-Files*, edited by David Lavery, Angela Hague, and Marla Cartwright.[1] But academic scholarship in the area that has come to be known as Cultural Studies generally pursues an agenda quite different from my own and has often seemed irrelevant to my particular project. In any case, I did not want to spend every other page of this book engaged in high-level theoretical disputes with other academics. I prefer to devote as much space as possible to discussing the television shows that are my real subject. I had originally planned to begin with a systematic effort to distinguish my theoretical position from what tends to prevail in Cultural Studies. I hope to return to that task at a later date; for the moment, readers can get a sense of how I differ from Cultural Studies by looking at a review I wrote of W. J. T. Mitchell's *The Last Dinosaur Book* under the title "Jurassic Marx."[2]

To give just the barest sketch of my quarrel with Cultural Studies, I would begin from the seemingly trivial point that academic analysis of popular culture strikes me—with some notable exceptions—as woefully humorless.[3] It is one thing to take popular culture seriously and to maintain a critical distance from it (I do so myself in this book). It is another to write about it in ponderous theoretical jargon and thereby to lose touch with its texture—its very "popularity." A great deal of work in Cultural Studies provides a variation on Nietzsche's formulation of Kant's joke—scholars writing about the interests of the common man in terms the common man could never understand. I have made a point of writing in plain English in this book and—without simply surrendering to the charms of popular culture—to attempt to understand it as much as possible in its own terms.

In particular I have tried to maintain my own sense of humor when discussing *Gilligan's Island* and *The Simpsons*. Although I cannot hope to match the comic genius of these shows (particularly the latter), I at least sought to have a little fun myself while writing about them. I have tended to be more serious about *Star Trek* and *The X-Files*, but even these shows have their lighter moments, and I occasionally have a little fun at their expense as well. In general I have tried to suit my style to my subject matter in this book. Thus, although I am obviously taking popular culture seriously, I hope that I am not taking it *too* seriously. Writing about popular culture strikes me as a case where style is significantly related to subject matter. The dense, obscure, jargon-laden, overly theoretical prose characteristic of much of Cultural Studies reflects its distance from and active hostility to the popular culture it claims to embrace. Many of the practitioners of Cultural Studies come at popular culture with an elaborate theoretical framework already in place, and television shows often become little more than grist for their Marxist mills. My decision to avoid the theoretical jargon that often seems *de rigueur* in Cultural Studies is thus quite deliberate. I hope thereby to articulate popular culture phenomena in terms that are not just more comprehensible to the common reader, but also truer to the phenomena themselves. My goal is not to understand these series in terms of a theoretical framework external to them, but rather to tease out the view of the world they develop themselves.

I of course inevitably come at popular culture with my own theoretical framework, but I hope that I have allowed it to be shaped and even altered by my active engagement with the concrete phenomena I have studied. In fact, because of my willingness to learn from popular culture, this book has turned out to be considerably, if not fundamentally, different from what I might have originally projected. When, in the late 1980s, I began giving the public lectures from which these chapters are ultimately derived, I concentrated on the relativism and even what seemed to me the nihilism in American popular culture. Had I written this book back then, it might well have resembled Thomas Hibbs's *Shows about Nothing*—a book I very much admire, but also one I have come to quarrel with.[4] From the beginning, I approached American popular culture with the concept of "the end of history" in mind. In many respects, my *Star Trek* chapter represents the oldest stratum of my argument, and I was thoroughly familiar with Francis Fukuyama's work—and the Hegel-Kojève view of history it embodies—before writing any of the original essays. In thinking about *Star Trek VI* and American popular culture in general, I was principally concerned with the relation of the postmodern to the posthistorical—how the relativistic tendency toward leveling artistic distinctions in postmodernism can be connected to forms of democratic leveling at the end of history. This concern remains in my book, particularly in the *Star Trek* chapter, but as I continued thinking about popular culture and began to come to terms with new phenomena in the 1990s such as *The Simpsons* and *The X-Files*, my perspective on the material changed, or at least broadened.

As long as I was thinking in terms of the "end of history"—a seemingly all-embracing concept if there ever were one—I was fixated on what was coming to an end in American popular culture—the dissolving of a consensus—and thus was mesmerized by its negative and even nihilistic tendencies. I was forgetting that the end of one thing can often be the beginning of another. What has been called the end of history may in fact only be the end of one particular phase of history, namely the era of the nation-state. Thus what looks nihilistic from the standpoint of the old ideology of the nation-state might turn out to be liberating from a new perspective. I first came to this recognition in the course of writing an essay on—of all things—pro wrestling, in which I began to wonder whether I really should be lamenting the loss of crude nationalist stereotypes in wrestling in the post–Cold War era.[5] This development may have signaled a decline in whatever modicum of moral fiber the "sport" ever had, but should we really be turning to wrestling for our moral values in the first place? Perhaps with its bizarre meta-morphoses, pro wrestling has been pointing in its own peculiar (and vulgar) way beyond the nation-state and its ideological domination in twentieth-century America. The title of my book reflects my new interest in exploring the liberating potential of American popular culture, rather than dwelling exclusively on its nihilistic tendencies.

At the time I wrote the wrestling essay in the fall of 1999, I was vaguely familiar with the "end of the nation-state" debate and in particular had already read authors, such as Benedict Anderson, who correlate the era of the nation-state with a certain level of technological development (print culture, for example). But it was only in the course of writing my *X-Files* essay in the summer of 2000—trying to work out the logic of this extraordinarily complex series—that I first began to formulate this book in terms of the concept of globalization and the end of the nation-state. Thus it was only after writing the *X-Files* chapter that I plunged into the literature on this subject, and in particular read the books by Ohmae, Guéhenno, and van Creveld that have turned out to be so useful to me. But I want to stress that I read them in light of *The X-Files* and not vice versa. That is, I did not analyze the TV series in terms of a framework derived from these theorists of the end of the nation-state. On the contrary, it was studying *The X-Files* that made me receptive to their ideas in the first place. I do not know if Jean-Marie Guéhenno, for example, has ever seen *The X-Files*—I suspect not—but his book *The End of the Nation-State* reads like a commentary on the series. That *The X-Files* should illuminate an important theoretical debate should not be all that surprising. As I will suggest, the producers of the series display signs of being familiar with a good deal of theoretical material themselves, including, for example, Marshall McLuhan's theories about print culture. If that is so, it only underscores my point that we should not approach popular culture with our own theoretical framework firmly and immovably in place. We should rather be prepared to modify our ideas in light of what we encounter in popular culture, which may at times have something theoretical to say itself. I fully recognize that much of popular culture may be mindless entertainment, but we should be awake to the possibility that in what former FCC chairman Newton Minow once famously called the "vast wasteland" of television, oases of quality and maybe even of thoughtfulness can be found. The producer of *Gilligan's Island*, Sherwood Schwartz, has revealed that he named the ill-fated vessel of his castaways—the tiny ship the *Minnow*—after the very FCC chairman who expressed such contempt for television—a good reminder that TV producers may not be as dumb as we sometimes think they are.[6] As skeptical as I myself may be about the intellectual level of television in general, I have tried to give the programs I discuss the benefit of the doubt and have found that the more I have reflected upon them, the more I have learned from them (above all from *The X-Files* but even, to my surprise, from the lowly *Gilligan's Island*).

In particular I have tried to respect the heterogeneity of the television programs I discuss. If Cultural Studies has one principal fault in my view, it is a tendency to impose a kind of homogeneity on the phenomena it discusses, viewing all TV programs, for example, as telling the same sad tale of racist and sexist stereotyping. I have tried to treat the shows I discuss as if they had a kind of artistic integrity and have looked for the ways in which each reflects a distinctive view of the world. I have organized this book around a single set of questions having to do with globalization, but I have emphasized the ways each show suggests different answers to these questions. At the same time as I point out the range of views of globalization I discuss, I want to stress that I fully recognize that globalization is not the only issue these shows raise. I do not offer this book as a comprehensive treatment of these particular shows, let alone the whole of American television in the second half of the twentieth century. There are many other legitimate approaches to these shows, and for all my doubts about Cultural Studies, the movement has produced much of value in its analyses of television in particular and popular culture in general. If I do not deal with some of the issues Cultural Studies tends to be obsessed with, the reason is that I have my own agenda in this book and cannot possibly exhaust all aspects of my chosen subject.

For example, some critics may complain that I do not discuss the significant gender issues raised by all four programs I am treating. As it happens, I touch upon gender questions briefly in each of my chapters, but I admit that I do not explore them as thoroughly as they deserve. I would offer the essay "'What Do You Think?': *The X-Files*, Liminality, and Gender Pleasure," by Rhonda Wilcox and J. P. Williams (in *"Deny All Knowledge"*), as a model of how gender analysis can be used to illuminate a television program, and indeed any series that entitled one of its episodes "Genderbender" cries out for interpretation in these terms. But since gender is precisely one of the topics Cultural Studies has already thoroughly mined, I felt that I could legitimately move on to other subjects in this book such as globalization, which to my knowledge has not yet been analyzed in depth as a thematic concern in American television.

◆

While I am outlining the limitations of this book, let me come back to the fact that I am a professor of English. As such, I have been trained to read texts, and that is what I do with the television programs I discuss in this book. I think that one of its strengths is that I treat these programs as if they were artistic texts and try to uncover what they themselves have to say about my central theme of globalization. Nevertheless, I acknowledge that there are genuine methodological difficulties in "reading" television programs as if they were coherent texts. Of course the whole business of interpreting texts has been increasingly viewed as problematic in the past fifty years or so, but at least in the case of literature one can generally speak of authors, who in some way stand behind the texts and "authorize" their meanings (even this claim is much disputed by my colleagues). But in the case of television programs, it is very difficult to speak of "authors," or even *auteurs*, to use the French term often invoked in the interpretation of movies. Most American television programs are corporate products, and the way a given episode finally appears on the air is seldom if ever the result of a single person's artistic intentions. People with genuine aesthetic aims, such as writers and directors, may have a say in the final product, but people with very different motives—network executives with their eyes on the bottom line, network censors with their hands on their blue pencils—may have equal or greater control over what eventually flickers on the screen. Thus it is genuinely problematic to speak of the artistic integrity of a given television program. A particular element in any program may have to be explained in terms of economic rather than artistic considerations.

This problem in interpretation is compounded by the peculiar nature of television as a medium, especially of series television. The need to meet weekly deadlines inevitably introduces an element of contingency into television programs and often forces producers to improvise on the spur of the moment. For example, one of the most interesting developments in the ongoing story of *The X-Files*—the plot arc centering around the "Duane Barry"/"Ascension" pair of episodes in its second season—was dictated by a simple biological fact, the pregnancy of Gillian Anderson, one of the stars of the series. The producers of the show needed to find a way to shoot around Anderson's condition and in fact came up with a brilliant solution—a plot arc in which the character Anderson plays, Dana Scully, is apparently abducted by space aliens. The way the *X-Files* team responded to this challenge is one indication of their talent, but anyone who would argue that the idea of Scully's abduction was part of the original conception of the series is just not familiar with its production history. This is not to deny that *The X-Files* found a way to make something meaningful to the series as a whole out of Scully's abduction—indeed it became the thematic heart of the second season. But this incident in the production history of *The X-Files* is a good reminder that chance often plays a role in artistic creation, and a brilliant creative move may be the result not of aesthetic foresight, but of the ability to adapt to changing circumstances and even moments of crisis.

This is true of all art, but especially of long-running television shows. It is difficult enough to maintain the aesthetic coherence of individual episodes on television with all the different people having a say in the final product. It is almost impossible to maintain strict continuity from one episode to another, and fans often delight in pointing out the inconsistencies that develop over time in any successful TV show. In a fit of madness, the producers of *The Simpsons* decided to build one episode ("The Principal and the Pauper") around the revelation that the principal of Bart's school, Seymour Skinner, was in fact an impostor and really named Armin Tamzarian. Of course to get the series back on track, they had to reinstate "Skinner" to his position of authority by the end of the episode. The producers evidently were so embarrassed by this plot twist that they later singled it out for condemnation in a retrospective "Behind the Laughter" episode. But no show can avoid this kind of occasional inconsistency, given the ruthless scheduling demands of weekly television programming. Waylon Smithers, the assistant to the evil businessman Montgomery Burns, appears as a black man in the second episode of the series, "Homer's Odyssey"—simply because the colorizing instructions to the Korean animators of *The Simpsons* somehow got garbled in transmission. It is probably fortunate that the show never even tried to explain this inconsistency. Given the sometimes haphazard or at least improvisatory character of television production, I have, then, not tormented myself in working up my argument with the thought that somewhere out there on the airwaves an odd episode may be lurking that contradicts my thesis. I have simply looked for an overall thematic continuity in the shows I discuss, a level of consistency appropriate to television as a medium. Indeed, just because television shows may develop minor inconsistencies from episode to episode does not mean that they are utterly incoherent. Indeed, one might argue that only because a series maintains an overall thematic continuity are we able to note particular moments of inconsistency.[7]

With all these factors complicating my task, I have a few working in my favor. For the purposes of interpretation, I am fortunate that the particular series I discuss offer the prospect of artistic integrity in ways that are unusual—though not unique—in television history. Each of these series creates a distinct world with a recognizable logic all its own, and a core of regular characters who appear from episode to episode. These factors tend to give *Gilligan's Island*, *Star Trek*, *The Simpsons*, and *The X-Files* a degree of imaginative continuity and coherence that makes it easier to speak about each series as a whole. Moreover, behind each of these series stands a creator figure who clearly put his stamp on it—Sherwood Schwartz in *Gilligan's Island*, Gene Roddenberry in *Star Trek*, Matt Groening in *The Simpsons*, and Chris Carter in *The X-Files*. These people are about as close to *auteurs* as television gets—especially Carter, who has written many episodes of *The X-Files* and also directed many—and sometimes even written and directed individual episodes—thus making him the television equivalent of Orson Welles. It helps in interpreting these particular shows to know that a single person did originally have a vision of what each should look like, and the record shows that in each case that person fought, sometimes vehemently, to preserve the integrity of his creation in the face of interference from network executives and other nonartistic forces. To be sure, we also know that each of these television creators had to accept compromises to get his show on the air in the first place and to keep it there. But the more one studies the history of these particular series, the more one sees that at least there was always someone fighting to keep them true to their original conception.[8] For that matter, studies of great literary artists such as Shakespeare and Dickens have shown the degree to which they were forced to compromise with theater companies and publishers in order to realize their imaginative conceptions in material form. In short, as nervous as I am about transposing interpretive techniques I learned in studying literature to the analysis of television programs, I think that the situation in the newer medium is not without legitimate analogies to what has prevailed in literary history.[9] Thus I am willing to take a chance and see if the experiment will work of reading select television series as if they had the depth and complexity of traditional literature.

Even in my interpretive approach to the television programs I discuss, I try to respect the heterogeneity of the phenomena. Cultural Studies tends to take a "one size fits all" approach to television shows, bracketing out the issue of quality and therefore the question of whether one program deserves to be "read" more carefully than another. By contrast, I would distinguish between a show such as *The X-Files*, which I think has genuine artistic merit, and a show such as *Gilligan's Island*, which I think is television at its most average and hence simply mass entertainment. (I would say that *Star Trek* and *The Simpsons* fall somewhere in between these two extremes.) Thus I would never look in *Gilligan's Island* for the kind of subtlety and complexity I think is present in *The X-Files*, particularly in its best episodes, which strike me as among the most aesthetically sophisticated productions ever to appear on television ("Clyde Bruckman's Final Repose," for example, to cite one of my favorite episodes that I did not get to discuss in this book).

Thus, with *Gilligan's Island*, I tend to paint with a broad brush, looking for overall tendencies and in particular structural patterns that embody the "meaning" of the series. I generally do not analyze individual episodes of this series in elaborate detail, as I do when I get to *The X-Files*. I was surprised to learn in researching *Gilligan's Island* how much thought actually did go into the series, but I still believe that it is worth distinguishing a show that was basically intended merely to amuse its audience from one such as *The X-Files* that has from the beginning sought to be thought-provoking as well as entertaining. Thus, in discussing *Gilligan's Island*, I am mainly interested in the way it more or less inadvertently reflects the democratic ideology of the United States, as well as a certain conception of globalization prevalent in the 1960s. I have much more respect for *The X-Files* and thus take more seriously the possibility that the show might have its own contribution to make to the globalization debate. Once again, I think *Star Trek* and *The Simpsons* fall somewhere in between the extremes of passively reflecting larger cultural attitudes and actively seeking to shape them. I want to stress, however, that all this is a matter of degree. I believe that all four shows reflect broader trends in the surrounding culture and a variety of economic, social, and political developments. In fact, I suggest that the way these shows reflect historical trends has been one source of their popularity; they hooked their audience in part by speaking to their specific concerns at different points in American history. That is one reason I take the shows up in historical order. At the same time, I think that all four shows were not just reflecting but also reflecting on historical changes, and even *Gilligan's Island* had something of its own to say about America in the 1960s.

◆

I would argue for a similar complexity when one examines the question of whether these television shows have had an effect on American society. *Star Trek* is the most overtly didactic of the series I discuss. We know that Gene Roddenberry and other people involved in the show wanted it to make a statement about the future of America, and on issues such as race relations and the Vietnam War, *Star Trek* sometimes offended its fans by becoming downright preachy. Both *The Simpsons* and *The X-Files* often seem to be straining to get messages across to their audiences, and Sherwood Schwartz's account of creating *Gilligan's Island* indicates that even he regarded his show as something of a soapbox for political pronouncements.

Whether these shows have actually had any real impact in shaping social and political attitudes in the United States is a complicated question and well beyond the scope of this book. Support for the Vietnam War eroded in America in the late 1960s; that *Star Trek* was responsible for this development I very much doubt, but I would hesitate to rule out its having played any role at all. It seems plausible that the shows the American public watches week after week have some effect in shaping their attitudes and opinions. That is certainly the assumption behind most complaints about violence on television. I am not a sociologist and thus I am not in a position to do the kind of empirical studies needed to explore the complicated question of the impact of individual shows on their audience. I occasionally look at some of the anecdotal evidence and gesture in the direction of this kind of question. For example, in discussing *The X-Files*, I begin by suggesting that the popularity of the show reflects the political disillusionment of the American people in the 1990s, and I further imply that the show's cynicism about the U.S. federal government is contributing to the delegitimating of the nation-state. I do not pretend to settle these issues in this book or even to begin to explore them in a systematic way. I merely offer them as important areas for future study.

The question of the social impact of a given television program is further complicated by the theory of subversion/containment associated with the movements known as Cultural Materialism and the New Historicism, and more basically with the thought of the French theorist, Michel Foucault.[10] This theory questions the naive understanding of subversive literature and other cultural forms. One would intuitively think that a work that embodies a subversive perspective on the government would have a subversive effect on society. Take the case of *The X-Files*—as we will see, it presents the U.S. government as corrupt, Machiavellian, and in general working against the interest of the American people. One would think, therefore, that to the extent the show had any impact on its audience, it would weaken their faith in their government and hence weaken its hold on them. But the subversion/containment theory paradoxically suggests just the opposite. An apparently subversive cultural form may actually strengthen the hold of the government it appears to criticize, working to contain subversive ideas even in the seemingly rebellious act of expressing them. For one thing, the argument runs, subversive cultural forms serve a kind of safety-valve function. They let people blow off steam—the resentment they have been building up against an oppressive regime is discharged when they merely see that resentment represented on stage or on television—without their actually having to do something about it. In this view, cultural forms serve to defuse potentially explosive social situations—which would explain why government authorities do not seem to attempt to close down "subversive" cultural forms, but may even encourage them.

Radical criticism of programs such as *The Simpsons* and *The X-Files* often takes this form, arguing that these shows actually serve the interest of the ruling class in the United States, despite appearing to criticize it. *The Simpsons* seems to satirize dominant institutions in America, such as big corporations, but, some critics ask, does it actually trivialize and hence blunt such criticism by presenting it within a cartoon context—thus making people laugh at their oppressors rather than getting angry at them?[11] Similar criticism has been leveled against *The X-Files*—does the show undermine its own criticism of the federal government by explicitly linking it to the lunatic fringe of UFO believers and self-proclaimed victims of alien abductions? Or as I have sometimes heard the criticism formulated: Does *The X-Files* end up diverting the American people from what should really be bothering them? The show traces the evil in the world to a shadowy conspiracy between a global syndicate and a band of invading extraterrestrials. If that were really the problem, it would let more conventional political institutions, such as Congress or the presidency, off the hook. I personally think that this criticism of *The X-Files* depends on an overly literal reading of the show, as if its audience were incapable of taking the alien plotline of the series as a metaphor for more fundamental—and real—problems in their lives. Still, these are legitimate questions to raise, and I bring them up myself to make it clear that I am aware of these complexities. But they are not the focus of my concern in this book. Although I am interested in the effect of particular TV programs on society, I am much more concerned with them as artistic forms that embody and express distinctive views of the world. I basically confine myself in this book to what I think I do best—reading "texts"—even when they take the somewhat anomalous form of TV shows. I wanted to use these methodological notes to indicate that I am aware of the complexities involved in dealing with television as a medium. But in writing this book, I have largely bracketed out these concerns and tried not to let them paralyze me as a critic. In the end, I made a conscious decision not to let methodological concerns interfere with the one task I have really set myself in this book—examining the way globalization has been portrayed, and shown to be problematic, in a representative set of American television programs.

NATIONAL TELEVISION AND THE DEMOCRATIC IDEOLOGY OF AMERICA

Ask not what your country can do for you. Ask what you can do for your country.

—John Fitzgerald Kennedy

"The Courage of the Fearless Crew": *Gilligan's Island* and the Americanization of the Globe

"A social microcosm?" asked Mr. Paley incredulously. "But I thought *Gilligan's Island* was a comedy!"
"It's a funny microcosm!" I replied in desperate haste.

—Sherwood Schwartz

The whole thing sounds so darn democratic.

—Thurston Howell III

Gilligan's Island must be the most successful bad show in the history of television. Though it has its amusing moments, ever since it originally aired in 1964, the show has been blasted by critics. At the time of its debut, Jack Gould wrote in the *New York Times*: "*Gilligan's Island* is quite possibly the most preposterous situation comedy of the season." Terence O'Flaherty of the *San Francisco Chronicle* was even more hostile: "It's difficult for me to believe that *Gilligan's Island* was written, directed, and filmed by adults. . . . It marks a new low in the networks' estimate of public intelligence."[1] Someone—I think it was Woody Allen—best captured the negative response when he quipped on the *Tonight Show*: "CBS has a great idea for a new series next fall—it's a comedy version of *Gilligan's Island*."

And yet, despite all the critical contempt, the show was popular with television viewers from the beginning, and when it was canceled by CBS, the reason was not low ratings but a scheduling difficulty involving *Gunsmoke*.[2] Last broadcast as a first-run program on September 4, 1967, *Gilligan's Island* went on to remarkable success in its afterlife in syndication, becoming one of the most watched programs in television history. Reruns are still regularly broadcast on cable channels such as TBS, TNT, and NIK, and audiences evidently continue to be delighted by the wacky misadventures of the hapless castaways: Gilligan, the Skipper, the Millionaire and his wife, the Movie Star, the Professor, and Mary Ann. As if the public could not get enough of the castaways' comic efforts to adjust to life on their tropic isle or to escape it, the show was remade as a cartoon series on ABC, *The New Adventures of Gilligan* (1974–77). Not to be left out, NBC reunited the original cast in three made-for-television movies (1978, 1979, and 1981).[3] In recent years, several television advertising campaigns have referred to the series, some of them featuring original cast member Dawn Wells.[4] In 1999 Wells also appeared on MTV in a continuing segment, "What Would Mary Ann Do?", offering advice on life in the tropics to guests at the MTV beach house in the Bahamas and thereby proving that *Gilligan's Island* is alive even for the MTV generation.[5] During the summer of 2000, when a game show called *Survivor* became the most popular program on American television, its tropical island setting inevitably led to comparisons with *Gilligan's Island* in all the media.[6] One of the most successful movies of 2001, *Cast Away*, points in the direction of *Gilligan's Island* in its title and explicitly refers to the series. In short, the show has achieved something of the status of a myth in contemporary America, becoming a reference point in popular culture for understanding the world.[7]

How could a show that originally generated so much critical hostility continue to captivate audiences more than three decades after it was originally canceled by CBS? Of course the very silliness of the show has been one of its main assets. It appeals to children, who enjoy seeing adults behave like infants. In some episodes, the castaways even reenact fairy tales, such as Jack and the Beanstalk or Cinderella.[8] But there have been many infantile shows on television and few have demonstrated the staying power of *Gilligan's Island*. At the risk of appearing to take too seriously what is often viewed as the defining case of mindless entertainment, I will argue that its popularity is somehow related to its political content.[9] Whether by design or happy accident, or more likely a combination of the two, the show turned out to provide a perfect reflection of the liberal democratic regime of the United States and has accordingly touched a responsive chord in its citizenry over the years.[10] A product of early-1960s America, *Gilligan's Island* managed to capture the mood of the country at the peak of its self-confidence, when it was still exuding the New Frontier spirit conjured up by John Kennedy, the spirit that was soon to triumph in the U.S. moon landing. If Americans still look to the show today to be entertained, it is with a kind of nostalgia. It offers them a chance to get back in touch with an earlier point in their history, when America's place in the world seemed clearer and more secure—when Americans optimistically thought that they had the answers to the world's problems and their own.

Gilligan's Island thus serves as a test case for the serious study of popular culture. No one—myself included—would ever claim that the show embodied a profound understanding of America and its democratic way of life. And yet the show could not help mirroring in some way the beliefs of the audience for which it was created and therefore it gives us a window into 1960s America. I will look first at the ways in which the show managed to celebrate a kind of democratic vision of man, exemplified in Gilligan, and try to work out the democratic logic of several of the more overtly political episodes. I will then look at the vision of community the show offered and trace the way it harks back to earlier, almost idyllic visions of a simpler, more natural America. Finally, I will examine how the show reflected America's conception of its global role in the 1960s, indeed its global supremacy.

In its own peculiar manner, *Gilligan's Island* is a patriotic show, celebrating America and its democratic way of life. As played by Bob Denver, Gilligan is the democratic hero par excellence, the perfect representative of the man in the street in all his ordinariness. He is the ultimate television Everyman, and as such an object of identification for all viewers. With apologies to Robert Musil, he is the true man without qualities. And this lack is precisely what the show celebrates in Gilligan. Unlike the other characters in the show, he has nothing to distinguish him and that constitutes his form of preeminence in the context of a democratic regime. Paradoxically, he is the hero who is missing all the traditional attributes of heroism. Indeed he has nothing of the traditional hero except a dogged desire to be one—a stubborn wish to be recognized for doing good for his community. His goodwill is in fact his one admirable trait, though his general incompetence prevents him from translating it into any solid accomplishments. By contrast, each of the other characters has a distinctive virtue that sets him or her apart from the crowd. Each is defined by a form of excellence, often the sort of claim to superiority that traditionally entitled outstanding individuals to rule over their fellow human beings. Thus the show subliminally reminds us of older aristocratic forms of constituting society. Only Gilligan has no distinctive excellence and hence none of the traditional claims to rule. In the democratic utopia of *Gilligan's Island*, he therefore emerges as the truly representative human being and the chief figure in the community, the man who sets its tone and generally determines its fate. It is no accident that the community is known as *Gilligan's* island.[11] As we will see, when the castaways seek to elect a president, they end up choosing Gilligan as their leader. He is living testimony to the democratic idea that you can have nothing to say for yourself and still deserve a voice in the community. He stands as an eternal monument to the great American democratic ideal: "On any given Sunday, anybody can rule anybody else."

In developing its democratic vision of the world, the show works to devalue traditional aristocratic notions by neutralizing conventional forms of heroism and excellence. The Skipper, Jonas Grumby (played by Alan Hale Jr.), is perhaps the best example in the series of a typical heroic figure. A physically imposing man (though a bit out of shape), he has a spirited nature and enjoys issuing commands and having them obeyed. He has served in the U.S. military, and projects the kind of authority that often flows from having led men in battle. The Millionaire, Thurston Howell III (played by Jim Backus), offers another model of preeminence and an equally familiar claim to rule: wealth and social position. He is reputed to be the richest man in the world and has all the advantages money can buy, including an education at the most prestigious university in the United States. His social polish and veneer of culture give him an obvious air of superiority and dispose people to honor his authority. Finally, among the men on the island, the Professor, Roy Hinkley (played by Russell Johnson), represents another traditional claim to rule: wisdom. His encyclopedic knowledge, especially his scientific and technological expertise, makes him the person the castaways often turn to for guidance in critical situations. As Mrs. Howell says in one episode: "Let's get the Professor—he'll know what to do—he's a professor."[12]

With their competing claims to rule, the men often come into conflict, for example, in the "Gilligan Meets Jungle Boy" episode (#19), when each wants to be the one to board an air balloon and seek out help. The Professor insists that logic prevail, but each man has his own conception of logic. The Skipper appeals to the military order of command: "It's logical for the captain to go," while Mr. Howell invokes the economic pecking order: "But I'm the richest man here." As the dispute deepens, all three get into the act and each appeals to a particular form of knowledge. The Skipper says, "I know navigation"; the Professor says, "I know air currents"; Mr. Howell says, "But I know the presidents of five major airlines." Though the appeal to knowledge might seem at first to suggest that wisdom is being invoked as the criterion for rule, closer inspection shows that the Skipper is typically

appealing to his military experience and Mr. Howell to his social connections, while only the Professor is trying to establish his authority
on the basis of a science, in this case meteorology. But in the democratic logic of the series, these claims to superiority cancel each other
out, and the uncivilized jungle boy ends up flying in the balloon.
Whatever virtues the Skipper, the Millionaire, or the Professor may
embody, they are never allowed to achieve a position of secure authority in the island community.

Unlike the men, the three women on the island make no claims to
rule. *Gilligan's Island* is not a feminist show and indeed has more than
its share of what would today be called sexist moments. But in "St.
Gilligan and the Dragon" (episode #20), when the men reject the
women's demands for equal rights, they secede from the community
and in many ways prove superior to the men.[13] Each does have her
distinctive form of excellence, as becomes evident in the episode that
features a Miss Castaway contest, an aristocratic effort to choose the
leading lady of the island, which involves the three excellent men
aligning themselves with the three excellent women ("Beauty Is As
Beauty Does," episode #38). The Skipper sponsors the Movie Star,
Ginger Grant (played by Tina Louise), and sings the praises of her
physical charms. Throughout the series, she tries to play the role of
Marilyn Monroe[14] and thus represents the traditional Hollywood ideal
of feminine pulchritude. In the quest to crown "the most beautiful
castaway in the whole wide world," Mr. Howell of course champions
his wife Lovey (played by Natalie Schaefer), who is distinguished by
her social grace. In response to the Skipper's preference for Ginger,
Mrs. Howell insists: "There's really more to beauty than perfection of
face and figure. It also means breeding and poise and a kind of charm
that comes with maturity." Mary Ann Summers (played by Dawn
Wells) at first seems to lack any of the aristocratic qualities of either
Ginger or Mrs. Howell; as she herself says: "Ginger's too glamorous
and Mrs. Howell's too darned cultured." But Mary Ann has her own
claim to fame. A wholesome young woman from Kansas, she embodies many of the traditional American virtues: She is innocent, opti-
mistic, hardworking, sincere, enthusiastic, kind, considerate, modest,
ever eager to help and please. And, unlike Ginger, she remains bliss-
fully unaware of her physical attractiveness. It is precisely Mary Ann's
all-American and specifically midwestern set of virtues that constitutes her distinctive form of excellence. In the Miss Castaway contest,
the Professor sponsors Mary Ann for her "sweetness and warmth."
Though it is not in her nature to make any special claims for herself,

she represents a form of moral goodness that makes even her stand out in a crowd.

But for all their claims to distinction, all three of the women fail to win the contest. Typically, Gilligan ends up as the ultimate authority in the situation. As the three other men soon realize, he is the one "uncommitted delegate" and "that leaves Gilligan to elect Miss Castaway." To everyone's surprise, he chooses Gladys, an ape he met on the island, because, as he explains: "We're all Americans except her. To enter a beauty contest, you have to be a native and she's the only one born on the island." Gilligan's sympathy for indigenous people reveals his democratic instincts; in his view, any inhabitant of the island has rights that must be respected. Dismissing all conventional claims to distinction—physical beauty, social poise, moral virtue—Gilligan sides with the most natural figure he can find on the island. The result of the episode is to link Gilligan with Gladys, who serves as the female equivalent of the man without qualities. She has no claim to winning the contest other than just being there. Like Gladys, Gilligan is a kind of cipher—distinguished only by his utter lack of distinction. In contrast to the other men on the island, he is not physically imposing, well-bred, or intelligent. He is a bumbler, good-natured to be sure, but chiefly characterized by his inabilities rather than his abilities, his failures rather than his successes. And yet in the inverted democratic logic of *Gilligan's Island*, he emerges as the reigning force in the community.

I have been speaking of Gilligan's nature in negative terms, but it is possible to redefine his character positively. If Gilligan has a virtue, it is a distinctively democratic one: agreeableness. Precisely because he is not outstanding in any way, he is extremely accommodating to other people and generally does what he is told to do. In the jungle boy episode, when the other castaways are disputing whether or not to send the child up in the balloon, Gilligan listens to one argument after another and tells each of the speakers that he or she has a good point. Finally an exasperated Skipper blurts out: "Gilligan, not everyone can have a good point. You don't have to agree with everyone, do you?" Gilligan's reply is of course: "You know something, Skipper? You've got a good point too." The reason Gilligan ends up voting for the ape in the beauty contest is that he does not want to insult Ginger, Mrs. Howell, or Mary Ann by expressing a preference for one over the others. In a rare act of diplomacy, he says: "All the ladies are very beautiful and each one deserves to win." But Gilligan's tact could easily be mistaken for an unwillingness to take a stand and make a decision. The man without qualities is also the man without opinions and hence well suited to the concessions to other people's views essential in a democracy. Gilligan's preeminent status on the island reminds us that virtue is relative to the regime. The very lack of character that would make him a nobody under an aristocratic regime gets reconstituted as compliance in a democratic regime and makes him its model citizen.

Gilligan thus becomes the ideological conscience of the island, the one who always recalls the other castaways to their democratic selves. This role is particularly evident in the episode in which the other castaways discover that Gilligan is keeping a diary of events on the island and become alarmed that he may be portraying them in a negative light ("Diogenes Won't You Please Go Home?", episode #31). The Skipper, for example, worries that Gilligan's diary may place the blame for the original shipwreck on his shoulders. Much of the episode is devoted to a series of heroic fantasies, in which—in *Rashomon* fashion—first the Skipper, then Mr. Howell, and finally Ginger reimagine and rewrite in their diaries the earlier episode in which Gilligan rescued them from a rampaging Japanese soldier.[15] When Mary Ann finally gets ahold of Gilligan's diary, she discovers that far from criticizing his fellow castaways, he has been idealizing them. Of the Millionaire he wrote: "I'm on the island with Mr. Thurston Howell III. I don't have to say who he is—he's so rich that everybody knows him. Only money isn't important to him. He treats me like I'm just as good as he is—which shows what a wonderful person he is." Though Gilligan recognizes Mr. Howell's aristocratic claims to distinction, in his democratic innocence, he reformulates the Millionaire's character on an egalitarian principle. He does something similar in his humble remarks about Ginger: "And then there's a real live movie star with us. Boy, I've been afraid to even ask for her autograph, let alone talk to her. But she's just like a real person and everybody loves her because she's so good." The other castaways are chastened by Gilligan's democratic vision of them and the egalitarian ideal it expresses. The Professor tells him: "We see ourselves as we are and you see us as we would like to be." Gilligan truly is the democratic heart and soul of the island and seems repeatedly able to bring the other castaways down to earth whenever their sense of self-importance threatens to puff them up.

But the peculiarly negative form Gilligan's democratic heroism takes—the fact that he is the man without qualities—creates complications for him. He is public spirited and hence aspires to be a more traditional hero and be applauded for conventionally heroic deeds. In "The Sound of Quacking" (episode #7), he dreams himself into the role of a lawman in the Old West, Marshall Gilligan (the episode was actually filmed in part on the set of CBS's long-running hit show *Gun-smoke*).[16] The "How to Be a Hero" episode (#23) is devoted to the issue of the problematic character of Gilligan's heroism. It begins with him trying to save Mary Ann from drowning, but all he can do is to fall into the lagoon himself, with the humiliating result that the Skipper must rescue them both. The Skipper is lionized for his courageous act; Mrs. Howell compares him to such traditional naval heroes as John Paul Jones and Horatio Hornblower. When all the attention showered on the Skipper leaves Gilligan feeling depressed, it is up to Mrs. Howell to analyze the problem. She tells the Skipper: "You're a hero and he's not—that makes him feel small and insignificant." As if she had been reading Hegel's *Phenomenology*, Lovey correctly points to the solution: "Gilligan needs recognition—something for his ego, I mean."

At the Skipper's instigation, the castaways decide to stage a situation in which Gilligan can believe that he has acted heroically. If he cannot be a real hero, at least he can become the simulacrum of a hero. After several failed attempts, in which Gilligan only manages to make things worse when he is trying to save first the Skipper and then Mr. Howell, his friends hit upon a workable plan. Since Gilligan has been talking about a headhunter loose upon the island, the Skipper decides to dress up as a savage, appear to capture the other castaways, and leave it to Gilligan to rescue them. The irony is that a headhunter really is on the prowl; typically Gilligan's foolishness in the eyes of his fellow castaways turns out to be a form of wisdom. He is able to defeat the savage only because he overhears the Skipper's plan for a masquerade. Since Gilligan thinks that the real headhunter is merely the Skipper in disguise, he is not afraid of him and eventually drives him off. Anticipating the famous opening of the movie *Patton* (1970), the episode ends with Gilligan speaking in front of an American flag and for once accepting the recognition he deserves. He concludes the episode with a succinct if somewhat ungrammatical formulation of the democratic premise of the whole series: "So I guess being brave just kind of comes natural." Less impressed by the conventional goods of the world than the other castaways, Gilligan is presented in the series as closer to nature (a fact shown by his affinity for Gladys and other native primates on the island). His function is often to teach the other castaways that the goods they are pursuing are merely conventional, and that they thus could be happy without the so-called benefits of mainland civilization for which they are often pining. In particular the series repeatedly stresses the conventionality of money by showing how meaningless Mr. Howell's vast wealth becomes in the natural context of the island; removed from the context of mainland civilization, his dollars tend to become mere pieces of paper.[17] As the man without qualities, Gilligan shows that the less one cares about conventional goods and the closer one comes to the natural state, the more suited one is to democratic existence.

♦

Gilligan's status as the archetypal democratic hero is appropriately confirmed in the one episode in which the castaways elect a leader, "President Gilligan" (episode #6). The episode characteristically begins with a testimony to Gilligan's incompetence. While digging a well with the Skipper, the Professor thinks of adding Gilligan to the team, only with the qualification that "he can't do anything wrong if he's just digging." But before Gilligan can prove the Professor wrong, a crisis of authority develops when the Skipper goes off to enlist Gilligan's services. It turns out that he is already working for Mr. Howell, who is planning the construction of Howell Hills Estate. With both the Skipper and Mr. Howell ordering Gilligan around, they quickly come into conflict. When the Skipper insists: "I gave him an order," Mr. Howell pointedly replies: "And I gave him a job." This exchange reveals the divided regime on the island—the Skipper's authority is military in nature, while Mr. Howell's is based on his economic power. Typically, the Skipper will brook no opposition and tries to silence Mr. Howell: "Look, I'm having enough trouble running the island without a mutiny." This early episode is the first to raise seriously the issue of authority on the island, the fundamental political question: who rules?[18]

Mr. Howell refuses to back down and reiterates the divided character of the island regime: "At sea, you're the Skipper; on land I am Chairman of the Board." With military and economic power contending for the right to rule, the Professor intervenes, not to assert his own claims as a wise man, but to state calmly the fact that no clear lines of authority exist on the island. Ever the conservative, Mr. Howell is shocked: "Good heavens, this is anarchy." With the social fabric of the island fraying and threatening to unravel, Ginger saves the day with an inspired suggestion: "Why don't we vote?" Being good Americans and products of a democratic regime, the castaways immediately and enthusiastically embrace the idea of electing a president, and none more warmly than Mr. Howell, who recognizes the political advantage his wealth will give him: "I'll spend millions on my campaign."

The election campaign shapes up into a contest between the two obvious candidates, the Skipper and the Millionaire. The show recognizes the dominant appeal of military authority and wealth as claims to rule throughout history. Oddly enough, the Professor never thinks of entering the race, but perhaps he realizes how little appeal wisdom normally has in the political marketplace. Soon we see the Skipper standing on a soapbox and practicing his political oratory on Gilligan, the ultimate representative of the voting public. The Skipper's slogan is: "Don't change leaders in mid-ocean" and he presents himself as "first at sea, on land, and first father of your island." Gilligan finds this rhetoric appealing, although it turns out that he thinks the Skipper is campaigning on behalf of George Washington. Mr. Howell takes a more direct route to political success: bribery. He offers Mary Ann a job as his secretary at $50,000 a year (an extravagant sum in 1964), he promises Gilligan the position of secretary of the navy in his administration, and he intimates that as president he could do a great deal to promote Ginger's movie career.

The outcome of the election is the best example of the series' tendency to devalue traditional aristocratic claims to rule and promote the democratic principle of the man without qualities. When the Professor reports the results of the election, everyone is shocked: Gilligan has been elected president. The Skipper received two votes, one from himself and one evidently from the Professor. Mr. Howell received two votes, one from himself and one from Ginger. In an early example of the political phenomenon that was later to be named the gender gap, Gilligan is elected when he votes for himself and Mrs. Howell and Mary Ann put him over the top. In what amounts to an exit poll, Mrs. Howell explains her vote to her husband: "It was time you let someone else run everything." She thereby reveals that Gilligan's victory was largely the result of a kind of protest vote. In particular two-thirds of the women on the island wished to see the conventional order overturned and one can justifiably conclude that Gilligan's chief qualification for office was his lack of qualifications in any traditional sense. The fact that he had never held a position of authority either on or off the island seems to have endeared him with a majority of the electorate, and it also seems to have helped that he was not even officially on the ballot and never campaigned. One might even say that Gilligan's victory was a portent of all the politicians in the United States who were soon to be running against "politics as usual" and trumpeting their positions as outsiders to the political establishment.

The Skipper is as disappointed as anybody with the result of the election, but he accepts it with his usual good humor and in the process articulates the fundamental principle of democracy as the series views it: "Now the people have made their choice and whether it's right or wrong, we're stuck with it." Confronted immediately by the power seekers and the power brokers, Gilligan wastes no time putting together his administration, which includes the Skipper as vice president and the Millionaire as chief justice of the Supreme Court. Mr. Howell is, after all, the castaway with the most legal experience, as he himself explains: "The Government has convicted me six times on antitrust suits and I've been investigated every year for income tax evasion." Betraying its roots in the 1960s, specifically the Kennedy-Johnson era, *Gilligan's Island* presents its hero as an activist president. His administration includes ambitious public works projects, like digging a new well. As his secretary of health and welfare, Ginger wants to build a hospital on the island. When President Gilligan astutely points out that they have no doctors to staff the hospital, Ginger replies, with the logic of government bureaucrats everywhere, "then I'll build a medical school."

Gilligan's reign as president has its high points, such as the lavish inaugural luau, but it quickly degenerates into squabbling and outright political conflict. Mr. Howell starts a movement to impeach President Gilligan, on charges of accepting a bribe—from the chief justice himself when he was a private citizen. Unfortunately we never learn the ultimate fate of the Gilligan administration. He does not appear to be successfully impeached, but neither does his presidency last into the next episode. Perhaps he resigns between episodes when he learns how heavily the burdens of high office weigh upon him. It would be in keeping with Gilligan's uniqueness as the man without qualities if he were able to step away from politics with no regrets. Far more striking is the fact that Gilligan's service as president is forgotten in all subsequent episodes. And yet even this outcome seems only appropriate for the ultimate democratic hero. Since he makes no claim to rule by nature in the first place, one would expect Gilligan to step back into the crowd as unobtrusively as he stepped out of it to assume office.

Gilligan's admirable term as president in the first season of the series is counterpointed by an episode that came early in the second season, "The Little Dictator" (episode #39), which shows the dark side of electoral politics and indeed offers the nightmare inversion of the democratic dream Gilligan normally embodies.[19] The episode begins with the arrival on the island of a deposed Latin American dictator named Pancho Hernando Gonzales Enrico Rodriguez, played to the hilt by the great character actor Nehemiah Persoff, fresh from his triumphs as Jake "The Greasy Thumb" Guzik in the Desilu series *The Untouchables* (1959–63). As might be expected, Rodriguez, who has a revolver with him, quickly takes over the island, illustrating the political maxim he has always lived by: "In my country there is a saying: he who has gun is the leader." Reminding us of the role of brute force in political life, the episode reveals the nasty alternative to democracy, or rather the way in which democracy can all too easily be perverted into autocracy when the gun rules.

Impressed that the island is "almost twice as big" as his native country of Equarico, Rodriguez demands recognition from his new followers, the castaways: "Show a little more respect for your provisional *Presidente*." When asked exactly how provisional his presidency will be, Rodriguez gives the dictator's standard answer: "Until it is safe to hold free democratic elections." Unfortunately, when asked when that will be, *El Presidente* replies: "You should live so long." But in fact his administration turns out to be brief, and while he rules, he focuses on economic issues, with Mr. Howell serving as his minister of finance. The Millionaire would like to see the island's currency based on the gold standard, but Rodriguez is more disposed toward the inflationary policies typical of a banana republic: "In my country all you need is printing press and paper." With memories of Kennedy's Alliance for Progress no doubt fresh in his mind, Rodriguez cautions Mr. Howell: "We want to stay undeveloped enough so we can get an American loan."

As seems to happen with embarrassing frequency in his career, Rodriguez is soon overthrown by a bloodless coup, leaving Mr. Howell to fret: "Poor fellow, I hope he has money in Switzerland." In a return to the basic principles of the series, Mrs. Howell holds out the promise of democracy to Rodriguez: "We're a free society, and you will be free to do or become whatever you want." But instead of accepting this warm invitation to participate in democratic life, Rodriguez pursues a new autocratic path: He will become the power behind the throne, with Gilligan as his front man. Listening to Rodriguez's flattery, Gilligan soon believes that he deserves to rule: "You really think I should be the leader here on the island?" Strangely enough, even Gilligan now seems to have forgotten he was once voted president of the island. All he can offer by way of political experience is "I was President of the eighth-grade camera club." But this is enough for Rodriguez: "You see, even then they recognized your leadership ability"—a claim somewhat undermined when Gilligan reveals that he was made president only because he owned the camera and was deposed as soon as he lost it.

In one of the many dream sequences the series featured, Gilligan fantasizes what it would be like to be put in power by the unscrupulous Rodriguez. Once again the show acknowledges Gilligan's preeminence on the island and places him at the center of the community, only this time we see the potentially sinister consequences of handing over rule to the man without qualities. Rodriguez tutors his apt pupil in the corrupt tactics of demagoguery, instructing Gilligan to offer the people anything they want. Soon Gilligan is standing on a balcony à la Mussolini, outfitted in a tacky military uniform, and pandering to the basest instincts of the populace that supports him. As the epitome of the common man himself, Gilligan knows how to appeal to the lowest common denominator in his audience. His speech to his people is brief and to the point: "Everybody go home, kick off your shoes, turn on the TV, and relax—and that's an order." With that political program, it is no wonder that he is soon referred to as "Gilligan the Great" and is, as the now sycophantic castaways tell him, "idolized by all the population."

But the show cannot remain true to the spirit of democracy and leave Gilligan in this fantasy of autocratic grandeur. Accordingly, the castaways begin trying to cut through the fog of propaganda Rodriguez has spread and show Gilligan the reality of what is going on under his regime, which turns out to be one disaster after another. In what may well be the most pointed political reference in the history of the series, Mr. Howell tells Gilligan: "I'll show you the economic state of your so-called Great Society" and points to a row of Depression-era shanties. Coming as this episode did in the 1965–66 season, the reference to Lyndon Johnson's economic program seems unmistakable, although one hesitates to claim that the show was suggesting that Kennedy's successor should be viewed on the model of a Third World dictator. At a minimum, though, the episode raises doubts about the corrupt economic policies rulers employ to gain power and the lies their agents spread to sustain the illusion of their benevolence.

By the end of the episode, Gilligan's dream has turned into a nightmare. Rodriguez tells him: "You are nothing but a puppet ruler" and to prove his point—in a scene reminiscent of Chaplin's *The Great Dictator* (1940)—he is shown pulling the strings and making Gilligan as marionette dance to his tune. The man without qualities as Pinocchio—this is a haunting image of how easily democratic politics can degenerate into its opposite. The very emptiness that is Gilligan's claim to rule makes him easily manipulated by a strong-willed autocratic leader such as Rodriguez operating behind the scenes. Seduced by the pseudoaristocratic trappings of a dictatorial regime, Gilligan has violated the democratic principles by which he has always lived.

His one attempt to present himself as better than his fellow castaways and entitled to rule them backfires and leaves him enslaved himself, a mere puppet. Presumably Gilligan is left chastened by his one experiment with autocracy; he generally does not try to assert himself again in this fashion in later episodes.[20] His brief flirtation with autocratic domination presumably teaches him the value of being just a face in the crowd and he returns to his role as the chief representative of the democratic spirit in the series. Typically *Gilligan's Island* suggests that Americans could be led astray from the true path of democracy only by a *foreign* influence.[21] With his heavy Spanish accent (Persoff was a master of dialects) and his fascist finery, Rodriguez stands for all the un-American forces in the world that threaten to subvert the democratic way of life. For Gilligan to be true to democracy, he must remain true to America and resist the siren song of foreign regimes and their autocratic policies.

◆

Gilligan's Island develops a consistent democratic ideology and celebrates what it presents as the distinctively American principle that no human being, however virtuous or outstanding in any way, is *entitled* to rule over another. Representing the average citizen at his most ordinary, Gilligan presides over a kind of democratic utopia on the island and is repeatedly called upon to act as its savior.[22] With a stupidity that turns out to be a deeper form of wisdom, he continually ruins even the most careful plans the castaways develop for getting off the island. Even when he is magically granted three wishes, he wastes two of them on ice cream (chocolate, then vanilla), and when he finally manages to wish the castaways off the island, he fails to specify how far off and they end up merely transported on a breakaway piece of land out into the lagoon.[23] But herein lies the deeper wisdom of Gilligan and ultimately his own claim to rule. Only he seems to appreciate the advantages of the island. Perhaps because he lacks the various civilized excellences of the other castaways, he is not as attached as they are to civilization and shows signs of actually preferring the more natural existence the island makes possible. The other castaways all want desperately to get off the island and return to mainland society. Only Gilligan intuitively understands that the island is a democratic paradise and that remaining there is in the castaways' best interest, no matter what they may think.

    Gilligan's Island in effect re-creates America in a purified form, distilling out its democratic logic in a microcosm of U.S. society, while trying to free it from some of its corrupt tendencies. One way the show accomplishes this goal is to go back into America's past. By transporting the castaways to a deserted island, the show in many respects takes them back to the nineteenth century when, it suggests, the United States was a simpler and more natural society. The key material fact of the castaways' lives on the island is the absence of regular electricity or any form of internal combustion engine. That dictates their living at a technological level that resembles nineteenth- rather than twentieth-century America (with some notable exceptions, including their possession of a functioning radio receiver—though not the all-important and ever-elusive radio transmitter). The castaways lead what might be described as a horse-and-buggy existence (though they lack a horse and a buggy). In many ways they resemble nineteenth-century American pioneers, subduing the wilderness with a few simple tools. They exude a kind of frontier spirit, which comports well with the fact that the series was created toward the end of the Kennedy era.[24] In several episodes, Gilligan ends up playing the role of a frontier marshall (if only in his dreams), and the show re-creates archetypes out of the American West. In general, *Gilligan's Island* harks back to earlier stages of American history. It would be too much to say that the show celebrates the original Jeffersonian ideal of an agrarian republic in America. After all, that vision did not allow for millionaires, professors, or movie stars. But there are ways in which *Gilligan's Island* does revive the old republican ideal of the self-sufficient community. With a little help from their luggage and the odd bit of ocean-going flotsam and jetsam, the castaways have to learn to take care of all their needs on their own and that includes raising all their food in a way that resonates with an older, agrarian vision of republican America (a number of episodes are devoted to the issue of food production on the island).[25]

Gilligan's Island looks back to one of the fundamental sources of democratic thinking in America, Rousseau and specifically his *Second Discourse*, and ends up championing the blend of nature and civilization that informed Rousseau's conception of the democratic republic. Though he is generally thought to hold up the state of nature as the ideal condition for humanity, he in fact celebrates a kind of halfway stage in human history as its peak.[26] The state of nature is in effect too primitive for Rousseau; man is virtually subhuman at that stage, incapable of speech and reason. When man leaves the state of nature, he does not fall immediately and fully into what Rousseau characterizes as the corrupt state of civil society. Rather Rousseau describes a period when man has developed some of his distinctive faculties and institutions but does not yet suffer all the drawbacks of civilization. This midway point between nature and civilization constitutes the golden age of humanity for Rousseau:

> Thus although men had come to have less endurance and although natural pity had already undergone some alteration, this period of the development of human faculties, maintaining a golden mean between the indolence of the primitive state and the petulant activity of our vanity, must have been the happiest and most durable epoch. The more one thinks about it, the more one finds that this state was . . . the best for man. . . . The example of savages, who have almost all been found at this point, seems to confirm that the human race was made to remain in it always; that this state is the veritable prime of the world.[27]

Here is how Rousseau specifically characterizes the best state for humanity:

> As long as men were content with their rustic huts, as long as they were limited to sewing their clothing of skins with thorns or fish bones, adorning themselves with feathers and shells, painting their bodies with various colors, perfecting or embellishing their bows and arrows, carving with sharp stones a few fishing canoes or a few crude musical instruments; in a word, as long as they applied themselves only to tasks that a single person could do and to arts that did not require the cooperation of several hands, they lived free, healthy, good, and happy insofar as they could be according to their nature, and they continued to enjoy among themselves the sweetness of independent intercourse.[28]

Fans of *Gilligan's Island* will immediately recognize how closely the life of the castaways corresponds to Rousseau's description of the golden age as a happy medium between the primitive and the civilized states. The famous "Ballad of Gilligan's Island" concentrates on what it lacks: "No planes, no lights, no motorcars, / Not a single luxury" and insists: "Like Robinson Caruso [sic], / It's primitive as can be."[29] But, granted that Robinson Crusoe led a more primitive life on his island than he did in London, Defoe has his hero bring some forms of technology to the island and jerry-build others over the years. Similarly, *Gilligan's Island* does not quite portray a world that is "as primitive as can be." Marooned on the island, the castaways do regress to a life far less sophisticated than they led back in the United States. Nevertheless, they still enjoy many of the benefits of civilization on the island. Indeed, as canny observers have noted, they packed a surprising number of the trappings of civilization aboard the *Minnow* for what was supposed to be only a three-hour tour, including three years of outfit changes. They take advantage of all the technology they brought with them to the island, especially their radio, and, through the Professor's inventiveness, they significantly increase the number of machines available to them.

Thus the castaways enjoy some technology without becoming slaves to it. They participate in some of the benefits of the division of labor without suffering the alienation characteristic of an advanced market economy. Having achieved a level of self-sufficiency Rousseau would have envied, they are ideally not dependent on others for their self-esteem and can maintain their dignity as free human beings. The jungle boy episode particularly explores the issue of technology on the island, with the Professor showcasing several of his inventions—a fan, a washing machine, and a sewing machine—all powered by foot pedals. When the Skipper observes admiringly that the first of these "works just like a fan," the Professor points out how his technology is actually superior by virtue of not being integrated into a larger market economy: "Better—you don't get a bill from the electric company every month." And yet later the Skipper adds a cautionary note: "Sometimes I think the Professor invents too many things." The Skipper sagely reminds his fellow castaways that the paradise of the island rests on a delicate balance between innovation and resistance to change. By avoiding the pitfalls of modern civilization according to Rousseau, Gilligan's island provides the setting for a truly democratic community.

Thus the underlying message of *Gilligan's Island* is that the castaways do not realize how fortunate they are. Mr. Howell wants to return to Wall Street to make more money, even at the expense of having to deal once more with the scheming of fellow Harvard graduates. Ginger dreams of getting back to Hollywood to resume her movie career, even though she knows full well the perils of the casting couch and other sinister aspects of the entertainment industry. And yet as episode after episode reveals, the castaways can pursue some of their more sophisticated activities right on the island, but without many of the complications that inevitably arise in mainland and mainstream America. As evidence of the degree of sophistication the castaways are able to achieve in their supposedly primitive state, in "The Producer" (episode #72), they stage a full-scale Broadway show—a musical version of *Hamlet*—in order to bring Ginger's talents to the attention of a theatrical impresario who has stumbled upon the island (Harold Hecuba, played by Phil Silvers with his usual panache).[30] Thanks to some camera equipment that surfaces in the lagoon in another episode, the castaways are even able to make their own movie ("Castaways Pictures Presents," episode #43). Set adrift to direct potential rescuers to the island, the movie, once found, goes on instead to win at the Cannes Film Festival, where it is mistaken for the work of either Ingmar Bergman or Vittorio De Sica. How much more sophisticated could the castaways get? And yet they are able to produce their movie without all the infighting and backstabbing endemic to Hollywood, although Mr. Howell does get a little overbearing as the film's director, and working on the set reawakens Ginger's vanity as a star when she insists: "Don't forget to photograph me from the left."

Gilligan's Island develops its idealized image of America by returning to Rousseau's vision of the democratic community. While retaining and reaffirming many of the achievements of American civilization, the show attempts to rein in its excesses and return its characters to a simpler and more natural way of life. Many of the plots are generated out of the opposition between nature and civilization.[31] The happy medium the castaways have achieved on their island is threatened by the two extremes, either attack from more primitive forces or invasion by representatives of all that is most dubious in modern civilization. Several episodes involve savages from adjacent islands, who for one reason or another become interested in the castaways. Often characterized as headhunters or cannibals, these figures are typical Hollywood stereotypes of native people. They are superstitious, speak pidgin English at best, and are prone to mistake the castaways—as representatives of a superior American civilization—for gods. In one of the later episodes ("High Noon on the Totem Pole," #91), the castaways come upon a native idol that appears to have the likeness of Gilligan at its top. The pole was carved by the Kapuki, a tribe of fierce headhunters. When some members of the tribe return to the island, the only way the castaways can save themselves is to convince the Kapuki that Gilligan is their long-lost king. Before the end of the episode, the murderous natives are indeed tamed and start to bow before the image of Gilligan. In the very last episode of the series ("Gilligan, the Goddess," #98), the plot works out so that an even more gullible group of natives, the Killiwanni, mistake Gilligan for a goddess.

Gilligan and his friends encounter a variety of candidates for Rousseau's natural man, including the jungle boy who turns up on the island (played by a very young Kurt Russell). Gilligan is the first to spot the jungle boy, but no one believes his report. He is able to befriend the jungle boy because, of all the castaways, he is the one closest to Rousseau's natural man, the one most in touch with the subhuman. As we have seen, he votes for an ape in the Miss Castaway contest and he repeatedly links up with various primates who appear on the island. When the Professor challenges Gilligan about the jungle boy: "You're sure it wasn't a monkey?" Gilligan begins making ape-like motions to show that he knows the difference. The Skipper says: "Gilligan, I've never seen you look so natural," raising the kind of issue Rousseau explores in footnote j of the *Second Discourse,* where he blurs the line between the human and the animal. In the way the castaways approach the jungle boy, the episode goes on to examine the question of what constitutes natural man. Ever obsessed with Hollywood, Ginger thinks that the boy needs a hair makeover above all. But the distressed look on his face as she tries to comb his hair leads the Movie Star to a surprisingly Rousseauian observation acknowledging the absence of self-alienation in natural man: "I guess we'd better let you look like you." The other castaways, however, are not content to leave well enough alone. They clothe the boy and try to teach him how to speak, in a process that quickly degenerates into the kind of "boy-girl" dialogue familiar from the Johnny Weissmuller *Tarzan* movies. Indeed, a frustrated Mrs. Howell finally exclaims: "I do wish I'd paid more attention to those Tarzan pictures." That Hollywood has hopelessly corrupted our conception of the state of nature is confirmed in a later episode, when an apeman named Tongo (played by Denny Miller) shows up on the island; he turns out to be an aspiring actor who is only posing as an apeman in order to win the starring role in a jungle movie.[32] In all these cases, the show works to devalue, discredit, and debunk any forces more primitive than the castaways. They defeat the meddlesome savages, tame and civilize the jungle boy for his own good, and expose the apeman as an impostor. These episodes thus validate the wisdom of the castaways in not regressing completely to a primitive state of nature, which is exposed as inferior or fraudulent.

The representatives of modern mainland civilization who show up on the island are in many respects an even sorrier lot and act as foils to show off the virtues of the castaways, who remain closer to nature. Revealing the excessive greed and deviousness of modern society, a number of hustlers and criminals happen upon the island, including a bank robber (played by Larry Storch) and a kidnapper (played by Don Rickles).[33] In all these cases, the castaways learn to control their own evil impulses, unite against the intruders, and thwart the efforts to disrupt their lives. The criminals are always presented as outsiders, that is, not true members of the island community, which is thereby certified as free of criminal elements itself. For all their faults, the castaways would never rob, kidnap, or kill anybody. Several episodes turn on false accusations against specific members of the island community, criminal charges of which they are always cleared in the end.[34] Three episodes employ the "evil twin" motif. Exact doubles of Mr. Howell, Gilligan, and Ginger show up at various points in the series and create confusion and havoc on the island as they introduce alien impulses into the community.[35] For example, Gilligan's double (created by the Russians through plastic surgery in order to spy on the island) shocks everyone with his uncharacteristic behavior, especially when he makes sexual advances toward Ginger. But in all three cases, the masquerades are eventually exposed and the true and good castaway is distinguished from the evil impostor coming from the outside world with its civilized excesses. When one adds up all the characters who come to the island from mainland civilization, it becomes clear that the castaways are better off where they are. Neither too primitive nor too corrupted by modern civilization, they are free to lead a virtuous democratic existence on their island.

◆

The castaways can thus be justifiably proud of their island community. In episode after episode, they prove themselves superior to ignorant natives from the local area or to city slickers and con men from the mainland. Here we approach the central paradox of *Gilligan's Island*. The very qualities that do not entitle the castaways to rule over each other do, in the terms of the series, give them the power and the right to rule over the rest of the world. This is only the ultimate working out of the political logic of democracy. Democracy demands that no human being is by nature superior to another, but this principle becomes the basis for asserting that democracy itself is superior to any other form of government. The principle of nonsuperiority thus generates a principle of superiority. What is not allowed to members of the community with respect to each other is allowed to the community as a whole with respect to other communities. No one is entitled to rule another in a democracy, but because of this commitment to freedom, democracy presents itself as entitled to prevail over all other forms of government.

This logic generates many of the story lines in *Gilligan's Island*. Again and again the castaways must learn the democratic lesson of how to cooperate with each other, and that usually means learning to tame their pride and vanity, to abandon their pretensions to rule, and to pitch in and work together for the common good.[36] That is why

Gilligan provides the natural focus for their community—he is by nature the least vain, pretentious, and opinionated of the castaways. But faced with external threats or challenges to their community, the castaways become justified in asserting themselves. The Skipper can use his belligerence to try to bully outsiders, Mr. Howell can use his wealth to try to bribe them, the Professor can use his cleverness to try to outsmart them, and even Ginger can use her feminine wiles to try to seduce them. An activity that appears questionable when directed against a fellow member of the island community becomes justified when the goal is to get the castaways off the island or to protect them against threats to their lives or welfare. The paradox of *Gilligan's Island* mirrors the larger paradox of the United States. As a democracy, it seems to be based on the principle of nonassertiveness on the domestic scene, but on the foreign scene it has proven to be a remarkably assertive nation, at least in the twentieth century. Time and again the United States has found itself in the seemingly self-contradictory position of trying to force freedom on other nations, to compel them to follow American models of democratic government against their will.

This is perhaps the most interesting way in which *Gilligan's Island* reflected the mood of the United States in the post–World War II era—its overwhelming self-confidence as a nation, its unshakeable faith in its own moral goodness, and its sense of its global mission as the chief representative of democracy. When one thinks about it, the premise of the show was really quite remarkable and revealing. A representative group of Americans could be dropped anywhere on the planet—even in the middle of the Pacific Ocean—and they would still feel at home—indeed they would *rule*. With a minimum of resources at their disposal, they could re-create the American way of life in a new wilderness, from its democratic organization to the panoply of labor-saving devices that at the time were making the United States consumer the envy of the world. Nothing about the remote and exotic locale of the island unsettles the castaways. They are never led to question their assumptions or beliefs. If anything, their displacement strengthens their attachment to America and its way of life. As we have seen, they remain faithful to the principles of American democracy, even in situations in which different forms of organization might begin to seem preferable. They stay fixated on home and the single goal of returning to the United States, and in the meantime do whatever they can to fashion a replica of America in the middle of the Pacific.

Gilligan's Island provides a powerful image of globalization in its original American form—namely the Americanization of the globe. For the castaways, as for most Americans in the 1960s, globalization is a one-way street—they have nothing to learn from the rest of the world, but the rest of the world has a great deal to learn from them. Notice their behavior when they arrive on the deserted island. They immediately take possession and give no thought to the question of whether anybody else might have prior rights to the territory. Evidence of earlier settlement by natives on the island and even their return never disturb the castaways' confidence that they have every right to occupy the territory. Accordingly they also feel perfectly justified in using any means available to defend the island against all comers. The foreigners who arrive on the island are often typecast as enemies of the United States, either a Japanese soldier left over from World War II or America's new antagonists in the Cold War—Russians in the form of Soviet spies and cosmonauts. The foreign is never presented as any kind of legitimate model in *Gilligan's Island*; rather it is always viewed as something to be resisted and if possible defeated. Foreigners are there for the castaways to teach them a lesson in American superiority.[37] *Gilligan's Island* reflects a basic faith in American democratic principles, and the show does not hesitate to project them universally. It suggests not just that Americans are better off living democratically, but that all peoples everywhere are. In the terms of the show, the castaways, like all good Americans, are beacons to the world.

Gilligan's Island embodies a belief not only in America's basic goodness but also in its strength. Together the castaways stand for everything that made America great and in particular established it as the preeminent power on Earth in the post–World War II era. And thus all the forces that are supposed to be moderated and subdued within the domestic order are set loose to make America supreme in the international order. The Skipper embodies American military might, the Professor represents American science and technological know-how, and the Millionaire reflects the power of American business, with its financial muscle and its entrepreneurial savvy. For all its silliness, *Gilligan's Island* is quite canny in showing the basis of America's global influence and power. The presence of the Movie Star among the castaways even hints at the source of America's cultural domination of the world—Hollywood. A number of the episodes self-reflexively deal with the entertainment business and suggest that America prevails, not only in running the world but also in creating our images of it. As we have seen, even stranded on the island, the castaways are still able to make movies that impress people in places as far away as France, and the show suggests that whoever makes the movies, rules the world.

Perhaps the canniest insight *Gilligan's Island* embodies is that American globalization first and foremost takes the form of a globalization of culture, spearheaded by an implacable entertainment industry that recognizes no geographic borders. The toughest characters who show up on the island tend to be from the entertainment business, perhaps because that is the form of power with which the creators of the show were most familiar. With its gallery of creepy producers and promoters,[38] *Gilligan's Island* seems to raise doubts about the business end of American popular culture, but it often seems to be celebrating the magic of Hollywood and in particular the power of motion picture technology to light up the world. In general, technology is the issue about which *Gilligan's Island* is most ambivalent and perhaps even incoherent. At times the show seems to be presenting the castaways as better off living at a level of technological development far lower than what they experienced back on the mainland. At other times, however, they seem to take great pride in the technological advances they make under the guidance of the Professor. The source of this incoherence is what might be called the tension between "domestic" and "foreign" policy on the island. Technology may complicate and corrupt the lives of the castaways, but it also seems necessary to protect them from would-be invaders.

The preoccupation of *Gilligan's Island* with the question of America's technological might and global influence is chiefly evident in the one Cold War theme that resonates throughout the series—the space race. One did not have to be a rocket scientist to write the scripts, but it helped if one wanted to be a character in an episode. Perhaps because the series was developed in the years immediately following the 1962 Cuban Missile Crisis, it dwells almost obsessively on the issue of U.S.-U.S.S.R. competition in space-age technology. As early as the 18th episode ("X Marks the Spot"), *Gilligan's Island* began to reflect American anxieties about ICBMs and nuclear weapons. Via their radio, the castaways learn that the U.S. Air Force, believing their island is deserted, is about to launch a test missile toward it. The castaways assume that they will be killed in the resultant nuclear blast, but fortunately technical problems with the warhead lead the military authorities to remove it and fire a harmless missile instead, merely to check its guidance system. For the castaways, then, the threat of nuclear annihilation turns out to be exaggerated. Their next encounter with space-age technology (in "Smile, You're on Mars Camera," episode #40) also turns out to be benign, but just as frustrating. An unmanned NASA probe meant for Mars ends up landing on the island

and sends images of the castaways' hut back to Cape Canaveral. Unaccountably the NASA scientists mistake the tropical island for the surface of Mars, and thus fail to identify and rescue the castaways.

The space race really heats up for the castaways in episode #45, "Nyet, Nyet—Not Yet," when a Soviet space capsule strays from its course and lands in the island's lagoon. The two Soviet cosmonauts, Ivan and Igor, ought to help rescue the castaways, but their paranoia makes them hesitate. Indeed the episode turns out to reflect Cold War paranoia on both sides. The Professor thinks the Soviets are trying to establish a base on the island, while the cosmonauts think that the castaways are participating in some secret American space program. The mutual distrust leads to duplicity from everyone. Ginger tries to divert one of the cosmonauts from his post guarding the capsule by inviting him for a midnight swim. Much of the episode is devoted to a typical *Gilligan's Island* comedy of errors when the two sides try to get each other drunk. Finally the cosmonauts are able to sneak off the island with the help of a Soviet submarine. All along they have been concerned that American authorities will discover the failure of their landing and thus be in a position to ridicule the Soviet space program. As the episode ends, the castaways hear on their radio that the Soviet news agency Tass is claiming that the cosmonauts were rescued successfully right on target in their home waters. The cosmonaut episode is as close as *Gilligan's Island* ever got to outright Cold War propaganda. The Soviets are shown to have inferior space technology, and moreover, they will go to any length to conceal their failures.

Even in its brief run, the producers of *Gilligan's Island* were given to recycling plot ideas, and in the third season ("Splashdown," episode #90), the castaways had another encounter with a space capsule. This time, for variety's sake, American astronauts are involved. A NASA space mission takes the astronauts right over the castaways' island, but Gilligan's bumbling thwarts their efforts to signal their compatriots to have them rescued. At least the American space technology functions better than the Soviet—the astronauts are able to stay on course—although even they prove unable to complete their mission to rendezvous with an unmanned space capsule (which Mission Control eventually blows up when it lands in the castaways' lagoon). All of this concern with space weaponry may seem out of place in a lighthearted comedy.[39] In fact, the way *Gilligan's Island* kept broaching serious Cold War themes is a good measure of how anxious Americans in the 1960s were about the space race and the threat of nuclear annihilation. The show obviously embodied fears about the dangerous weapons both the United States and the Soviet Union were developing at the time, and a number of the episodes seem to express a specific concern that U.S. weapons might in effect backfire and harm innocent Americans. At the same time, the unrelenting silliness of the show worked to trivialize whatever serious issues it brought up, and in the end it served to reassure the American public that they really were safe even in the new world of nuclear weapons and ICBMs (which time and again in the series turn out to be harmless after all). Moreover, with episodes parading out relentless Japanese soldiers, ambitious Latin American dictators, and devious Soviet spies, *Gilligan's Island* keeps reminding its audience that as long as America has enemies in this world, the castaways as well as all U.S. citizens should be happy that American scientists are developing the most powerful explosives, the most accurate missiles, and in general the most effective military machine on Earth.

Ultimately, as the surprising number of Cold War episodes in *Gilligan's Island* suggests, the U.S.-U.S.S.R. rivalry supplied the ideological underpinning of the series. External conflict helped define the internal order the show celebrated. Precisely because the Soviets and other foreign nations stand for tyranny and oppression, Americans can pride themselves on their embrace of freedom and democracy. In the end, Americans represent good in *Gilligan's Island* because foreigners represent evil. In particular patriotism gets defined in the show in the context of the international order. When Mr. Howell is trying to get Gilligan to vote for Mrs. Howell in the Miss Castaway contest, he appeals to patriotic motives—and since Soviet communism is the great contrary against which America defines itself in the series, that means he tells Gilligan that a vote for Mrs. Howell is a vote for "free enterprise." The confidence in American superiority *Gilligan's Island* exudes is rooted in a simple bipolar view of world politics typical of the Cold War era.

Thus the Cold War supplied the background against which *Gilligan's Island* projected its image of American global supremacy, but no one wanted the show to become too serious, and ultimately the U.S.-U.S.S.R. competition remained in the background. The show of course foregrounds the castaways and, above all, Gilligan. It is one thing to point to America's superior technology as the source of its global preeminence. It is another to point to Gilligan. But that in a way is precisely the fantastic claim the show makes—that a cross section of American society is capable of ruling anywhere in the world, and in particular the most average and ordinary American citizen can take on all comers and thwart any plans they may have to infringe upon U.S. sovereignty. Though the Professor is a genius and Mr. Howell the richest man in the world, in the end the point of *Gilligan's Island* is that it does not take the best and the brightest America has to offer for the United States to prevail in the world. Gilligan can do the job. America is so great that it does not even have to field its first team in international competition. Throughout the 1960s the United States was trying to prove exactly this point in the realm of athletics, when it constantly sent its "amateurs" up against Soviet "professionals" in the Olympics and other sports events. In retrospect one might say that Gilligan's weekly triumphs presaged the U.S. hockey team's miraculous upset victory over the Soviets at the Lake Placid Winter Olympics in 1980.

In this context, we can now see why it is in fact appropriate that the castaways often behave like children. The show wants to picture them that way because Americans like to think of themselves as the world's children. Ever since the nineteenth century, Americans have tended to portray Europeans as sophisticated and morally corrupt, while picturing themselves as childlike in their innocence and naïveté. As we have seen, there is something innocent about the characters of *Gilligan's Island*, especially Mary Ann—who represents sexual innocence in particular—and Gilligan, who is as completely without guile as a human being can be. To be sure, the other castaways are somewhat ambiguous morally. The Skipper is a bit of a blowhard and a bully, the Professor can come across as a pompous know-it-all at times, Mr. Howell is greedy and devious, and Ginger is not above exploiting her sexual allure. Still, the show ultimately suggests that the castaways, for all their faults, are basically good people. This both justifies their world domination and makes it appear all the more remarkable. If they triumph over all their adversaries, it is not due to any sinister grand design on their part, but simply to the fact that they do not know their own strength. Other nationalities, such as the Russians or the Japanese, may have schemes for world domination in *Gilligan's Island*, but the Americans just watch it fall into their laps, as a simple recognition of their various forms of superiority as Americans. How can Americans be bent on world conquest when Gilligan is their leader? The fact that he is usually responsible for their victories over their enemies is evidence of the fundamental innocence of American power. In a suspicious and cynical mood, one might even say that Gilligan provides the ideological cover for American expansionism; he gives a democratic facade to the various forms of power represented by the other castaways. Indeed the show manages to create an image of American global domination without the slightest tinge of imperialist intent. The castaways just happen to occupy the island as a result of a disaster at sea. They quickly become its rightful owners and all other peoples, including local natives, are presented as invaders. *Gilligan's Island* manages to portray its Americans as essentially in a defensive posture, even when they are occupying territory far out in the middle of the Pacific Ocean.

In its own simplistic way, *Gilligan's Island* portrays America at the peak of its self-confidence, convinced of both its moral goodness and its power to back up its claims to superiority. The historical moment of the show is thus important. Created in the first half of the 1960s, *Gilligan's Island* could still hark back to World War II, when the United States established its moral leadership by leading a crusade against the antidemocratic forces of Germany, Italy, and Japan. In the early 1960s the United States could still present itself as the moral leader of the Free World, engaged in a long drawn-out struggle with the antidemocratic forces of the Soviet Union and Communist China. Thus *Gilligan's Island* captured America almost at its last moment of self-proclaimed innocence on the world stage. Events such as the U-2 spy plane incident and the Bay of Pigs debacle had already begun to erode America's claims to purity in international affairs, but soon deeply divisive issues—above all the Vietnam War—were to shatter America's own faith in its moral goodness, as well as in its ability to maintain its world leadership. No wonder Americans still like to watch *Gilligan's Island*. It takes them back to a time when it was still possible to offer Gilligan as an image of America's place in the world—a simple, good-hearted soul wanting simply to be left alone and with no designs on lording it over others, but entirely capable of frustrating anybody who tries to encroach upon his turf.

In short, when Americans first looked at *Gilligan's Island* in the 1960s, they saw their own reflection, and they liked what they saw. Evidently many still do. The show offered a sanitized image of American global domination and, as we have seen, an idyllic picture of domestic relations in America. In retrospect, we can see that *Gilligan's Island* toyed with many of the significant fault lines in American society that were beginning to tear the country apart in the 1960s. Several episodes deal with the growing tension between men and women provoked by feminist reconceptions of sexual roles. The portrayal of the Professor as an egghead points to the alienation of intellectuals left over from the Eisenhower era. The show even raises the issue of the generation gap and hints at the emerging power of the counterculture. In one episode, what is billed as America's most popular rock-and-roll band, the Mosquitoes, arrives on the island and disrupts its order, prompting first the men and then the women to form their own bands, with ridiculous results.[40] The episode glances at the new power of popular music in American culture, though of course it displays no understanding of how truly explosive this power was to become in the middle to the late 1960s. Perhaps most importantly, *Gilligan's Island* plays with the class divisions in 1960s America, using Mr. Howell's ostentatious wealth to suggest the gap between the rich and the poor, and all the social tensions it provoked.

But for all the fault lines in American society the show exposes, it usually succeeds in covering them over by the close of individual episodes. The castaways generally learn how to work together for the common good and typically find a way to transcend their differences. From viewing *Gilligan's Island*, one would never guess how troubled a time the 1960s became for the United States, both abroad and at home. On the international scene, America's growing involvement in the Vietnam War led many to question its role as a global leader. On the domestic scene, issues such as civil rights and the counterculture created bitter divisions in American society. With these problems beginning to surface, television viewers could turn to *Gilligan's Island* for relief from the troubled times. The show provided an idealized view of the American community, able to achieve harmony domestically despite its differences and able to rule the world without actually having to exercise any nasty forms of domination. It is not surprising that Americans still turn to *Gilligan's Island*. It appeals to their nostalgia for an earlier day, when a combination of American technology, business, and military might—and above all American *goodwill*—seemed capable of bringing peace and prosperity to the whole earth. As the "Ballad of Gilligan's Island" tried to tell viewers week after week, thanks to "the courage of the fearless crew," the American ship of state might be tossed, but it would never be lost.

EPILOGUE

The continuing relevance of *Gilligan's Island* in American culture was confirmed in the surprise hit movie of the summer of 1999, *The Blair Witch Project*. Presenting itself as a documentary, this movie claims to offer film and video footage shot by a young woman (Heather) and her two assistants (Josh and Mike) as they try to track down the story of mysterious and sinister forces in a wooded area in rural Maryland. The movie cleverly puts together what appear to be unedited scenes to tell a story of increasingly nightmarish events, culminating in the death, or at least the disappearance, of the young filmmakers. Made on an absurdly low budget, by Hollywood standards, *The Blair Witch Project* was a huge box office success, partly because of a brilliant publicity campaign linking television ads to a web site (the first effective use of the Internet to market a movie).[41] But what interests us is that this incredibly hip movie, representing everything new in the entertainment business, takes us in one extended sequence all the way back to *Gilligan's Island*. Roughly a third of the way into the movie, when the filmmakers have lost their way and just before things really begin to go bad for them, they are gathered around a campfire and Josh begins singing the theme song from *Gilligan's Island*. This innocent gesture provokes a surprisingly sharp response from Heather, who has organized the Blair Witch Project and is leading the expedition. As if she somehow finds the *Gilligan* theme a threat to her authority, she points out: "This ship has a good captain, not a fat, beer-guzzling guy in a blue shirt." This insult to Alan Hale Jr. does not go unchallenged and soon the two men are disputing Heather's characterization of *Gilligan's Island*, among other things pointing out the total absence of beer on the television show. The argument only deepens Heather's sense of the relevance of the castaways' situation to their own, as she tells Josh: "You're kind of like the captain and Mike's kind of like your Gilligan." At this point Josh has had enough of Heather's ignorance: "Let's not call it the captain anymore, you illiterate TV people, it's the Skipper."

It would be easy to dismiss the *Gilligan's Island* references in *The Blair Witch Project* as a bit of comic relief before the real horrors begin, but in fact this sequence goes right to the thematic core of the movie. *Blair Witch* embodies precisely the nostalgia for *Gilligan's Island* I have been discussing and in the process documents how far American pop culture traveled between the early 1960s and the late 1990s. As we have seen, *Gilligan's Island* reflected the global self-confidence of Americans in the 1960s—they could be dropped in the most remote corner of the earth and they would not get lost for a moment; they would remain comfortably in control and in charge. *Blair Witch* shows the exact opposite in the 1990s—a representative group of Americans wandering in suburban Maryland can get hopelessly lost and in fact perish just a day's walk from their own car. The young filmmakers themselves cannot believe what is happening to them; Heather says later in the movie: "It's very hard to get lost in America these days, and it's even harder to stay lost." But despite their efforts to draw upon their reserves of American patriotism—the filmmakers end up singing snatches of "America the Beautiful" and "The Star-Spangled Banner" as they try to hike out of the woods—they never do find their way and all they leave behind is the film and video record of what appears to be their destruction. Whereas the *Gilligan* characters are so confident as Americans that they cannot get lost anywhere on the planet, the *Blair Witch* characters seem so disoriented that they cannot maintain their bearings even in their own backyard.

What changed between the making of *Gilligan's Island* and the making of *The Blair Witch Project* to explain these diametrically opposed situations? It would take another whole chapter to explore fully what the film is trying to say about America at the end of the twentieth century, especially about changing sex roles, and so I will confine myself to one observation here. The characters in *Blair Witch* live in a world that has lost the certainties Americans thought they possessed in the early 1960s. For one thing, America in the 1990s has been globalized itself, with all the disorientation that entails. The castaways in *Gilligan's Island* were too busy Americanizing the rest of the world to be influenced or changed by the foreigners they encountered, and they never hesitated to apply purely American standards to anyone who crossed their path. The characters in *Blair Witch* are still self-confident as Americans and convinced that they are entitled to impose their categories on the world. Early in the movie, Heather expresses pride in all the technology at her disposal as an American: "We got so much . . . battery power we could fuel a small world country for a month." But her confidence starts to break down when she and Josh plan their camera work. She gets upset with his calculations: "You measured for meters? We're not in Europe." This talk of the metric system points directly to the issue of globalization. The United States has refused to conform to the measuring system employed by most of the world, and that leaves the filmmakers confused. Josh insists: "The lens has meters on it," but Heather remains stubborn: "It also has our system." She claims: "This is an American camera," and assumes that as Americans they have no need to adapt to the practices of the rest of the world. And yet, given the contemporary global economy, I very much doubt that the camera was in fact manufactured in America; at most it was assembled in the United States, but the parts must have been made abroad, thereby leading to confusion—the filmmakers do not know whether to employ the metric system or not.

When Americans have to use technology designed for Europeans, with their "unnatural" way of measuring things, we have come a long way from *Gilligan's Island*. *Blair Witch* is trying to say something about the confusion of Americans in the 1990s, especially young Americans, who now have a whole new range of technology at their disposal—a globalized and increasingly mobile technology (video cameras, DAT recorders, and so on). This new technology seems to offer them a new freedom, but at the same time it leads them astray in the wilderness, where they lose their bearings and are destroyed. For our purposes, it is fascinating that when *The Blair Witch Project* tries to portray Americans lost in the late 1990s, it uses *Gilligan's Island* as its reference point of stability. Over thirty years after it went off the air, *Gilligan's Island* is still serving as an image of 1960s America, with all its self-confidence and sureness of its purpose in the world. The way *Blair Witch* makes use of *Gilligan's Island* helps highlight the transformation of the meaning of globalization I am tracing in this book—from the Americanizing of the globe to the globalizing of America.

Shakespeare in the Original Klingon: *Star Trek* and the End of History

They looked like insects. How could I know they were intelligent enough to have weapons?

—"The Cage," *Star Trek*

In space, all warriors are cold warriors.

—General Chang, *Star Trek VI*

◆

Though the producers of *Star Trek* may have seemed overoptimistic at first in assigning a five-year mission to the Starship *Enterprise*—the original television series lasted only three seasons—through reruns, movies, and later television incarnations, *Star Trek* has proven to be one of the most enduring and significant phenomena in American popular culture. To celebrate the twenty-fifth anniversary of the original television program, in 1991 Paramount released *Star Trek VI: The Undiscovered Country*, the last in the series of movies to employ exclusively the old crew of the *Enterprise*. In an attempt to round out their story, the producers came up with a plot that provides a convenient opportunity to review the career of Captain Kirk and his fellow galactic voyagers.[1] The original television show was a product of the Cold War era, with pointed references to the Vietnam War in particular. Accordingly, *Star Trek VI* is based on the collapse of the Soviet Union. The enemy race of the Klingons suffers a disaster resembling the Chernobyl explosion and as a result no longer constitutes a viable threat to the United Federation of Planets. The projected peace between the Klingons and the Federation corresponds to the end of the Cold War. Nicholas Meyer, the director of *Star Trek VI*, reports that

Leonard Nimoy, the actor who plays Mr. Spock, came to him with the proposal: "Let's make a movie about the [Berlin] wall coming down in outer space."[2]

Star Trek VI strongly suggests that the crew of the *Enterprise* have lost their function now that their version of the Cold War is over. Indeed at several points in the film, Kirk and the others worry that they may have become antiques. When the crew first appears on screen, Dr. McCoy wonders whether they have come for a retirement party. Later, Spock asks Kirk: "Is it possible that we two—you and I—have grown so old and so inflexible that we have outlived our usefulness?" In fact, the *Enterprise* crew are in the process of putting themselves out of business. If they bring about peace in the galaxy, there will be no need for them anymore. Their heroism is necessary only while the United Federation of Planets has powerful enemies such as the Klingons. Thus *Star Trek VI* raises doubts about the future. Will the world of galactic peace be a less interesting world, a world without heroes? The movie has a strange way of raising this question—it associates Shakespeare with the Klingons. It is the Klingons who keep referring to Shakespeare in the film; somehow they have appropriated his works. In a joke on the old Soviet propensity to take credit for all sorts of Western inventions, the Klingon Chancellor Gorkon even claims: "You have not experienced Shakespeare until you have read him in the original Klingon." As strange as it may seem at first, associating Shakespeare with the warlike Klingons is appropriate. Many of Shakespeare's tragic heroes are military aristocrats, such as Othello, Macbeth, Coriolanus, and Mark Antony. Thus it is fitting that the military leader of the Klingons, General Chang, should die quoting Shakespeare. But this is a disturbing moment—it suggests that the extermination of the Klingon military aristocracy will also mean the extermination of Shakespeare. *Star Trek VI* sets up a provocative series of associations: The end of the Cold War will mean the end of history, which in turn will mean the end of heroism, which in turn will mean the end of Shakespeare and heroic literature.

◆

Before analyzing the full implications of these associations, I must review the intellectual background to *Star Trek VI*—the controversial "end of history" debate, which is actually referred to in the film. At a climactic moment, Kirk says: "Some people think the future means the end of history. Well, we haven't run out of history quite yet." The phrase "end of history" was popularized by Francis Fukuyama in an article with that title in *The National Interest*; he then expanded the article into a book called *The End of History and the Last Man*.[3] Fukuyama derives the idea of the end of history from Hegel, who developed it in his *Phenomenology* and his lectures on the philosophy of world history. Fukuyama especially draws on the reading of Hegel developed by his great twentieth-century interpreter, Alexandre Kojève.[4] In a sense, Fukuyama merely updated the Hegelian idea of the end of history, relating it to the collapse of communism in Eastern Europe and the Soviet Union. He argues that the end of the Cold War means the global triumph of liberal democracy. Everybody around the world is now embracing the principles of freedom and representative government in politics and the free market in economics. This, then, is what Fukuyama means by the end of history—history has reached its goal with the worldwide recognition of the principle of freedom.

Fukuyama may seem to be portraying the fulfillment of a prophecy made by Hegel, but Hegel did not merely foretell the end of history, he proclaimed it. Rather than arguing that at some distant point in time history would come to an end, he believed that it had already ended in his own day. In his view, the French Revolution was the crucial event. By overthrowing the principle of traditional aristocratic legitimacy, it established once and for all the new principle of political freedom. In Hegel's day, the Napoleonic Wars had begun to spread this principle throughout Europe and hence throughout the world. Hegel recognized that for a long time backwaters of unfreedom would remain in the world, but he argued that eventually freedom would spread everywhere. The momentous events of his day allow us to see the end of history in the sense of its goal. With the French Revolution, for the first time we can see concretely where all history has been headed. In updating Hegel by referring to the collapse of communism, Fukuyama can argue that some very large backwaters of unfreedom have now been eliminated, but in a sense he is merely reiterating Hegel's original claims.[5]

As responses to Fukuyama have repeatedly shown, many people are misled by the phrase *end of history*, usually because they confuse two senses of the word *end*: *end* as *terminus* and *end* as *goal*.[6] Hegel and Fukuyama may at times conflate these two senses, but their emphasis is always on *end* as *goal*. Thus most people who have challenged the idea of the end of history would discover, if they examined their premises, that they in fact believe in it.[7] The idea of the end of history does not mean that one day events will just stop happening. That is why most people miss the point when they try to refute Hegel by saying: "What do you mean history ended in 1806?" (the moment when Napoleon defeated the last forces of the Holy Roman Empire at the Battle of Jena and when Hegel wrote his *Phenomenology*). People object: "What about Waterloo in 1815? What about the revolutions of 1848? What about everything we read about in nineteenth- and twentieth-century history books?" But the point Hegel and Fukuyama make is not that history is over in the sense that events have stopped happening, but that history is over *in principle*. The Hegelian argument is that history is the development of freedom and in that sense we have already reached the final stage. Freedom, democracy, and representative government have been recognized all over the world as the only legitimate principles of government. That does not mean that these principles have been universally put into practice; that is why Fukuyama speaks of the backwaters of unfreedom that remain. But any regime contrary to the principle of representative government has to rely on force and oppression to maintain itself. Today nondemocratic governments no longer have legitimacy in the way monarchies and aristocracies once did. In the twentieth century the most tyrannical regimes have in fact claimed to be representative of the will of their people. However false those claims may have been, they constitute a recognition of the fact that representative government is now generally thought of as the only legitimate principle of rule.[8]

Thus, in a very real sense, we all seem to be Hegelians. Those who disagree with this claim should ask themselves: "Can I imagine slavery ever being *legitimately* reinstituted anywhere on this planet? Can I imagine any form of aristocracy being *legitimately* restored?" Anyone who answers "no" to these questions is granting the point that history is ultimately headed in one direction—toward the establishment of the principle that self-determination for all people is the only legitimate form of government—again, not necessarily the only *existing* form of government but the only *legitimate* one. In fact, we are so much the heirs of Hegel and modern liberalism today that we have a difficult time even imagining what premodern principles of legitimacy were like. Who today thinks in terms of real aristocracies, and not the tourist attractions that some constitutional monarchies maintain? Just consider the vocabulary of our routine political discourse. We are always speaking of political parties as progressive or conservative, thus implying that history moves in one direction, and in particular in the direction of increasing liberalization. Any attempt to restore a premodern form of legitimacy is regarded as hopelessly reactionary. In short, anyone who uses terms such as *progressive, conservative,* or *reactionary* is thinking in Hegelian terms—one either goes with the flow of history, or tries to stall it or turn it back.[9]

Hence when most people challenge the idea of the end of history, they really are affirming it. The argument often runs: "What do you mean, the end of history? With peace and the triumph of democracy, there is no end to what humanity can now accomplish. With the potential of a free humanity finally realized and released, together we can do anything." But that is just the point—the triumph of democracy and the establishment of the principle of freedom are all that the "end of history" means to Hegelians such as Fukuyama. Thus, *Star Trek*'s Captain Kirk is a closet Hegelian, as is former president George H. Bush. On September 23, 1991, Bush delivered a speech to the United Nations, which, in a clear challenge to Fukuyama, centered on the theme of "the resumption of history." But what did Bush mean by that phrase? Here is his argument:

> Communism held history captive for years. . . . This revival of history ushers in a new era teeming with opportunities and perils. . . . [H]istory's renewal enables people to pursue their natural instincts for enterprise. Communism froze that progress until its failures became too much for even its defenders to bear.[10]

Thus, for Bush, the "resumption of history" is simply the triumph of democracy and free enterprise. He went on to say: "People everywhere seek government of and by the people, and they want to enjoy their inalienable rights to freedom and property and person." Bush even developed the idea of backwaters, with a certain cigar-smoking despot in mind: "The people of Cuba suffer oppression at the hands of a dictator who hasn't gotten the word, the lone holdout in an otherwise democratic hemisphere, a man who hasn't adapted to a world that has no use for totalitarian tyranny." In short, what Bush means by the "resumption of history" is exactly what Hegel, Kojève, and Fukuyama mean by the "end of history."[11] The same is true for the strangely similar speech by Captain Kirk about the end of history I quoted earlier from *Star Trek VI*.

To analyze this point completely, we would have to examine all the forms of premodern, nondemocratic legitimacy, but two are of special importance: aristocracy and theocracy. Aristocracy is based on the idea that some people are born to rule others. Simply by virtue of their birth, they are entitled to govern, as if something in their blood makes them superior by nature to other human beings. Modern partisans of democracy are understandably appalled by the idea of aristocracy, to the point where they reject it totally and even find it hard to comprehend. Theocracy is based on the idea that by virtue of some kind of direct line to God, some people have a divine right to rule. In theocracy, God provides a higher principle and hence a claim to rule not necessarily authorized by one's fellow human beings. With the well-established principle of the separation of church and state, Americans and other democratic peoples reject the principle of theocracy as well. But as a form of government, it is at least more comprehensible than aristocracy, because examples of theocracy are available in the world today, particularly in certain Islamic nations. The resurgence of theocracy has been offered as one of the most serious challenges to Fukuyama's thesis, but again, most of his critics view theocracy only as an ugly fact of contemporary political life and not as a legitimate form of government, least of all a desirable alternative to democracy or the wave of the political future. Whenever people refer to contemporary theocracies as "throwbacks to the Middle Ages," they are implicitly affirming the Hegelian view of history as progressing toward freedom.

Still, the presence of theocracy in the world today raises theoretical and practical problems for democracy. It claims to be tolerant and to welcome diversity, but one thing it has always had difficulty tolerating is antidemocratic principles and forces. To quote Bush's UN speech again: "The United Nations should not dictate the particular forms of government that nations should adopt, but it can and should encourage the values upon which this organization was founded." To veteran *Star Trek* fans, this rhetoric should have a familiar ring to it. As we will see, it sounds a great deal like the famous Prime Directive. But how do you encourage democratic values without encouraging a particular form of government, namely, democracy? Even democracy has its limits; for all its sense of tolerance, it has a hard time tolerating intolerance, such as the religious intolerance of theocratic regimes. Democracy must also outlaw aristocracy. The United States Constitution forbids patents of nobility; Article I, section 8, number 8 states: "No title of nobility shall be granted by the United States." Very few people could quote this provision of the Constitution from memory; few are even aware of it, and indeed it sounds quite quaint to our modern ears.[12] But this provision reflects the fact that at the origin of the American regime, its founders believed that democracy had to break fundamentally with the alternative principles of government, such as aristocracy and theocracy, that had dominated the world for centuries.

◆

This paradox at the foundation of democracy—that the one thing it cannot tolerate is intolerance—stands at the heart of *Star Trek* as well. Reflecting from the start the political ideology of the United States, the original television episodes of *Star Trek* are fundamentally democratic in spirit. The explicit mission of the *Enterprise*—"to seek out new life and new civilizations"—appears to capture the spirit of democratic diversity and what is now called multiculturalism. But I would like to reformulate the mission of the *Enterprise*—"to seek out new civilizations and *destroy* them" if they contradict the principles of liberal democracy. Above all, Kirk and his crew set out to eliminate any vestiges of aristocracy or theocracy in the universe. In short, their mission was to make the galaxy safe for democracy. In that sense, the original *Star Trek* was already dealing with the issue of globalization, which is basically another name for the phenomenon we have been calling the end of history. The end of history is the globalization of liberal democracy, first the establishment of the principle that representative government is the only legitimate form of government and then the worldwide diffusion of that principle. We saw that *Gilligan's Island* rests on the premise that the principles of American democracy are applicable anywhere on the globe. *Star Trek* reflects an even deeper faith in the universality of American democratic principles—they can be projected anywhere in the galaxy. But *Star Trek* is a more serious show than *Gilligan's Island*, and thus even as it offers the prospect of universalizing democratic principles, it raises doubts about the legitimacy and desirability of that outcome. *Gilligan's Island* unself-consciously and almost innocently ends up suggesting that the way to globalize democracy is simply to Americanize the globe. The impulse to identify democratic globalization with Americanization is in many ways even stronger in *Star Trek* and the show often comes close to presenting the end of history as nothing more or less than a kind of galactic Pax Americana. But already in the original television series, one can sense unease with the notion of a homogeneously Americanized galaxy and it thus prepared the way for the even more serious doubts raised in *Star Trek VI*.

The television series broached the issue of whether globalization should simply take the form of Americanization in terms of the Prime Directive, the cornerstone of democratic respect for diversity in the United Federation of Planets. The Prime Directive insists that no political community should try to remake another in its image.

Originally called the Non-Interference Directive, it established the principle that the Federation would not try to impose its way of life on other cultures in the universe. But as any regular viewer of *Star Trek* knows, in many episodes, Kirk chooses to interfere in a newly discovered planet's affairs, irrevocably altering its history, and always directing it toward what we have been calling the end of history, namely, the principle of increasing freedom. When examined more closely, the Prime Directive turns out to be the principle of not interfering in the *self*-development of a planet. Thus it is already based on a democratic premise, that development is always self-development. Because in *Star Trek* the highest principle in the universe is democratic self-determination, Kirk can interfere in a planet's history if someone or something else is interfering with its autonomous development. This principle is illustrated in an episode called "A Private Little War," in which the Klingons are arming one side on a primitive planet to help them enslave the other. Accordingly, Kirk decides to arm the other side in order to achieve a balance of power, even at the price of speeding up the technological development of the planet. He cannot let the aristocratic Klingons get an advantage in the system of interplanetary alliances. *Star Trek* takes a dim view of any form of aristocracy or theocracy establishing or spreading its influence. If someone claims the natural or divine right to rule anyone else in the galaxy, Kirk automatically reaches for his phaser.

In *Star Trek* no form of superiority—above all, not mental superiority—justifies ruling over others. As shown by the treatment of the villain Khan Noonian Singh in both the television episode "Space Seed" and the movie *Star Trek II* (1982), the show is especially hostile to the idea of eugenics, that someone could be bred to be genetically superior and hence entitled to rule. This hostility even extends to Plato's *Republic*, the subject of one bizarre episode called "Plato's Stepchildren." The *Enterprise* comes upon a planet called Platonius, where the crew encounter a group of space travelers who once visited Earth in the time of ancient Greece. In their own words, "they liked Plato's ideas," and they have taken over a planet and tried to institute Plato's republic, with, as they say, "a few adaptations." They have undertaken a "mass eugenics program" and have been "bred for contemplation and self-reliance."

The Platonians have a philosopher-king, who makes the claim: "Ours is the most democratic society conceivable—anyone can, at any moment, be or do anything he wishes, even to the point of becoming ruler of Platonius, if his mind is strong enough." But that principle is not democratic in the terms of *Star Trek*, since rule on Platonius is founded on an aristocratic principle, a claim to a superior intellectual nature. Moreover, the episode exposes that claim to be a fraud. It turns out that the psychokinetic powers that allow the Platonians to rule are merely the result of something in the soil of their planet. Under the guidance of Dr. McCoy, Kirk takes twice the normal dose of the element and becomes mentally twice as powerful as the reigning philosopher-king. Kirk is thereby able to put Plato's republic out of business on this planet, with the memorable dismissal: "Despite your brains, you're the most contemptible beings who ever lived in this universe." So much for Plato's philosopher-king as far as *Star Trek* is concerned.

This particular episode is deeply biased against any notion of aristocracy. Almost as if the writers had read Hegel, Platonius is presented as a planet of many masters and one slave, emphasizing Hegel's central criticism of aristocracy, namely, the idleness of the masters. When the slave is given the chance to acquire his own psychokinetic power, he refuses because he does not want to "just lie around like a big blob of nothing and have things done for [him]." Even the philosopher-king concludes at the end: "we have become bizarre and unproductive." *Unproductive* is one of the most serious criticisms that can be leveled against a culture in *Star Trek*, which generally takes a bourgeois view of galactic developments. In the ideology of *Star Trek* everybody in the universe is supposed to be putting in a hard day's work, and aristocratic luxury and leisure are frowned upon and derided.

Star Trek is also hostile to theocracy, with a strong sense that no form of divine origin or inspiration justifies rule. Theocracy is unacceptable even in the case of a god providing paradise for his subjects. In an episode called "The Apple," Kirk and the crew come upon a planet where the inhabitants seem to be living in the Garden of Eden. But the price they pay for their innocent and idyllic happiness is that they serve a god called Vaal with blind obedience. Kirk and McCoy refuse to tolerate this situation. Only Spock defends it: "This may not be an ideal society but it is a viable one." To that McCoy objects in ringing liberal democratic rhetoric: "These people aren't living, they're existing. They don't create, they don't produce, they don't even think. They should have the opportunity to choose—we owe it to them to interfere." So much for the Prime Directive, which evidently always loses when it conflicts with the Hegelian-Marxist premium on productivity and work. Kirk is quite satisfied with himself once he has destroyed the god of the planet and starts explaining to the bewildered people how their lives will change: "That's what we call freedom—you'll like it a lot."

Despite all the protests to the contrary throughout the series, Kirk has a strong normative sense and tells the people of Vaal: "You'll learn something about men and women—the way they're supposed to be." At the end of the episode, when he is challenged about violating the Prime Directive, Kirk insists: "We put those people back upon a normal course of social evolution." Here is a clear statement of the premise of *Star Trek*—planetary history moves in one direction, the development of freedom.[13] As this antitheocratic episode shows, *Star Trek* is profoundly humanistic in spirit. It repeatedly demonstrates that nothing higher than the human exists in the universe, no higher principle to which human beings might be subordinate, that might justify some form of hierarchy. Above all, despite occasional moments of obligatory piety, *Star Trek* strongly implies that there are no gods. The *Enterprise* travels all over the universe, but finds no genuine gods or even God— despite a sustained effort in *Star Trek V* (1989). All Kirk and his crew encounter are impostors. Indeed, with its strong Enlightenment spirit, *Star Trek* repeatedly exposes the divine as an illusion.

The paradigm for this tendency is an episode entitled "Who Mourns for Adonais?" The *Enterprise* runs into the Greek god Apollo, and of course Kirk destroys him. That is to say, far out in space, the crew find a powerful being who they eventually realize once appeared to human beings on Earth as the god Apollo. This being has mysteriously withdrawn into space, along with the other Greek gods, but they have all faded away. Only Apollo has succeeded in waiting, in the faith that human beings would eventually come to him in space, thus giving him a chance to reclaim them as worshipers. That is what he wants to do with the crew of the *Enterprise*. The underlying suggestion of this episode is that aristocracy fundamentally *is* theocracy, a situation of men posing as gods. Naturally, Kirk cannot tolerate this outcome; he will not worship anybody or anything (some might say because he is too busy worshiping himself). With his democratic pride, what he most vigorously resists throughout the series is any form of servitude or slavery. Though he claims to be peace-loving, his spiritedness rouses him to violent behavior if peace ever seems to require him to surrender his autonomy in any form, especially if his command of the *Enterprise* is challenged. Thus, he will not yield even in the face of a power who at least at first sight appears to be higher than a human being, namely a god. Having destroyed Apollo, the crew in fact wonder whether they did the right thing. After Apollo fades away at the end, McCoy sadly says: "I wish we hadn't had to do this." Even Kirk uncharacteristically for once shows remorse: "They gave us so much. The Greek civilization, much of our culture and philosophy, came from a worship of those beings. In a way they began the Golden Age. Would it have hurt us, I wonder, just to have gathered a few laurel leaves?" To be sure, it is a little late for Kirk to be asking this question—he has just blasted Apollo's power into oblivion with his phasers. And earlier he was making more characteristic statements, such as "You're no god to us, mister" and "If you want to play God, that's your business," and above all "We don't bow to every creature who happens to have a bag of tricks."

Once again democratic ideology demands that Apollo's superiority be exposed as a merely technological advantage, not a superiority of nature. He has an *external* source of his extraordinary powers, much as the Platonians did. In *Star Trek,* he cannot be shown as possessing an *internal* source of his superiority; he cannot be intrinsically or *by nature* superior to human beings. Thus, although Apollo has some kind of different internal organ, it only allows him to channel an external power source. Any would-be divinity must always be debunked in *Star Trek* and exposed as a kind of cheap trick. Apollo's magic may have worked on primitive shepherds in ancient Greece, but it will have no effect on James Tiberius Kirk; as he says, "we've come a long way in 5000 years." The result of breaking Apollo's spell is to destroy possibly the greatest single archaeological find in the history of the universe—an authentic Greek god. This episode teaches a basic truth about Kirk—as in *Star Trek IV* (1986), he is willing to save whales, but he feels compelled to kill gods.[14] Kirk can be quite solicitous of the welfare of lower beings, but he cannot accept the idea that there might be something higher than humanity in the universe, something to which human will might have to be subordinated. Kirk does not want to have to face up to the implications of Apollo's claim: "There's an order of things in this universe—your species has denied it." "Who Mourns for Adonais?" is one of the most interesting *Star Trek* episodes, providing probably the most sympathetic treatment of any being claiming to be higher than humanity. But though it conveys an almost Hölderlinian sense of nostalgia for the ancient gods, even in this episode the supposedly divine being must be destroyed.

◆

Thus, *Star Trek* strangely parallels *Gilligan's Island,* and the two shows, admittedly in differing ways, reflect America's self-confidence in its democratic ideology in the 1960s. Like *Gilligan's Island,*

Star Trek champions the democratic principle of equality and frowns on anyone who claims the right to rule other people by nature and without their consent. *Star Trek* in fact takes the argument of *Gilligan's Island* a step further. If *Gilligan's Island* follows the Declaration of Independence in claiming that all men are created equal, *Star Trek* tries to universalize the principle—extending it literally throughout the universe—and show that all rational beings are created equal. Whatever planet they approach, Kirk and his crew are continually trying to prevent one group of creatures from being enslaved by another and thus to get everyone in the galaxy to recognize the superiority of the principles of American liberal democracy.

In particular the show reflected the moral fervor of the Civil Rights movement of the 1960s and often worked to promote the cause of racial equality. One episode, "Let That Be Your Last Battlefield," was a thinly veiled allegory of American race relations. The *Enterprise* gets a request for political asylum from a refugee whose race is colored half-white and half-black. He is being relentlessly pursued by another being from his planet, who is also colored half-white and half-black, but with the colors reversed. When the *Enterprise* finally gets to the home planet of these embattled beings, the crew discover that the entire population has been wiped out in an act of mutual racial genocide. Despite this frightening example, the white-black and black-white creatures vow to continue their bitter feud to the death. The episode is obviously a parable about the arbitrariness and destructiveness of racial prejudice and provides perhaps the clearest statement of the 1960s liberalism of *Star Trek*. Its message is that whatever their color, all rational beings are mirror images of each other and need to learn how to live together in peace.[15]

Since *Star Trek* routinely portrayed encounters with alien beings, the series often got to deal with the issue of prejudice, and how it might be overcome. Several episodes present the crew's need to get over their initial fear of and hostility to alien beings who behave in strange ways simply because their natures are so different.[16] Some of the episodes explore the problematics of interplanetary miscegenation, usually driven by Captain Kirk's womanizing tendencies. *Star Trek* prided itself on having presented "the first interracial kiss on national television"[17]—between Kirk and his communications officer, Lieutenant Uhuru, in the "Plato's Stepchildren" episode. The scene may seem tame by contemporary standards—and the series weakened its force by making the kiss result, not from genuine passion between Kirk and Uhuru, but from a kind of spell cast over them. Nevertheless, at the time (1968), this screen moment was considered quite daring and generated a good deal of controversy. By raising the race issue, *Star Trek* went well beyond *Gilligan's Island* in its championing of American liberalism, as might be expected from a show that only rarely ventured into comic territory and generally tried to present itself as serious television fare—adult science fiction. As evidence that *Star Trek* took the principle of equality more seriously, the show was not content to leave it to a bungler like Gilligan to champion the cause of liberal democracy. Comparing *Star Trek* to *Gilligan's Island*, one might say that just as the Professor got recast as Mr. Spock, the Skipper was reconfigured as Captain Kirk.[18] The later show offers a highly competent military figure as the active protector and promoter of democracy, making it clear that as far as *Star Trek* was concerned, the principle of equality is no laughing matter. In *Gilligan's Island* the characters, as we have seen, more or less blunder into Americanizing the globe. The characters in *Star Trek*, by contrast, are actively on a mission and are working hard to Americanize the whole galaxy.

Thus, the Cold War was more central to *Star Trek* than it was to *Gilligan's Island*, providing not just a subtext but in a sense the main text of the later series. The way the show celebrates the American regime depends heavily on a sense that, however flawed it may be, it is superior to the political alternatives. The autocratic aliens *Star Trek* routinely trots out make American-style democracy look good, even when it is not at its best. This is important because, unlike *Gilligan's Island*, *Star Trek* was willing to raise serious doubts about justice in America. In addition to criticizing race relations in the United States, it questions class relations. One episode called "The Cloudminders" portrays a world in which hardworking miners are oppressed by a self-indulgent ruling class—"the Stratos-dwellers"—who live in luxury far above the planet's surface in a city in the clouds. Drawing heavily upon Fritz Lang's *Metropolis* (1926), this episode is a transparent Marxist allegory about capitalists exploiting the proletariat. Kirk champions the miners and works to get the ruling class to grant them equality. Thus, while upholding the principle of equality, *Star Trek* does not claim that the United States perfectly embodies it. If anything, the show repeatedly criticizes America for not living up to its own democratic ideals and suggests that in terms of race and class, inequality still exists in the United States.

But in the view of *Star Trek*, America's failure to live up to its ideals is corrigible. This was the vision of 1960s liberalism—America is not a perfect country, but it is working to perfect itself, and thus can still

serve as a beacon to the world. As long as there are men like Captain
Kirk, who will stand up for equality and liberty, there is hope for
America to lead the world (and perhaps the galaxy) into a brighter
democratic future. That is why enemy races are central to the dramatic
logic of *Star Trek*. Judged by the standard of its own ideals, America
may seem deficient. It is only by comparison with hostile and undemocratic regimes that America can lay claim to superiority. Injustice
in America can be corrected, but these alternative regimes have no
mechanism for righting their wrongs because they are undemocratic
in principle and hence unjust to the core.

The structure of the *Star Trek* universe basically reflected the
geopolitics of the Cold War era. On one side is the United Federation
of Planets, in some ways just a galactic projection of the United States
of America, but perhaps more accurately a mirror of what used to be
called the Free World, the system of antitotalitarian, anticommunist
nations led by America. On the other side are two enemy races, the
Klingons and the Romulans, both characterized as militaristic, autocratic, and antagonistic to the principles of freedom, equality, and democracy. The series to some extent differentiated the Klingons from
the Romulans; the former were presented as more barbaric and warlike, the latter as more devious and treacherous. The division of the
Federation's enemies into two parties may have reflected the fact that
during the Cold War the United States and its allies faced a pair of political antagonists—the Soviet Union and Communist China, nations
that formed an uneasy alliance against the Free World and often had
their own differences. With the Federation representing one political
pole and the Klingons and the Romulans the other, the remaining
planets in the *Star Trek* universe form a kind of galactic Third World,
or what used to be known as the nonaligned nations in the Cold War.
Many *Star Trek* plots turn on competition between the Federation and
the Klingons or the Romulans to win the allegiance of these nonaligned planets.

Whatever the specific correspondences between the political pattern of *Star Trek* and the international system of the 1950s and 1960s, the
series clearly reflected a Cold War atmosphere and championed American democracy as an alternative to Communist totalitarianism. While
the show often criticizes military belligerence, and in particular portrays the warlike aristocracy of the Klingons negatively, *Star Trek* is in
many ways itself militaristic in spirit, celebrating the martial heroism
of Kirk and his crew and portraying their gleaming military hardware
in loving detail. Though focused on the Cold War, the show harked

back to World War II and still fed upon the nationalism generated by America's role in that global conflict. The very name of the starship— the *Enterprise*—clearly refers to one of America's most famous naval vessels in World War II. The episode called "Balance of Terror" is a re-creation of a World War II submarine warfare drama, with echoes of films such as *Run Silent, Run Deep* (1958), and *The Enemy Below* (1957).[19] In "Patterns of Force," Kirk and Spock get involved in the affairs of a strange planet where one of the captain's teachers from Starfleet Academy has re-created Nazi Germany.[20] In short, *Star Trek* drew upon memories of World War II to create a sense of the justice of the American cause, subliminally suggesting that when Kirk battles Klingons or Romulans, he is like a U.S. commander in the European or the Pacific Theater, fighting for freedom against the forces of tyranny.

As we saw, the chief manifestation of the Cold War in *Gilligan's Island* is the space race between the United States and the Soviet Union, which is featured in several episodes. One episode of *Star Trek* deals directly with the 1960s space race. In "Assignment: Earth," the *Enterprise* travels back in time to 1968 and Kirk and Spock struggle with a strange figure named Gary Seven, who is trying to sabotage a rocket launch at Cape Kennedy.[21] But it is pointless to try to track down isolated moments when *Star Trek* refers to the 1960s space race. The *Star Trek* TV series simply is the 1960s space race writ large, a dramatization of the competition between the United States and the Soviet Union. After all, the basic premise of the series is that in the future the ideological struggle between rival powers will be played out in space—the final frontier. The show continually implies that a political system will best demonstrate its superiority by its ability to colonize and generally win over other planets. *Star Trek* in effect gave its blessing to the U.S. space program of the 1960s by suggesting that the future of America as a world power hinged on its ability to keep abreast of its rivals in space technology and indeed surpass them. That is why several episodes turn specifically on the issue of whether the technology of the Federation's starships is equal to that of the Klingons or the Romulans (whether, for example, the Romulans can develop a cloaking device to make their ships invisible to their enemies—a strange premonition of American stealth technology in the 1990s).[22] At a time when Americans were genuinely insecure about whether their space technology was the equal of the Soviets', *Star Trek* offered reassurance to the TV public. As the stand-ins for American military might, the Federation's starships are generally state-of-the-art, and whatever technological shortcomings they may display are generally made up for by the superiority of American strategy and tactics, as well as a dose of good old Yankee ingenuity. (Chief Engineer Scott is able to jerry-rig a solution to any problem on the *Enterprise*.)

The final frontier of *Star Trek* thus was a science-fiction re-creation of the 1960s New Frontier and James Tiberius Kirk was in many respects an idealized version of John Fitzgerald Kennedy. (Note how both the fictional TV series and the real president invoked the frontier tradition of the American West.[23]) Kennedy was of course closely associated with the issue of space in the American imagination. One of his chief issues in the 1960 presidential campaign was the so-called Missile Gap with the Soviet Union and he made the space program and specifically the mission of landing a man on the moon one of the centerpieces of his presidency. And Kennedy always linked the issue of space to the Cold War; the point above all was for Americans to get to the moon before the Russians. Thus, *Star Trek* is a good reminder that American liberalism was at one time quite compatible with a militant anticommunism. Kirk is in fact a Cold Warrior very much on the model of JFK. He justifies his belligerence by insisting that he stands for democracy and freedom and is merely trying to secure the rights of people throughout the galaxy against tyrannical alien powers.

Star Trek thus develops more fully the paradox we saw adumbrated in *Gilligan's Island*—assertiveness in foreign policy based on the principle of nonassertiveness in domestic policy. Again and again *Star Trek* questions the right of anybody to run the life of another being and erects this principle into the foundation of the United Federation of Planets—the Prime Directive that forbids any planet from interfering in the affairs of another planet. And yet precisely this principle of noninterference ends up providing the justification for Kirk interfering in the affairs of one planet after another. The show is continually calling for a peaceful domestic order in which no being can lord it over another. At the same time, though, *Star Trek* shows its heroes claiming to be superior because of their allegiance to democracy and willing to go to war to defend or advance its cause. The analogies to the way America conducted itself as a world power in the 1960s are obvious.

◆

For all its Cold War mentality, *Star Trek* ended up raising doubts about America's role as leader of the Free World and champion of democracy. Ultimately the show mirrored the crisis American liberalism experienced in the second half of the 1960s, a crisis that almost tore apart the Democratic Party and led to the birth of the New Left. We have already discussed one of the factors that drove a wedge between liberalism and American patriotism, causing some to question whether the United States can simply be identified with the cause of justice in the world. *Star Trek* shows that in the 1960s liberals began to lose faith in America when they began to question whether it was truly living up to its own democratic principles, and especially the principle of equality. *Star Trek* tries to hold to the old liberal line that America may have its faults, but it is still the best game in town. Yet one can see in its treatment of the issue of class and especially the issue of race that it sometimes approaches the more radical position of the New Left that was to dominate college campuses by the end of the 1960s—that America is domestically an oppressive nation and in fact the enemy of equality for certain categories of its citizens.

But foreign policy issues turned out to be more important than domestic in *Star Trek*. The show reflected the self-doubts liberals began to experience in the late 1960s about their anticommunism and above all their commitment to the Cold War. Though the show is in its own way quite militaristic, it displays at times a strong pacifist streak. Several episodes dwell upon the evils of war, and even the normally bellicose Kirk sometimes regrets the havoc he is often forced to wreak in the name of peace.[24] *Star Trek* took the threat of nuclear annihilation more seriously than *Gilligan's Island* did. Several episodes deal with the theme of weapons of mass destruction that get out of control, sometimes coming back to haunt their inventors and even annihilate them.[25] Anxieties about the Cold War arms race were evident throughout popular culture in the 1960s, most notably in Stanley Kubrick's apocalyptic film *Dr. Strangelove* (1964). The producers of *Star Trek* never went as far as Kubrick's black comedy, but the show's enthusiasm for the Cold War was often tempered by a concern that championing the cause of democracy through military means, however nobly conceived, might result in the destruction of humanity in a nuclear holocaust. This fear came to be summed up in the 1960s in the famous slogan "Better Red Than Dead." *Star Trek* never fully embraces this position, and indeed Kirk often in effect speaks out against it. Nevertheless, the show reveals the increasing uncertainty of American liberals in the 1960s, as they began to wonder whether even the defense of their cherished democratic principles justified militant opposition to the communist world.

The foreign policy issue that finally shattered American liberalism, and in particular split the Democratic Party, was of course the Vietnam

War, and it surfaces in a number of *Star Trek* episodes. Though *Gilligan's Island* (1964–67) and *Star Trek* (1966–69) seem quite close in time, in one respect they stood on either side of a historical watershed, and that was the bitter division in America over its involvement in Vietnam. There are several reasons why *Star Trek* is more conflicted in its commitment to American ideology than *Gilligan's Island*, but I would argue that the principal factor is the effect of the Vietnam War as the 1960s wore on in undermining the ideological self-confidence of the American people. One *Star Trek* episode devoted to the Vietnam issue is "A Private Little War," in which, as we have seen, the Klingons arm one side in a planetary civil war and Kirk, representing the Federation, arms the other. The Cold War context is obvious, and "Kirk himself cites the parallel in the situation, and mentions that a balance of power must be employed on the planet exactly as it was implemented in 20th-century conflicts on 'Old Earth.'"[26] The references to Vietnam are evidently clearer in the first draft of the screenplay, written by Don Ingalls. "The tribesmen dressed in Mongolian-type clothes, and Apella (the puppet of the Klingons) was described as a 'Ho Chi Minh' type."[27] Echoing the controversies that were raging in the United States at the time about its commitment in Vietnam, this episode features McCoy pointedly questioning Kirk's strategy on the planet. "A Private Little War" suggests the futility of the conflict; the Klingons and the Federation seem bogged down in a trivial dispute that matters little to either party. But the criticism goes deeper, as the episode questions whether the Federation, for all its high ideals, is really helping the tribe it claims to be championing and not just condemning them to a life of constant warfare.

The Vietnam War surfaces again in an episode called "The Omega Glory," as Kirk, Spock, and McCoy are drawn into another planetary civil war, this time between an Asian-looking tribe, the Kohms, and a tribe called the Yangs. In another transparent allegory, the Kohms clearly stand for the communists and the Yangs for the Yankees (as Spock says at one point, "the parallel is almost too close"). But contrary to the spirit of the Cold War, the episode does not simply take the anticommunist side. In fact it presents the Yangs as more barbaric than the Kohms; it is the Yangs who are described as "savages." Still, Kirk ultimately allies himself with the Yangs by speaking their "worship words," which turn out—due to some strange process of intergalactic parallel evolution—to be a badly garbled version of several patriotic American texts, including the Pledge of Allegiance and the Preamble to the U.S. Constitution.[28] When Kirk accuses the Yangs of saying these words "without meaning," the episode threatens to reduce the foundational texts of American democracy to fetishes in the hands of a primitive tribe. The Yangs just repeat their sacred texts like a mantra and make an idol out of a tattered replica of the American flag. Thus *Star Trek* risks suggesting that the democratic principles it normally champions have no intrinsic value; they may be just a myth one people happens to believe in. The episode hints that American anticommunism might be based, not on genuine devotion to principle, but on ritual adherence to hollow tradition.

Drawing upon all his histrionic talent, Kirk gives an intensely dramatic reading of the Preamble and tries hard to save the day for the spirit of American democracy: "Among my people, we carry many such words as this—from many lands, many worlds—many are equally good, and are as well respected. But wherever we have gone, no words have said this thing of importance in quite this way." Even in his attempt to celebrate the U.S. Constitution, Kirk betrays the nervousness about American exceptionalism *Star Trek* occasionally betrayed. On the one hand, he feels compelled to say that there is nothing special about the Constitution as a text (it is just one among many); on the other hand, he insists that it is somehow uniquely important. Explaining the first words of the Preamble ("We the people"), Kirk tries to wean the Yangs away from the primitive aristocracy they have developed in their barbarism. He tells them that their sacred document "was not written for the chiefs or kings, or the warriors, or the rich or powerful, but for all the people." From this idea, Kirk draws a conclusion that surprises the warlike tribe, who have devoted themselves to exterminating their racially distinct enemies: "These words . . . were not written only for the Yangs, but for the Kohms as well. They must apply to anyone or they mean nothing." This statement neatly sums up the tendency of *Star Trek* to universalize American principles, but in context it gives them a new twist. If the Yangs are to obey their version of the U.S. Constitution, they must end their hostilities and embrace their Kohmunist neighbors. In general "The Omega Glory" conveys a sense of the arbitrariness of the conflict between the Kohms and the Yangs, implying that there is no reason to prefer one side over the other. In that sense, the episode seems to be a parable directed against the spirit of the Cold War, and indeed suggests that if Americans were really true to their principles, they would end their fighting in Vietnam. Indeed, "The Omega Glory" dares to imagine a parallel universe in which the Kohms at one point defeated the Yangs in all-out bacteriological warfare.

In deconstructing any meaningful opposition between the Yangs and the Kohms and thus running counter to the normal Cold War polarities of *Star Trek,* "The Omega Glory" shows what a difference the Vietnam War made in the late 1960s. Faced with stinging criticism from foreign quarters, Americans themselves began to wonder if their nation had been right to intervene in Southeast Asia. And the behavior of U.S. forces in the war led many to question if America was as morally superior to its opponents as it had long assumed. In short, the Vietnam War undermined the ideological self-confidence the Cold War had generated in the American people, their faith that their country was simply good and stood for democracy and freedom, while the Soviet Union and other communist nations were simply evil and stood for totalitarianism and tyranny. The Vietnam War led many people to view the United States and the Soviet Union as simply mirror images of each other, two superpowers pursuing their geopolitical interests, masking them behind a variety of ideological screens.[29]

Even this negative reinterpretation of the Cold War surfaces at times in *Star Trek.* In an episode called "A Piece of the Action," the series takes one of its typical Cold War plots—the intervention of a starship in a hitherto isolated planet's affairs—and gives it a new twist. Imitating a book of American twentieth-century history left behind by Federation interlopers, the inhabitants of the planet have re-created the world of Chicago mobsters in the 1920s. This is one of the more amusing episodes in the history of the series, but it has potentially serious undertones. It seems to reduce the ideological conflicts the series normally presents (democracy versus autocracy) to mere gang warfare—with each side simply grabbing for its "piece of the action." The suggestion seems to be that the two sides in the Cold War may be no better than gangsters themselves. Ultimately, *Star Trek* is ambivalent in its view of the Cold War, and in particular the place of the United States in world affairs. In many respects the television series was a perfect embodiment of Cold War ideology, presenting the United States as the true representative of freedom, equality, and democracy in the world and its nondemocratic opponents as the true representatives of evil. But the series sometimes worked against its own investment in Cold War polarities, questioning the value of any armed conflict and moreover raising doubts about whether one side truly is morally superior to the other. *Star Trek* thus shows how crucial the Cold War was to American self-consciousness and self-definition in the 1960s. If one accepted Cold War categories, then Americanizing the globe seemed justified, but if one questioned those categories, then the triumph of American ideology became problematic.

◆

We can now see why *Star Trek VI*, dealing as it does with the end of the Cold War, occupies such a pivotal position in the whole history of the series of television programs and movies. With the ideologically bracing effect of the Cold War removed, *Star Trek VI* was freer than the original TV series to raise the issue whether the cause of America can simply be identified with the cause of democracy. We have seen that in the original TV series colonizing space serves as a metaphor for globalization. The way the Federation attempts to spread the principle of freedom throughout the galaxy provides an image of America's mission to democratize the Earth. But what is on one level presented metaphorically in *Star Trek* must on another level be taken literally. The attempt to galacticize democracy in fact presupposes that it had already been globalized on Earth. In the television series, the planet Earth has long since been united under one democratic regime. For obvious reasons, the show was deliberately vague about the details of Earth's history after the 1960s, but it periodically threw out hints and we may surmise that at some point the planet achieved world government, and evidently under American leadership. The uniting of the Earth was of course pointedly symbolized on the bridge of the *Enterprise*, where the command structure of the starship is supposed to mirror the full integration of the world's nations. The multinational, multiracial composition of the *Enterprise* crew was one of the major liberal statements *Star Trek* was trying to make. The chief officers on the starship include an Asian, Mr. Sulu, an African, Lt. Uhuru, and, most strikingly, a Russian, Mr. Chekov.[30] The series may have shown the Cold War re-created and continuing in outer space with the Klingons as surrogates for the Russians, but in literal terms it assumed that the conflict had been settled on Earth, so amicably that Americans and Russians could now serve together in the same military unit (admittedly with some good-humored tension remaining between them).[31]

But the multinational character of the command of the *Enterprise* is largely a facade. There is no question who is really in charge of the starship; it is Captain Kirk, and he is emphatically an American (born and bred in the heartland of Iowa). The *Star Trek* TV series tried not to dwell on this fact, but wherever one looks in the program one sees unmistakable signs of American domination. The idea is even projected onto a higher plane at the level of the United Federation of Planets. The unspoken premise of the *Star Trek* TV series is that Americans dominate the Earth, and the Earth dominates the United Federation of Planets. Thus one can conclude that the United Federation of Planets is in effect an Americanized institution. At every level of political association the series portrays, it thus raises the same questions: Can beings be united only on the basis of one superior way of life prevailing over all the others, and will that way of life always be specifically American? According to *Star Trek*, human beings seem to be united into a single planet only on the basis of American democratic principles. When human beings go on to federate with species from other planets, it seems to be on the basis of these same principles, now viewed as representing humanity as a whole. Thus the humanization of the galaxy in *Star Trek* appears to be simply a continuation of the original Americanization of the Earth. Indeed, in identifying the cause of democracy with the cause of humanity, *Star Trek* comes perilously close to identifying both with the cause of America. In *Star Trek VI*, we return to the basic metaphor of the original TV series—human beings trying to make the principle of freedom prevail throughout the galaxy stand for Americans trying to make their democracy prevail all over the Earth, and especially over their Cold War opponents. *Star Trek VI* in some ways represents the epitome of American triumphalism, as it celebrates America's final defeat of its enemies in the Cold War. But at the same time, the movie calls that triumph into question and makes us wonder whether America's victory will lead to a great loss as the galaxy is culturally homogenized under its domination.

As the movie opens, with the very existence of the Klingon home planet threatened, the path seems cleared for a new galactic order. Seeking peace, the United Federation of Planets is willing to extend a helping hand to its traditional enemies. But reactionary hard-liners on both sides are trying to prevent détente from developing between the Federation and the Klingons. The rhetoric of the film is largely multicultural, suggesting that the Federation is not exclusive but rather tries to embrace any new culture. But in an important sense, that multicultural rhetoric threatens to become hollow. The Klingons will be embraced, but only insofar as they abandon what makes them distinctively Klingon, their warlike ways. That is what motivates the Klingon hard-liners—they feel that they will lose their cultural identity if admitted to the Federation. In this context, one sees the importance of the moment near the end of the film when Kirk says to Spock: "Everybody's human."[32] This is supposed to be the great all-embracing affirmation of the film, but Spock answers as a Vulcan: "I find that remark insulting." *Star Trek VI* raises the question whether "to be human" is the highest claim that can be made in the universe. Is humanity coextensive with goodness? Or is that claim an insult to other ways of life in the universe? As one of the Klingons bitterly puts it, is the United Federation of Planets ultimately a *"Homo sapiens*-only club?"[33]

On these fundamental questions, the film vacillates. One view represented is that humanity simply happens to have discovered principles of justice that turn out to be universal. That explains why a *prime directive* is possible, a universally valid law based on the principle of self-determination. One might argue that there is nothing uniquely human about this principle; it has a Kantian formalism to it, as the kind of law that applies to all rational beings and not just to human beings. Nevertheless, the principle looks suspiciously like good old human justice. And the Federation is led by humans who seem committed to spreading human domination throughout the universe. Thus there seems to be an internal contradiction in the principles of the Federation, which cannot decide if it is promoting the cause of universal justice or merely the cause of the human race. This contradiction was already reflected in an interesting dialogue between Spock and McCoy back in the television episode "The Apple." Upset about interfering in another planet's affairs, Spock says to McCoy: "You insist on applying human standards to nonhuman cultures. I remind you that humans are only a tiny minority in the galaxy." But this genuinely multicultural perspective provokes a sharp reply from McCoy: "There are certain absolutes, Mr. Spock, and one of them is the right of humanoids to a free and unchained environment, the right to have conditions which permit growth." Here is the key to the ethos of *Star Trek*—the right to self-determination generates the one absolute in its universe. Spock counters with another candidate for an absolute: "Another is their right to choose a system that seems to work for them." But the imperative of freedom always seems to prevail in *Star Trek*, especially when it comes into conflict with any society that smacks of military aristocracy, even if creatures such as the Klingons express satisfaction with their nondemocratic way of life. *Star Trek* keeps returning to the same galactic imperative: "You may live under any planetary government you choose—as long as it is democratic."

Aristocracy never seems to get a fair hearing in *Star Trek*, which, like most science fiction, tends to present it as atavistic, a throwback to the distant past. We may contemplate it with a certain antiquarian and even archaeological curiosity, but we are never to regard aristocracy as a viable alternative to liberal democracy. It is indeed a curious fact that in science fiction stories, extraterrestrial rulers often look like figures out of our past history on Earth, a history that turns out to be aristocratic and often specifically imperial. Space aliens may have superior technology, but they often still carry swords and hail emperors in togas.[34] Time and again, space travelers from Earth journey to remote planets only to find themselves in ancient Greece or Rome. We have already seen an example of this in "Who Mourns for Adonais?" In two other television episodes, "Bread and Circuses" and "The Gamesters of Triskelion," Kirk and several crew members end up involved in Roman-style gladiatorial contests. Nilo Rodis, the art director for *Star Trek VI*, reports that in planning the sets for the big trial scene—perhaps the most widely viewed medical malpractice suit in galactic history—Nicholas Meyer said: "The Klingons are kind of like Romans throwing Christians to the lions."[35] Science fiction looks to the future, but it is paradoxically haunted by memories of the aristocratic past of humanity. The evocation of ancient Roman grandeur in *Star Trek* and other science fiction stories reflects a nostalgia for earlier forms of greatness, but the emphasis on gladiatorial combat is a way of stamping aristocratic life as barbaric.[36] The very fact that aristocracy is usually pictured in science fiction in images out of ancient history is a way of rejecting it as hopelessly outdated in the eyes of democratic liberals at the end of history. Science fiction allows us to flirt imaginatively with aristocratic ways of life, while ultimately rejecting them in order to reaffirm the superiority of liberal democracy.

Thus, for all the multicultural rhetoric of *Star Trek VI*, we are left wondering if the film is genuinely willing to contemplate embracing ways of life that fundamentally differ from American democracy in political terms. The ideology of multiculturalism has a tendency to aestheticize the issue of difference, focusing on ethnic variations in costume or cuisine. Dealing with purely cultural differences—phenomena such as folk dances or folk songs—it is easy to celebrate difference, because nothing vital is at stake. With aesthetic differences, it is possible to avoid genuine and substantive clashes of principle. But what if another culture has a different attitude toward life and is willing to enslave or even exterminate other beings? What if it has a different attitude toward multiculturalism itself? One culture may think it is superior to all other cultures, and therefore entitled to rule them. Some Klingons do not want to become human; they would rather maintain their genuine difference, a difference involving not something superficial such as costume but a substantive political principle.

The Klingons are a martial people who genuinely love war and live for it; hence they have no desire to embrace peace, especially under human domination. If Spock is any indication, even the Vulcans are not sure they want to be fully humanized.

Thus *Star Trek VI* cannot decide whether humanity represents merely one principle among many in the universe or the universal principle of justice. The film appears to celebrate the achievement of a universal galactic peace founded on human principles, which are identified with the principles of liberal democracy. But at the same time, the film seems to express misgivings about that result. It suggests that universal peace will result in the homogenization of the galaxy. To make the universe safe and harmonious will require losing what makes the universe interesting. "Genuine clashes of legitimately opposing principles" is Hegel's formula for tragedy, which is why the end of history necessarily means the end of tragedy as well.[37] For Hegel, tragedy is the engine of history—violent clashes of opposing principles keep driving humanity on to the next stage of history, until it reaches the end, when one single principle universally prevails as legitimate. With two principles, we have the formula for heroism on both sides, as each spurs the other on. But that means that at the end of history, heroes will no longer be necessary because conflict has been transcended. This explains Kirk's concern in the film: "How on earth can history get past people like me?" What we are witnessing in *Star Trek VI* is the crew of the *Enterprise* making themselves obsolete. With the strongly valedictory sense of the conclusion, we are left with the feeling of a diminished world.[38]

After the violent heroes have played out their struggle, perhaps tamer, more efficient beings will run the world. That may explain why the last person we see in charge of a commissioned starship in *Star Trek VI* is Captain Sulu. As the one Japanese character, he used to be subordinate to Kirk, but now he has command of his own starship, a technologically more advanced one. The film seems to be making a strange suggestion—if the Klingons are the Russians, and the Federation the United States, have the two sides fought each other for years only to leave the world in the hands of the Japanese? Now we see what happens when productivity is made the ultimate standard of value in the universe. Sulu is the only one of the original crew still working at the end of the film, still on active duty. Perhaps the suggestion is that the Japanese will preside over the end of history, a point already made by Kojève in a crucial footnote in his Hegel commentary: "The recently begun interaction between Japan and the Western

World will finally lead not to a rebarbarization of the Japanese but to a 'Japanization' of the Westerners (including the Russians)."[39] Kojève argues that customs such as the Japanese tea ceremony provide the prototype of behavior at the end of history. Posthistorical and post-modern existence consists of acts of ritual emptied of their original meaning in an aristocratic culture and reenacted merely for the sake of form, thus transmuting once authentic rituals into acts of pure snobbery, such as the tea ceremony. *Star Trek VI* opens with a shot of Captain Sulu drinking a cup of tea.

◆

These are disturbing suggestions, but as a professor of English, I am even more troubled by the treatment of Shakespeare in the film.[40] One reason the reactionary Klingons appear to be the dramatically more interesting characters is that they are given most of the best lines, which is to say, most of the lines from Shakespeare. By linking Shakespeare with the Klingons, the film associates him with the form of heroism that is dying out in the universe at the end of history. Some of the quotations from Shakespeare in *Star Trek VI* are essentially trivial, such as "To be, or not to be" or "Parting is such sweet sorrow." These are Shakespeare clichés, quotations sure to be known by the audience; their only function is to be recognized by the audience as Shakespeare quotations. Other passages quoted are less well known but seem to be more meaningful. Several contribute to the valedictory mood of the film: Falstaff's "We have heard the chimes at midnight" or Prospero's "Our revels now are ended," a line from Shakespeare's own farewell to the theater in *The Tempest*. The most pointed of these valedictory passages comes from *Richard II*: "Let us sit upon the ground / And tell sad stories of the death of kings."[41] Referring to the deposition of a monarch, these lines constitute a farewell to the old regime, and, more generally, to all forms of predemocratic legitimacy.

A cluster of Shakespeare quotations appears in the film just before General Chang is blown out of space, lines that suggest that what is being destroyed is the old heroic ethos of the warrior. Chang quotes *Henry V*: "Once more unto the breach, dear friends" and "The game's afoot!" (*Henry V*, III.i.1, 32), as well as Mark Antony in *Julius Caesar*: "Cry 'Havoc!' and let slip the dogs of war" (III.i.273). The most resonant of these quotations comes from *Julius Caesar* (III.i.60): "I am constant as the northern star." Caesar speaks these words just before he dies, when the Senators have come to ask pardon for Publius Cimber.

Refusing to go back on his word, Caesar identifies himself in this scene with the constancy of a god—"Hence! wilt thou lift up Olympus?" (III.i.74). Thus, in effect, Caesar is killed directly as a result of his claim to divinity. As Shakespeare shows particularly in the case of Cassius, the Roman Senators cannot stand the thought of anyone claiming to be of a higher order than they are, and hence claiming the right to rule them as a god. The way *Star Trek VI* alludes to this kind of republican spiritedness at this climactic moment is appropriate. Kirk's killing Chang resembles his earlier destruction of Apollo; he must strike down any being who claims to be qualitatively superior by nature.

One last quotation in this cluster seems at first out of place, but it is the most interesting and disturbing of all. For one moment, Chang stops identifying with Shakespeare's warriors and chooses a different model, quoting *The Merchant of Venice* (III.i.64–67): "If you prick us, do we not bleed? If you tickle us, do we not laugh? . . . And if you wrong us, shall we not revenge?" These lines from Shylock's famous speech constitute a last—and futile—plea from the Klingon warrior for genuine multicultural tolerance. *The Merchant of Venice* is Shakespeare's play about multiculturalism, and its argument about our common humanity culminates in this eloquent speech by Shylock. But if one looks closely at Shylock's claims, one notices that his idea of a common humanity is based solely on the fact that we share the same physical form, the same body. As Allan Bloom points out:

> Shylock justified himself by an appeal to the universality of humanity. . . . Men can only be men together when they mutually recognize their sameness; otherwise they are like beings of different species to each other, and their only similarity is in their revenge. But, sadly, if one looks at the list of similar characteristics on which Shylock bases his claim to equality with his Christian tormentors, one sees that it includes only things which belong to the body; what he finds in common between Christian and Jew is essentially what all animals have in common. . . . (Shylock characteristically mentions laughter as a result of tickling. He and Antonio would not laugh at the same jokes.) . . . Shylock asserts that the brotherhood of man can only come into being on the basis of the lowest common denominator. . . . It is the body; all the higher parts of the soul must be abstracted from, because they express men's opinions and beliefs about what is good and bad, virtue and vice. These, men do not share; these beliefs make men enemies.[42]

Bloom's analysis of Shylock suggests that the quotation from *The Merchant of Venice* greatly complicates *Star Trek VI*, since the human body cannot provide a common basis for the whole galaxy. Who knows what happens when you tickle a Klingon? We learn in the film, for example, that Klingons do not have tear ducts.[43] As *The Merchant of Venice* shows, it is difficult enough to assert a common humanity in one city here on Earth. To do so throughout the entire galaxy would obviously be much more difficult. As the chameloid Martia says in *Star Trek VI*: "not everybody keeps their genitals in the same place"— sound advice for interplanetary travelers. The uncertainty of *Star Trek VI* is reflected in the way the movie alternates between two generalizations: "everybody's human" and "not everybody keeps their genitals in the same place."

Thus Chang's quotation from *The Merchant of Venice* raises doubts about the democratic ideology of *Star Trek*. Shylock calls attention to the hypocrisy of Venice. The city claims to be a genuinely multicultural community, indifferent to racial or religious distinctions, treating all its citizens alike. But Shakespeare shows that in fact Venice operates very differently, treating Shylock as a second-class citizen, much as it does Othello.[44] In the end, Venice refuses to ignore what it regards as genuine differences in principle between Christians and Jews. Eventually the city forces Shylock to become a Christian. Perhaps this outcome provides a clue to the United Federation of Planets' goal; ultimately it wants Klingons such as Chang to "convert." His identification with Shylock points to the Federation's hypocrisy in trying to establish its galactic hegemony under the banner of multicultural toleration. To the Federation, Chang is an alien and cannot cease being one until he abandons all that he stands for, the code of a Klingon warrior. In short, aliens have a real problem with what modern Americans and the United Federation of Planets regard as inalienable rights. Despite its multicultural rhetoric, *Star Trek VI* suggests that peace between warring cultures will require a process of homogenization, in which one culture will be ultimately absorbed into the other and the resulting world will inevitably be less interesting because less diverse.

Star Trek VI thus raises the question: Will the end of history mean the end of Shakespeare and, more generally, the end of those higher human possibilities that inspired heroic literature? After examining the specific Shakespeare quotations in the film, one is left with a number of nagging questions. Do the Shakespeare quotations provide a serious aristocratic countermovement to the democratic thrust of the movie as a whole? Or does Shakespeare merely serve as window dressing in the film, an attempt to give it the aura of high art? In short, do the Shakespeare quotations amount to anything more than postmodern pastiche?[45] Indeed the way the quotations are often jumbled together threatens to become comic. All the lines from Shakespeare are ripped out of context, perhaps just to give a pseudo-Shakespearean elevation to the film. One of its writers, Denny Martin Flinn, gives an account that suggests that the multiplication of Shakespeare quotations was more or less an accident: "Once we got [Christopher] Plummer, Nick [Meyer] said, 'This guy can really do this stuff' and kept adding more and more."[46] What seems to be important about the quotations is simply the fact that they are from Shakespeare; their specific content seems largely irrelevant. The average member of the audience would not even recognize half of them and surely would not be able to remember the original contexts from which they come. The aristocratic world of Shakespeare is evidently not being presented as a genuine alternative to the democratic world of the film. *Star Trek VI* simply tries to absorb Shakespeare, to bite off chunks of his dialogue and spit them out as its own.

Thus the use of Shakespeare in the film illustrates the very process it deals with in portraying the Klingon-Federation conflict—the effacement of difference. The way *Star Trek VI* tries to absorb Shakespeare into a popular film demonstrates the dangers of homogenization the main plot suggests. The film appears to be making a positive statement about the universality of Shakespeare, that his works apply everywhere in the galaxy. Flinn reflects this attitude when he comments: "In *Star Trek II*, [Meyer] put [Dickens's *Tale of Two Cities*] in Shatner's [Kirk's] hands . . . and he made a marvelous statement that no matter how information is delivered to us in the 23rd century, no matter how electronic it all becomes, great literature will still exist."[47] Flinn's sentiments sound uplifting, but all he really means is that in the twenty-third century great literature will still physically exist, perhaps even in the traditional form of books. But what Flinn cannot guarantee is that people will still know how to read these books, that is, to read them with understanding. In *Star Trek VI*, the price of including Shakespeare in the dialogue is to blur everything that is distinctively Shakespearean, as the passages get lost in the babble of other voices. The effect resembles that of T. S. Eliot's *The Waste Land*—quotations from great literature jumbled together with banal dialogue from ordinary life.

In that sense, *Star Trek VI* provides us with a troubling vision of the postmodern condition. At the end of history, all of past culture is spread out and equally available to contemporary artists, who can pick and choose what they want from the vast museum, or rather supermarket, of historical art. Hence the end of history works to efface distinctions—between past and present, between noble and base, be-

tween high art and popular culture. *Star Trek VI* thus helps us to reflect
on the connection between the posthistorical and the postmodern. In
particular it suggests how postmodernism as a cultural attitude is related to the democratic leveling at the end of history.[48] *Star Trek VI* is
itself a postmodern film, embodying an awareness of its place in film
history. At many points the characters seem to know that they are
playing roles, most notably at the end when Kirk proclaims: "Once
again we've saved civilization as we know it." Throughout, the film is
very self-conscious about its use of cinematic conventions, for example, the sense of riding off into the sunset at the conclusion. In short,
Star Trek VI accepts its own belatedness and tries to make the best of
it. The film makes no effort to conceal the fact that it is related to a long
line of prior films; indeed it repeatedly plays with the fact that it
comes at the cinematic equivalent of the end of history. If one takes the
film's political and literary background seriously, it leaves us with disturbing questions about the end of history and the postmodern culture
to which it gives birth.

In particular *Star Trek VI* raises doubts about the globalization of
democracy and America's role in the process. The original television
series, produced at the height of the Cold War, shows how rivalry with
the Soviet Union helped generate U.S. nationalism and encouraged
the country to view itself as the champion of democracy in the world.
But even the TV show occasionally wavered in this faith, sometimes
questioning whether America was living up to its own democratic
principles, sometimes perhaps even questioning those principles
themselves, or at least their universal validity—particularly when the
Cold War began to lose its ideological clarity in the jungles of Vietnam.
Star Trek VI carries on and deepens this process of interrogating America's claim to set an example for the world and reveals that with the
end of the Cold War, the United States began to open up to more genuinely multicultural perspectives and to wonder whether it had the
right to set universal standards. *Star Trek VI* presents the Americanization of the globe as problematic, thereby setting the stage for our
exploration of a new development—the globalization of America.

GLOBAL TELEVISION AND
THE DECLINE OF THE
NATION-STATE

The era of big government is over.

—William Jefferson Clinton

Simpson Agonistes: Atomistic Politics, the Nuclear Family, and the Globalization of Springfield

> Oh, Marge, cartoons don't have any deep meaning. They're just stupid drawings that give you a cheap laugh.
>
> —Homer J. Simpson

> Democracy loosens social bonds, but it tightens natural bonds. It brings relatives together at the same time that it separates citizens.
>
> —Alexis de Tocqueville

When Senator Charles Schumer (D-N.Y.) visited a high school in upstate New York in May 1999, he received an unexpected civics lesson from an unexpected source. Speaking on the timely subject of school violence, Senator Schumer praised the Brady Bill, which he helped sponsor, for its role in preventing crime. Rising to question the effectiveness of this effort at gun control, a student named Kevin Davis cited an example no doubt familiar to his classmates but unknown to the senator from New York: "It reminds me of a *Simpsons* episode. Homer wanted to get a gun but he had been in jail twice and in a mental institution. They label him as 'potentially dangerous.' So Homer asks what that means and the gun dealer says: 'It just means you need an extra week before you can get the gun.'"[1] Without going into the pros and cons of gun control legislation, one can recognize in this incident how the Fox Network's cartoon series *The Simpsons* shapes the way Americans think, particularly the younger generation. It may therefore be worth taking a look at the television program to see what sort of political lessons it is teaching. *The Simpsons* may seem like mindless entertainment to many, but in fact it offers some of the most sophisticated comedy and satire ever to appear on American television. Over the years, the show has taken on many serious political issues: nuclear power safety, environmentalism, immigration, gay rights, women in the military, and so on. Paradoxically it is the farcical nature of the show that allows it to be serious in ways that many other television programs are not.

I will not, however, dwell on the question of the show's politics in the narrowly partisan sense. *The Simpsons* satirizes both Republicans and Democrats. The local politician who appears most frequently in the show, Mayor Diamond Joe Quimby, speaks with a heavy Kennedy accent[2] and generally acts like a Democratic urban machine politician. By the same token, the most sinister political force in the series, the cabal that seems to run the town of Springfield from behind the scenes, is portrayed as Republican. On balance, it is fair to say that *The Simpsons*, like most of what comes out of Hollywood, is pro-Democrat and anti-Republican. One whole episode was a gratuitously nasty portrait of former President George H. Bush,[3] whereas the show was surprisingly slow to satirize President Bill Clinton.[4] Nevertheless, perhaps the single funniest political line in the history of *The Simpsons* came at the expense of the Democrats. When Grandpa Abraham Simpson receives money in the mail really meant for his grandchildren, Bart asks him: "Didn't you wonder why you were getting checks for absolutely nothing?" Abe replies: "I figured 'cause the Democrats were in power again."[5] Unwilling to forego any opportunity for humor, the show's creators have been generally evenhanded over the years in making fun of both parties, and of both the right and the left.[6]

Setting aside the surface issue of political partisanship, I am interested in the deep politics of *The Simpsons*, what the show most fundamentally suggests about political life in the United States. The show broaches the question of politics through the question of the family, and this in itself is a political statement. As we will see, *The Simpsons* turns to the family as the source of value in life precisely out of a disillusionment with politics in general and national politics in particular. Indeed, the American nation-state plays a marginal role in the lives of the Simpson family and their neighbors. In episode after episode, the show mirrors the way Americans have become increasingly concerned with local and global issues at the expense of national issues. In *Gilligan's Island* as a representative TV program of the 1960s, we saw a tendency to project the American nation-state and its politics on the rest of the world. One might say that the premise of the series was that beyond the borders of the United States the world is just a deserted island, a blank space on which Americans are free to impose their way of life (give or take an encounter or two with hostile natives or scheming foreigners).

By contrast, *The Simpsons* portrays its characters as having a surprising awareness of the rich diversity of life outside the United States, especially surprising because the show at the same time portrays the Simpsons leading a decidedly small-town existence in their home, Springfield, USA. It is not simply that at various times members of the Simpson family journey to distant countries such as France, Japan, and Australia and, unlike the *Gilligan* castaways, turn out to be genuinely open to foreign influences. Even more significantly, over the years *The Simpsons* has portrayed the globalization of Springfield, the way the whole world flocks to this American small town. Sometimes it is just a matter of foreign celebrities such as Elton John or Paul and Linda McCartney turning up on the Simpsons' doorstep—an apt image for the way television now brings stars from all around the globe right into the homes of average Americans, making these "virtual neighbors" sometimes seem more real than their actual neighbors.[7] But Springfield's globalization goes deeper than the occasional intrusion of famous foreigners into its way of life. *The Simpsons* shows Springfield globalized right down to the minute details of its citizens' daily lives, and nowhere more than in the center of their civic existence—not their city hall but the local convenience store, which is run by an immigrant from India with the very un-American-sounding name of Apu Nahasapeemapetilon.[8]

Apu's Kwik-E-Mart is the place where the local and the global intersect in *The Simpsons*. The characters of *Gilligan's Island* are portrayed as staunchly self-sufficient, producing whatever they need for themselves. Reflecting the great changes in the United States and the larger world between the 1960s and the 1990s, the characters in *The Simpsons* have become dependent on immigrants such as Apu to provide them with their daily necessities (beef jerky, porn magazines, and Homer's beloved donuts). As we will see, *The Simpsons* does a remarkable job of portraying how globalized the texture of life has become even in an average American small town of the 1990s. And yet, for all its globalization, Springfield remains a small town, with a small-town outlook on life, and at times resists the globalizing forces it at other times embraces. Indeed, from a political point of view, what is most striking about *The Simpsons* is the way the show feels a need to anchor its portrait of an American family in a portrait of a typical and largely traditional American small town. Over the years, the way the show has filled out our view of the Springfield community, with its kaleidoscopic cast of characters, has made *The Simpsons* feel more real and paradoxically less "cartoonish" than many other television programs.

Because of their complex interaction, its cartoon characters are more human, more fully rounded, than the supposedly real human beings in many situation comedies. *The Simpsons* shows the family as part of a larger but still local community and in effect affirms the kind of small community that can sustain the family. That is at one and the same time the secret of the show's popularity with the American public and the most interesting political statement it has to make.

The Simpsons indeed offers one of the most important images of the family in contemporary American culture, and in particular an image of the nuclear family. With the names taken from creator Matt Groening's own childhood home, *The Simpsons* portrays the average American family: father (Homer), mother (Marge), and 2.3 children (Bart, Lisa, and little Maggie).[9] Many commentators have lamented the fact that *The Simpsons* now serves as one of the representative images of American family life, claiming that the show provides bad role models for parents and children. The popularity of the show is often cited as evidence of the decline of family values in the United States. But critics of *The Simpsons* need to take a closer look at the show and view it in the context of television history. For all its slapstick nature and its mocking of certain aspects of family life, *The Simpsons* has an affirmative side and ends up celebrating the nuclear family as an institution. By television standards, this is no minor achievement. For decades American television has tended to downplay the importance of the nuclear family, while offering various one-parent families or other nontraditional arrangements as alternatives to it. The one-parent situation comedy actually dates back almost to the beginning of network television, at least as early as *My Little Margie* (1952–55). But the classic one-parent situation comedies, such as *The Andy Griffith Show* (1960–68) or *My Three Sons* (1960–72), generally found ways to reconstitute the nuclear family in one form or another (often through the presence of an aunt or uncle) and thus still presented it as the norm. (Sometimes the story line actually moved in the direction of the widower getting remarried, as happened to Steve Douglas, the Fred Mac-Murray character, in *My Three Sons*.)

But starting with shows in the 1970s such as *Alice* (1976–85), American television genuinely began to move away from the nuclear family as the norm and suggest that other patterns of child rearing might be equally valid or perhaps even superior. Television in the 1980s experimented with all sorts of permutations on the theme of the nonnuclear family, in shows such as *Love, Sidney* (1981–83), *Punky Brewster* (1984–86), and *My Two Dads* (1987–90). This development partly re-

sulted from the standard Hollywood procedure of generating new series by simply varying successful formulas.[10] But the trend toward
nonnuclear families also expressed the ideological bent of Hollywood
and its impulse to call traditional family values into question.[11] Above
all, although television shows usually traced the absence of one or
more parents to deaths in the family, the trend away from the nuclear
family obviously reflected the reality of divorce in American life (and
especially in Hollywood). Wanting to be progressive, television producers set out to endorse contemporary social trends away from the
stable, traditional, nuclear family. With the typical momentum of the
entertainment industry, Hollywood eventually took this development
to its logical conclusion: the no-parent family. Another popular Fox
program, *Party of Five* (1994–2000), portrayed a family of children gal-
lantly raising themselves after both their parents were killed in an au-
tomobile accident. "Kids on their own, that's the franchise" was the
way one of the show's creators, Amy Lippman, explained its premise
to *TV Guide*.[12]

Party of Five cleverly conveys a message some television producers
evidently think their contemporary audience wants to hear—that children can do quite well without one parent and preferably without
both. The children in the audience want to hear this message because
it flatters their sense of independence. The parents want to hear this
message because it soothes their sense of guilt, either about abandoning their children completely (as sometimes happens in cases of divorce) or just not devoting enough "quality time" to them. Absent or
negligent parents can console themselves with the thought that their
children really are better off without them, "just like those cool—and
incredibly good-looking—kids on *Party of Five*." In short, for roughly
the past two decades, much of American television has been suggesting that the breakdown of the family does not constitute a social crisis
or even a serious problem. In fact it should be regarded as a form of
liberation from an image of the family that may have been appropriate in the 1950s but was no longer valid in the 1990s. It is against this
historical background that the statement *The Simpsons* has to make
about the nuclear family has to be appreciated.

Of course television never completely abandoned the nuclear family, even in the 1980s, as shown by the success of such shows as *All in
the Family* (1971–83), *Family Ties* (1982–89), and *The Cosby Show*
(1984–92). And when *The Simpsons* debuted as a regular series in 1990,
it was by no means unique in its reaffirmation of the value of the nuclear family. Several other shows were taking the same path at the

time, reflecting larger social and political trends in society, in particular the reassertion of family values that has been adopted as a program by both political parties in the United States. Fox's own *Married with Children* (1987–98) preceded *The Simpsons* in portraying an amusingly dysfunctional nuclear family. Another interesting portrayal of the nuclear family was ABC's *Home Improvement* (1991–99), which recuperated traditional family values and even sex roles within a postmodern television context. But *The Simpsons* is in many respects the most interesting example of this return to the nuclear family. Though it strikes many people as trying to subvert the American family or to undermine its authority, in fact, it reminds us that antiauthoritarianism is itself an American tradition and that family authority has always been problematic in democratic America. What makes *The Simpsons* so interesting is the way it combines traditionalism with antitraditionalism. It continually makes fun of the traditional American family. But it continually offers an enduring image of the nuclear family in the very act of satirizing it. Many of the traditional values of the American family survive this satire, including the value of the nuclear family itself.

As I have suggested, one can understand this point partly in terms of television history. *The Simpsons* is a hip, postmodern, self-aware show.[13] But its self-awareness focuses on the traditional representation of the American family on television. It therefore presents the paradox of an untraditional show that is deeply rooted in television tradition.[14] *The Simpsons* can be traced back to earlier television cartoons that dealt with families, such as *The Flintstones* (1960–66) or *The Jetsons* (1962–63). But these cartoons must themselves be traced back to the famous nuclear family sitcoms of the 1950s and 1960s, such as *The Adventures of Ozzie and Harriet* (1952–66), *Father Knows Best* (1954–63), and *Leave It to Beaver* (1957–63). *The Simpsons* is a postmodern re-creation of the first generation of family sitcoms on television.[15] Looking back on these shows, we easily see the transformations and discontinuities *The Simpsons* has brought about. In *The Simpsons*, father emphatically does *not* know best. And it clearly is more dangerous to leave it to Bart than to Beaver. Obviously *The Simpsons* does not offer a simple return to the family shows of the 1950s. If for no other reason, the Simpsons differ fundamentally from the Nelsons, the Andersons, or the Cleavers because television plays such an important role in their lives. The original sitcom families on television were not routinely shown watching TV themselves; in fact they were generally portrayed as untouched by the new medium that was in reality already beginning to reshape American family life in the 1950s. By contrast, the Simpsons are always shown watching television; indeed it is one of the few activities that brings the family together and television programs provide them with the bulk of the experiences they have in common. That is why the Simpsons are a postmodern TV family; their values are profoundly shaped by television itself, and thus they are very different from the original families portrayed in 1950s sitcoms, who lived in a kind of blissful ignorance of the medium that was giving them life. But even with all these crucial differences, *The Simpsons* provides elements of continuity with its 1950s sitcom ancestors that make the show more traditional than may at first appear.

The Simpsons has indeed found its own odd way to defend the nuclear family. In effect the shows says: "Take the worst-case scenario— the Simpsons—and even that family is better than no family." In fact, the Simpson family is not all that bad. Some people are appalled at the idea of young boys imitating Bart, in particular his disrespect for authority and especially his teachers. These critics of *The Simpsons* forget that Bart's rebelliousness conforms to a venerable American archetype and that this country was founded on disrespect for authority and an act of rebellion. As early as the 1830s, Alexis de Tocqueville was commenting on the way American democracy works to create a more democratic family, and in particular to weaken the authority of fathers over their sons: "(T)he distance that formerly separated a father from his sons has diminished; and . . . paternal authority has been, if not destroyed, at least altered. . . . [F]rom the moment when the young American approaches manhood, the bonds of filial obedience are loosened day by day. Master of his thoughts, he is soon after master of his conduct."[16] Tocqueville has often been credited with remarkably prophetic powers in anticipating developments in twentieth-century America, and here it seems that he even foresaw *The Simpsons*. He had a premonition of how Bart would behave toward Homer:

> As the social state becomes democratic and men adopt for their general principle that it is good and legitimate to judge all things by oneself, . . . the power of opinion exercised by the father over the sons becomes less great, as does his legal power. . . . When the father of a family has few goods, he and his son live in the same place constantly and are occupied in common with the same work. . . . [T]herefore there cannot fail to be established between them a sort of familiar intimacy that renders authority less absolute and that ill accommodates to external forms of respect.[17]

The Simpsons evidently has roots way back in the early days of the American republic, and indeed one can find anticipations of Bart in some of the classics of nineteenth-century American literature. Bart is an American icon, an updated version of Tom Sawyer and Huck Finn rolled into one. For all his troublemaking—precisely because of his troublemaking—Bart behaves just the way a young boy is supposed to in American mythology, from the *Dennis the Menace* comics to the *Our Gang* comedies.[18]

As for the mother and daughter in *The Simpsons*, Marge and Lisa are not bad role models at all. Marge Simpson is very much the devoted mother and housekeeper; she also often displays a feminist streak, particularly in the episode in which she goes off on a jaunt à la *Thelma and Louise* (1991).[19] Indeed she is very modern in her attempts to combine certain feminist impulses with the traditional role of a mother. In "The Way We Was" (#7F12, 1/31/91), we learn that back in 1974 Marge and Homer first met in detention hall in high school; he was there for smoking, but she was there for the quintessential feminist gesture: burning her bra. Moreover, despite generally accepting her role as a housewife, Marge tries to cultivate her artistic talent in a number of episodes, including "Brush With Greatness" (#7F18, 4/11/91), in which we learn that she once painted a portrait of Ringo Starr. Lisa is in many ways the ideal child in contemporary terms. She is an overachiever in school, and as a feminist, a vegetarian, and an environmentalist, she is politically correct across the spectrum. She repeatedly stands up to corporate America and other sinister forces, displaying her integrity when she refuses to shill for cigarettes in "Lisa the Beauty Queen" (#9F02, 10/15/92) and when she takes on the toy industry in "Lisa vs. Malibu Stacy" (#1F12, 2/17/94).

The real issue, then, is Homer. Many people have criticized *The Simpsons* for its portrayal of the father as dumb, uneducated, weak in character, and morally unprincipled. Homer is all of those things, but at least he is there. He fulfills the bare minimum of a father: He is present for his wife and above all his children. In one episode, when he drags his feet at spending time with Bart and Lisa, his son challenges him: "Oh, quit complaining; it's half the work of a divorced dad," but Homer defends himself with surprising mathematical sophistication: "Yeah, but it's twice as much as a deadbeat dad."[20] Whatever one wants to say against Homer Simpson, he is not a "deadbeat dad." To be sure, he lacks many of the qualities we would like to see in the ideal father. He is selfish, often putting his own interest above that of his family. As we learn in one of the Halloween episodes, Homer would sell his soul to the devil for a donut (though fortunately it turns out that Marge already owned his soul and therefore it was not Homer's to sell).[21] Homer is undeniably crass, vulgar, and incapable of appreciating the finer things in life. He has a hard time sharing interests with Lisa, except when she develops a remarkable knack for predicting the outcome of pro football games and allows her father to become a big winner in the betting pool at his favorite hangout, Moe's Tavern.[22] Moreover, Homer gets angry easily and takes his anger out on his children, as his many attempts to strangle Bart attest. When Homer takes the National Fatherhood Institute Test in "Saturdays of Thunder" (#8F07, 11/14/91), his score is miserably low, and even he has to admit: "I don't know jack about my boy."

In all these respects, Homer fails as a father. But on looking closely, we are surprised to see how many decent qualities he has. First and foremost, he is attached to his own—he loves his family because it is *his*.[23] His motto basically is: "my family, right or wrong." This is hardly a philosophic position, but it may well provide the bedrock of the family as an institution, which is why Plato's *Republic* must subvert the power of the family. Homer Simpson is the opposite of a philosopher-king; he is devoted not to what is best but to what is his own. That position has its problems, but it does help explain how the seemingly dysfunctional Simpson family manages to function.

For example, Homer is willing to work to support his family, even in the dangerous job of nuclear power plant safety supervisor, a job made all the more dangerous by the fact that he is the one doing it. In the episode in which Lisa comes to want a pony desperately, Homer even takes a second job working for Apu at the Kwik-E-Mart to earn the money for the pony's upkeep and nearly kills himself in the process.[24] In such actions, Homer manifests his genuine concern for his family, and as he repeatedly proves, he will defend them if necessary, sometimes at great personal risk. Often Homer is not effective in such actions, but that makes his devotion to his family in some ways all the more touching.[25] Homer is the distillation of pure fatherhood. Take away all the qualities that make for a genuinely good father— wisdom, compassion, even temper, selflessness—and what you have left is Homer Simpson with his pure, mindless, dogged devotion to his family. That is why, for all his stupidity, bigotry, and self-centered quality, we cannot hate Homer. He continually fails at being a good father, but he never gives up trying, and in some basic and important sense that makes him a good father.[26]

◆

The most effective defense of the family in the series comes in the episode in which the Simpsons are actually broken up as a unit.[27] This episode pointedly begins with an image of Marge as a good mother, preparing breakfast and school lunches simultaneously for her children. She even gives Bart and Lisa careful instructions about their sandwiches: "Keep the lettuce separate until 11:30." But after this promising parental beginning, a series of mishaps occurs. Homer and Marge go off to the Mingled Waters Health Spa for a well-deserved afternoon of relaxation. In their haste, they leave their house dirty, especially a pile of unwashed dishes in the kitchen sink. Meanwhile, things are unfortunately not going well for the children at school. Bart has accidentally picked up lice from the monkey of his best friend, Milhouse, prompting Principal Skinner to ask: "What kind of parents would permit such a lapse in scalpal hygiene?" The evidence against the Simpson parents mounts when Skinner sends for Bart's sister. With her prescription shoes having been stolen by her classmates and her feet accordingly covered with mud, Lisa looks like some street urchin straight out of a Dickens novel.

Faced with all this evidence of parental neglect, the horrified principal alerts the Child Welfare Board, who are themselves shocked when they take Bart and Lisa home and explore the premises. The officials completely misinterpret the situation. Confronted by a pile of old newspapers, they assume that Marge is a bad housekeeper, when in fact she had assembled the documents to help Lisa with a history project. Jumping to conclusions, the bureaucrats decide that Marge and Homer are unfit parents and lodge specific charges that the Simpson household is a "squalid hellhole and the toilet paper is hung in improper overhand fashion." The authorities determine that the Simpson children must be given to foster parents. Bart, Lisa, and Maggie are accordingly handed over to the family next door, presided over by the patriarchal Ned Flanders. Throughout the series, the Flanders family serves as the doppelgänger of the Simpsons. Flanders and his brood are in fact the perfect family according to old-style morality and religion. In marked contrast to Bart, the Flanders boys, Rod and Todd, are well behaved and obedient. Above all, the Flanders family is pious, devoted to activities such as Bible reading, more zealous than even the local Reverend Lovejoy. When Ned offers to play "bombardment" with Bart and Lisa, what he has in mind is bombarding them with questions about the Bible. The Flanders family is shocked to learn that their neighbors do not know of the serpent of Rehoboam, not to mention the Well of Zahassadar or the bridal feast of Beth Chadruharazzeb.

Exploring the question of whether the Simpson family really is dysfunctional, the foster parent episode offers two alternatives to it: on the one hand, the old-style moral/religious family; on the other, the therapeutic state, what is often now called the nanny state.[28] Who is best able to raise the Simpson children? The civil authorities claim that Homer and Marge are unfit as parents. They must be reeducated and are sent off to a "family skills class," which is based on the premise that experts know better how to raise children. Child rearing is a matter of a certain kind of expertise, which can be taught. This is the modern answer—the family is inadequate as an institution and hence the state must intervene to make it function. At the same time, the episode offers the old-style moral/religious answer: What children need is God-fearing parents in order to make them God-fearing themselves. Ned Flanders does everything he can to get Bart and Lisa to reform and behave with the piety of his own children.

But the answer the show offers is that the Simpson children are better off with their real parents—not because they are more intelligent or learned in child rearing, and not because they are superior in morality or piety, but simply because Homer and Marge are the people most genuinely attached to Bart, Lisa, and Maggie, since the children are their own offspring. The episode works particularly well to show the horror of the supposedly omniscient and omnicompetent state intruding in every aspect of family life. When Homer desperately tries to call up Bart and Lisa, he hears the official message: "The number you have dialed can no longer be reached from this phone, you negligent monster." In *The Simpsons*, Big Brother is not just watching; he is actively intercepting our phone calls. Throughout this episode we see social tyranny masquerading as humanitarianism in a particularly creepy manner.

At the same time we see the defects of the old-style religion. The Flanderses may be righteous as parents but they are also self-righteous. Mrs. Flanders says: "I don't judge Homer and Marge; that's for a vengeful God to do." Ned's piety is so extreme that he eventually exasperates even Reverend Lovejoy, who at one point asks him: "Have you thought of one of the other major religions? They're all pretty much the same."

In the end, Bart, Lisa, and Maggie are joyously reunited with Homer and Marge. Despite charges of being dysfunctional, the Simpson family functions quite well, because the children are attached to their parents and the parents are attached to their children. The premise of those who tried to take the Simpson children away is that there is a principle external to the family by which it can be judged dysfunctional, whether the principle of contemporary child rearing theories or that of the old-style religion. The foster parent episode suggests the contrary—that the family contains its own principle of legitimacy. The family knows best.[29] This episode thus illustrates the strange combination of traditionalism and antitraditionalism in *The Simpsons*. Even as the show rejects the idea of a simple return to the traditional moral/religious idea of the family, it refuses to accept contemporary statist attempts to subvert the family completely and reasserts the enduring value of the family as an institution.

As the importance of Ned Flanders in this episode reminds us, another way in which the show is unusual is that religion plays a significant role in *The Simpsons*.[30] Religion is a regular part of the life of the Simpson family. Several episodes revolve around churchgoing, including one in which God even speaks directly to Homer.[31] Moreover, religion is a regular part of life in general in Springfield. In addition to Ned Flanders, the Reverend Lovejoy is featured in several episodes, including one in which no less than Meryl Streep provided the voice for his daughter.[32]

This attention to religion is atypical of contemporary American television. Judging by most television programs today, one would never guess that Americans are by and large a religious and even a churchgoing people. Television generally acts as if religion played little or no role in the daily lives of Americans, even though the evidence points to exactly the opposite conclusion. Many reasons have been offered to explain why television generally avoids the subject of religion. Producers are afraid that if they raise religious issues, they will offend orthodox viewers and soon be embroiled in controversy.[33] Television executives are particularly worried about having the sponsors of their shows boycotted by powerful religious groups.[34] Moreover, the television community itself is largely secular in its outlook and thus generally uninterested in religious questions. Indeed, much of Hollywood is often outright antireligious and especially opposed to anything labeled religious fundamentalism (and it tends to label anything to the right of Unitarianism as "religious fundamentalism").[35]

Religion has, however, been making a comeback on television in the past decade, in part because producers have discovered that an audience niche exists for shows such as *Touched by an Angel* (1994–).[36] Still, the entertainment community has a hard time understanding what religion really means to the American public, and it especially cannot deal with the idea that religion could be an everyday, normal part of American life. Religious figures in both movies and television tend to be miraculously good and pure or monstrously evil and hypocritical. While there are exceptions to this rule,[37] generally for Hollywood, religious figures must be either saints, laboring against all odds for good, or religious fanatics, full of bigotry, warped by sexual repression, laboring to destroy innocent lives in one way or another.[38]

But *The Simpsons* accepts religion as a normal part of life in Springfield, USA. If the show makes fun of piety in the person of Ned Flanders, in Homer Simpson it also suggests that one can go to church and not be either a religious fanatic or a saint. One episode devoted to Reverend Lovejoy deals realistically and rather sympathetically with the problem of pastoral burnout.[39] The overburdened minister has just listened to too many problems from his parishioners and has to turn the job over to Marge. The treatment of religion in *The Simpsons* is parallel to and connected with its treatment of the family. *The Simpsons* is not proreligion—it is too hip, cynical, and iconoclastic for that. Indeed, on the surface, the show appears to be antireligious, with a good deal of its satire directed against Ned Flanders and other pious characters. But once again we see the principle at work that when *The Simpsons* satirizes something, it acknowledges its importance. Even when it seems to be ridiculing religion, it recognizes, as few other television shows do, the genuine role that religion plays in American life.

It is here that the treatment of the family in *The Simpsons* links up with its treatment of politics. Although the show focuses on the nuclear family, it relates the family to larger institutions in American life, such as the church, the school, and even political institutions themselves, including city government. In all these cases, *The Simpsons* satirizes these institutions, making them look laughable and often even hollow. But at the same time, the show acknowledges their importance and especially their importance for the family. Over the past few decades, television has increasingly tended to isolate the family—to show it largely removed from any larger institutional framework or context. This is another trend to which *The Simpsons* runs counter, partly as a result of its being a postmodern re-creation of 1950s sitcoms. Shows such as *Father Knows Best* or *Leave It to Beaver* were set in small-town America, with all the intricate web of institutions into which family life was woven. In re-creating this world, even while mocking it, *The Simpsons* cannot help re-creating its ambience and even at times its ethos.

Springfield is very much the typical American small town. Obviously the show makes fun of small-town life—it makes fun of everything—but it simultaneously celebrates the virtues of the traditional American small town. One of the principal reasons why the dysfunctional Simpson family functions as well as it does is that they live in a traditional American small town. The institutions that play an important role in their lives are not remote from them or alien to them. The Simpson children go to a neighborhood school (though they are bussed to it by the ex-hippie driver Otto). Their friends in school are largely the same as their friends in their neighborhood. The Simpsons are not confronted by an elaborate, unapproachable, and uncaring educational bureaucracy. Principal Skinner and Mrs. Krabappel may not be perfect educators, but when Homer and Marge need to talk to them, they are readily accessible. The same is true of the Springfield police force. Chief Wiggum is not exactly a crack crimefighter, but he is well known to the citizens of Springfield, as they are to him. The police in Springfield still have neighborhood beats and have even been known to share a donut or two with Homer.

Similarly, politics in Springfield is largely a local matter, including town meetings at which the citizens of Springfield get to influence decisions on important matters of local concern, such as whether gambling should be legalized or a monorail built. In one of the earliest episodes, "Homer's Odyssey" (#7G03, 1/21/90), Homer learns that if he simply shows up at a town council meeting, he can get Springfield to enact all sorts of safety improvements at his suggestion. Mayor Quimby may be a demagogue (as his Kennedy accent suggests), but at least he is Springfield's own demagogue. When he buys votes, he buys them directly from the citizens of Springfield. Everywhere one looks in Springfield, one sees a surprising degree of local control and autonomy. The nuclear power plant is a source of pollution and constant danger, but at least it is locally owned by Springfield's own slave-driving industrial tyrant and tycoon, Montgomery Burns, and not by some remote multinational corporation. (Indeed, in the exception that proves the rule, when the plant is sold to German investors in "Burns Verkaufen der Kraftwerk," Montgomery soon buys it back to restore his ego.)

◆

In sum, for all its postmodern hipness, *The Simpsons* is profoundly anachronistic in the way it harks back to an earlier age, when Americans felt more in contact with their governing institutions and family life was solidly anchored in a larger but still local community. The emphasis on local politics in *The Simpsons* grows out of a disillusionment with politics at the state and national levels. The characters in the show proceed with their lives as if what happens in Washington, D.C., or their state capital were largely irrelevant to their existence, and the show implies that they are better off for doing so. It is in fact a standing joke in the series that we as audience are never to learn the identity of the state in which Springfield is located. If a character is about to mention the state's name, he is immediately cut off, or if we see Springfield on a map, somehow its state location is obscured. The state capital, teasingly named Capital City, occasionally plays a role in the series, but not an important one. For Ned Flanders, it is a place he has to go to "fill out some forms" when his wife and mother-in-law are being held hostage by terrorists in the Holy Land.[40] Homer has a fling with a power plant coworker, Mindy Simmons, at the National Energy Convention in Capital City.[41] But that is just the point—the state capital in *The Simpsons* is not an integral part of the lives of its characters but only the place for some kind of interlude, a break in their routine that will have no lasting effect on their existence.

In one episode, Homer has such success as the mascot of the local baseball team in Springfield, the Isotopes, that he is promoted to the big time and gets a chance to be the mascot of the Capital City Capitals.[42] For once, the Simpsons pull up stakes in Springfield and head for life in the fast lane in their state capital. They are at first charmed by all the novelties a major metropolitan area has to offer. "Kids, look! Street crime!" Homer announces as they enter Capital City and he proudly shows Bart and Lisa a mugger robbing a woman, something they did not normally get to see back in Springfield. But things do not work out for Homer in Capital City. The mascot routines that electrified the crowds in small-town Springfield fall flat in the big city. As one vocal Capitals fan puts it: "These cornball antics may play in the sticks, but this is Capital City." The Simpsons are evidently not cut out for life in the big city and return, chastened by their experience, to Springfield, where Homer can still be a hero at Moe's Tavern. The Simpsons basically view their state capital, not as the center of their existence, but as a mere tourist attraction—a nice place to visit, but they wouldn't want to live there.

The one episode of *The Simpsons* that focuses on state politics is central for understanding its view of politics in general and why the show places a premium on family life. In "Two Cars in Every Garage and Three Eyes on Every Fish" (#7F01, 11/1/90), Mr. Burns faces a crisis when Bart and Lisa catch a three-eyed fish near his nuclear power plant. This evidence of genetic mutation resulting from improper nuclear waste disposal leads regulatory authorities from Washington to threaten to shut down Burns's business. At Homer's suggestion, he decides to run for governor so that he will be in charge of the laws that regulate power plants and can do as he pleases. Burns seems at first to have little chance against a popular incumbent governor, Mary Bailey, but he is able to use his vast fortune to mount a highly effective media campaign against her. Here is the basis for the suspicions *The Simpsons* directs against politics on anything but a local scale. As Mayor Quimby makes clear, local politics may be corrupt but at least the citizens of Springfield know Quimby for the corrupt politician he is because they can observe him up close and on a day-to-day basis. Once one moves beyond the local level, however, politics inevitably becomes mediated and the voting public must rely on the image a politician manages to project. Thus, the less local a political race is, the more likely it becomes that political illusion will replace political reality.

Burns's gubernatorial campaign becomes a textbook case of everything that is wrong with media politics. He begins as the most unpopular man in Springfield; he is well known to his neighbors as a skinflint, a curmudgeon, and a slave driver in the workplace. His staff tells him that in an initial poll "98 percent of the voters rate you as despicable or worse." Yet with a little help from media consultants, Burns starts to surge in the polls. (The frequency with which polls are reported during this episode is itself a telling comment on media politics.) Burns's team of advisors includes a speechwriter, a joke writer, a spin doctor, a makeup man, and a personal trainer to remake his public image, as well as a muckraker, a character assassin, a mudslinger, and a garbologist to attack his opponent. Together these experts help Burns to turn the public against Mary Bailey and also to make him seem like the kind of politician the people want. In an obvious allusion to one of Michael Dukakis's less successful efforts to project a presidential image in his 1988 campaign, Burns poses for the cameras on top of a battle tank. Burns's media tactics may seem transparently false and deceptive, but *The Simpsons* shows him succeeding with voters around the state. His staff is eventually happy to report: "The voters now see you as imperial and godlike."

"Two Cars" becomes the most important episode in *The Simpsons* for showing the way that politics and the family intersect. The gubernatorial race divides the Simpson family. As a public-spirited voter,

Marge supports Mary Bailey. Homer is guided, as always, by pure self-interest and feels that he must vote for his boss, Mr. Burns. Conversations between Homer and Marge may get a little heated at dinnertime, but Lisa for one is delighted by the debates at home: "Oooh, a political discussion at our table. I feel like a Kennedy!" The plot works out so that the fate of the gubernatorial race comes to rest in the hands of the Simpson family. Burns's advisors hit upon a scheme to ingratiate him with the public by demonstrating that he has the common touch. In a carefully staged media event, he will be shown having dinner in the home of one of his workers—Homer Simpson. Burns understands the strategy: "Every Joe Meatball and Sally Housecoat in this Godforsaken state will see me hunkering down for chow with Eddie Punchclock. The media will have a field day."

Burns's advisors clearly appreciate the appeal of family values as a campaign issue, but their attempt to exploit the Simpson household for political purposes backfires. Marge ostensibly goes along with the Burns plan, but when it comes time for dinner, she serves up the three-eyed fish to her husband's boss. Though Burns gamely tries to eat it, once he spits it out right in front of the television audience, his hopes of becoming governor are dashed, as the headlines proclaim: "Burns Can't Swallow His Own Story." In effect, in this episode the truth and honesty bred in the family triumph over the lies and duplicity generated by the media world of politics. "Two Cars" suggests that the turn to the family as the locus of value in *The Simpsons* is at least in part a reaction against the corruption of political life in the modern mediated world. Moreover the episode underlines the need to protect the family against the insidious demands of politics and the intrusive eyes of the media.

Politics at the national level fares no better at the hands of *The Simpsons*. The federal government rarely makes its presence felt in Springfield, and its inhabitants seem largely indifferent to what happens far away in Washington, D.C. For national politics to get the attention of the Springfielders, it must somehow be made local, as happens, for example, when former President George H. Bush moves right across the street from the Simpsons ("Two Bad Neighbors"). Evidently Homer will not even acknowledge the federal government's existence unless it turns up on his doorstep. Even with Bush as his neighbor, he remains unimpressed by the mere fact that a man once headed the federal government, and he is not at all in awe of the former president. Bush seems totally out of place in Springfield, except for the fact that he sounds very much like Ned Flanders (not all that surprising considering that both are voiced by Harry Shearer). Homer and the ex-president do not get along and soon end up literally at each other's throats.

In a telling moment, Marge points out that Homer did not vote for Bush or anybody else for that matter in the last national election, and Homer replies: "I voted for Prell to go back to the old glass bottle. After that, I became deeply cynical." Typically, Homer cares more about the consumer products he deals with on a daily basis than he does about national political issues. And, however comically presented, his cynicism is crucial to the series. As thick-headed as he is, even Homer has learned to discount and distrust the promises politicians routinely make. Occasionally he is taken in by grand schemes propounded by one public figure or another, but in the end he is just shrewd enough to see through them and always comes back to his family as the bedrock of his life and the one thing that truly matters to him.

What turns Homer into Bush's implacable enemy is the fact that the former president spanks Bart after the mischievous boy accidentally destroys his memoirs. Out of fundamental indifference, Homer will put up with a lot from the federal government, but not with one of its representatives interfering directly in his family life: "First Bush invades my home turf, then he takes my pals, . . . now he steals my right to raise a disobedient, smart-alecky son! Well, that's it!" Homer's anger is mollified at the end of the episode only by the intervention of another former president who has evidently also moved to Springfield, Gerald Ford—who kindly invites him over for beer, nachos, and televised football. These two do hit it off, exclaiming Homer's signature phrase "D'oh!" in tandem as they simultaneously trip on their approach to Ford's home. In *The Simpsons*, only a president reduced to Homer's level of bumbling is fit to be welcomed into Springfield. Thus the show works to demystify and demythologize national politics. In its lighthearted but ultimately corrosive way, *The Simpsons* suggests that our national leaders, however high we may place them on pedestals, are really no different from us as average citizens—and certainly no better.

Institutionally, the federal government does reach its tentacles into Springfield, but that only raises further doubts about it in *The Simpsons*. The FBI shows up in town periodically, sometimes helping the local law enforcement authorities but often proving to be meddlesome and intrusive. In "Cape Feare" (#9F22, 10/7/93), the Simpsons actively seek help from the FBI to protect them from a paroled criminal who is out to murder Bart for putting him in jail in the first place. The

FBI's Witness Protection Program does not turn out to provide much protection for the Simpsons (renamed "The Thompsons"), though Homer's inability to grasp the basic concept of adopting a new identity takes a good deal of the blame away from the federal officers. FBI agents in effect become the villains in "Mother Simpson" (#3FO6, 11/19/95), an episode in which they are shown relentlessly pursuing Homer's mother for a terrorist incident she was involved in in her youth. One FBI episode of *The Simpsons*, "The Springfield Files" (#3G01, 1/12/97), was really just an excuse to link up with the show's neighbor series on Fox, *The X-Files*. Its heroes, Mulder and Scully, prove even more ineffective in penetrating the mysteries of Springfield than they are with the monsters and aliens they encounter on their own show. In the end, all Mulder can do is to mutter portentously about the "Voodoo priests of Haiti, the Tibetan numerologists of Appalachia, the unsolved mysteries of *Unsolved Mysteries*." In the one revealing moment in this episode, a sign at the Springfield branch of the FBI reads: "Invading Your Privacy for 60 Years," a motif picked up elsewhere in the series. The *Complete Guide to The Simpsons* (221) points out that in the preceding episode, "El Viaje Misterioso de Nuestro Jomer" (#3F24, 1/5/97), people with really fast and sharp eyes might notice that in the floorboards between the first and second floors of the Simpson house, the telephone wires are labeled "NSA," "FBI," "ATF," "CIA," "KGB," and "MCI" (221), thus hinting that a bit of wiretapping may be going on. Here as elsewhere *The Simpsons* suggests that the U.S. government is busily engaged in spying on its own citizens and hence no better than the foreign governments from which it claims to be protecting them (indeed the American CIA and the Russian KGB seem to be presented as moral equivalents).

The other federal agency that has an impact on the daily lives of the Springfielders is the IRS and the series presents it in a very negative light. In an episode ominously entitled "Bart the Fink" (#3F12, 2/11/96), the host of the local kiddie show, Krusty the Klown, gets in trouble when Bart inadvertently alerts federal authorities to his hero's secret offshore bank account in the Cayman Islands. Accused of tax evasion, Krusty sees his life come crashing down around him. To pay his back taxes, he will have to give the IRS 75 percent of his salary for fifty years. When he carelessly remarks: "But I don't plan to live that long!" an IRS official quickly recalculates: "Better make it 95 percent." The federal government ends up running Krusty's TV show, which in typical bureaucratese is renamed: "The IRS Presents Herschel Krustofski's Clown-Related Entertainment Show." Krusty is so upset by the way the IRS takes over his life that he has to fake his own suicide to escape its clutches.

The Simpsons has generally tried to avoid recycling plot ideas, but its animus against the IRS is evidently so strong that two seasons later it built another episode around taxmen marauding in Springfield. In "The Trouble with Trillions" (#5F14, 4/15/98), Homer has to scramble to meet the April 15 deadline on his taxes, having failed to follow the example of model citizen Ned Flanders. Flanders in fact got started on his tax return already on January 1 and tends to err on the side of the government in listing his deductions: "Let's see, cash register ink. Well, that's a business expense, isn't it? Oh, but then I do enjoy the smell of the stuff, don't I? Better not risk it." If Ned is generous to the federal government, the reason is that he appreciates what it does for us all. When his son asks what taxes pay for, he explains: "Why, everything! Policemen, trees, sunshine, and let's not forget the folks who just don't feel like workin', God bless 'em!" Homer is not so charitable in his view of paying his taxes—in fact he is visibly upset that just one year after doing so he is being asked to do it again—and in his rush to meet the deadline, he reaches for any deduction he can get: "Okay, Marge, if anyone asks, you require twenty-four-hour nursing care, Lisa's a clergyman, Maggie is seven people, and Bart was wounded in Vietnam."

Homer manages to make the midnight deadline at the post office, but unfortunately his hastily prepared tax return does not survive the careful scrutiny at IRS headquarters; after all, as one official proudly points out: "This government computer can process over nine returns a day." Charged with tax fraud, Homer is forced by the IRS to work with the FBI to help track down other tax evaders. Homer becomes what Lisa calls "a tool of government oppression" and is soon ratting on his friends at Moe's Tavern. Ultimately the IRS and the FBI ask Homer to betray his corporate loyalty and spy on Mr. Burns. The federal government believes that Burns stole a trillion-dollar bill it once printed to finance post–World War II reconstruction in Europe (this detail in itself is an interesting comment on the inflationary monetary policies of the federal government and Burns characterizes himself as "standing up against America's reckless spendthrift politicians"). Homer leads the FBI to Burns and the trillion-dollar bill but then helps him to escape when he argues: "I'm not the thief—the government is." Burns hates to see the money wasted on "aid to ungrateful foreigners, do-nothing nuclear missiles, and tomb polish for some unknown soldier."[43]

In strong language, Burns vows: "Let's start our own country, free from the relentless tyranny of Uncle Sam." With Homer's help, Burns heads for Cuba, hoping to buy the island from its communist ruler with the stolen bill. Without knowing it, Burns comes upon Castro at an opportune moment, indeed in the very last throes of the Cold War, as he sorrowfully admits to his cronies: "Comrades, our nation is completely bankrupt; we have no choice but to abandon communism." When his toadies ritually protest, Fidel simply tells them: "We all knew from day one this mumbo-jumbo wouldn't fly." But the wily Cuban dictator saves his regime by cheating Burns out of the trillion-dollar bill. When Castro turns down Burns's request—"Will you at least allow us to live in your socialist paradise?"—he is forced to return to the United States empty-handed, even more bitter than usual, as he tells Homer: "It's hard to believe there's a worse place than America, but we found it." Even Burns's last-ditch effort to reconcile himself to America has a sardonic edge to it: "Oppression and harassment are a small price to live in the land of the free." Of course much of the satire in this episode is directed against Burns and his extreme antigovernment views, but he is given a suspiciously eloquent statement of his case and we cannot help feeling that he is treated shabbily by every government figure he meets. The fact that we end up sympathizing with Burns in this episode is the ultimate indictment of the IRS—it is so sinister that it can turn even the central villain of *The Simpsons* into a hero.[44]

With the FBI and the IRS combining to make life a living hell for select citizens in Springfield, it is tempting to mistake *The Simpsons* for an outright libertarian show.[45] One must remember how often the show displays sympathy for traditionally left-wing causes that call for government intervention in the economy, such as environmentalism.[46] Still, it is very difficult to find a moment when *The Simpsons* portrays the federal government doing anything good for its citizens. Even when officials in Washington try to do the right thing, they get fouled up in their own procedures. With a comet hurtling toward Springfield, the U.S. Congress takes up a bill to evacuate the town, but before it can pass, one congressman adds a rider authorizing "thirty million dollars of taxpayer money to support the perverted arts"—thereby dragging the rescue measure down to defeat.[47]

A good measure of the demotion of the federal government in *The Simpsons* is the diminished role it assigns to the American space program. As we saw in *Gilligan's Island*, the space race was very much on the minds of Americans in the 1960s, and everything having to do with NASA had a certain cachet to it. Although *Gilligan's Island* presented space flight in a comic light, it did not actually make fun of astronauts (at least not the Americans). In *Gilligan's Island*, NASA represents the cutting edge of technology and as such is offered as a symbol of American global preeminence. By contrast, in *The Simpsons*, NASA's fortunes have sunk so low that it must turn to Homer of all people to try to recoup its reputation and rekindle America's love affair with spaceflight. As "Deep Space Homer" (#1F13, 2/24/94) opens, Bart and his father are watching an American space launch on TV, but they find it unspeakably boring. The episode then cuts to NASA headquarters, where an official makes the dramatic announcement: "We've run into a serious problem with our mission." But this is not a case of "Houston—we have a problem"—now NASA is worried about its public image, not its operations. The official reports: "These Nielsen ratings are the lowest ever" and spells out the real problem: "We're in danger of losing our funding. America isn't interested in space exploration anymore."

As Homer and Bart suggest, the American TV audience simply finds space launches have become too routine. Moreover, by 1994, when this episode first aired, NASA had lost its ability to present space exploration as part of a space race, that is, a competition between the United States and its powerful rival, the Soviet Union. The presence of Soviet cosmonauts in *Gilligan's Island* added drama to its space episodes, but they are of course conspicuously absent from *The Simpsons* in the post–Cold War era. Thus NASA in *The Simpsons* finds it must turn from the Cold War to class war to regain the public's interest.[48] The NASA scientists survey what Americans are watching on television, and in particular observe the 1990s sitcoms *Home Improvement* and *Married with Children*. Being rocket scientists, the NASA officials are quick to catch on: "They're all a bunch of blue-collar slobs." NASA thus decides to win back the American TV audience by finding a blue-collar slob to be their new astronaut hero, what TV reporter Kent Brockman later refers to as an "Averagenaut." After some competition, Homer emerges as the blue-collar representative to be sent into space, and he actually manages to save the mission from a near-disaster (caused, to be sure, by his own bumbling in the first place). In effect, in this episode, rather than having Homer turn to the federal government for salvation, a federal agency must turn to Homer to salvage its reputation. And it does not help the federal government's image that the episode reveals that the real goal of the space mission is to put an IRS surveillance satellite in orbit.

One episode actually set in Washington, D.C., takes a very dim view of the operation of the federal government.[49] Lisa gets to take the whole Simpson family with her to the nation's capital when she makes it to the finals of the *Reading Digest* "Patriots of Tomorrow" contest. This episode captures perfectly the tone of hackneyed patriotic speeches in the first version of Lisa's paean to the United States government, called "The Roots of Democracy":

> When America was born on that hot July day in 1776, the trees in Springfield were tiny saplings trembling towards the sun and as they were nourished by Mother Earth, so too did our fledgling nation find strength in the simple ideals of equality and justice. Who would have thought such mighty oaks or such a powerful nation could grow out of something so fragile, so pure?

But while waiting for the competition in Washington to begin, Lisa observes a congressman being bribed by a lobbyist. Her belief in the federal government shattered, she prepares a new speech, renamed "Cesspool on the Potomac," indicting the crooked congressman and damning the whole D.C. community: "The city of Washington was built on a stagnant swamp over two hundred years ago and very little has changed. It stank then and it stinks now. Only today, it is the fetid stink of corruption that hangs in the air."

With this approach, Lisa of course loses the patriotism contest, but when a senator hears of her disillusionment, he informs the FBI of the congressman's perfidy and he is soon caught by a sting operation. Typically, *The Simpsons* does not let its cynicism go too far—in the end it must reassure the American public that their system of government really does work, and though it may be subject to corruption, it also includes mechanisms for dealing with that corruption. Still, it is remarkable how far *The Simpsons* is willing to take its corrosive satire of national politics. "Mr. Lisa Goes to Washington" attacks the federal government at its foundation, the patriotic myths upon which its legitimacy rests. It makes fun of the very process by which patriotism is inculcated in the nation's youth, the hokey contests that lead children to outdo each other in progovernment effusions (on Lisa's scorecard at the Springfield regionals, she receives only a 9 for "organization," but a 10 for "jingoism").[50]

In a related episode, aptly titled "Lisa the Iconoclast" (#3F13, 2/18/96), the bright young girl is once again at work undermining political myths. In preparation for Springfield's bicentenary, Lisa researches an essay on the town's revered founder, Jebediah Springfield.

Unfortunately Lisa uncovers the fact that Springfield's eponymous hero was "really a vicious pirate named Hans Sprungfeld." The town is not grateful to Lisa for revealing the dark truth about its founding father. Lisa uncharacteristically receives an F on her essay from her teacher, Miss Hoover, who comments: "This is nothing but dead white male–bashing from a P.C. thug." The curator of the Springfield Historical Society, Hollis Hurlbut (named, incidentally, after two freshman dorms at Harvard), finally convinces Lisa that the town needs its myths, and knowing the truth about Jebediah Springfield is less important than encouraging the civic pride his false legend inspires. Once again *The Simpsons* ultimately backs off from its thoroughgoing attack on patriotism and leaves us with an uplifting scene of the town celebrating its heritage in a parade. And yet if one looks closely at the newspaper Homer is reading, one can see the headline: "Parade to Distract Joyless Citizenry." Time and again, *The Simpsons* suggests that the political rhetoric of the United States is just a distraction, an attempt to hide the truth about government and its corruption from the American people. By focusing on Springfield's town hero, "Lisa the Iconoclast" may seem to be directed against local politics, but by raising the issue of founding fathers and bicentennial celebrations, its satire casts a wider net. In attacking the power of political mythmaking itself, it calls into question politics at all levels, but particularly at the national level. People can in effect see their local government (all too clearly at times) but their belief in their national government must rest largely on myths. Thus to raise doubts about our understanding of the founding fathers is to weaken the legitimacy first and foremost of the national government.

◆

Given the negative portrait of national politics in *The Simpsons*, it is thus not surprising that the Springfielders are attached to their local community and not to larger political units. But the devaluation of politics on the national level in the show has other consequences. The Springfielders' disillusionment with and lack of concern for national politics lead them to think globally even as they act locally. *The Simpsons* can thus serve as a representative of the new developments in television in what I am calling the global era. Working to reduce the power of the national networks, cable TV and other technological breakthroughs have allowed television to become at once more local and more global as a medium. To be sure, *The Simpsons* is not itself a cable TV program; shown by the Fox Network, the series is in fact an example of broadcast television. But the rise of Fox in the 1980s and 1990s was one of the central events in the great change in the television landscape that is often called the cable revolution but should perhaps more properly be called the globalization of television. As a fourth network challenging the supremacy of the seemingly entrenched and untouchable Big Three—CBS, NBC, and ABC—Fox was instrumental in undermining the centrality of the traditional national networks in American culture, and it did so precisely by promoting untraditional TV programming such as *The Simpsons*. Many analysts have attributed the success of Fox largely to *The Simpsons*. William Shawcross, for example, writes: "'The Simpsons' was the show that fanned Fox's flame and gained it the respect of the television industry. . . . [P]rograms like 'The Simpsons' made Fox the darling of media buyers. . . . Bart Simpson had done the impossible. He had created a fourth national network."[51]

The Simpsons illustrates the economic logic of globalization that has transformed television. The show is largely created in the United States, but to save money, the episodes are in fact animated in Korea. This outsourcing of the production of the show is typical of the modern globalized economy. For all the obvious logistical problems, it is still cheaper to have the cartoons drawn halfway around the world. Moreover, as a Fox program, *The Simpsons* is ultimately financed by an Australian, media mogul Rupert Murdoch. Murdoch actually appears in one episode ("Sunday, Cruddy Sunday," #AABF08, 1/31/99), describing himself as a "billionaire tyrant." Thus *The Simpsons* itself is a perfect example of globalization: an American show financed by an Australian and animated by Koreans, now shown all around the earth. No wonder globalization emerges as one of the recurrent themes in the show.

For small-town people, the Springfielders are in their own way remarkably cosmopolitan, especially when compared to their antecedents in the sitcoms of the 1950s. The Springfield of *Father Knows Best* did not have a convenience store, but if it did, it would not have been operated by a practicing Hindu like Apu. Unlike Bart and Lisa Simpson, Bud and Kathy Anderson of *Father Knows Best* never met a Hindu, practicing or otherwise, in their lives. One can say that this merely mirrors the realities of life in the United States at the end of the twentieth century, but that is just the point. Without trumpeting the fact, *The Simpsons* effectively portrays the globalization of America in the 1990s. Simply by virtue of living when they do, the Simpson family has opportunities that were denied to their counterparts in sitcoms in the heyday of the national networks. *Leave It to Beaver* devoted a whole episode to the chaos that results when Wally and the Beav simply take a bus beyond the borders of Mayfield. *My Three Sons* thought it was being quite daring when it took the Douglas family to Hawaii for a two-part episode. By contrast, the Simpsons have taken trips to Australia and Japan and taken them in stride. It is of course much easier to transport characters halfway around the globe in a cartoon. But the jet-setting of the Simpsons still points to a fundamental transformation in their lives that the show consistently documents. For all their small-town mentality, they have become citizens of the world.

A fundamental reason for the demotion of the nation as a concern in the minds of the Springfielders is the fact that *The Simpsons* portrays a world fundamentally at peace and this in turn leads to a broadening of the cultural horizons of the characters in the series. It is appropriate that the show made its debut as a full-length program at the end of 1989 (in a Christmas special on December 17), that is, shortly after the fall of the Berlin Wall and hence the "official" end of the Cold War. Real war is no longer a threat in the world of *The Simpsons*. Bart is sent in one episode to a military academy, but it is to punish him, not to train him for a life of combat in the army.[52] In the many visions the show offers of Bart's future, it never imagines him having to go to war for his country. In fact, in "Homer's Phobia," when Homer is worried that the influence of a friendly gay man (voiced by John Waters) may be affecting Bart's sexual orientation, he and Moe momentarily think of turning to the military to make a man out of the boy, but the bartender quickly points out that this option has been foreclosed by the success of 1990s diplomacy: "There's not even any war anymore, thank you, Warren Christopher."

For real wars, *The Simpsons* must look back to the past. One episode deals with Grandpa Simpson's service in World War II,[53] and Principal Skinner is constantly referring to his experiences in Vietnam (in one episode the truth about his past in the Vietnam War comes back to haunt him).[54] The elimination of war as a palpable threat significantly reduces the importance of the nation-state in the minds of the Springfielders. They no longer feel that the government is necessary to protect them from aggressive foreigners, and they no longer think in terms of giving up their lives in battle for the sake of the United States. Hence their nation cannot possibly mean as much to them as it did to Abraham Simpson in his youth, when Americans were marching off to fight the Germans and the Japanese in a kind of national crusade. In the world of *The Simpsons*, the Germans now can try to purchase Mr. Burns's nuclear power plant and the Japanese open up a sushi restaurant in Springfield (The Happy Sumo), admittedly nearly killing Homer in the process, but not as a hostile act of war.[55]

The Simpsons rests so firmly on the premise of peace in the post–Cold War era that the show can even play with the idea of nuclear annihilation. In one of the Halloween episodes, one segment deals with the hellish aftermath when Springfield is hit by a neutron bomb from France, delivered in retaliation for a rude remark about the French made by Mayor Quimby.[56] The absurdity of this segment underscores the point—if the French are all that Americans need worry about anymore, then they need not really worry at all. *The Simpsons* even toys with the idea that the end of the Cold War may have been a Russian trick. In the episode called "Simpson Tide" (#4G04, 3/29/98), Homer joins the naval reserve, not because he has a sudden surge of patriotism but because he has been fired from his job at the nuclear power plant. In one imaginative sequence, the Russians reveal that the end of their hostilities with the West was just a ruse, as a seemingly peaceful parade in Red Square mutates into an old Soviet-style display of aggressive military might. Lenin's corpse springs back to life, solemnly intoning: "Must crush capitalism," and in the most emblematic moment, the Berlin Wall suddenly pops back up. Just by raising the possibility of this reversal, *The Simpsons* reveals how crucial it is in fact to the series that the Cold War really is over. In the absence of a credible threat to the United States, and hence in the absence of the need for the national government to defend the citizens of Springfield, they are free to pay less attention to national concerns, to neglect many of the demands the nation-state has traditionally made, and to devote themselves to local matters. But the end of the Cold War also frees the Springfielders to take a more global view of their lives. No longer feeling threatened by foreign enemies, they are more open to influences from abroad and are willing to enter into dealings with people from other nations.

This is the subject of one of the earliest episodes of *The Simpsons*, and still my personal favorite, "The Crepes of Wrath," a marvelously absurd episode, but one that also shows the remarkable range of cultural reference in the series. Bart pushes his luck with Principal Skinner too far and ends up in an exchange-student scheme, largely designed just to get him out of the country. Bart is sent to France, and in his place an exchange student from Albania, named Adil Hoxha, comes to Springfield Elementary School. To my knowledge, *The Simpsons* is the only American TV program that has ever played with the name of an Albanian dictator (Enver Hoxha). "The Crepes of Wrath" is the show's backhanded tribute to the end of the Cold War. By 1990 one had to go to the depths of darkest Albania to find anyone still committed to Communist ideology and hence implacably opposed to the United States. Indeed, in trying to explain Albania to Homer, Lisa tells her father that its "main export is furious political thought." This episode can be viewed in two ways, as reflecting either the parochialism of Americans or their cosmopolitanism, their orientation toward the local or toward the global. On the one hand, "The Crepes of Wrath" offers a compendium of American prejudices against foreigners. The French live up to their stereotype of being hostile to Americans when Bart is treated miserably in France. The men in whose care he is placed, Ugolin and Cesar, force him to work like a slave in their vineyard and even use him to test the wine they have laced with antifreeze. As for the innocent-looking Adil, he turns out to be an American's worst nightmare—a sinister secret agent working for a foreign enemy. He exploits Homer's American hospitality to obtain secret information about the Springfield nuclear power plant, which he dutifully broadcasts back to his Communist masters in Albania. In short, the episode seems to confirm the nasty suspicions Americans tend to harbor about foreigners—they are all evil and anti-American at heart.

On the other hand, the episode does show Springfield welcoming Adil with open arms, and even as the evidence against him mounts, Homer is so receptive to his foreign guest that he refuses to believe that the young boy has done anything wrong. Bart grudgingly sums up his trip abroad: "So basically, I met one nice French person," but the fact is that a gendarme did save him from his plight. More to the point, the only reason the policeman rescued him is that Bart suddenly found himself explaining his predicament in fluent French. After failing to learn the language by study, Bart picked it up by osmosis, just as Principal Skinner predicted: "When he's totally immersed in a foreign language, the average child can become fluent in weeks." Once he actually goes abroad, even the unstudious Bart Simpson is open to the influence of a foreign culture and he ends up quite a devotee of all things French by the close of the episode. He returns from France wearing a beret and bearing all sorts of French gifts for his family, including a toy guillotine for Lisa. Homer ends the episode saying proudly: "You hear that, Marge, my boy speaks French"—not realizing that Bart has just used his newly acquired mastery of the language to call his father a "buffoon." For an American cartoon, "The Crepes of Wrath" has a remarkably polyglot texture, with whole scenes not just in French but even in Albanian.

Principal Skinner sums up the ambivalent response of Springfield to foreigners when he originally introduces Adil at school:

> You may find his accent peculiar. Certain aspects of his culture may seem absurd, perhaps even offensive. But I urge you all to give little Adil the benefit of the doubt. In this way, and only in this way, can we hope to better understand our backward neighbors throughout the world.

Here is the strange combination of being both open and closed to the rest of the globe that characterizes Springfield. Skinner may regard all foreigners as backward, but he would still like to understand them better. And, when one adds up what happens in "The Crepes of Wrath," one finds a Springfield strangely integrated into the world community, with its children being educated in France and foreigners coming to learn about the workings of its advanced technology. Though a small town, Springfield has an international airport, with direct flights from Paris according to the PA announcements we hear, and, even more remarkably, from Tirana, the capital of Albania. It is a small world after all.

Thus, for all its parochial qualities, Springfield emerges as a globalized community in *The Simpsons*. Even after Adil is returned under a cloud to his native Albania, the town continues to have a foreign exchange student in the person of Uter, complete with his German accent and *Lederhosen*. One of Springfield's most distinguished residents also has a heavy German accent, Rainier Wolfcastle, the actor who plays the action hero McBain (obviously modeled on the Austrian-born movie star Arnold Schwarzenegger). Perhaps the presence of so many German speakers in Springfield explains the interest of German businessmen in buying the nuclear power plant from Burns. The prospect of this foreign takeover reflects the increasingly multinational nature of business at the end of the twentieth century. We see Burns's flunky, Waylon Smithers, using audiotapes labeled "Sycophantic German" to get ready for his new bosses, learning such useful phrases as: "You looken sharpen todayen, mein herr" ("Burns Verkaufen der Kraftwerk"). As for the polyglot character of Springfield, this small town even has a Spanish-language sitcom on its Channel Ocho, featuring the famous Bumblebee Man. When Lisa takes the wrong bus and gets lost in Springfield, she discovers to her surprise whole ethnic neighborhoods in the town, including one in which everybody speaks Russian.[57] As we see in the episode called "Mom and Pop Art" (#AABF15, 4/11/99), Springfield is sufficiently Europeanized to support a trendy art community. Filled with homages to masterpieces of European art, from Rousseau's *Sleeping Gypsy* to Dali's *The Persistence of Memory*, this episode deals with Homer's brief triumph as an "outsider artist," due to the support of a group of foreign admirers, semi-affectionately referred to as "Eurotrash." But perhaps the most telling detail of the episode is the fact that Homer obtains his art supplies from "Mom & Pop Hardware," which turns out upon closer inspection to be "A Subsidiary of Global Dynamics, Inc." In late 1990s Springfield, a seemingly local business operation is really part of a multinational corporation. *The Simpsons* truly grasps the dynamics of the contemporary world, as everywhere one turns the local is globalized and the global is localized.

In one particularly bizarre subplot (in "In Marge We Trust"), Homer finds to his dismay that halfway around the earth his face has mysteriously become the logo for a Japanese soap product called "Mr. Sparkle." The episode features a brilliant parody of a Japanese TV commercial that reveals how aware the creators of the show are of what is happening on television around the globe. Indeed, as part of portraying the globalization of the world, *The Simpsons* repeatedly portrays the globalization of television. And in an odd case of life imitating art imitating life, *The Simpsons* has itself emerged as a perfect example of globalized television. The program is now shown all around the world and has been dubbed into over twenty languages, often illustrating the complexities and paradoxes of contemporary globalized culture. As an example of local variations on a global theme, *The Simpsons* is dubbed into French in both France and Quebec and thus ends up existing in "two parallel francophone universes" according to an article in the Canadian magazine *Saturday Night*. The dubbers in France and Quebec often come up with different solutions to the problem of translating American idiom. "Where American Homer describes his shrewish sisters-in-law as the 'gruesome twosome,' French Homère labels them *les sorcières Siamoises* (the Siamese witches), in Quebec, they're called *deux airs de boeuf* (the two grouches)."[58] Sometimes the seemingly simple act of translation can take on a political dimension. "The French are confident enough to let an anglicism or two slip into the dub. In Quebec, apparently, the fear is that if you give the English an inch, they'll swamp your whole language. So Homer's doughnuts remain *les donuts* in France, but in Quebec become *les beignes*" (16). Who would have thought that Homer's donuts could spark such cultural controversy? But evidently translating *The Simpsons* into French raises all sorts of issues of race and class, as the dubbers in both France and Quebec scramble to find local

The logic of globalization in *The Simpsons* is thus largely economic, as the role of Apu and the Kwik-E-Mart makes clear. In that sense, the globalization of America in *The Simpsons* rests on a more fundamental Americanization of the globe. Only when the basic political and economic issues have been settled in favor of America do its citizens become open to the whole range of products and customs available around the world. Thus, although the characters in *The Simpsons* are indeed globalized in a way that the characters in *Gilligan's Island* are not, they are still Americans at heart. They may be less attached to their national government, but they remain by and large convinced that their way of life as Americans is superior, particularly their economic way of life.[63] To the extent the Springfielders look beyond their local borders, it is mainly to see what the outside world has to offer in terms of exotic or at least different consumer goods and lifestyles—but they are not looking for alternatives to their system of government. The whole world has in effect become Springfield's shopping mall, and international merchants such as Apu are now presiding over the global rummage sale. That is the deepest way in which the premise of *The Simpsons* is the end of the Cold War. The show assumes that the issue between communism and capitalism has been decisively settled in favor of free markets, and only in that context can America proceed with globalization.

"The Crepes of Wrath" toys with this issue in a debate between Adil and Lisa. As a communist from Albania, Adil argues against American capitalism: "How can you defend a country where five percent of the people control ninety-five percent of the wealth?" The feisty Lisa replies: "I'm defending a country whose people can think and act and worship any way they want!" Typically, *The Simpsons* reduces this serious ideological confrontation to a childish game, as Adil and Lisa stubbornly answer each other again and again: "Can not!" "Can too!" Homer intervenes to try to settle the argument judiciously: "Please, please, kids, stop fighting. Maybe Lisa's right about America being the land of opportunity and maybe Adil has a point about the machinery of capitalism being oiled with the blood of the workers." This is a fascinating moment—here in early 1990, shortly after the Berlin Wall came crashing down, *The Simpsons* takes one last seminostalgic look back at the ideological history of the twentieth century, when the conflict between capitalism and socialism genuinely divided the world and people were willing even to die for one way of life or the other. Attributing the evenhanded view of the debate between capitalism and socialism to Homer is the way *The Simpsons* makes the po-

sition appear laughable. By 1990 everybody but a few die-hard Alba-
nians and Homer Simpson knows that Lisa is right and capitalism is
the only viable economic system. Even Homer eventually comes
around to championing the free market economy with Adil, con-
fronting the contentious Albanian with American abundance where it
matters most to him: "American donuts—glazed, powdered, rasp-
berry filled—now how's that for freedom of choice?" Once again we
see that consumer goods mean more to Homer than any political ideology, or rather, consumer goods *are* his political ideology.

Thus *The Simpsons* ends up giving an insightful portrait of what is
happening in America at the end of the twentieth century and the beginning of the twenty-first. With the end of the Cold War, Americans
are no longer as dependent on their national government to protect
them and feel freer to pursue both local and global concerns instead of
their traditional national concerns. This development has been reinforced by the way Americans have become disillusioned with government in general and their national government in particular. Though
The Simpsons has generally shied away from dealing with the specific
scandals that rocked the federal government in the last few decades, it
generally portrays government at all levels—local, state, and national—as mired in corruption. *The Simpsons* also portrays Americans
gradually wising up to the media tricks by which politicians attempt
to manipulate them. Thus the series shows that just when politics becomes less important in people's lives, it also becomes less legitimate.
People are increasingly less disposed to believe in the integrity of their
leaders or the desirability of their grand political schemes.

With all these factors conspiring to undermine politics on the national level, the show portrays the Simpsons as more likely to be concerned with what is happening across the river in Shelbyville or across
the globe in Tokyo or Canberra than they are with what is happening in
Washington, D.C. The *Simpsons* episode most fully devoted to the theme
of globalization is probably the one portraying the family's trip to
Japan.[64] It begins appropriately in a newly opened cybercafe in Springfield and focuses on the new importance of the Internet in American life,
showing how the latest technological developments are working to integrate the global community. We are told right at the beginning about
the Internet: "It's more than a global pornography network." Indeed,
we see that even someone as dense as Homer is now making full use of
the globalizing potential of the Internet. For once, Lisa speaks with
pride of her father: "Wow, Dad. You're surfing like a pro." Homer himself is proud of his mastery and begins to detail his accomplishments:

"I'm betting on jai alai in the Cayman Islands, I invested in something called News Corp." Only when Lisa points out that News Corp is the parent of the Fox Network and Homer tries in vain to unload his stock do we begin to suspect that perhaps he is not up to the intellectual demands of cyberspace. As if to confirm our suspicions, the Simpsons soon lose all their vacation money to a cyberthief.

But the contemporary globalized world offers myriad possibilities, and through a financial seminar, the Simpsons learn of cheap vacation opportunities at the local airport. In a continuing validation of Springfield's globalization, we discover that its airport is now offering daily departures to London, Paris, Tokyo, and Kingston, Jamaica. The Simpsons manage to make the flight to Tokyo and get a full education in Japanese culture, starting when Homer and Bart encounter the Emperor of Japan at a sumo wrestling match. Their disrespectful treatment of his Imperial Highness lands them in jail, but even that turns out to be a culturally educational experience. As Homer explains to Lisa, displaying a surprising command of classic Japanese literature: "In jail, we had to be in this dumb Kabuki play about the 47 Ronin, and I wanted to be Yoshi, but they made me Ori." Bart adds: "Then we had to do two hours of origami followed by flower arranging and meditation." As the ultimate measure of the orientalizing of Homer and Bart, we next hear them speaking fluent Japanese. The subtitles reveal that they have even absorbed the inward-turning, exclusionary character of Japanese culture, as Homer asks Bart: "Should we tell them the secret of inner peace?" and the boy replies (still in subtitled Japanese): "No, they are foreign devils."

At the same time as we see the Simpsons adapting to Japanese culture, we see how the Japanese have adapted to American culture. The Simpsons go to eat at a restaurant in Tokyo called Americatown, filled with U.S. memorabilia and a waiter who introduces himself: "Howdy gangstas! I am average American Joe salaryman waiter!" Lisa is upset at encountering this simulacrum of her own country in Japan, where she had hoped to find a different way of life: "We didn't come halfway around the world to eat at Americatown." Faced with an all-American menu, she asks sarcastically: "Don't you serve anything that's even remotely Japanese?" The episode is filled with signs of how eagerly the Japanese have taken to American culture, including Woody Allen doing a commercial for Japanese television. The only way the Simpsons can earn their way back to the United States is to humiliate themselves on a Japanese game show. In the television studio, they finally find a difference between Japanese and American culture. As the game-show host explains to them: "Our game shows are a little different from yours. Your shows reward knowledge. We punish ignorance." The Simpsons survive their ordeal on "Happy Smile Super Challenge Family Wish Show," and in the end, nothing can stop them from returning to America, not even a last-minute appearance by the Japanese monster Godzilla.

The outcome of this episode is typical of the series and suggests that in the end the Simpsons are more attached to the local than to the global, and indeed the global is ultimately important in the series only insofar as it can be made local, that is, part of Springfield. For all its cosmopolitanism, the show keeps returning to the traditional American theme of "there's no place like home." When the Simpsons go to foreign countries such as Japan or Australia, it is basically as tourists, with no intention of staying. By contrast, *The Simpsons* in effect shows the whole world beating a path to Springfield's door. As Apu and several other characters in the show make clear, when foreigners come to Springfield, it is often to stay—with the hope of participating in the American dream, which is to say, the American economy. Thus, for all the success of *The Simpsons* in capturing the increasingly globalized texture of American life, ultimately the interest of the local prevails in the show and Springfield remains a small town, with small-town politics. And politics in Springfield is noticeably unideological, as is appropriate to the post–Cold War era. The local political issues are very local in nature and purely pragmatic—whether to build a freeway or a monorail, whether to legalize gambling or criminalize alcoholic beverages.

The nonideological nature of politics in Springfield does not mean that one cannot find political parties in the town. What it does mean is that, although *The Simpsons*, as we have seen, may display a sentimental preference for Democrats, it does not take the ideology of either party seriously. Despite efforts to differentiate Republicans from Democrats, the show tends to be cynical about both parties and often suggests that their differences are superficial in the face of one underlying and overriding similarity—the willingness of either party to do anything to gain and hold on to power and to place its own interest above that of the people. In "Sideshow Bob Roberts" (#2F02, 10/19/94), the Democratic regime of Mayor Quimby is challenged by insurgent Republicans. Led by a Rush Limbaugh look-alike named Burch Barlow, the Republicans first run a slick radio talk show campaign to get Quimby to pardon Krusty's former second banana on TV, Sideshow Bob, from prison and then run the ex-convict against the incumbent mayor in the next election. The episode suggests that media politics has even infected the local level in Springfield, and presents Barlow as a radio demagogue. He says: "Let's just junk those dumb-o-crats and their bleeding-heart smellfare program" and calls Quimby an "illiterate, tax-cheating, wife-swapping, pot-smoking Spend-o-crat" (to which Quimby replies: "Hey, I am no longer illiterate"). The episode goes over the top in its caricature of the Republicans as evil. At one point Sideshow Bob tells Bart and Lisa: "No children have ever meddled with the Republican Party and lived to tell about it." And the secret cabal that runs the Republican Party in Springfield is an assem-blage of the most sinister forces in the town, including Mr. Burns and what the *Complete Guide* describes as "a green vampire-like hu-manoid" (153). And yet the fact that the Republicans are attacking the thoroughly corrupt Mayor Quimby makes it hard simply to side with the Democrats in this episode.

The Republican cabal also includes the radio personality Barlow of course and the movie star Rainier Wolfcastle. The suggestion seems to be that the rich Republicans control the media in Spring-field and use that power to oust Quimby from office. The notion of Republicans controlling the media may seem laughable, but even more implausible is the idea that important media figures would be living in Springfield. Here is one respect in which the portrayal of the local community in *The Simpsons* is unrealistic. In Springfield, even the media forces are largely local. There is of course nothing strange about having a local television station in Springfield. It is perfectly plausible that the Simpsons get their news from a man, Kent Brockman, who actually lives in their midst. It is also quite be-lievable that the kiddie show on Springfield television is local, and that its host, Krusty, not only lives in town but also is available for local functions such as supermarket openings and birthday parties. But what are authentic movie stars such as Rainer Wolfcastle doing living in a hick town like Springfield? And what about the fact that the world-famous *Itchy & Scratchy* cartoons are produced right in downtown Springfield? Indeed the entire *Itchy & Scratchy* empire is apparently headquartered in Springfield. This is not a trivial fact. It means that when Marge campaigns against cartoon violence, she can picket *Itchy & Scratchy* headquarters without leaving her home-town.[65] The citizens of Springfield are fortunate to be able to have a direct impact on the forces that shape their lives and especially their family lives. In short, *The Simpsons* takes the phenomenon that has in fact done more than anything else to subvert the power of the local in American politics and American life in general—namely the media—and in effect brings it within the orbit of Springfield, thereby placing the force at least partially under local control.[66]

The unrealistic portrayal of the media as local helps highlight the overall tendency of *The Simpsons*—to present Springfield as a kind of classical polis; for all its veneer of globalization, the town is just about as self-contained and autonomous as a community in today's world can be. This once again reflects the postmodern nostalgia of *The Simpsons*; with its self-conscious re-creation of the 1950s sitcom, it ends up weirdly celebrating the old ideal of small-town America.[67] Again I do not mean to deny that the first impulse of *The Simpsons* is to make fun of small-town life. But in that very process, it reminds us of what the old ideal was and what was so attractive about it, above all the fact that average Americans somehow felt in touch with the forces that influenced their lives and maybe even in control of them. In a presentation before the American Society of Newspaper Editors on April 12, 1991 (broadcast on C-SPAN), Matt Groening said that the subtext of *The Simpsons* is: "The people in power don't always have your best interests in mind."[68] This is a view of politics that cuts across the normal distinctions between left and right and explains why the show can be relatively evenhanded in its treatment of both political parties and has something to offer to both liberals and conservatives. *The Simpsons* is based on distrust of power, and especially of power remote from ordinary people. The show celebrates an old-style community, in which everybody more or less knows everybody else (even if they do not necessarily like each other). By re-creating this older sense of community, the show manages to generate a kind of warmth out of its postmodern coolness, a warmth that is largely responsible for its success with the American public. This view of community may be the most profound comment *The Simpsons* has to make on family life in particular and politics in general in America today. No matter how dysfunctional it may seem, the nuclear family is an institution worth preserving. And the way to preserve it is not by the offices of a distant, supposedly expert, therapeutic state, but by restoring its links to a series of local institutions, which reflect and foster the same principle that makes the Simpson family itself work—the attachment to one's own, the principle that we best care for something when it belongs to us.

The celebration of the local in *The Simpsons* is confirmed in an episode called "They Saved Lisa's Brain" (#AABF18, 5/9/99), which for once explores in detail the possibility of a utopian alternative to politics as usual in Springfield. The episode begins with Lisa disgusted by a gross-out contest sponsored by a local radio station, which, among other things, results in the burning of a traveling van Gogh exhibition. With the indignation typical of youth, Lisa fires off an angry letter to the Springfield newspaper, charging: "Today our town lost what remained of its fragile civility." Outraged by the cultural limitations of Springfield, Lisa complains: "We have eight malls, but no symphony; thirty-two bars but no alternative theater." Lisa's spirited outburst catches the attention of the local chapter of Mensa, and the few high-IQ citizens of Springfield (including Dr. Hibbert, Principal Skinner, the Comic Book Guy, and Professor Frink) invite her to join the organization. Inspired by Lisa's courageous tirade against the cultural parochialism of Springfield, Dr. Hibbert challenges the city's way of life: "Why do we live in a town where the smartest have no power and the stupidest run everything?" Forming "a council of learned citizens," or what Kent Brockman later refers to as an "intellectual junta," the Mensa members set out to create the cartoon equivalent of Plato's *Republic* in Springfield. They begin by ousting Mayor Quimby, who in fact leaves town rather abruptly once the matter of some missing lottery funds comes up.

Taking advantage of an obscure provision in the Springfield charter, the Mensa members step into the power vacuum created by Quimby's sudden abdication. Lisa sees no limit to what the Platonic rule of the wise might accomplish: "With our superior intellects, we could rebuild this city on a foundation of reason and enlightenment; we could turn Springfield into a utopia." Principal Skinner holds out hope for "a new Athens," while another Mensa member thinks in terms of B. F. Skinner's "Walden II." The new rulers immediately set out to bring their utopia into existence, redesigning traffic patterns and abolishing all sports that involve violence. But the abstract rationality and benevolent universalism of the intellectual junta soon prove to be a fraud. The Mensa members begin to disagree among themselves, and it becomes evident that their claim to represent the public interest masks a number of private agendas. At the climax of the episode, the Comic Book Guy comes forward to proclaim: "Inspired by the most logical race in the galaxy, the Vulcans, breeding will be permitted once every seven years; for many of you this will mean much less breeding; for me, much much more." This reference to *Star Trek* appropriately elicits from Groundskeeper Willie a response in his heavy Scottish accent that calls to mind the *Enterprise*'s Chief Engineer Scott: "You cannot do that, sir, you don't have the power." The Mensa regime's self-interested attempt to imitate the *Republic* by regulating breeding in the city is just too much for the ordinary citizens of Springfield to bear.

With the Platonic revolution in Springfield degenerating into petty squabbling and violence, a *deus ex machina* arrives in the form of physicist Stephen Hawking, proclaimed "the world's smartest man." When Hawking voices his disappointment with the Mensa regime, he ends up in a fight with Principal Skinner. Seizing the opportunity created by the division among the intelligentsia, Homer leads a counterrevolution of the stupid with the rallying cry: "C'mon you idiots, we're taking back this town." Thus the attempt to bring about a rule of philosopher-kings in Springfield ends ignominiously, leaving Hawking to pronounce its epitaph: "Sometimes the smartest of us can be the most childish." Theory fails when translated into practice in this episode of *The Simpsons* and must be relegated once more to the confines of the contemplative life. The episode ends with Hawking and Homer drinking beer together in Moe's Tavern and discussing Homer's theory of a donut-shaped universe. As the executive producer of *The Simpsons*, Mike Scully, explained: "It was a chance to get the world's smartest man and the world's stupidest man together in the same place."[69]

In a way, Scully's remark sums up what *The Simpsons* accomplishes week after week: bridging the gap between the high and the low in our culture. The show can be enjoyed on two levels—as both broad farce and intellectual satire. "They Saved Lisa's Brain" contains some of the grossest humor in the long history of *The Simpsons*. (I have not even mentioned the subplot concerning Homer's encounter with a pornographic photographer.) But at the same time, it is filled with subtle cultural allusions; for example, the Mensa members convene in what is obviously a Frank Lloyd Wright prairie house. In the end, then, this episode embodies the strange mixture of intellectualism and anti-intellectualism characteristic of *The Simpsons*. In Lisa's challenge to Springfield, the show calls attention to the cultural limitations of small-town America, but it also reminds us that intellectual disdain for the common man can be carried too far and that theory can all too easily lose touch with common sense. Ultimately *The Simpsons* seems to offer a kind of intellectual defense of the common man against intellectuals, which helps explain its popularity and broad appeal. Very few people have found *The Critique of Pure Reason* funny, but in *The Gay Science*, Nietzsche felt that he had put his finger on Kant's joke: "Kant wanted to prove in a way that would puzzle all the world that all the world was right—that was the private joke of this soul. He wrote against the learned on behalf of the prejudice of the common people, but for the learned and not for the common people."[70] In Nietzsche's terms, *The Simpsons* goes *The Critique of Pure Reason* one better: It defends the common man against the intellectual, but in a way that both the common man and the intellectual can understand and enjoy.

Mainstreaming Paranoia:
The X-Files and the
Delegitimation of the Nation-State

The X-Files is very nineties, because everything is left in doubt. There's no closure, no answers. . . . Obviously, it's tapping in to something the nation wants. I think it has to do with religious stirrings—a sort of New Age yearning for an alternate reality and the search for some kind of extrasensory god. Couple that with a cynical, jaded, dispossessed feeling of having been lied to by the government, and you've got a pretty powerful combination for a TV show. Either that, or the Fox network has an amazing marketing department.

—David Duchovny

Although we may not be alone in the universe, in our own separate ways, on this planet, we are all alone.

—Jose Chung

Imagine a television program that takes UFOs and other extraterrestrial phenomena seriously. Moreover, it assumes not only that aliens have actually visited our planet, but also that the United States government is actively involved in a vast conspiracy to hide that fact from the American people in a plot that reaches up to the highest levels in the chain of command. The series goes on to link that cabal to other subjects beloved of conspiracy theorists, Watergate, for example, or the Kennedy and King assassinations. The series furthermore connects all these conspiracies to the international military-industrial complex and views the history of the United States since World War II as one huge exercise in militarism, beginning with a deal with its former Nazi enemies and including Nazi-like atrocities during the Vietnam War. With such a dark view of the U.S. government and its role in world politics, would such a series ever be permitted on the air by network

TV executives? If programmed, could it possibly last a whole season? Would not the American public at some point wake up to the subversive character of the series and hoot it off the air?

I am of course not making up this series but simply describing the Fox Network's flagship program *The X-Files*. Contrary to all normal TV rules, a show with such a controversial view of U.S. history has been a solid success, completing seven seasons on the air and still going, getting high ratings consistently, being widely syndicated in reruns already, and gathering fans all around the world as well as a cult following in America. The remarkable and unpredictable success of *The X-Files* has to tell us something about the United States in the 1990s; it has to reflect a fundamental shift of mood in the country.[1] To be sure, the show did not reveal its deepest secrets all at once, and one might argue that it initially hooked its viewers with intriguing science fiction plots and only gradually hit them with its shocking claims about the U.S. government. But even in its pilot episode, *The X-Files* was already suggesting that the federal government is hiding something and the dominant mood of the show has always been distrust of authority. Though not inconceivable, it is difficult to believe that a show with such dark content could have achieved equivalent success in the 1970s or 1980s. Try to imagine a network in the 1970s casting James Garner as the hero in a series called *Jim Garrison: DA* or Mark Lane hosting a PBS series called *Great Performances: The Assassinations*.

The success of *The X-Files* in the 1990s would seem to reflect a growing cynicism in the American people about their government—a distrust of their leaders and a new disposition to believe the worst about them, no doubt fueled by the seemingly endless series of political scandals that emanated out of Washington in the 1970s, 1980s, and 1990s. Accounts of the genesis of the show reveal that when Fox executives were concerned about its political content, they were reassured by audience surveys:

> Strangely enough, little mention was made at first of the show's politics, considering that the pilot and subsequent hours begin with the premise that the government is behind widespread, covert activity to prevent the public from learning about the existence of UFOs. [Fox executive Sandy] Grushow does remember Jon Neswig, the head of Fox's sales department, raising the issue when the show was first screened, resulting in "some sparks flying in the room." Still, when Fox tested the show with what are called focus groups . . . to gauge viewer response, no one even questioned the notion. "The thing that was amazing to me in that test marketing was that, to a man, everyone believed that the government was conspiring" to cover things up, [*X-Files* creator Chris] Carter marvels.[2]

The X-Files found a way to exploit this political disillusionment of the American people, tapping into their developing sense that their government does not have their best interest in mind. The fact that the show has been popular in many countries around the globe suggests that it may reflect even broader developments, a worldwide sense that politicians have failed to live up to their claims to be the saviors of humanity.[3] But the political disillusionment goes even deeper. People do not just blame individual politicians for betraying their professed ideals; they have a more disturbing feeling that their political institutions themselves are failing, and above all, they have come increasingly to question whether their national governments can solve their problems. Indeed, some now believe that the nation-state is the problem, not the solution, interfering with the free play of global economic forces and thus reducing people's liberty and standard of living. Historians may someday look back at the 1990s as the decade in which, for a wide range of people, the nation-state began to lose its legitimacy. If so, they may view *The X-Files* as one of the cultural reflections of this development. The show took government conspiracy theories that had long been regarded as the lunatic fringe of political discourse in the United States and brought them into the mainstream.[4] Indeed it transformed ideas that for decades had been regarded as virtually paranoid into the weekly fare of television everywhere.[5]

One can see what an extraordinary development *The X-Files* represents in American popular culture by concentrating on the fact that, for all its science fiction and horror elements, it is fundamentally a series about the FBI. But as a TV advertiser might put it, this is not your father's FBI—and certainly not J. Edgar Hoover's. Far from being the "hero" of the series, as one might expect on American television, the federal agency is virtually the "villain" in *The X-Files*. Hoover actually appears in an episode called "Travelers" that goes back into FBI history, and he is portrayed in a very negative light as a rabid anticommunist, willing to go to any lengths to rid America of the Red Menace. At one point, he says: "If we are to defeat the enemy, we must use their tools! . . . We must do those things which even our enemies would be ashamed to do." One of the writers of the episode, Frank Spotnitz, reports:

> We hired a retired FBI agent to serve as a technical advisor on the script. This was a gentleman who'd been with the Bureau for twenty or thirty years, and he was very offended by our script. He was angry that we would even suggest that J. Edgar Hoover—whom he still calls "Mr. Hoover"—would be involved in any of the plots, or take any of the positions that he takes in the script. Then he told me that he'd never actually

seen our show. "But if this is the type of story that you're telling," he told me, "I can't imagine that it would be very popular."[6]

So much for the ability of retired FBI agents to read the mood of the United States in the 1990s. Active agents did not do much better. Chris Carter reports that he initially got very little help from the FBI when he sought background information for the show. It was only after *The X-Files* had become a hit that he started hearing from individual agents, some of whom arranged a tour of FBI headquarters in Washington for Carter and the show's stars, David Duchovny and Gillian Anderson. Carter says that his relations with individual contacts in the FBI are better now: "I've been able to call and get good expert advice or information from these people. Still, officially, they can't say they endorse the show or that they are in any way connected to the show."[7] Given the way *The X-Files* portrays the FBI, the lack of official endorsement is hardly surprising.

To be sure, the individual FBI agents featured in the series, Fox Mulder and Dana Scully, are presented as heroic figures, but almost everything they accomplish they achieve in spite of the Bureau, not because of it. *The X-Files* presents the FBI as a vast government bureaucracy, with bewildering, Byzantine, and even Kafkaesque layers of authority that make it impossible for Mulder and Scully to get clear guidance or support in their efforts to right the wrongs of the world. At times, *The X-Files* shows the FBI hindering the work of Mulder and Scully simply out of bureaucratic inertia, incompetence, and all-around thickheadedness. But as the series developed, it began to suggest that the opposition to Mulder and Scully is the product of sinister forces working within the FBI or at least exerting pressure on it from other branches of the federal government. We gradually learn that the agency that more than any other over the years has represented the federal government's ability to uncover threats to its citizens is being used as part of a plot to cover up the greatest threat the American people have ever faced—a worldwide conspiracy to aid aliens in taking over the earth.

In general, *The X-Files* is more likely to show the failures of the FBI than its successes. Indeed, in their very nature, the X-Files are tributes to the FBI's limitations—mysterious cases, chiefly involving paranormal phenomena, that the Bureau has failed to solve over the years. They have become the special province of Fox Mulder, who is interested in any case involving mysterious or unexplained phenomena for a personal reason. He believes that years ago his younger sister was abducted by space aliens, and he seeks to find extraterrestrial causes behind paranormal events to validate his suspicions about his sister and to help him locate her, or at least find out what happened to her. In the pilot episode, higher-ups in the FBI assign Dana Scully to Mulder as a partner in the hope that she will discredit his investigations. Her scientific expertise as a medical doctor is supposed to allow her to debunk his explanations of phenomena in terms of occult causes. If there are genuinely mysterious forces abroad in the world, evidently the FBI does not want to know about them—and it does not want anybody else to know about them either.

Thus, in its basic premise, *The X-Files* suggests that the government is incapable of dealing with a whole side of human life. It neglects the deepest mysteries and leaves them to a figure it proceeds actively to marginalize (symbolically, Mulder's office is in a basement corner of the FBI building in D.C.).[8] It does everything it can to thwart his efforts to uncover the truth and, if he ever does, to prevent him from making it known to the public. The show in fact emphasizes that the government does not represent the public interest but has a hidden agenda that largely reflects the self-interest of those in power. All this runs counter to the way the FBI has traditionally been presented in American popular culture.[9] Probably no branch of the federal government has gotten more of a free ride from the mass media than the FBI. Bureau agents have been the darlings of movies, radio, and television throughout their history, and especially in the 1930s, 1940s, and 1950s. The notion of a federal police force was originally very controversial—many felt that it was an unjustified extension of the federal government's power, beyond what is specified in the Constitution—but we seldom get even a hint of such controversy in media representations of the FBI. In perhaps the most celebratory treatment Hollywood ever produced—a movie called *The FBI Story* (1959)—the question of why a *federal* bureau of investigation is necessary comes up briefly, but the answer is almost comic in its simplicity: "The country's growing, and crime will grow with it." This makes the FBI sound like a franchise operation on the model of McDonald's—"over one billion criminals captured"—but it completely begs the constitutional question and leaves us wondering why local police forces are not adequate to dealing with the problem of crime, no matter how much it may be growing. Supporters of the FBI would of course answer that the agency was needed to deal with new developments in crime that local police forces were incapable of handling, such as criminals crossing state lines in speedy automobiles. Opponents would counter that much of the "growth in crime" was actually the result of the federal government outlawing innocent activities or at least "victimless crimes," as it did during Prohibition.

These are admittedly complex legal and political issues and people may legitimately disagree about them, but the point is that none of these arguments are vetted in *The FBI Story*. The FBI was heavily involved in the film and supervised all aspects of its production.[10] It is not surprising, therefore, that the film comes across as outright propaganda for the FBI. *The FBI Story* stresses that the agency, at least under Hoover's reign, is above politics; that its agents are God-fearing, self-sacrificing public servants, willing to give their lives to protect their country and their families; that it is technologically sophisticated and able to ferret out any criminal; and, above all, that, in Superman-like fashion, the Bureau is on the side of truth, justice, and the American way.

The FBI Story may be extreme in its blanket endorsement of J. Edgar Hoover and the agency he ran for decades, but it is representative of the general tendency of Hollywood and other elements of American popular culture to take a positive view of the FBI (with some notable exceptions, especially during the Vietnam and Watergate era).[11] Hoover himself was quite aware of the importance of public perception of the FBI and was very canny about cultivating its public image. For decades popular culture worked to make Americans proud of their FBI, and to view it as a symbol of the integrity of their government. The FBI was portrayed as policing the borders of America in every sense of the term, protecting it against a wide range of enemies, foreign and domestic. During World War II, it countered the sabotage and espionage efforts of German and Japanese agents working in the United States. During the Cold War, FBI surveillance was extended to agents from the Soviet Union and other communist nations. Many FBI stories have dealt with attempts to violate U.S. borders—smuggling operations, for example, and especially attempts to sneak illegal aliens into the country. The FBI has been shown fighting domestic terrorism, and in particular working to thwart assassination attempts on public figures such as the president. Many movie and television FBI dramas deal with the FBI's war on organized crime, pictured as a national syndicate that is the mirror image of the Bureau's own national organization.[12] In its efforts to eliminate gangsters, the FBI was shown going after bootleggers and rumrunners during Prohibition, and, more recently, after drug dealers.

The various functions of the FBI sometimes link up. For example, gangsters are often shown to come from specific immigrant groups, sometimes living in the United States illegally. Occasionally this tendency has gone too far. The FBI television show *The Untouchables* (1959–63), for example, came under fire for always portraying its villains as Italian Americans. But such ethnic stereotyping in some ways goes to the heart of the typical Hollywood FBI story. Portraying the FBI often turns into an exercise in defining what is American by defining what is un-American. The FBI agent is himself frequently the very image of the all-American hero; Jimmy Stewart, for example, plays the lead in *The FBI Story*. The FBI hero is set against a variety of villains who all in some way challenge the mainstream conception of the American way of life. In *The FBI Story*, for example, when the Bureau is trying to track down a Soviet spy on a Sunday, the Jimmy Stewart character remarks: "Since he was a communist, we knew he couldn't be going to church." The film reduces the ideological conflict to the simplest possible terms—Americans believe in God and Soviet communists do not. As epitomized by its efforts at policing national borders, the fundamental role of the FBI seems to be to draw a sharp line between America and everything that is not America.[13] In one subgenre of the FBI drama, the Bureau takes on the subversive activities of counterfeiters and thereby works to ensure the integrity of U.S. currency. The federal government gets to define what counts as money in America, and the FBI's job is to make sure that no private individuals get in on the act. Protecting the symbols as well as the realities of national sovereignty is the noble mission of the FBI in traditional representations in the media.

The X-Files works to deconstruct this myth in its portrayal of the FBI. Instead of the clear-cut oppositions of the classic American FBI drama, it serves up a murky twilight world in which it is difficult if not impossible to tell the good guys from the bad guys. With double, triple, and sometimes quadruple agents at work, *The X-Files* always keeps its audience guessing who is working for America and who against it, or, for that matter, whether the American government is on the side of right or wrong. Far from presenting neat distinctions between the United States and its enemies, the central plotline of *The X-Files* suggests that at various times American authorities have been in collusion with Nazi scientists or linked up with covert Soviet operations. Rather than showing the FBI protecting American public figures against assassins, *The X-Files* in one particularly dark episode ("Musings of a Cigarette-Smoking Man") half-seriously suggests that a figure closely linked to the agency may have been responsible for killing John Kennedy and Martin Luther King Jr. Mulder and Scully are of course consistently presented as heroes and in that sense "good guys," but even they sometimes appear as morally ambiguous, at least in each other's eyes. A number of the *X-Files* plots work to give Mulder and Scully reasons to be suspicious of each other and set them at cross-purposes, sometimes because weird circumstances contrive to produce an exact double of one or the other, who functions as a kind of evil twin.[14] This kind of doubling is characteristic of *The X-Files*, whose central mode is duplicity. Where the classic FBI drama gives us moral and political clarity, *The X-Files* time and again delivers ambiguity, thereby reflecting a loss of faith in the national government that the Bureau represents.

◆

To illustrate these points, I will discuss a typical and not particularly distinguished *X-Files* episode from the fifth season, "The Pine Bluff Variant." At the beginning of the episode, Mulder is acting very suspiciously. Participating in the surveillance of an FBI suspect, he has evidently helped him escape. His actions are so odd that Scully begins to doubt his loyalty and starts tailing him to find out what he is up to. It turns out that Mulder's apparent treachery is actually part of a plot for him to infiltrate a domestic terrorist operation. By helping the suspect escape, he is trying to get in the good graces of an organization called the New Spartans, who are portrayed as a stereotypical right-wing militia group, which has "the expressed goal of overthrowing the federal government." To further their ends, they seem to be pursuing a course of bio-terrorism, using some kind of genetically engineered weapon said to be derived from the secret laboratories of the former Soviet Union. Their plan appears to strike at the very heart of U.S. sovereignty; in his undercover role, Mulder learns that the New Spartans are going to use the cover of robbing a bank (aptly named the First Sovereign Bank of Pennsylvania) to contaminate the American money supply with their bio-weapon (specifically they are going to spray a whole Federal Reserve shipment of banknotes with a flesh-eating microbe). "The Pine Bluff Variant" thus seems to offer a veritable compendium of the elements of a standard FBI drama: domestic terrorists challenging the authority of the federal government, with a sinister connection to a foreign enemy, and a plan for attacking the integrity of the American currency.

Up to this point the plot of "The Pine Bluff Variant" is convoluted enough, leaving even Scully bewildered when she is pulled over on the road by armed men: "Exactly what agency are you guys from?" But the episode has one last plot twist for its viewers. It seems to be telling a predictable story of a right-wing conspiracy against the federal government. In general, *The X-Files* presents right-wing conspiracies more negatively than it does left-wing conspiracies. In fact, I cannot think of a single case where it presents anything that could be described as a left-wing conspiracy. With its generally left-wing political sympathies, *The X-Files* tends to regard all conspiracies as right-wing, including of course the military-industrial conspiracy at the center of its main plot.[15] But for all the negative stereotyping of the right-wing militia figures in "The Pine Bluff Variant" (one of them is a skinhead), it turns out that the federal government—or at least an element within it—is the real villain of the episode. We find out at the end that the U.S. attorney who has been working with the FBI to uncover the terrorist plot has known about it all along and seems to have participated in it and perhaps even planned and authorized it.

Earlier in the episode, when Scully wonders if the killer microbe could have been "developed by the Russians," a doctor from the federal Centers for Disease Control tells her: "I've seen everything in the Russian arsenal; they've got nothing this sophisticated." When Scully tells her stalwart boss, Assistant FBI Director Walter Skinner, that the weapon must have been "developed domestically," he toes the official line: "The United States has no bio-weapons. President Nixon dismantled our program in 1969." The mention of Nixon is of course not exactly calculated to convince the audience of the federal government's integrity, and Scully goes on to contradict her superior: "Yes, sir, that's what we've been told," but "the bio-weapons program may have continued in secret." Blurring the line between America and its enemies, the episode ultimately invites us to think of the U.S. military as perhaps more sinister than the Russian. It makes Mulder's earlier remark to the New Spartans sound prophetic: "The only reason I tolerate your methods is that the government's are worse."

Even by the normal standards of *X-Files* murkiness, this episode leaves it unclear why a federal official would be involved in a plot to contaminate the money supply. But *The X-Files* constantly shows shadowy government figures experimenting on an unsuspecting American public, in particular trying out various toxins on them. In the climactic confrontation, the U.S. attorney rebukes Mulder: "Our government is not in the business of killing innocent civilians," but the FBI agent insists: "Those were tests on us, to be used on someone else." By the end of "The Pine Bluff Variant," the characters appear to have switched sides so often that our ability to tell the good guys from the bad guys has been completely eroded.[16] We are left thoroughly confused and tempted to agree with Mulder when he himself says of the plot as it is unfolding: "It doesn't make sense." The only thing that is clear is that *The X-Files* has chosen to invert the normal pattern of the FBI drama. In a plot twist that should endear the show to monetarists everywhere, here it is the federal government and perhaps the Federal Reserve itself that is shown tampering with the money supply, and not the private individuals vilified in the standard counterfeiting story line. In Mulder's last words to the U.S. attorney, he insists: "The money's as dirty as you are." Sticking to his guns, the federal official asks Mulder which side he is on, demanding to know if he wants "to bring down the federal government—to do the very work that that group you were part of is so bent on doing. What do you want—laws against these men or laws protecting them?" Mulder's reply goes to the heart of *The X-Files*: "I want people to know the truth." And the official's answer shows where the battle lines are drawn on the show: "Well, sometimes our job is to protect those people from knowing it." That the federal government might have an interest in concealing the truth from the American people goes against everything that FBI dramas have traditionally tried to show.[17]

As damaging as the serious criticism of the federal government in *The X-Files* may be, in a way the show's comic episodes can be even more corrosive. In perhaps the funniest of all episodes, "Jose Chung's *From Outer Space*," a science fiction writer concocts fictionalized versions of Mulder and Scully and ultimately passes a damning judgment on the latter: "Seeking the truth about aliens means a perfunctory 9-to-5 job to some, for although Agent Diana Lesky is noble of spirit and pure at heart, she remains nevertheless a federal employee."[18] Rarely have the words "federal employee" been delivered with such ringing contempt on American television. *The X-Files* is just as likely to treat the national government with derision as with suspicion. Sometimes it shows all-powerful shadowy forces running the lives of Americans with sophisticated methods of surveillance and mind control. At other times, however, the show delights in portraying federal officials as inept, bumbling, and hence easily outwitted by private citizens, who display more intelligence and initiative.

But perhaps the most damaging revelation *The X-Files* has to make about the federal government is its growing irrelevance in the lives of its citizens. The show reveals Americans more and more being shaped by local and global forces in their world, with the nation-state consequently caught in a squeeze, increasingly pushed out of its seemingly central role in American life and relegated to the margins. Though pictures of the president and the attorney general routinely grace the FBI offices in the series, that is all they are—mere pictures. *The X-Files* strongly suggests that our public officials are just figureheads, manipulated from behind the scenes by mysterious power brokers. It is remarkable how small a role prominent officials such as the president or central institutions such as Congress have to play in *The X-Files*. It is obscure government agencies that have the real power, such as FEMA (the Federal Emergency Management Agency), which according to one conspiracy theorist in the *X-Files* movie forms "the secret government" of the United States and will take over openly once the planned alien invasion finally begins. Arguably the most extraordinary message *The X-Files* has for its audience is that the public figures they see in Washington, who seem to represent the nation-state in all its flag-waving glory, are in fact inconsequential in the grand scheme of things. According to *The X-Files*, it is people whose faces we do not know who, in effect, govern our lives, and they do not do so in the name of the nation-state. In "Musings of a Cigarette-Smoking Man," the dark villain tells one of his coconspirators: "How many historic events have only the two of us witnessed together? How often did we make or change history? And our names can never grace any pages of record. No monument can bear our image. And yet once again, tonight, the course of history will be set by two unknown men— standing in the shadows." History made by unknown men standing in the shadows—that is the governing vision of *The X-Files* and its ultimate subversion of the ideology of the nation-state.

I want to begin to explore the challenge to the nation-state's legitimacy in *The X-Files* by concentrating on one subset of episodes, which corresponds to one subgenre of traditional FBI stories. I will look at several episodes that deal with the issue of immigration, and specifically the problem of illegal aliens, and show how differently *The X-Files* treats this material when compared to standard FBI dramas. Because those who are not fans of the series may regard the episodes that deal with space aliens as preposterous, I prefer to begin with those that treat recognizable and "real world" problems, even if in a characteristically bizarre manner that emphasizes the monstrous aspect of the immigrant aliens. I hope to show that as fantastic as the *X-Files* plots may become, they tend to be rooted in genuine economic, social, and political concerns. Later in the chapter I will, for example, discuss the way *The X-Files* relates the problem of the nation-state to the problem of technology. And all along I will

be considering the larger meaning of "aliens" in the series and specifically the connection it develops between illegal aliens among immigrants and the space aliens featured in its main plot—what Chris Carter
refers to as its "mythology." I will argue that alienation in all senses of
the term is one of the central concepts of *The X-Files*. The show characterizes the nation-state above all in terms of its "alienating" effect, revealing that it draws its strength from its ability to "create" aliens, but it
may also be ultimately undermined by the alien forces it unleashes.

It is impossible to discuss in detail all the episodes of a long-
running series such as *The X-Files*, but I have tried to select a representative set that gives an idea of the variety and yet the unity of the
show—some of them from the main plot involving the alien conspiracy, some of them with independent story lines; some of them among
the best of the episodes artistically, some of them, quite frankly, weak
as dramas; some of them completely fantastic in their plots, some of
them comparatively down-to-earth. By discussing a number of
episodes, I hope to give a sense of the show's scope and depth, and especially its range.[19] For all its indulgence in special effects and its
comic-book love of blood and gore imagery, *The X-Files* is an unusually
thoughtful and thought-provoking television program. The more I
have studied it, the more I have been impressed by the consistency of
its engagement with and exploration of a set of serious and central concerns. For that, its creator and presiding genius, Chris Carter, must be
credited. From all accounts of the show's production, he is responsible
for maintaining its high level of quality and its consistency of viewpoint. Given the nature of television shows, it is hard to regard them as
the product of a single artistic consciousness. They generally are corporate products and often suffer as a result in terms of artistic purpo-
siveness and unity. Thanks to Carter's hands-on control of the series—
the fact that he writes and directs many of the episodes and supervises
the creation of all of them—*The X-Files* is an exception to this rule.[20]

◆

The X-Files rests on a fundamental pun on the word *alien*, which can refer to extraterrestrial beings or immigrants, especially as used in the
phrase "illegal aliens."[21] The central plotline of the series presents extraterrestrial beings as the ultimate illegal aliens, with a mysterious
plan to take over the earth. As FBI agents, Mulder and Scully seek to
police these illegal aliens and check their violation of U.S. borders, but
their efforts at containment are thwarted by the fact that the aliens are

working with American officials, some of them perhaps within the FBI itself. By the same token, several of the independent episodes of the series deal with the experience of immigrants to the United States, which is presented as strangely parallel to that of the extraterrestrials. The immigrant is often presented in *The X-Files* as a monster, or at least as somehow monstrous in the eyes of ordinary U.S. citizens. Like an extraterrestrial being, an immigrant is perceived to be alien to the American way of life and hence a threat to its preservation. In that sense, *The X-Files* presents the alien of science fiction as only a special case of a more general alienation, a point made at the beginning of the comic episode "Jose Chung's *From Outer Space*," when the titular character announces: "I always felt like such an alien myself that to be concerned with aliens from other planets—that just seemed so redundant."

Several individual *X-Files* episodes deal with aliens in the sense of immigrants: Chinese, Africans, Haitians, Mexicans, Eastern Europeans, Jews, and so on. The show is particularly fascinated by the hybrid character of the immigrants—we refer to them as Chinese Americans or African Americans, for example, and not simply as Americans. The general thrust of the show is that immigrants do not fully assimilate into the culture of the United States. They always remain somehow alien, still bound by the culture of their homeland. The main plot of *The X-Files* reveals a similar concern with hybridity, since for several seasons it centered around a scheme to create an alien-human hybrid. The focus on hybridization in *The X-Files* is one way in which the show rejects conventional nationalist ideologies. Nationalism rests on simplistic polarizations between *us* and *them* and above all develops a notion of distinct national identity, often based on ideas of cultural homogeneity, monolingualism, and even racial purity. With its constant images of hybridity, *The X-Files* works to deconstruct the simple binary oppositions on which nationalism depends. At first in the series, the aliens seemed to provide a perfectly clear and homogeneous image of the Other—prototypical creatures from another planet, indistinguishable from each other but strikingly distinct in appearance from human beings. But as the central plotline developed, we learned of a rebel faction of aliens who clouded this picture, especially since their chief representative, a character known as the Bounty Hunter, is a shape-shifter, who can easily assume the form of any human being he chooses. This pattern is typical of *The X-Files*—what began as a simple opposition gradually lost its sharp outlines and developed into a very muddy picture indeed, in which it became increasingly hard to tell one side from the other.[22] The general dissolution of boundaries in *The X-Files*—even between extraterrestrials and human beings—reflects a dissatisfaction with the clear-cut categorizations on which nationalism and the ideology of the nation-state rest.

The emphasis on hybridity in *The X-Files* works to debunk the narrative myth about immigrant experience that in many ways stands at the center of American culture. The United States is supposed to be the great melting pot; it takes "the wretched refuse of your teeming shores"—"your tired, your poor, your huddled masses yearning to breathe free," according to the Statue of Liberty—and it turns them all into Americans. If an alien obeys the law and follows the established procedures, he will become a full-fledged American; if he does not— if he is an "illegal alien"—he cannot become an American. This myth has been embodied over the years in countless FBI dramas about policing U.S. borders. Together with federal immigration officials, the FBI heroes break up attempts to smuggle aliens into the United States. Often a central character in these dramas is a naturalized U.S. citizen with the same ethnic background as the illegal aliens. This character experiences divided loyalties, torn between the old country and his new home in the United States. But he usually resolves his dilemma in favor of his adopted American identity, betraying his comrades from his homeland and helping the FBI heroes to apprehend them. The popularity of this kind of drama over the years reflected a faith in America as a nation-state. The immigrant must learn to leave the old country behind him once and for all and become fully American, and if he sides with the FBI and the national government for which it stands, he will be completely accepted into the American mainstream, perhaps even as an American hero himself.

One *X-Files* episode that deconstructs this immigrant myth is set in San Francisco's Chinatown and is called "Hell Money." Mulder and Scully are investigating a strange series of deaths involving Chinese Americans. They were "all recent immigrants," Mulder points out, and a local police official adds more specifically: "We've got a big influx of immigrants from Hong Kong, trying to get out before 1997." For roughly the first half of the episode, we as viewers are privy to information denied to Mulder and Scully. We witness members of the Chinatown community engaged in a mysterious ritual or game involving urns and markers with Chinese characters on them, but because much of the dialogue is in Chinese (Cantonese to be more precise) and only some of it is subtitled, we at first have little idea of what is going on. In general, *The X-Files* is unusual among television shows in the way it incorporates dialogue in foreign languages into its scripts, often going to great lengths to make sure that it is correct and authentic.[23] Most producers would balk at the idea of using subtitles in a television program, fearing that they would automatically lose their audience. But the *X-Files* producers have generally been willing to violate the normal rules of television and have occasionally even left large chunks of foreign dialogue untranslated.[24] This in part results from their desire to maintain the show's intellectual veneer, but it also reflects a respect for foreign cultures rare in American television. Since globalization is such an important theme in the show, the producers have evidently made a conscious decision to incorporate something of the new polyglot texture of contemporary life into the series. In the "Anasazi" episode, Italian, Japanese, and German are all spoken in the opening sequence, not to mention Navajo (which, as we will see, comes to feature prominently in the plot of the three-part arc of which this episode is the beginning).

The unusual proportion of dialogue in Chinese helps create the aura of mystery in "Hell Money" and also contributes to an alienating effect in Bertolt Brecht's sense. The Chinatown citizens seem all the more alien to us when we cannot even understand their speech, and their speaking Chinese is a powerful indication that they have not assimilated into what is supposed to be their new American homeland. One thing I particularly like about this episode is the way it forces the viewer to figure out what is going on and does not bother with elaborate *post hoc* explanations once the mystery clarifies. It turns out that the Chinese Americans are engaged in a macabre form of gambling. They have staked money in a lottery and draw from one urn for the right to draw from another, which in turn determines if they win a fortune or must sacrifice a bodily organ to be sold on the medical market. It is bad enough when a gambler draws the Chinese character for "eye," but if one draws the character for "heart," it is clearly a death sentence. That explains the mutilated corpses of Chinese Americans that have been turning up in the Bay Area. In a sick joke, Scully says of one of the victims: "He really left his heart in San Francisco."

The episode focuses on the plight of one Chinese American named Hsin, who has entered the game in the desperate hope of winning the money necessary to pay for a blood marrow transplant his daughter needs to save her life. In Hsin, we see the dark side of the immigrant experience. He has clearly come to America to better his life and his daughter's, but things have not worked out as he planned. His great fear is that he may lose his life in the game and his daughter will be condemned to die "alone with strangers"—the ultimate fate of the alien (and one suffered by numerous extraterrestrials in the course of the series). Hsin is particularly concerned that in coming to the United States he may have betrayed his traditional way of life in China: "Do our ancestors scorn us for leaving our home?" He speculates that his daughter's illness may be a punishment for his abandoning his homeland to come to America.

The other central character in the episode is a young Chinese American police officer named Glen Chao. He is the borderline figure who normally appears in this kind of immigrant drama, with one foot in the traditional Chinese community and one foot in the fully modernized and Americanized world of the San Francisco police department. In some ways, Chao defends the integrity of the Chinatown community, but he seems to side with the economic rationality that is the hallmark of Western culture, especially in its American form. When Mulder asks him about the Chinese ghost stories that seem at first to lie behind the mysterious murders, Chao replies: "I find it hard to argue with two thousand years of Chinese belief, but the truth is I'm more haunted by the size of my mortgage payments." Scully, however, questions Chao's commitment to the side of the West: "You feel some kind of protectiveness toward the Chinese community." At this point Chao challenges the way Scully and Mulder seem to be operating with belittling Western stereotypes of the East and suggests that the oriental world may be more opaque than they think: "This isn't some pretty little lacquer box you can just take the lid off and find out what's inside."

"Hell Money" carries its image of the inscrutable East a bit too far and the episode could be accused of orientalism itself, of exploiting Western stereotypes of Chinese behavior. In particular the Chinese are pictured as insanely obsessed with gambling. But to be fair to the producers, they seem to be trying to maintain a sense of the cultural distinctiveness of the Chinese community in "Hell Money," and what from one angle looks like ethnic stereotyping from another looks like respect for Chinese custom and its ability to maintain its integrity even in the face of powerful forces trying to dissolve it. The episode shows Chinatown to be a close-lipped, tight-knit community, with all the pluses and minuses that entails. On the negative side, the show keeps hinting that the community is corrupt, with allusions to Chinese gang warfare and suggestions that organized crime may be behind the murders. And it turns out that Chinatown *is* corrupt. The game is rigged so that the hapless participants will never win the jackpot. Moreover, Chao is revealed to be working for the gambling syndicate, who expect him to defend their interests: "We've paid you well to protect the game from foreigners"—an interesting comment, in which the American police are recast as the aliens vis-à-vis the Chinese immigrant community.

Thus "Hell Money" might be said to confirm the worst American prejudices about the Chinese and immigrants in general—they refuse to adapt to the United States; they wall themselves off from the larger American community; they remain mired in their old-fashioned ways; and they are superstitious, relying on luck to better their condition rather than hard work. But at the same time, "Hell Money" displays a deep sympathy for the plight of the Chinese Americans and gives them dignity in their quiet suffering. The father is shown genuinely caring for his daughter and even willing to risk his life for her. In general the very fact that the Chinatown community is shut off from outsiders gives it an authentic cohesion; it may seem bizarre to nonmembers, but it is revealed to have its own logic and to function in its own way. Moreover, the community is ultimately able to police itself. For all his complicity in the crooked game, Chao in the end turns on his masters, exposes their corruption, and brings their evil scheme to a close. In this kind of immigrant drama, it is almost always the FBI agents who are active in seeing that justice gets done for the immigrants (who are presented as passive and unable to help themselves). Typically, *The X-Files* suggests just the opposite—in an American society that is largely indifferent to the suffering of immigrants, Chinatown must take care of itself and only a Chinese American—who speaks Chinese—can protect Chinese Americans. Indeed at the end, the American authorities find that they cannot prosecute the gambling syndicate, even though they have caught the criminals red-handed. The Chinese community closes its ranks against outsiders and no one is willing to testify against the wrongdoers; as Mulder says: "They put up a wall of silence." All the American authorities are able to deliver is the bone-marrow transplant for Hsin's daughter.

In trying to assess where the sympathies of this *X-Files* episode ultimately lie, one can view the horrific organ lottery as negative stereotyping of Chinese Americans as gamblers, but perhaps the episode presents it as a reflection on America, not China. Perhaps the episode is offering a powerful image of the immigrant experience as one gigantic gamble, a kind of lottery with potentially big rewards but even greater risks. America promises a new life to its immigrants, but the episode seems to be asking: Does it really offer them a better deal than this organ lottery? The show seems to be hinting that the odds really are not much better for the vast influx of immigrants; for every one who succeeds, hundreds suffer in silence or, even worse, perish. The episode culminates emotionally in an unnerving dialogue between Scully and the Chinese American doctor who has been operating on the lottery losers. He is presented strangely sympathetically, as a spokesman for the traditional character of Chinese culture: "My people live with ghosts, the ghosts of our fathers, and our fathers' fathers. They call to us from distant memory, showing us the path." When Scully accuses him of exploiting the Chinese immigrants, of "preying upon their hopelessness and their desperation," the doctor reveals that he was once an immigrant himself: "Yes, they were desperate, just as I was desperate when I first came to this country." The fact that the doctor is himself representative of the immigrant experience casts Scully's further charges against him in a new light: "You cheated them out of life, by promising them prosperity when the only possible reward was death." In the inverted logic of *The X-Files*, one is forced to ask: Is this a statement about the doctor's treatment of the immigrants or America's? America too lures immigrants "by promising them prosperity," but as this and several other *X-Files* episodes suggest, it does not always deliver on that promise and instead often hands its immigrants over to misery and sometimes even horrible deaths.

"Hell Money" takes us right to the thematic heart of *The X-Files*: the contrast between a traditional and a modern community.[25] The episode is shadowed by ancient Chinese legends; when Mulder is originally searching for an explanation for the murders, he turns to Chao's talk of the "Chinese Festival of the Hungry Ghosts." "Ghosts or ancestral spirits have been central to Chinese spiritual life for centuries," Mulder says, displaying his usual interest in occult phenomena and his respect for non-Western beliefs and ways of life. The glimpses the episode provides of traditional Chinese culture center around its ancestor worship. We see a tradition-bound way of life, rooted in and guided by the past, in which children listen to and obey their parents. When asked why one of the Chinese murder victims was incinerated, Mulder replies: "It would sure teach him to respect his elders."

"Hell Money" juxtaposes the traditional Chinese way of life with the new regime offered immigrants in the United States, powerfully symbolized by the grotesque lottery. The Chinese Americans are now willing to sacrifice everything on the altar of money, even the family ties basic to their native culture. They are selling their body parts for money; the market for organs provides another powerful symbol of how America has transformed the traditional Chinese way of life.

Everything is up for sale in America; all communal beliefs and ancestral traditions are stripped away, leaving a pure, soulless economic rationality in which even vital organs can be harvested for profit.[26] The heart is literally and figuratively torn out of the Chinese community in America and put on the auction block.

This is how *The X-Files* in general presents the process of modernization—the transformation of a traditional community rooted in religious beliefs into a purely rational society based solely on economic motives. In *The X-Files* prophets are continually displaced by profits. The lottery in "Hell Money" is in fact one of the most striking emblems *The X-Files* offers of modernity—a world in which the only thing men have in common is their greed. The episode's title points to its central idea that money and the pure economic rationality it represents create a new hell for modern man. The name refers to a kind of false money used in a Chinese ritual for appeasing the ghosts of the dead, but the larger suggestion is that all money is fake, a false goal relentlessly pursued by modern man, who thereby plunges himself into a hell of his own making.

The X-Files thus presents immigrant experience as a special case of the general process of modernization, the replacement of traditional community by economic and technological rationality. The tension between spirituality and rationality is of course the guiding idea of the whole series. It generated the very conception of Mulder and Scully as a complementary pair. Mulder is the spiritual member of the team, guided by his intuition and always searching for supernatural or paranormal explanations of events, while Scully—the trained doctor—is the rational one, skeptical about nonscientific accounts of phenomena and always reaching for a purely natural cause for even the strangest occurrences.[27] Over the years the series has played with this polarity and deconstructed it, like any other binary opposition it offers its viewers. In some episodes Mulder and Scully switch roles, with him becoming skeptical and her falling back upon what turn out to be deeply ingrained religious beliefs (she is Catholic).[28] But even in these variations on the *X-Files* theme, the basic principle remains the same, as the show juxtaposes faith and reason. What the immigrant episodes highlight is that *The X-Files* views this contrast not only in personal and psychological terms, but also in geographic and historical ones. The show develops the contrast in terms of the opposition between Third World countries and the United States, and thus also in terms of the opposition between older forms of community, usually based on religion or myth, and the modern community, based on rationality and hence on bureaucratic organization. The central action of *The X-Files* is the globalization of modernity, the relentless advance of bureaucratic rationality into every corner of the earth, seeking to eradicate all pockets of tradition, myth, religious belief, and in general resistance to the technological worldview.[29]

The mysterious worldwide conspiracy at the center of *The X-Files*—the strange and uneasy alliance between a technologically advanced alien civilization and a shadowy group of world leaders in industry and government—is the show's uncanny symbol for the globalization of modernity. In the vision of *The X-Files*, modernity is a world of laboratories, hospitals, clinics, morgues, offices, factories[30]—a sterile world of science and technology—dedicated to turning out a new breed of human beings, fully adapted to the new world economic order, who would thus appear "inhuman" to members of traditional communities. One of the central symbols of *The X-Files* is cloning, manufacturing identical human beings.[31] In general, the series suggests that the shadowy forces attempting to run the modern world are trying to homogenize humanity, to make all human beings alike because that will make them more easily controlled and more capable of taking their places in the modern automated factory and office. The global conspiracy in *The X-Files*, sometimes referred to as the Syndicate, is using all the sophisticated technology at its disposal to turn human beings into machines, into cogs in machines. That is why immigrants must be stripped of their cultural heritage; immigration is presented as a form of internal globalization in *The X-Files*, the destruction of everything that makes people culturally distinct, as they are assimilated into a mainstream society centered on economic rationality.[32]

Thus *The X-Files* shows conventional notions of nationalism threatened and indeed undermined by the relentless march of global modernity. In *The X-Files* the nation-state is caught in a gigantic pincer movement. On the one hand, modern rationality is trying to globalize itself and in the process works to obliterate all communal distinctions, including national differences. On the other hand, the pockets of resistance to modernity in the series all take prenational or subnational forms. The most likely candidate to stand up to the evil forces in *The X-Files* is an Indian shaman or a voodoo priest. Conventional national authorities, such as an FBI deputy director, generally prove powerless in dealing with the international conspiracy because they are somehow implicated in the globalizing process themselves. In *The X-Files* the nation seems incapable of resisting internationalism, since it already incorporates too much of the principle of rationality to halt its further spread across national boundaries. After all, the nation itself came into existence by obliterating local boundaries, customs, and traditions, partially in the name of economic rationality. Having triumphed over local communities, the nation-state becomes merely local itself when confronted with the drive toward world community.

The X-Files thus rejects the nation-state as a solution to the human problem, as symbolized by its basic conception that the FBI is incapable of dealing with the new threats in the world. Mulder succeeds only to the extent that he abandons his role as an officer of the federal government—a mere cog in a bureaucratic machine that is itself part of the problem. Only to the extent that Mulder can overcome his modernity and recover the role of shaman himself—become a sort of postmodern shaman—can he hope to triumph over his adversaries.[33] *The X-Files* frequently celebrates the pockets of resistance left to the globalization of modernity, whether they come from Third World countries or social and cultural backwaters within the United States. Mulder is constantly linking up with these forces of resistance, for example with Native Americans in the Anasazi trilogy.[34] One reason the show is sympathetic to immigrants is that they have not yet been globalized; they represent what still remains of cultural difference in a world that is threatening to become numbingly homogenized.

◆

"Teliko" is another one of the most important *X-Files* episodes dealing with immigrant experience and develops many of the same themes as "Hell Money." The episode begins in an airplane carrying passengers from West Africa to the United States. As if to stress the fact that they are foreigners, some of them are in native dress and both the signs on the plane and the instructions given to the passengers are in French (without subtitles). The plane, coming from the Francophone nation Burkina Faso, bears a strange genetic mutation—a man named Samuel Aboah, who murders a fellow passenger on board and then goes on to kill a series of African Americans in the Philadelphia area. The strange characteristic of the murders, which attracts Mulder and Scully to the case, is the albinism of the corpses; whatever kills these black men blanches them white. The central symbol of this episode thus points again to the problematic character of attempting to bring immigrants into the American mainstream. Turning blacks white would seem to be the ultimate triumph of the American claim to be able to assimilate and integrate aliens into its culture, but unfortunately the process kills the people involved. If there were any doubt that the episode is concerned with the cultural assimilation of African Americans in the United States, Mulder makes a snide comment when he hears about the albino corpses: "There's a Michael Jackson joke in this somewhere, but I just can't find it." As a black man who has supposedly used plastic surgery and other means to make himself look as white as possible, Michael Jackson is an apt symbol of the central concern of "Teliko"— are African Americans another example of immigrants who must be stripped of their distinct culture to become accepted into the American mainstream?[35]

The episode offers a rather contrived medical explanation for Aboah's murders. He comes, as Mulder eventually explains, from "a clan of sub-Saharan albinos linked by this common congenital deficit"—lacking a pituitary gland, he must extract the organ from his victims to get the hormones he needs to live, and the process has the side effect of turning their corpses white. But in typical *X-Files* fashion, the episode offers a parallel supernatural explanation for the events. Questioning a diplomat at the Burkina Faso Embassy in Washington, Mulder learns of a native African legend that accounts in its own way for Aboah's freakish behavior—he is some kind of spirit-demon. Minister Alpha Diabira tells Mulder: "My people, the Bambara, are farmers. I grew up learning the old stories—believing them as only a child can believe." We see here how ambivalent the *X-Files* is about non-Western sources of knowledge. The Africans are superstitious, and there is even a suggestion that their beliefs are childish. But Mulder does not scorn the legends Diabira tells him—through Mulder we get the strong impression that African legends do a better job of accounting for Aboah's behavior than American medicine does. In response to an effort to belittle folktale explanations, Mulder undercuts any attempt to distinguish Western science from non-Western myth: "All new truths begin as heresies and end as superstitions." According to Diabira, Aboah is an example of "the Teliko, the spirits of the air," strange nocturnal creatures who prey upon human beings. And with his knowledge of the "old stories," Diabira has understood what is happening long before the FBI agents could, even with all the modern diagnostic resources of the federal government at their disposal.

One characteristic of the Teliko is especially appropriate to the role of immigrant-alien: They are able to squeeze into extremely tight places and thereby hide themselves.[36] Aboah uses this ability to catch his victims by surprise (in an airplane lavatory, for example) and also to try to evade the police and eventually to escape after he has first been captured. In symbolic terms, the episode is suggesting that to be an immigrant in America can be a very tight squeeze. Far from being a land of freedom for its aliens, America forces them into various forms of restraint. The fact that the Teliko succeed only to the extent that they know how to make themselves *small* corresponds to immigrant experience in several ways. The alien in America is generally better off if he makes himself invisible, or at least draws a minimum of attention to himself as a foreigner. Moreover, America tends to pigeonhole its aliens, forcing them into the narrow confines of ethnic categories. Finally, the alien often has to accept inferior and specifically cramped living conditions and in general has to make do with the limited opportunities America offers him. The shadowy and marginal existence Aboah leads is one more example of how negatively *The X-Files* portrays the immigrant experience in America.

The episode also works to associate the immigrants directly with the word *alien*, thus offering a clue as to how "Teliko" fits into *The X-Files* as a whole. When Mulder questions an immigration official about the strange events in Philadelphia, he pointedly says: "You're in charge of most of the case work for aliens immigrating from Africa and the Caribbean." At one point the camera dwells on Aboah's immigration documents, clearly revealing that he is designated a "resident alien." The immigration official, Marcus Duff, takes Aboah's side and tries to shield him from the FBI. When Aboah's efforts to evade arrest are taken as evidence of his guilt in the murders, Duff asks the authorities to sympathize with how the harassed immigrant views the world, and in particular to picture the kind of life he probably fled: "If you had ever been beaten by the police or had your home burned to the ground for no other reason than that you were born, then you would understand." Later, when Scully asks why a mutant like Aboah would choose to come to America, Mulder has a simple answer: "Free cable. I don't know—the same reasons that anybody comes to this country: liberty, the freedom to pursue your own interests." Aboah may be a monster, but Mulder makes him sound just like any other American immigrant. When Duff initially speaks to Aboah, he empathizes with his alienation, evidently because he identifies with it: "I know how lonely it is, believe me, being in a strange place, far from your family." But Duff reassures Aboah that as soon as he overcomes his alien status, he can become fully part of America: "But once you become a U.S. citizen, I can help you bring over every brother, sister, aunt, uncle, and cousin." Under the circumstances, these well-meaning words have an ominous ring for the audience and play upon a common anxiety concerning immigrants—that these monstrous aliens will overwhelm America with their numbers, especially because of the premium on extended families in their native cultures.

Indeed, "Teliko" succeeds in doing what *The X-Files* generally excels at—grounding the fear of the supernatural in everyday anxieties.[37] Few of us fear African spirit-demons, but many of us do fear immigrants, and "Teliko" links the mythic fear to the real. At first the authorities think that Aboah is carrying a disease that causes death and albinism, thus reflecting one of the primary anxieties concerning immigrants, that they bring with them alien bacteria and viruses that can infect and perhaps devastate America. In particular "Teliko" subtly raises the specter of AIDS; when Scully is discussing the case with a representative of the Centers for Disease Control, she suggests that some kind of "autoimmune" disorder may be involved. That statement, coupled with the references to Africa throughout the episode, points to the most feared disease of the 1990s, one closely associated by the American public with immigrants, and specifically black immigrants. "Teliko" goes on to link American anxieties about immigrants with similar fears about the urban underclass. One of Aboah's victims is a typical representative of that group—a young black who works in a fast-food restaurant. Already succumbing to Aboah's power, he is unable to board a bus, prompting the driver to ask hostilely: "What's your problem: you on drugs or something?" Drugs and disease—the episode concentrates on two problems the American mainstream associates with both immigrants and the urban underclass. In fact when Mulder first learns about the murders, he views them as reflecting a larger social problem in the inner city (and in words that might equally apply to the AIDS epidemic): "Young black men are dying, and nobody seems to be able to bring in a suspect. The perception being that nobody cares."

The episode thus suggests that Aboah, as an immigrant from Africa, has much in common with the African Americans he preys upon. In perhaps the most ironic moment in the episode, a black policeman investigating the crimes looks at the African's mailbox and says: "Aboah? What the hell kind of name is that?" The African American policeman has lost touch with his African heritage and fails to perceive what he has in common with the man he is hunting down. "Teliko" suggests that the immigrant and the inner-city black are mirror images of each other, both victims of the prejudices of mainstream America. But the American system succeeds in preventing the two groups from making common cause; indeed "Teliko" suggests that it gets them to work at cross-purposes, fighting each other rather than the regime that oppresses both. Neither the immigrant nor the inner-city black is treated as fully a part of the American nation-state, which seems to have all the power and to deploy it against anyone alienated from the system.

But at the same time "Teliko" suggests that the nation-state is in trouble. When Mulder finds out that one of the few clues in the case is a seed from a rare West African plant, he turns for elucidation, not to the FBI or any other national organization, but to the United Nations. He contacts the mysterious Marita Covarrubias, an assistant in the secretary general's office, who had recently been introduced as a series character in the episode called "Herrenvolk," where she was presented as knowledgeable in agricultural matters. The turn to the UN in the fourth season of *The X-Files* marked a further globalization of the show's outlook and an extension of the worldwide conspiracy it portrays into the ranks of the premier international organization on earth.[38] What Covarrubias tells Mulder is extremely ominous for the future of the nation-state: "Thousands of exotic species cross into U.S. soil every day undetected." The realities of international travel and trade have made it impossible to maintain the integrity of any nation-state, or, as Covarrubias puts it, "in practical terms, borders are little more than lines on maps."[39]

The episode emphasizes the way in which the new cosmopolitan world intersects with the world of the American inner city. As one segment of the show begins, the camera pans from a billboard with a picture of a happy white couple posed in Egypt with the Sphinx to the urban black who will be Aboah's next victim. The pointed contrast between the wealthy jetsetters and the poor inner-city dweller is obvious, and the scene reminds us that Africa and America may be linked in negative as well as positive ways. We soon see that the couple is part of a travel advertisement, whose slogan ironically is: "It *is* a small world after all." These Disney words could serve as the bitter motto for the whole episode and indeed for *The X-Files* in general. The technological developments such as jet aircraft that have facilitated international travel and thus shrunk the world bring new threats in their wake.

In this new globalized world, *The X-Files* suggests that we must learn to come to terms with the alien rather than rejecting it as monstrous. Scully's final summation of the case of Samuel Aboah somewhat tendentiously tries to teach this lesson: "Science will eventually discover his place in the broader context of evolution. But what science may never be able to explain is our ineffable fear of the alien among us." Scully's statement is one of the most explicit attempts in the series to connect the special theme of the alien as immigrant with the larger theme of the alien as extraterrestrial. As often happens in *The X-Files*, the episode calls for us to sympathize with what we regard as monstrous, and yet at the same time insists on portraying the alien as monstrous in the first place. Despite Scully's cosmopolitan rhetoric, "Teliko" ends up giving a very dark portrait of the globalizing world.

◆

An equally dark picture emerges in a related episode called "Fresh Bones," which deals with Haitian refugees in an internment camp in North Carolina, who are hoping to get political asylum in the United States. The episode gave the show the chance to work up a voodoo plot, but again the supernatural fears are rooted in real-world anxieties. At the time the show first aired (on February 3, 1995), Haitian refugees were still very much in the news, and many Americans were upset about their shores being invaded by these foreigners.[40] The episode pits a kind of Haitian freedom fighter, named Pierre Bauvais, against an authoritarian camp commander, named Colonel Wharton. Wharton is bitter about the deaths of some of his soldiers while he was stationed with the American occupying forces in Haiti, and he is retaliating against the refugees now under his jurisdiction by mistreating them, including ordering them beaten. When Scully accuses him of "physical abuse of political refugees," Wharton defends his actions: "Nobody ever said this was a hotel, but it's hardly a concentration camp." But in fact the show has the audacity to present an American INS Processing Center as virtually indistinguishable from a concentration camp, complete with armed guards and prison-like conditions. When Mulder questions his shadowy informant, Mr. X, about the camp, he replies: "The Statue of Liberty is on vacation. The new mandate says if you're not a citizen, you'd better keep out." "Fresh Bones" strongly suggests that America has betrayed its ideal of open borders and gives the most negative treatment in any *X-Files* episode of U.S. immigration policy.[41]

In response to the colonel's brutality, Bauvais draws upon his voodoo powers to retaliate against the soldiers and eventually Wharton himself, who, as a result of a voodoo spell, is being buried alive as the episode ends. "Fresh Bones" is filled with all the standard paraphernalia of voodoo stories: clouding of men's minds, zombies, ritual symbols, and so on. The voodoo gives the episode the supernatural aura of an *X-Files* episode, but it also fits the thematic pattern of the series. American society represents the rational pole in the episode, but its rationalism is here presented as authoritarianism, assuming the ultimate nightmare form of the bureaucratic state: the concentration camp. Poised against the power of modernity is the atavistic power of voodoo, the spiritual pole in this episode, with Bauvais as the shaman, drawing upon the folk wisdom of his people to fight back against their oppressors. Bauvais' power is given a political dimension—"He thinks he's some kind of revolutionary" is one acrid comment made about him, and when he is finally allowed to speak for himself, he claims to be a champion of liberty: "My country was born on the blood of slaves—freedom is our most sacred legacy." By drawing upon the history of slavery in Haiti, the episode manages to make Bauvais sound more American in his values than Wharton. Indeed, the basic irony of "Fresh Bones" is that it is the illegal alien Bauvais who speaks on behalf of liberty and the American commander who in effect speaks on behalf of slavery and oppression.

This inversion of American values is worked out in the plot of the episode as a whole. Normally in this kind of story, voodoo is presented as the truly sinister force, often as the embodiment of pure evil. The fact that zombies are usually black suggests that voodoo often serves in popular culture as a symbol of the evil of slavery, and in general functions as a typical Gothic image of the old regime. Involving as it does priests, superstition, rituals, and slaves in the form of zombies, voodoo stands for everything from which modern democracy and hence America are supposed to liberate us. Accordingly, in a typical voodoo story, an American happens upon some form of zombie regime, usually on some Caribbean island and often involving an evil plantation owner, who stands for the antebellum South and its cruel slave owners. When the hero manages to overthrow the voodoo power, it is thus presented as a triumph of American democracy, which is viewed as the great counterforce for liberty in the world.

In "Fresh Bones," voodoo does at first appear to be a source of monstrous evil in the world, and in particular responsible for the deaths disrupting the community. But as Mulder and Scully investigate the case, they discover that the really evil figure is not the voodoo priest but the American colonel. Voodoo typically represents an evil that is foreign to America and that reflects the lingering power of the past, an atavistic force bound up with old-style superstition and the antiquated institution of slavery. But "Fresh Bones" suggests that the real evil is American and very much a product of the present—indeed a result of contemporary American immigration policy. And about this evil Mulder and Scully can do very little, if anything. Just to deal with Bauvais, they need the help of a young black boy named Chester Bonaparte, who we learn at the end actually died six weeks earlier in a riot at the camp and thus must have been some form of spirit when he aided the FBI agents. Hence the episode works to deconstruct the simple opposition between voodoo superstition and American rationalism (a point reinforced when Wharton himself resorts to voodoo). Even the powerful FBI would apparently be powerless to deal with voodoo if it did not have some sort of spiritual force on its side.

Just as we saw in "Hell Money," ultimately the immigrant community in "Fresh Bones" has to defend itself. Normally in this kind of voodoo story, an American must intervene in a foreign community to save it from itself, often with the specific twist that a white American is necessary to liberate black natives from being tyrannized by other blacks. But in *The X-Files*, to the extent that the Haitians get any justice at all, they must act on their own. Mulder and Scully uncover the wrongs being committed at the refugee camp, but the episode shows that they will not be able to do anything about them. When Mulder confronts his shadowy contact toward the end of the episode, Mr. X flatly tells him: "These people have no rights" and Mulder realizes that a government cover-up is in the works: "They're making the camp invisible." In "Teliko" Mulder and Scully manage to deal with the monstrous evil in the sense that they expose and neutralize the power of Samuel Aboah. But there is no indication that they have dealt with the underlying problems and the larger evil they have uncovered in the American inner city. This pattern is typical of *The X-Files*. The point of the traditional FBI drama is that the forces of the federal government can genuinely bring justice to the world. The FBI identifies the sources of evil in the world, which are typically un-American and even anti-American, arrests them, and sees that they are successfully prosecuted, thereby ridding the nation of its threats and problems. No *X-Files* episode ever has any such neat closure or sense that federal government forces can right the wrongs of the world. As happens in "Fresh Bones," often in *The X-Files* when the FBI agents seek the source of evil, they find it in another branch of the federal government itself and thus end up powerless to do anything about it. Lack of narrative closure is one of the most distinctive aspects of *The X-Files* as a series, but it is not simply a plot device to maintain audience interest from episode to episode.[42] The narrative closure of the traditional FBI drama reflected a faith in the federal government's power to set the world right, to bring not just the story but evil itself to an end. Given the skepticism in *The X-Files* about the power and the very legitimacy of the nation-state, the stories cannot tie up all the loose threads at their conclusions because the series has no such faith in the corresponding ability of the FBI or any other government institution to master the world and see that justice ultimately prevails.

◆

In view of the interest in immigrant experience in *The X-Files*, it seemed inevitable that the show would eventually get around to treating Mexican Americans, and it finally did so in the fourth season in an episode called "El Mundo Gira." This story dealing with the plight of migrant workers in California is in my opinion one of the sillier *X-Files* episodes, largely because it awkwardly grafts a story of vengeful brothers onto its central monster plot and deliberately gives a Mexican soap opera feel to the whole production (in English, the title means "The World Turns," with an obvious allusion to the American soap opera *As the World Turns*).[43] Moreover, the monster itself, *El Chupacabra*, is one of the least successful in the history of the series. Though evidently based on authentic Mexican folklore, the story of a "goatsucker" is hard to take seriously, especially when according to the medical explanation offered in the episode it takes the form of what amounts to an extremely advanced case of athlete's foot. Still, "El Mundo Gira" is important because it goes further than any other *X-Files* episode in identifying the immigrant alien with the extraterrestrial alien. The story is presented as if told by a middle-aged Hispanic woman named Flakita to her female friends. She herself refers to it as a "fairy tale" but insists that she witnessed the events with her own eyes. The episode consistently associates the migrant workers with folktales and legends, and stresses the orality of their culture, chiefly through the fiction of Flakita telling the tale. The immigration official, Conrad Lozano, who is the FBI's chief source of information about Mexican Americans, keeps explaining the importance of the oral tradition for them: "These people love their stories. It's the one thing that keeps them from going mad when they're out there standing on the street corner waiting for work." Indeed, Lozano claims that the proliferation of stories among the migrant workers is an index of their misery: "Their lives are small. So they have to make up these fictions just to keep on going—to feel alive. Because they are strangers here.

They feel hated, unwanted. . . . And because they cannot turn to the law, they make up these fantastic tales."

Like several *X-Files* episodes, "El Mundo Gira" thus contrasts the oral culture of an immigrant community with the literate culture of mainstream America, which seeks scientific explanations for what the migrant workers explain mythically. On the mythic level, "El Mundo Gira" is the story of the strange Chupacabra creature, which destroys goats and people alike. In the scientific explanation the episode offers, the deaths result from a mysterious enzyme carried and spread by the migrant brothers. The enzyme reduces the body's ability to deal with funguses and thus makes affected people liable to massive, quick-spreading, and deadly infections. This time, the episode makes the connection between AIDS and immigrants explicit; when explaining the medical pathology to Mulder, Scully points out that fungal infection "can be lethal to AIDS patients." But typically the episode leaves it open whether the mythic or the scientific explanation best accounts for the destruction spreading through the community. And when Mulder suggests an extraterrestrial source for the deadly enzyme—he says it may have come from a meteorite—Lozano comments: "So you've got your own 'stories' too," thus equating modern science with archaic myth.

In the most interesting development in the episode from our point of view—unfortunately also the silliest—as the story nears its conclusion and one brother tries to murder the other for killing the woman they both loved, Flakita explains that she saw four extraterrestrial aliens show up from the sky and intervene to carry off one of the brothers. Identifying the aliens as themselves Chupacabras, Flakita makes the equation of the immigrant and the extraterrestrial as monstrous aliens complete. As happens in oral cultures, however, versions of what really took place at the end multiply, leaving us wondering if the extraterrestrial creatures were real or only figments of Flakita's imagination. Confronted back at FBI headquarters with the conflicting accounts, Assistant Director Skinner seems to speak for the audience when he says: "Frankly, I'm confused by this story." When Mulder replies: "I don't blame you" and Scully adds: "We can't really explain it ourselves," the producers seem to be throwing up their arms and admitting that they did not know exactly what to make of the story.

Despite the confusing ending, the episode clearly condemns the way American business exploits migrant workers for their cheap labor. Commenting on the difficulty of policing illegal aliens and developing a motif we have already seen in the show's presentation of immigrants, Lozano says: "These people are invisible—you look at them and you don't see them."[44] Echoing what he says about urban blacks in "Teliko," Mulder sums up the episode by saying of the mistreatment of migrant workers: "The truth is, nobody cares." Once again in "El Mundo Gira," *The X-Files* tries to create sympathy for anyone regarded as alien by mainstream America and the vocabulary emphasizes how the immigrant episodes of the series mirror the main plot about extraterrestrials. Lozano says of the American reaction to the migrant workers: "To most people, they're aliens in the true sense of the word." In perhaps the most pointed comment in the episode, Scully tells Mulder: "I think the aliens in this story are not the villains, they're the victims." This is the reversal of the conventional perspective that *The X-Files* is constantly striving to bring about. The illegal aliens in "El Mundo Gira" *are* the monsters, and at the end both brothers are shown mutated into horrific Chupacabras themselves. But the show insists that it is America's mistreatment of the migrant workers that has turned them into monsters.

Once again an *X-Files* investigation into alien horrors turns into an indictment of American national policy with regard to immigrants. In one version of the conclusion, the immigration official, who is Mexican American himself, ends up killed by the fungal infection, an apparently apt punishment for his participation in the oppression of his own people. And Mulder and Scully never succeed in apprehending the suspects, or at least they are unable to keep them in custody. When last seen the infected brothers seem to be wandering freely, as is only appropriate for migrant workers. Indeed, the episode once again stresses the porousness of borders in the modern world—the migrants seem to move back and forth between Mexico and the United States with ease. Lozano at first thinks Mulder is wasting his time when he tries to prevent one of the brothers from returning to Mexico. But then the immigration official adds: "File your paperwork. By the time they process it, he'll probably be back here anyway." As in many *X-Files* episodes, including those dealing with the extraterrestrials' plan to use a virus to disseminate their influence on Earth, the central symbol of "El Mundo Gira" is infection, and the migrant workers seem to pass across national borders as easily as the microbes that spread disease. Faced with the new migratory world of the globalized economy, the nation-state seems powerless. Mulder and Scully accomplish little or nothing in "El Mundo Gira" and once again prove incapable of dealing with the underlying problems they uncover in the way America treats its migrant workers.

◆

The four episodes we have discussed are the principal ones dealing with immigrants as aliens; they all highlight immigration as an issue and feature immigration officials or their equivalents in alternately sympathetic and sinister roles. (Significantly, all four officials who get involved with the immigrant community—Chao, Duff, Wharton, and Lozano—die horrible deaths.) Having dealt with Asian, African, Caribbean, and Mexican immigrants, to fill out our picture of immigration in *The X-Files* we can turn to episodes that deal with immigrants from Eastern Europe, "The Calusari," which takes up Romanians, and "Kaddish," which takes up Hasidic Jews. These two episodes do not specifically treat immigration as an issue, but they do deal with the problematic character of the immigrant experience. "The Calusari" is a blatant rip-off of *The Exorcist* (1973), complete with speaking in tongues, telekinesis, and the ever-popular projectile vomiting. It is a tribute to the quality and production values of *The X-Files* that the episode does not simply pale by comparison with what is after all one of the most powerful horror movies ever made. "The Calusari" is no *Exorcist*, but for a television show it does a remarkable job of capturing much of the force of the film and adds a few twists of its own to the plot. The episode begins with a chilling scene of a little child run over by a miniature train at an amusement park and goes on to tell the story of his older brother, Charlie Holvey. Charlie is the son of an American State Department official, who in 1984 married a Romanian woman named Maggie and now lives with her and her mother in Arlington, Virginia. Charlie is a troubled child, with a long record of illness, and his problems are in part attributed to the migratory character of a government official's life: "The family moved around a lot." At first we are led to believe that Charlie's difficulties may also be caused by his Romanian grandmother, especially when we learn that "superstition rules Golda's life." She openly speaks of him as a "devil child" and performs weird rituals over him, for which she enlists the aid of a bizarre group of men, dressed in Old World garb, called the Calusari.

All this seems extremely un-American—Charlie should be out playing Little League baseball—and Scully's reaction is to turn him over to a social worker, in the hope that she will be able to straighten him out with the latest techniques of child psychology. But in the central reversal of the episode, it turns out that Golda is right and Scully wrong—Charlie is in fact possessed by a demon, the spirit of his stillborn twin brother, Michael. The demon in Charlie lured his younger brother to his death and goes on to kill his father and his grandmother, and at the end of the episode comes close to killing Scully. Taking a cue from *The Exorcist*, "The Calusari" insists on the reality of evil and presents as shallow the tendency of Americans to psychologize it away. In the person of the social worker, the episode is questioning the capacity of the therapeutic state to make good its claim to solve the family's problems or the world's. Like a typical government official, the social worker believes that the most important thing is to get Charlie out of the hands of his family and above all to counteract the effect of any traditional form of upbringing, symbolized by his grandmother's role in his life.[45] Mulder, by contrast, has suspected all along that supernatural forces are at work and thus at a crucial point he calls back the Calusari to perform an exorcism on Charlie, which is the only thing that saves him and Scully as well. We learn of the Calusari: "in Romania they are responsible for the correct observances of sacred rites," and once again in *The X-Files*, a traditional religious approach succeeds where modern science fails. The episode begins with the New World blaming the Old for its troubles, but in the end it is the Old World that must save the New.

The episode reveals that having married an American, Maggie developed a contempt for her mother Golda and her Romanian superstitions. But as the disasters mount in her life, Maggie begins to wonder if she is being punished "for abandoning the old ways," much as Hsin did in "Hell Money." She goes on to say of her mother: "I was raised to believe as she did in spirits, the unseen world. When I married and came to this country, I left all that behind." But as we have seen repeatedly, *The X-Files* shows that immigrants to America cannot so easily escape their heritage. "The Calusari" presents another tragedy of displaced immigrants, whose efforts to adapt to America threaten to destroy them. Specifically, the episode suggests that there is something callow and naive about America in its refusal to accept the spiritual reality of evil. Europe knows better, because its experience goes back much further and is more profound. In explaining "the evil" to Mulder, the Calusari speak of biblical figures such as Cain and Lucifer, but they also mention Hitler, reminding us that Europe has experienced depths of evil foreign to America. The episode ends with the leader of the Calusari warning Mulder about the evil: "It is over for now. But you must be careful—it knows you." But the real question is whether Mulder knows the evil. The problem with America is its lack of historical memory. Obsessed with the future and the spread of economic rationality, it thinks it has left the irrational past behind it and especially its European heritage, a complex legacy that includes much that is problematic if not outright evil. The Romanian woman in "The Calusari" thought she had solved all her problems by marrying an American and moving to the United States. But in fact, the episode suggests, this kind of globalizing movement creates its own problems, given the unsettling and alienating effects of uprooting people from their homelands and committing them to the migratory existence epitomized by the life of a State Department official. And in the end, the FBI can do nothing to help the State Department. Once again, the immigrant community must fall back upon its own traditional resources to protect itself.

◆

This theme is also central to "Kaddish," a related episode that goes deeper into the historical and political subtext of "The Calusari." With its mention of Hitler and the use of a swastika in one of the rituals, the earlier episode had pointed in the direction of the evil of Nazism. "Kaddish" centers directly on the problem of anti-Semitism, dealing with a group of American neo-Nazis. The episode tells the story of Isaac Luria, a Hasidic Jew murdered by young thugs inspired by an anti-Semitic hate merchant, who, among other things, publishes a pamphlet entitled "How AIDS Was Created by the Jew" (once again, the show connects anti-immigrant sentiments with fears about AIDS). As we eventually learn, Luria's bride-to-be, Ariel, resurrected him in the horrific form of a golem, a traditional figure out of Jewish mysticism, animated by Kabbalistic spells in order to wreak vengeance on the enemies of the Jewish community.[46] Resurrected as a golem, Luria kills off his murderers one by one, including the anti-Semitic publisher, and is only stopped when Ariel finally realizes that she must undo her spell and break the cycle of revenge. But though the episode seems to suggest that private vengeance is wrong, in fact it shows that if the Jewish community does not protect itself, no one else will. Mulder even sees something righteous in the form the revenge takes; upon learning of the first murderer's death, his comment is: "Very Old Testament." When Mulder and Scully show up at Ariel's apartment, her father, Jacob Weiss, gets upset by their investigation into the murder of the anti-Semites: "But where were you when *Isaac* needed your protection? When we called them, the police, they said we were paranoid. That there was nothing to worry about. They always say that whenever someone threatens the Jew."

This is a good example of how *The X-Files* works to validate para-noia. As the old saying goes, "You're not paranoid if everybody's out to get you," and when Mulder asks Weiss if Luria had been specifi-cally threatened, he replies: "The threat is *always* there." "Kaddish" ex-poses the weakness of the modern nation-state—it is unable to deal successfully with the kinds of ethnic tensions created by the increas-ing globalization of society. The Jews may try to form a safe enclave in the Williamsburg section of Brooklyn, but they end up right across the street from people who hate them with a passion.[47] Drawing upon the long history of Jewish persecution is a powerful way for the show to lend credibility to what is normally understood as paranoia. Mulder defends Jacob Weiss by showing Scully the neo-Nazi pamphlet and saying: "it's hard to fault his attitude when you see something like that." Indeed, after what Hitler did in Europe, it is difficult to call any Jewish response to anti-Semitism "paranoid." Nazism has long served as the one symbol of absolute evil in American culture; no matter how relativistic people may be about other subjects, they can almost always be counted on to condemn Hitler and Nazism. Nazism has been fea-tured prominently in *The X-Files* over the years, providing the show with a striking example of everything that is wrong with nationalism. The producers have carefully worked references to Nazism into the main plot. In one of the most striking revelations in the course of the series, in the Anasazi trilogy we learn that Nazi scientists have been and still are deeply involved in the alien conspiracy. Drawing upon the historical fact that a number of German scientists, including Werner von Braun, did work in the American space program after World War II and elaborating on rumors of more insidious ways the United States used German refugees, the show proposes that after Germany's defeat, American authorities enlisted some of its top scien-tists to work on various ways of dealing with the planned alien inva-sion, especially the project of creating an alien-human hybrid. Since Nazi scientists such as Dr. Josef Mengele were notorious for their bio-logical experiments and especially their willingness to work on live human subjects, they supplied a model of the sort of sinister biotech-nology projects that fascinate the producers of *The X-Files*.

For *The X-Files* Nazi science represents the hypertrophy of moder-nity: the unbridled technological impulse, the willingness to treat hu-man beings as things, the sacrifice of all human values in the name of scientific knowledge. Thus connecting Nazi scientists with the global conspiracy to work with the aliens is a brilliant stroke on the part of *The X-Files*.[48] The Nazi connection helps to characterize the conspiracy as an example of modernity run amok. In particular the global scope and aspirations of the conspirators are emphasized by partnering them with members of a would-be master race, who themselves hoped to conquer the world by means of their superior technology. Perhaps more importantly, the Nazi connection works to deconstruct the familiar political binaries on which America's sense of its national identity and especially its world mission rests. Popular culture is filled with reassuringly patriotic images of American good guys versus Nazi bad guys (think of the first Indiana Jones movie, *Raiders of the Lost Ark* [1981]). And yet *The X-Files* blurs this fundamental distinction by suggesting that elements of the U.S. government enlisted the aid of Nazis for decades. The Americans thus compromised their claims to moral superiority over their former opponents, especially since they asked the Nazi scientists to continue and expand their experiments, and with the same ultimate aim—world domination through biotechnology.

The incorporation of Nazis into the alien conspiracy reflects the general strategy of *The X-Files* to make it impossible to tell the good guys from the bad guys on the international scene, and thus to undercut the claims of any particular nation-state to moral superiority. America's other main opponents in World War II, the Japanese, also turn out to be involved in the alien experiments.[49] And *The X-Files* works to deconstruct the other great international binary opposition of the twentieth century: the Cold War. In the "Tunguska"/"Terma" pair of episodes, the show takes us to Russia and we learn that Soviet science has been engaged in alien experiments, somehow connected to the mysterious 1908 explosion in Siberia of a meteor, asteroid, or other extraterrestrial object. It is unclear whether the Russians are working in opposition to or in conjunction with similar experiments on alien material in the West. The situation is complicated by the presence in these episodes of the treacherous Alex Krycek, a double, triple, or perhaps even quadruple agent. Our inability to sort out who Krycek is working for mirrors our larger uncertainties in *The X-Files*. We thought we knew that Germans and Americans were enemies in World War II and that Russians and Americans were enemies in the Cold War. We now learn that the two sides may have been working together in nefarious ways in some kind of conspiracy that transcends national boundaries and allegiances. In a traditional FBI drama dealing with international intrigue, we would expect to see individuals arrayed against each other as representatives of their conflicting nations. Instead, in *The X-Files* we see heroic individuals such as Mulder and Scully or rogue agents such as Krycek struggling on their own against a vast state apparatus that no longer seems tied to any particular country and may in fact be pursuing interests directly contrary to those of particular nations.

The theme of Nazism thus connects the main plot of *The X-Files* to individual episodes such as "Kaddish." If FBI agents do not know who they are really working for or what their government stands for anymore, how are poor immigrants supposed to tell the good guys from the bad guys and trust the so-called duly constituted authorities? Jacob Weiss is outraged by Mulder's intervention on behalf of Luria's murderer and wants to know which side he is on: "And now you've come here. Not to help us, but to ask for our help. So you can impose your justice on the only man who has taken justice into his own hands." Taking justice into one's own hands becomes a logical response to the world *The X-Files* portrays. Every immigrant episode shows that the state is unable to live up to its most basic responsibility of protecting the lives of its citizens or would-be citizens, and thus the immigrants are left to protect themselves as best they can. Given the fundamental culture clashes a globalizing society produces, there no longer even seems to be agreement as to who is a member of a given nation and who is not. Under these circumstances, the very concept of paranoia begins to lose its meaning. The definition of the paranoiac depends on being able to define a "normal person"; the paranoiac's mental illness emerges only against a background of what a "reasonable" person would believe. In that sense, a concept of paranoia must be rooted in a community of belief; thus, in a world of clashing cultural communities, one man's paranoia becomes another man's religious faith.

And that is exactly what *The X-Files* shows again and again, especially in the immigrant episodes. "Kaddish" gives a bizarre twist to this idea. The anti-Semitic publisher also characterizes himself as a man who has unjustly been called paranoid. Indeed, in presenting himself as a heroic battler against the International Jewish Conspiracy, he comes across as the mirror image of Mulder. When he says: "We're working to spread the truth. . . . I am exposing their lies," he sounds just like Mulder in many episodes. I do not know if the producers intended this parallel, and in some ways find it hard to believe that they did. Yet in a way the parallel between Mulder and the neo-Nazi as conspiracy theorists fits the overall pattern of *The X-Files*. The Jew, the FBI agent, the anti-Semite—each in his own way could be called "paranoid" in "Kaddish"—at least by the "other side." The effect of *The X-Files* is to make it difficult if not impossible to distinguish paranoia from some kind of genuine secret knowledge. All the immigrant episodes turn on access to a kind of esoteric wisdom; the key to dealing with the monstrous turns out to be understanding its foreign and hence secret origins, and that always involves learning about some archaic myth or legend, which in turn requires knowing a foreign language. In this respect, "Kaddish" is paradigmatic of *The X-Files* immigrant episodes. The Kaballah is the form of esoteric wisdom par excellence, and the FBI must go to a scholar of Jewish mysticism to solve the mystery. At one point Mulder is forced to confess: "I don't speak Hebrew—I don't know what that means." Ultimately the episode turns on knowledge of an esoteric text, the *Sefar Yezirah*, the Book of Creation, which explains the origin of the golem, but only in Hebrew. Indeed, words in the sacred language of Hebrew are the key to animating the golem, and deanimating it actually depends on a pun that works only in Hebrew (turning *emet*, which means "truth," into *met*, which means "death"). Sacred languages in one form or another run throughout the immigrant episodes, from voodoo rituals in French to exorcism chants in Romanian. All the episodes we have discussed include significant chunks of dialogue in a foreign language, some of it untranslated in a way that is quite "foreign" to American television. *The X-Files* thus highlights the problem of nationalism as a problem of language. Many have argued that the national community is fundamentally a linguistic community, and the difficulties multilingual nations have faced lend support to this claim.[50] The plots of many *X-Files* episodes, particularly those dealing with immigrants, are generated by people not speaking the same language, literally and figuratively. If not to speak someone's language is to appear monstrous in his eyes, then the polyglot communities produced by the contemporary globalization of the world become deeply problematic and in their own way monstrosities. The complicated linguistic texture of *The X-Files* shows that a central concern of the series is the dissolution of the legitimacy of the traditional nation-state.

◆

Language, especially spoken language, thus proves to be a fundamental point of resistance to the nation-state and a source of independent power, sometimes able to accomplish what the forces of national governments cannot do. The nation-state cannot of course do without language, but it usually works to impose a single, standard language upon its people, largely brought about by the shift from oral to literate culture. Once a language is written down, and above all once it takes the form of books and other printed matter such as newspapers, it can be standardized.[51] In general, modern technology works to transform the nature of language, and in particular to strip it of its mythic dimension and make it serve the cause of economic rationality. In the modern nation-state, language becomes the common currency of trade and thus one of the chief flashpoints in the battle between traditional communities and modern communities. The standardization of language in the modern community is a central example of the cultural homogenization the nation-state works to produce. Analyzing the immigrant episodes of *The X-Files* has given us the opportunity to look at the forces the nation-state seeks to absorb into its modernized, technological regime. It is time to turn to the issue of technology itself in *The X-Files*, and especially its problematic relation to the nation-state.

From the standpoint of the nation-state, technology is a double-edged sword. On the one hand, the nation-state very much depends on technology to create, maintain, project, and increase its power. Some have even argued that the nation-state is correlated with a certain level and stage of technology.[52] On the other hand, precisely if that is the case, technological developments may sooner or later make the nation-state obsolete. That is, new technologies may make it possible to perform by other means the functions that have long been associated with the nation-state and also provide new ways for private citizens to neutralize, evade, or negate the seemingly overwhelming power of the nation-state. The complexity of the issue of technology and the nation-state is well illustrated by the case of totalitarian regimes. In *1984* George Orwell famously suggested that modern technology, such as two-way television, would enable governments to clamp down on their citizens in hitherto unimaginable ways and permit a bureaucratic elite to perpetuate a tyranny over every corner of society. In actual fact, however, technology has turned out to be the Achilles heel of many totalitarian regimes.[53] With its closed society and centrally planned economy, the Soviet Union proved incapable of matching the technological progress facilitated by the open societies and free markets of the West. Moreover, dissidents within the Soviet Union found ways to undermine the regime by using new technologies such as copying machines and personal computers.[54] Totalitarian regimes may be only a special case of the vulnerability of the nation-state to new technologies. The nation-state may live and die in connection with a certain level of technological development. Created in tandem with the printing press, the telegraph, the telephone, and the railroad, the nation-state may be brought to an end by the jet plane, cable television, the cellular phone, and the Internet. These are of course highly speculative issues, but *The X-Files* has never shied away from speculation. And it has repeatedly explored the question: Does new technology provide the lifeblood or the death knell of the nation-state? Some episodes seem to present the state's technological grip on society as inescapable and all-powerful, while others suggest that technology can be the greatest weapon against state power.

The X-Files often portrays the modern technological world negatively, suggesting that people are being dehumanized by the machines with which they have surrounded themselves. In particular the show presents technology as imprisoning. Several episodes have been based on the idea of people becoming trapped in videogames or other forms of virtual reality.[55] A typically negative view of the modern technological economy can be found in an episode from the fifth season, "Folie à Deux." It tells the story of an office worker who goes berserk, rebelling against his boss, accusing him of being a monster (literally), holding his boss and his coworkers hostage, and killing one of them, who he claims was dead already—a zombie controlled by the evil power of the boss. The episode takes off from a common kind of story of office violence, when a worker snaps under the pressure of his job and takes his frustration out on his colleagues. But *The X-Files* offers a twist on this pattern; in this case, the "crazy" worker turns out to be right. His boss *is* a monster, a strange bug-like creature able to cloud people's minds and convince them that he is human, thus allowing him to feed upon them in some mysterious way and turn them into zombies. "Folie à Deux" thus offers one of the show's best exercises in legitimating paranoia, becoming especially powerful when Mulder figures out that the seemingly insane office worker is in fact telling the truth. Everyone (including Skinner and even Scully) begins to think that Mulder is insane too, and he ends up confined to a hospital bed (and thus a sitting duck for the bug-monster himself) until Scully has a change of heart and rescues him. The episode dramatizes the pathos of being the sole person who knows the truth in a world fallen prey to a mass delusion, a common motif in science fiction movies, going back to *Invasion of the Body Snatchers* (1956).

The episode is a transparent Marxist allegory, and as such one of the most left-wing in the history of *The X-Files*. In the person of the boss, it identifies capitalism as monstrous and portrays the process of alienation as it is defined by the young Marx and his followers, such as Georg Lukács. The boss is explicitly accused of "sucking the humanity" out of his workers. The rebellious worker tries to warn his colleagues and wants to go on television to alert the whole community to the problem. He accuses the boss of trying to turn his workers into "insects, not people—mindless drones." In the ringing rhetoric of class conflict, the worker charges: "He wants to take away who we are, to control us." In typical *X-Files* fashion, the episode manages to root its horror fantasy in the genuine realities of economic life. As "Folie à Deux" opens, we see the protagonist in a perfectly ordinary setting— a telemarketing office. He is trying to sell the most middle-class of products—vinyl siding—over the phone and is engaging in a promotional patter that is all too familiar to everyone viewing the show.[56] Before we know what the episode is about, we witness the phone salesman mindlessly following a script outlined for him on a computer screen. We are thus subtly prepared for what will turn out to be the central theme of the episode—how people lose their souls and are turned into machines by a modern economy. In a reversal of the perspective of "Fresh Bones," we see that the modern world produces its own kind of zombies, the walking dead of the automated office. The doctor who performs an autopsy on the man killed by the berserk office worker is surprised by the officially recorded time of death: "It sure looks to me like he's been dead longer than that." In a vision that goes back at least as far as T. S. Eliot's *The Waste Land*, "Folie à Deux" offers a modernist image of the deadening effect of twentieth-century urban existence and the regimented, despiritualized life it imposes on workers.

The episode does a marvelous job of creating the image of the boss (while reminding us that it is just that—an artificially created and delusive image). To everyone, including us in the audience, the boss appears to be the very opposite of a monster. He handles everything smoothly, seeming to run his office in a calm and effective manner, even if we may be put off by the cloyingly benevolent atmosphere he tries to create, epitomized by the office's motto: "Dial and smile." What is truly monstrous about the boss is that he is so *nice*. In his central confrontation with Mulder, he never once loses his even temper, while the normally cool FBI agent becomes increasingly agitated, thus convincing Skinner that Mulder is the one in the wrong. With evil thus successfully masquerading as good, the central idea of "Folie à Deux" becomes profoundly Marxist, that capitalism creates a false consciousness in its workers. The episode is continually suggesting that modern society has robbed us of our humanity, but we do not know it. In fact we have become so blindly content with our death-like existence that we reject as crazy anyone who questions it. The episode thus becomes an exercise in consciousness-raising, in getting us to be alienated from society in a positive sense, to cut through the illusions it imposes on us and allow us to realize how monstrous our lives have become, how inhuman and unfree.

"Folie à Deux" presents the problem of technology in purely economic terms, suggesting that the capitalist system enslaves its workers, all the more so because they do not recognize their slavery for what it is. But a number of *X-Files* episodes present technology in an even more sinister light because they show big business linked up with big government, especially in the all-important and all-pervasive communications industry. When the "Jose Chung" episode half-jokingly has Mulder refer to "the military-industrial-entertainment complex," it provides a clue to a central theme of the series, that covert government control of the media is the most insidious aspect of technological tyranny. Perhaps the most Orwellian episode of *The X-Files* is "Wetwired," which rather self-consciously deals with the issue of the impact of television on society.[57] Mulder and Scully are investigating a strange outburst of murders in a suburban community in Maryland. Perfectly sane and ordinary people have suddenly become delusional and murdered family, friends, and neighbors for no apparent reason. The only link the agents can find among the various crimes is television, and they end up watching hundreds of videotapes of cable news recorded by one of the killers. Scully thinks that this may help solve the mystery because "recent studies have linked violence on television to violent behavior." It is odd to hear the issue of television violence raised on a television program itself, especially one that often features violence of a peculiarly disturbing nature and that might therefore be regarded as culpable if television does have a negative impact on its viewers. Mulder, who is portrayed throughout the series as something of a television addict himself (with a particular predilection for pornography), rises to the occasion and defends the medium: "Those studies are based on the assumption that Americans are just empty vessels ready to be filled with any idea or image that's fed to them, like a bunch of Pavlov dogs."

Mulder speaks eloquently on behalf of human freedom, but viewing hundreds of hours of CNN could drive anybody crazy, and we soon see Scully glued to the TV, watching with exactly the kind of docile passivity Mulder argued was the false assumption behind the behavioral studies. Scully starts acting strangely and becomes suspicious of everybody and everything. In a scene borrowed from Francis

Ford Coppola's brilliant movie *The Conversation* (1974), she tears up her apartment searching for electronic bugs in phones and other places.[58] We learn that somebody has added what is significantly called a "foreign signal" to the cable TV transmissions in this town and it apparently activates the deepest fears of the viewers, creating a "virtual reality of their own worst nightmares." For example, the first murderer was watching a news broadcast about a war criminal in the former Yugoslavia described as a "modern-day Hitler." Since his parents were Holocaust victims, viewing scenes of parallel atrocities in Bosnia sets him off on his murder spree. (The references to Hitler and ethnic cleansing in the Balkans show how this technology episode is linked to the immigrant episodes.) In Scully's case, the doctored TV signals tap into her anxieties about her FBI colleagues and the question of who she is really working for and with. In short, in a weirdly self-reflexive comment on its own impact, *The X-Files* shows television turning a normal person paranoid.[59] Scully thinks that she sees Mulder conspiring with the Cigarette-Smoking Man, his professed worst enemy and the most sinister figure in the entire series. In her paranoia, Scully comes close to killing Mulder and only after the effect of the TV transmissions has worn off is she able to reflect on what happened. She tells Mulder that she thought: "Everybody was out to get me," giving him the perfect reply: "Now you know how I feel most of the time." Once again, *The X-Files* suggests how thin the line is between "true" and "false" paranoia.

The murders in the Maryland town turn out to be linked to some dark experiment in mind control involving cable television. To help solve the mystery, Mulder turns to his friends, the Lone Gunmen, three recurrent characters in the series who are his experts on high-tech matters, especially involving computers, and whose very name points in the direction of the Kennedy assassination.[60] The Lone Gunmen are one of the most brilliant strokes of *The X-Files*—nerds as heroes. They are the perfect representatives of the new hacker culture that evolved with the personal computer and the Internet. They live for breaking codes and gaining access to supposedly secure computer files, especially when government secrets are involved. And in the world of *The X-Files*, they are the ultimate paranoiacs. When they have something to tell Mulder, they are cautious and make the one direct reference to Orwell in the episode: "We don't want to talk about it over the phone. Big Brother may be listening." The Orwellian implications of this comment are borne out by the episode as a whole, which is haunted by the specter of government corruption and tyranny. The episode begins in a shady Washington, D.C., neighborhood. When one of Mulder's informants comments: "This area's always been known for its criminal element," the FBI agent adds: "Especially when Congress is in session." Like many *X-Files* episodes, "Wetwired" keeps reminding us of the Watergate affair. (Mulder's principal informant in the first season is named Deep Throat.) Mulder's meeting with an informant in an underground parking garage particularly evokes the Watergate story as Woodward and Bernstein recount it, especially when Mulder is told "Just follow the evidence," echoing the famous line: "Follow the money." The allusions to actual government conspiracies such as Watergate give a certain plausibility to the fictional government conspiracy "Wetwired" portrays.[61]

As often happens in *The X-Files*, we never learn exactly what the TV experiment was trying to achieve or who was behind it. But we can assume that the federal government was involved, because Mulder gets much of his information about what happened from Mr. X, who is linked to high circles in Washington. In the last scene, we see him reporting to the Cigarette-Smoking Man, who is evidently implicated in the plot. We learn from the Lone Gunmen that the experiment involved planting subliminal messages in the TV transmissions, and they explain that "both Russian and American scientists have been working with this for decades"—another example of Cold War convergence in the series. Mulder's reference to the "naked lady in the ice cube" is an acknowledgment of Wilson Bryan Key and his book *Subliminal Seduction*, an exposé of secret advertising techniques that served as one of the inspirations for this episode.[62] In his last exchange with Mr. X, Mulder suggests that the strange TV signals may have been an attempt to influence the way people behave in important situations—"what to buy, who to vote for." As if that were not sinister enough, Mr. X darkly hints: "You think they'll stop at commerce and politics?" For all we know, the government may be rigging the Nielsen ratings and thus may have been responsible for the cancellation of Chris Carter's other series, *Millennium*.

"Wetwired" thus offers the paradox of a television show that exposes the sinister effects of television. The episode seems to be in the typical over-the-top mode of *The X-Files*, making the outrageous suggestion that the federal government is using television in a subliminal way to manipulate its citizens' minds and perhaps even how they vote. But as usual, the paranoid fantasies of *The X-Files* have a genuine grounding in reality. "Wetwired" cleverly reminds us how all-pervasive television has become in our lives. We see televisions everywhere in the episode, even in Scully's hospital room. And with its references to CNN and the Home Shopping Network, "Wetwired" suggests that television shapes the way we view our world and our preferences as consumers. The Lone Gunmen's reference to "Madison Avenue" implies that it may not take a government conspiracy to turn television into a corrupting influence. Marshall McLuhan argues that we are too obsessed with the question of the content of television— what specific messages it conveys. For him, the far more significant issue is the very medium of television, which in itself has more of an impact in changing us as human beings.[63] "Wetwired" also seems ultimately less concerned with who controls television than with the way television controls us. The real horror in "Wetwired" is a world in which anybody would tape hundreds of hours of CNN broadcasts, let alone watch them, and unfortunately, that world is not far from the one we already live in. The episode seems to say: "Forget about government conspiracies: television is already running our lives." The central concern of the episode is the passivity of average television viewers, which makes them captives of the TV screen and puts them at the mercy of the medium. Mulder tries to dismiss that view of television's effect in his early remarks, but everything in the story, especially Scully's behavior, seems to contradict him and reinforce the idea that Americans in fact "are just empty vessels waiting to be filled with any idea or image that's fed to them."

◆

In "Blood," an episode closely related to "Wetwired," ordinary people are provoked into murders by reading messages off the LED screens that have, like television, become ubiquitous—on cash registers, gasoline pumps, microwave ovens, personal computers, and dozens of other everyday devices.[64] The episode links the digital readouts to a typically convoluted X-Files plot, involving hallucinogenic drugs such as LSD, an experimental pesticide, and a scheme to send subliminal messages through electronic machines. Once again, we seem to be dealing with an experiment in manipulating the minds of ordinary people, an experiment that may or may not have gone awry. These two episodes, along with others, suggest that technology is fundamentally a method of thought control and thus a powerful weapon in the hands of governments trying to maintain and extend their power over their people. But there are hopeful signs, even in "Wetwired." After all, Mulder does uncover and seems to thwart the scheme to use television for mind control. Most importantly, he is able to use technology to battle technology. The Lone Gunmen boast that they were able to "use freeware off the Net" to unravel the mystery of the device that altered the TV transmissions. In the hacker culture, we see how truly double-edged the sword of technology can become for the nation-state. The very means the state tries to use to maintain its grip on power can be used as a weapon against it, and the question *The X-Files* poses is: Who can stay ahead in the technology race, the government or the private individuals resisting its tyranny?

This is a central issue in the Anasazi trilogy, one of the most popular sets of *X-Files* episodes, frequently voted their favorite by fans in television polls. The Anasazi trilogy provides an epitome of *The X-Files* as a whole and represents the series at its best and worst. It has some of the most dramatic, inventive, and exciting sequences in the history of the series, but also some of the most pretentious and overwritten dialogue, filled with New Age platitudes and moments that seem to be lifted from Oliver Stone's even more pretentious motion picture epic about Jim Morrison, *The Doors* (1991). Nevertheless, it takes us to the heart of *The X-Files*.[65] The first episode, "Anasazi," begins with the momentous news that a hacker named the Thinker—described as "an anarchist—and a snoop"—has broken into secret computer files at the Defense Department and downloaded the greatest prize of all—every bit of information the government has collected since World War II about UFOs and extraterrestrials. We see here a striking image of the vulnerability of the nation-state in the new world of advanced computer technology. Secrets the federal government had carefully and successfully guarded for decades can be obtained by a single individual at the touch of a keyboard. The shocking news of the security breach circulates quickly around the world among members of the Syndicate, prompting the Cigarette-Smoking Man to meet with Mulder's father, William, who we learn in the course of the three episodes was deeply involved in the original experiments with aliens. The Cigarette-Smoking Man is bitterly aware of how technological developments have changed the terms of the game: "Who could have predicted the future, Bill—that the computers you and I only dreamed of would someday be home appliances capable of the most technical espionage?" In the struggle between the vast state apparatus and the lonely individual, the personal computer seems to be the great equalizer, as the efforts of a single hacker promise to expose the conspiracy Mulder has been fighting unsuccessfully for years. At the same time, however, we see that the new capacity for worldwide communication allows the Syndicate to respond immediately and in unison to the threat.

Though the Thinker is soon killed by the usual shadowy forces, he manages to get a digital tape with the secret files to Mulder. There is, however, a catch: The files are encrypted in Navajo, a language with a unique syntax that makes it very difficult for nonnative speakers to understand. Navajo was actually used by the United States in the Pacific Theater during World War II as the ultimate unbreakable code—deployed by a special corps of Navajo Code Talkers. The centrality of Navajo in the plot of the Anasazi trilogy is perhaps the best example of the importance of language as a theme in *The X-Files*[66] and links these episodes to those that deal with immigrants. More generally, the importance of Native Americans in the Anasazi trilogy casts an interesting light back on what we saw in the immigrant episodes. Those episodes present various forms of immigrants to the United States as the aliens, and mainstream Americans as the natives. But as the presence of the Navajo and other Indian tribes in *The X-Files* repeatedly reminds us, White Anglo-Saxon Protestants are *not* the true native Americans. The people who now take pride in being Americans are descended from immigrants who gained their title to the country only by displacing the original inhabitants. The Anasazi trilogy, and the general importance of Native Americans in *The X-Files*, works to deconstruct the simple alien-native binary. The Navajo are among the original natives of the American continent, and yet they and their language now appear profoundly alien to the people who regard themselves as mainstream Americans. Moreover, the Anasazi trilogy hints at some special relation between the Navajo and the extraterrestrial aliens, which suggests why so many UFO sightings and purported landing sites are in the American Southwest. The Anasazi are historically a Native American people who mysteriously disappeared hundreds of years ago. *The X-Files* hints that they were an early example of alien abductees, and one of the Navajo in the episode translates their name: "It means the ancient aliens."[67] Later episodes (especially "Biogenesis") have developed the alien–Native American connection further along increasingly bizarre lines, as we learn that the deepest secrets of the aliens themselves seem to be encrypted in Navajo. In fact, the ultimate revelation of *The X-Files* seems to be that what we now call the aliens were in fact the original inhabitants of the planet Earth, or at least the ones who seeded life on it. There could be no more complete inversion of the alien-native binary. Ultimately *The X-Files* pursues the theme: "We have met the aliens and they are us."

Native Americans such as the Navajo become another example in *The X-Files* of a subculture within the borders of the United States that is alien to mainstream America. Accordingly, the Anasazi trilogy develops most fully the central opposition we have seen in *The X-Files* between traditional and modern cultures, with the Navajo representing one pole and the global conspiracy representing the other, and the two forces are indeed pitted against each other throughout the trilogy.[68] At first, the contest seems to be grotesquely uneven, as all the scientific and technological resources of a multinational military-industrial complex are brought to bear against a ragtag band of hapless Navajo in the desert, whose only resource seems to be their incomprehensible language. As we have already seen, modernity appears at its worst in the Anasazi trilogy. It is in these episodes that we learn that Nazi science was transplanted to America by the U.S. government itself. Flashback scenes of strange creatures being gassed in railroad cars draw a parallel between the Nazi treatment of Jews and the American treatment of the alien-human hybrids.[69] And hovering in the historical background is the mass extermination of Native Americans that was the precondition of the white man's occupation of the western territories. When, in a scene that seems like an update of a John Ford movie such as *Cheyenne Autumn* (1964), the Cigarette-Smoking Man leads a brutal military raid on a Navajo home, it stands for hundreds of such incidents in the ugly past. Almost as if they had read Horkheimer and Adorno's *Dialectic of Enlightenment*[70] (itself a reaction to Nazi atrocities), the producers of *The X-Files* seem to be tracing how civilization paradoxically passes over into barbarism. The supposedly more advanced culture, the one that prides itself on its sophisticated science and technology, turns out to act far more brutally than the supposedly primitive culture it subdued.

But this dialectical reversal of the "higher" civilization and the "lower" suggests the possibility of a reversal of the power relations between traditional and modern culture. In the Anasazi trilogy, all the power seems at first to be on the side of modernity, but only when one looks at strictly material power. The power of spirituality is on the side of the Navajo, as is stressed in the second episode of the trilogy. The military-scientific-industrial-technological-governmental conspiracy has done its best to kill Mulder, but the Navajo are able to revive him, using one of their ancient rituals called "The Blessing Way," which gives the episode its name. Acting the key *X-Files* role of the shaman, the head of the Navajo group, an old code talker named Albert Hosteen, leads a comatose Mulder on a spiritual journey, during which his body is revitalized and his soul is taught lessons by the departed spirits of his old friend and informant, Deep Throat, and his recently murdered father. The traditional character of the ceremony is stressed: Hosteen points out that everything is done "in accordance with our ancient traditions," just as they have been "passed down by our ancient Navajo ancestors." (We might be reminded here of the importance of the ancestral in episodes such as "Hell Money" and "The Calusari.") As a traditional culture, the Navajo draw strength from the past. By contrast, modern culture is always oriented toward the future and seeks to eradicate the past, even all memory of the past. A representative of the global conspiracy known as the Well-Manicured Man, newly introduced in this sequence, replies to Scully's question about the goals the Syndicate is pursuing: "We predict the future, and the best way to predict the future is to invent it." "The invention of the future" versus "the preservation of the past" are the terms in which *The X-Files* presents the contrast between modern and traditional culture. When we recall the Cigarette-Smoking Man's remark to Mulder's father—"Who could have predicted the future?"—we realize that the Syndicate may not be as powerful as it seems and that its opponents may have ways to "fight the future" (which became the slogan of the one *X-Files* movie thus far). Viewed in these terms, the Navajo are not simply powerless vis-à-vis modernity; on the contrary, as a traditional culture they have the potent force of memory on their side.[71]

This contrast is articulated in the long monologue with which Albert Hosteen begins "The Blessing Way":

> There is an ancient Indian saying that something lives only as long as the last person who remembers it. My people have come to trust memory over history. Memory, like fire, is radiant and immutable, while history serves only those who seek to control it, those who would douse the flame of memory in order to put out the dangerous fire of truth. Beware these men, for they are dangerous themselves—and unwise. Their false history is written in the blood of those who might remember and those who seek the truth.

Though somewhat overwritten, this speech is one of the central utterances in *The X-Files*. In opposing memory to history, it contrasts the oral culture of the Navajo with the literate culture of modern America.[72] The key to history is that it is *written*, and the fact that it is here said to be written in blood suggests a preference in *The X-Files* for oral culture over literate. Written history represents the culture of control, an attempt to impose a single pattern on events, even at the expense of the truth. When modern man generally says that he prefers history to memory, what he means is that he regards history as reliable and memory as unreliable. We say that memories vary from person to person, whereas history gives us a single authoritative account. But *The X-Files* suggests that history is not simply to be preferred to memory, as the official print culture would have it. History too easily becomes the preserve of the nation-state, which exerts direct or indirect control over the print media and what they set down in writing. As Albert Hosteen suggests, history conceived as a single authoritative account is too important a prize for the powerful men who control the state to leave in private hands. As the Anasazi trilogy and *The X-Files* as a whole suggest, history is always *nationalized*. Ultimately the nation-state gets to write its own history—to stamp out dissident views and alternate accounts of events and leave its citizens with a single story of its origins and growth, a story invariably flattering to the nation-state's self-conception of its legitimacy. The ongoing plotline of *The X-Files* might be characterized as a battle over who is going to tell the story of our time, the official print organs of the nation-state or the alternative nonprint media, represented in the Anasazi trilogy by the Navajo oral tradition.

Sharing McLuhan's perspective, *The X-Files* embodies a deeply negative attitude toward print culture. Print is the medium of the nation-state, of the official, government-sanctioned truth.[73] Any account that appears in the newspapers in *The X-Files* is likely to be false. For example, in the Anasazi trilogy, the conspirators manage to plant cover stories in the papers to explain away their murders of figures such as the Thinker. As the Cigarette-Smoking Man cynically comments: "The media attention will amount to no more than a few scattered obituaries." In *The X-Files* the only way to get at truth is through word of mouth or its postmodern equivalent, the Internet. The series reverses the normal rules of evidence that dominate the modern nation-state. In the terms of *The X-Files*, hearsay is always preferable to official written documents. Mulder spends his entire career tracking down rumors, urban legends, and tall tales, trying to validate them in opposition to what official channels of communication are willing to stamp as the truth in print.

Whether consciously or not, *The X-Files* thus develops the connection between print culture and the nation-state, a point that has been made by writers from Marshall McLuhan to Benedict Anderson. Anderson correlates the rise of the nation-state with the rise of the newspaper and the novel, arguing that the borders of a national community effectively get defined by the borders of a reading public.[74] Oral culture is tribal; only print culture permits the standardization of language that in turn makes it possible for people from different regions, classes, professions, and ethnic backgrounds to communicate with each other and form the larger unit of a nation-state.[75] The nation-state has established itself the moment that people in general abandon their local sources of information, reject rumor as unreliable, and accept the idea: "It must be true—I read it in the papers." And it is precisely this impulse that *The X-Files* labors mightily to undo and reverse. The premium on oral culture in the Anasazi trilogy thus represents an assault on the validity of the nation-state and its government-sanctioned print culture.

Appropriately the Anasazi trilogy ends in the third episode, "Paper Clip," with the triumph of oral culture over the representatives of the state apparatus. The conspirators are determined to get back the stolen computer files and to suppress all knowledge of their existence, even if they have to kill Mulder and Scully. To protect them, Assistant Director Skinner offers to make a deal with the Cigarette-Smoking Man. He will exchange the missing files for a guarantee of the safety of Mulder and Scully, as well as their reinstatement in the FBI. Doubting that Skinner still has the files, the Cigarette-Smoking Man refuses to deal with him. At this point, in what amounts to his finest hour, Skinner speaks his most famous words in the history of *The X-Files*: "This is where you pucker up and kiss my ass."[76] Skinner claims that he has had Albert Hosteen memorize the files, which are after all in Navajo, and "in the ancient oral tradition of his people," he has passed them on to twenty other members of his tribe. "So unless you kill every Navajo in four states," Skinner tells the Cigarette-Smoking Man, "that information is available with a single phone call." Though such an act of genocide does not strike us as beyond either the Cigarette-Smoking Man's capabilities or his inclinations, evidently Skinner has checkmated him. Oral culture wins the day in the Anasazi trilogy precisely because of its ability to disseminate and multiply the truth rather than to centralize and standardize it, as print culture tends to do. In its use of Navajo code talking as a plot device, *The X-Files* found a brilliant way to dramatize the power of oral culture.[77]

In the flush of victory, Skinner sarcastically remarks to the Cigarette-Smoking Man: "Welcome to the wonderful world of high technology." Skinner is of course being ironic and gloating that he has overcome all the sophisticated resources the Syndicate has deployed against him by the seemingly most primitive means of communication, the oral tradition of an Indian tribe.[78] But the connection he suggests between oral tradition and high technology is borne out by the arc of the trilogy, which begins with a postmodern computer hacker and ends with a premodern Navajo code talker—each in his own way able to frustrate the massive state apparatus. The Anasazi trilogy suggests that the nation-state and its correlative print culture are in effect caught between oral culture and electronic culture, between what precedes the print era and what will succeed it. The central issue of the Anasazi trilogy is cultural memory—how a culture maintains its "files"—and the episodes offer striking images of the three stages that have emerged in history.[79] We go from the most contemporary medium—computer files—to the most ancient—oral tradition. As different as these two media are, they have something in common—neither is written down in conventional print.[80] In between the printless media of computer files and Navajo code talking, *The X-Files* shows us the filing system of the nation-state, which is deeply tied to writing and specifically print. Alerted by a clue from a Nazi scientist they tracked down, Mulder and Scully journey to an abandoned mine in West Virginia, where they come upon an extraordinary sight: a veritable mountain of federal government paper, collected in seemingly endless rows of filing cabinets, filled, as they discover, with medical records and DNA samples for a significant portion of the U.S. population, including Scully herself and Mulder's elusive sister. We later learn that these files are connected to the genetic experiments to create an alien-human hybrid. But in themselves they constitute one of the most powerful symbols *The X-Files* offers of the nation-state. In a vision worthy of Michel Foucault and his obsession with Bentham's panopticon, we see the fundamental activity of the nation-state—spying on and collecting data about its citizens—reminding us that the root of *statistics* is the *state*. "Paper Clip" suggests that in a profound sense these filing cabinets *are* the nation-state, which reveals its nature most clearly in its efforts to manipulate and control its population by means of a centralized data bank.[81] Penetrating into the depths of the mine's caves, Mulder and Scully think that they have finally found the sinister heart of the power arrayed against them.

And yet, as ominous as the massive government filing system may be, there is something almost laughable about its very mass. In the context of the trilogy, what once represented the cutting edge of information technology now looks old-fashioned and even out-of-date and hopelessly clumsy. We realize that all the information in these filing cabinets could fit on a few computer disks, and indeed Skinner may have been carrying around in his coat pocket for several days an equivalent amount of data on a single digital tape. The hall of records serves as an excellent image for the stage of technology represented by the nation-state. Historically it did mark an advance beyond oral tradition, which is inadequate to the record keeping required by a modern mass society. The complex records of modern economic and other social transactions must be recorded in some form, and the nation-state did help to make that process possible, with its various bureaus and other data-keeping institutions. At a certain stage of information technology, when data keeping required massive amounts of space, the nation-state with its massive centralized resources had a competitive advantage. But computers have changed all that, making it possible to combine the flexibility and portability of oral tradition with the storage capacity, permanence, and reliability of print culture. Ironically then, the nation-states helped pave the way for the technological advances that may ultimately render them obsolete. Nation-states have always been particularly concerned with information technology and spurred the development of the first electronic computers, largely for military purposes. But once computers were developed and became increasingly available to private citizens, they made possible new forms of data collection and processing that allow individuals to bypass the state and its centralizing informational function. (A similar story was replayed in the development of the Internet out of what originally amounted to a Defense Department project.)

The Anasazi trilogy suggests that, paradoxically, the advance into the paperless and printless world of computers may allow humanity to recapture something of the old freedom of the preprint era of oral tradition. Oral and electronic cultures are united by their tendency to proliferate versions of the truth, to replace the single standardized and authorized accounts characteristic of print culture with multiple stories. What the officially sanctioned print culture tries to stigmatize as rumor, hearsay, and mere gossip is the lifeblood of both the oral tradition of a tribe and the chat rooms of the Internet. Once again *The X-Files* seems to be dramatizing the theories of McLuhan, who argues that electronic media are taking us back to the world of oral culture, after a long detour through print culture.[82] That may well be the fundamental way in which advances in technology are leading us beyond the nation-state. If the nation-state can be correlated with the era of print culture, then the spread of computer technology may ultimately spell its doom, at least in the form in which we have known it. The Anasazi trilogy might be renamed "Requiem for a Filing Cabinet." As comic as the image of the abandoned files in the mineshaft may be, there is also something faintly elegiac about the scene. The government seems to have given up on its central project of recording and classifying all its citizens. In the bureaucratic equivalent of the elephants' burial ground, we seem to be witnessing the end of the era of the nation-state.

◆

The history of *The X-Files* itself is an example of the larger process it tries to portray of the denationalization, retribalization, and globalization of culture in our day. Along with *The Simpsons*, *The X-Files* is one of the programming successes that made the upstart Fox Network a viable alternative to the long-standing Big Three of television: CBS, NBC, and ABC. As such, *The X-Files* is very much at the center of the revolution in television and hence in American culture that began with the spread of cable TV in the 1980s and culminated in what I am calling the global era in the 1990s.[83] Television always had the potential as a medium to decenter national cultures, but drawing upon their experience with radio, national governments moved quickly to bring the fledgling TV medium within their orbits as soon as it became an important player on the mass entertainment scene. In Europe and elsewhere, television was in fact nationalized and for decades governments jealously guarded their monopolies on broadcast programming. The limitations of over-the-air TV transmission at first facilitated efforts by nations to police their television "borders." Even in the United States, where television stations were allowed to develop as private corporations, the national government managed to exercise control over the medium through licensing agreements, legislation, and regulatory agencies such as the FCC. Partially as a result of government regulation and partially as a result of the existing level of technology, in the classic era of broadcast television in the 1950s, 1960s, and 1970s, the American scene was dominated by just three networks: CBS and NBC at first and soon joined by ABC. These networks did develop distinct profiles at various times, appealing to different segments of the audience, and on the whole they offered a variety of programming, certainly more than was available under the nationalized TV regimes in Europe. But as the very term *broadcasting* indicates, the national networks inevitably aimed at national audiences, and in many ways the first three decades of American television reinforced the nationalizing effects of print culture in the United States. Aiming for reasons of advertising revenue at the largest possible audience, the networks often pitched their programming to the lowest common denominator, or at least tried to find what would unite their audience rather than divide it. The result, with of course some notable exceptions, was a general uniformity in the values portrayed on the national television networks in the 1950s, 1960s, and 1970s and a tendency toward homogeneity in the programming. The national networks produced national programming and in that sense helped foster a sense of a national culture that in turn bolstered the nation-state.

The new technology of cable television, coupled with the new possibilities created by satellite TV transmissions, gradually changed all this. With the explosion of channels available on cable, it became possible to replace broadcasting with what became known as narrowcasting. Programming could be tailored to specific segments of the audience, and the result was a proliferation of specialty channels on cable, such as the History Channel, Comedy Central, the Cartoon Network, the Sci-Fi Channel, the Health Network, the Food Network, the Weather Channel, the Travel Channel, and even the Golf Channel. Reversing its earlier tendency, television began to fragment and divide up its audience. (This development actually appealed to advertisers, who realized that they could target their audience better with narrowcasting—you may reach fewer people on the Golf Channel, but at least you have a good idea that those you reach will want to buy golf equipment.)[84] One of the most striking reflections of this trend has been the development of foreign-language channels on American cable, most notably in Spanish but in other languages as well, wherever a significant demand exists for them in various parts of the country. Linguistically, television originally reflected the traditional melting-pot image of the United States, as all Americans were forced to view their TV in English. Today television reflects a new mosaic image of American culture, in which different subcultures retain their distinct identities and even in some cases their distinct languages. The repeated use of foreign languages we have seen in *The Simpsons* and *The X-Files* of course mirrors this development.

To be sure, the original national networks have maintained much of their power and still are major players in the television industry. But over the past two decades, they have watched their share of the viewing audience gradually eroded and they can no longer count on being the ones to set television trends and, in that sense, to be the principal shapers of American culture.[85] That a pathbreaking show such as *The X-Files* appeared on Fox and not one of the "major" networks is itself a revealing fact. Increasing competition has diluted the centralizing power of the original national networks. Satellite transmission has made possible the emergence of the so-called superstations, such as

TBS out of Atlanta and WGN out of Chicago—local stations that have in effect gone national, bypassing the original networks and beaming their signals across the country. The cable news channel CNN represents perhaps the most important development in television in recent decades—the first truly international television station. Though headquartered and largely based in the United States, CNN has bureaus all over the world and can take advantage of satellite transmission to bring news from any one corner of the globe to any other. CNN first proved the strength of its global resources during the Gulf War, when its live transmissions from Baghdad put the news bureaus of the national broadcast networks to shame. TBS and CNN, both as it happens developed by media mogul Ted Turner, together show the two directions in which television has been moving for the past two decades. It is becoming at once more local and more global, increasingly bypassing the national level and leaving the traditional broadcast networks with a shrinking share of the market.[86]

The result can be seen in American television programming, which has opened up to a wider range of interests, sometimes more parochial and sometimes more cosmopolitan than what prevailed when the national networks dominated. *The X-Files* is a good illustration of this development. As I have argued already, it is hard to believe that *The X-Files* would ever have been programmed by any of the original national networks, though one might counter with the fact that some of its obvious precursors, such as *Kolchak: The Nightstalker* (1974–75)[87] and *Twin Peaks* (1990–91),[88] did make it on to ABC. But these shows were never as politically controversial as *The X-Files* has turned out to be. In any case, one can say that *The X-Files* had a much better chance of being scheduled by an upstart network such as Fox, which in a sense had nothing to lose and was looking to carve a distinctive niche for itself in the television market.[89] It thus had to take chances in its programming and go with innovative and original television concepts. The results were not always artistic masterpieces, as shown by examples such as *Married with Children* (1987–98), *21 Jump Street* (1987–90), and *Beverly Hills 90210* (1990–2000). And sometimes a genuinely brilliant and innovative show such as Chris Elliott's *Get a Life* (1990–92) proved to be a ratings flop. But both *The Simpsons* and *The X-Files* show Fox at its best: creative shows that have also consistently attracted large audiences. They demonstrate how genuine television excellence can be generated in part by the commercial needs of a new network in the cable era. Fox is owned by another media mogul, Rupert Murdoch, Australian by birth, with major entertainment and communication holdings around the world, especially in both the United Kingdom and the United States.[90] The financial underpinnings of *The X-Files* reveal another way in which the show reflects the increasing globalization of culture. Backed by Murdoch's organization, the show has at one time or another been viewed in 120 different countries around the world, if not quite from A to Z, at least from Afghanistan to Yemen.[91]

But the success of *The X-Files* cannot be attributed to the machinations of a multinational media conglomerate. Though well financed from the top down, the show is one of the most remarkable examples in the history of television of support building for a show from the bottom up. At the time of its debut, it was not heavily promoted by Fox or touted in advance by television critics. In the fall of 1993 Fox was betting its promotional budget on a show called *The Adventures of Brisco County Jr.* (1993–94), which has long since passed into oblivion. (It originally aired right before *The X-Files* and never provided the strong lead-in audience that new shows are supposed to require to succeed.)[92] To an unusual degree in the case of a successful show, news of *The X-Files* initially spread by word of mouth. Even more remarkably, a new factor came into play: the Internet.[93] One might well call *The X-Files* the first television success of the wired generation. Given its subject matter and its style, the show attracted the sort of people who, at exactly the same time, were beginning the Internet revolution. As we have seen, the show has catered to this audience segment, with plots that involve the Internet and other high-tech developments, and even created a set of characters, the Lone Gunmen, who are virtually poster boys for the wired generation.

As a result, *The X-Files* quickly became the subject of Internet chat rooms, and web sites devoted to it proliferated, spreading news of the show to potential fans, who were hooked once they tuned in.[94] As the case of *The X-Files* demonstrates, the Internet can powerfully reinforce the new ability of television to target specialized audiences. Once a start-up network took a chance on the show, the various *X-Files* web sites helped the producers to get word of it out to just the kind of audience that was most likely to be receptive to it. *The X-Files* thus provides the prototype of what may well be the future of mass entertainment—a powerful symbiosis between television and the Internet. In addition to helping establish and spread the show's popularity, the Internet has even influenced the course of its development. Chris Carter admits to monitoring the many web sites devoted to *The X-Files*, and he listens to fans' reactions and their suggestions for future plotlines.[95]

The show has benefitted from this unprecedented Internet feedback from its fans, perhaps opening up a new chapter in the interaction between television programs and their audience.[96]

The result has been a kind of tribalization of the audience of *The X-Files*, the flip side of the globalization television is helping to bring about in the contemporary world. Even as it serves to subvert and break down national boundaries, it works to create new subcommunities within the nation-state. What has been striking about *The X-Files* from its inception has been the fanatical devotion of its regular viewers, who think of themselves as a group apart. Fans quickly coined a name for their "tribe"—"X-Philes"—and the show soon achieved cult status, allowing for the sort of merchandising possibilities that are reserved for only the biggest of pop culture phenomena, such as *Star Trek* and the *Star Wars* movies. Fans of *The X-Files* can identify with each other by means of clothing and all sorts of paraphernalia featuring the show's logo, including action figures of Mulder and Scully.[97] This kind of commercial totemism gives the show's popularity its postmodern tribal quality. Clearly something more is going on in *The X-Files* phenomenon than just large numbers of people enjoying a television show. Its more fanatical devotees feel that their identities are somehow bound up with *The X-Files*. The communal nature of the response to the show is evidenced by the fact that within two years of its debut fans were already flocking to conventions organized to allow them to share their enthusiasm.[98] Within a remarkably short time (facilitated by the Internet), *X-Files* fans formed a distinct community within the broader television audience, displaying a fascination with the peculiar content of the show, the details of its production, and of course the private lives of its cast members.

The cult status of *The X-Files* shows every sign of spontaneous generation on the part of fans, but the producers of the show have evidently not been averse to helping it along. The show seems to have been tailor-made to become a cult hit. As anyone viewing it for the first time can testify, with its convoluted plots and ongoing mysterious conspiracies, it seems at first impenetrable to the uninitiated. Many of the episodes, as we have seen, deal explicitly with religious cults and esoteric knowledge. As if the program were trying to replicate in its audience what it shows in the world at large, *The X-Files* seems designed to separate its viewers from the mainstream and establish them as one of the tribal communities it consistently portrays as pockets of resistance to globalized modernity. The show has developed a secret language all its own, one which its devoted fans delight in, partly because it gives them a feeling of belonging to an in-group.[99] Woe to the innocent first-time viewer of *The X-Files* who dares discuss it with a group of hard-core fans. He will soon discover how embarrassing it can be not to know that "Cancer Man" is another name for the Cigarette-Smoking Man, or that this one character may have been responsible for just about every high-level political assassination since Lincoln (and the book is still out on that one as long as the show continues and it allows for time travel plots).

Obviously fans of *The X-Files* do not belong to a tribe in any traditional anthropological meaning of the term, and yet in some ways the show performs an analogous function for them, filling some kind of void in their lives.[100] Learning the secret language of the show gives them a feeling of solidarity as members of a special group, as well as giving them a distinctive vocabulary with which to discuss issues that concern them. The possibilities of this kind of tribalization are only heightened by its connection with the Internet. Many of the fans of *The X-Files* are united not only by the esoteric knowledge of the show they share but also by the fact that they obtained it through the Internet. Their actual passwords into the Internet become metaphorical passwords into a new form of common culture, and they take pleasure in thinking that what they enjoy is denied to the technologically uninitiated.[101] As we saw in the Anasazi trilogy, the most up-to-date technology paradoxically allows people to recapture something of an earlier tribal existence in a weird synthesis of the postmodern and the premodern. *The X-Files* as a cult phenomenon may presage a kind of high-tech balkanization of national cultures, as segments of a once broader audience take advantage of the Internet to seek out like-minded people wherever they may be and form their own smaller cultural units. At the same time, this tribalization of culture can easily pass over into a form of globalization. When I e-mail friends in Australia about the latest episodes of *The X-Files* (the United States still has an edge and gets the new shows first), I am struck by the fact that for the moment I have more in common with someone in Canberra who likes the show than I do with someone in my hometown, Charlottesville, who does not even know it exists. In general, the Internet allows people to break with traditional community configurations and group themselves with anyone they choose on the basis of perceived cultural affinities. The main point of all this talk of globalization and tribalization is that television in the cable and the Internet era is redrawing the cultural map in ways that increasingly ignore traditional national boundaries.

These developments are evident in the very production process of *The X-Files*. We have been talking about the show as American, and yet for its first five seasons it was shot in Vancouver, Canada, largely out of financial motives. For a number of reasons, it was cheaper to film the show in Vancouver than in the Los Angeles area.[102] *The X-Files* can thus serve to illustrate the economic logic of globalization—what used to be known as the Law of Comparative Advantage and now is generally referred to as the "outsourcing" of production to foreign countries, chiefly to take advantage of cheaper labor costs. The challenge to *The X-Files* producers was to give their Canadian locations an American look, and in fact they succeeded so well that most viewers were unaware that for the first five years the show was not being filmed in the United States. Of course Hollywood has long excelled at making scenes shot in the Los Angeles area appear to have been filmed in other places, and no extraordinary magic was needed to do the same in Vancouver. Still, given the fascination of *The X-Files* with the theme of virtual reality, it seems only appropriate that for years the show was engaged in a game of virtual reality itself. The way the show created a simulacrum of America in episode after episode ran strangely parallel to its own scripts, in which the Syndicate was constantly pulling off similar tricks to deceive Mulder and Scully with phantom locales and the biotechnological equivalents of Potemkin villages. The remarkable ability of the conspirators to disassemble an entire installation overnight to discredit the FBI agents' reports simply mirrored a production company's ability to stick to a tight schedule and strike a set as soon as filming is done.

And yet producing five years of *The X-Files* in Canada could not fail to leave its mark on the series. William B. Davis, the actor who plays the Cigarette-Smoking Man so brilliantly, is Canadian, and many of the guest roles and bit parts have been filled by Canadians, who were sometimes more convenient to cast.[103] They played their parts admirably, but we are left with odd moments in some episodes when a character supposedly from Texas or North Carolina speaks with a recognizably Canadian accent.[104] Location shooting proved to be even more of a problem. The topography and weather of British Columbia have not always corresponded to the scenes the producers wished to depict, most notably in the Anasazi trilogy. One can find a wide variety of terrains in British Columbia, but something equivalent to the high desert of the American Southwest is not among them. Thus the show had to struggle to create the illusion of Navajo country in British Columbia:

The New Mexico locations were created at a rock quarry in Vancouver painted red with 1,600 gallons of paint. "It was such an incredible find," locations manager Louisa Gradnitzer says, with even the weather cooperating on the day of filming, as the sun broke through to truly approximate the Southwestern United States—one area deemed virtually impossible to duplicate in lush Vancouver. After painting the quarry, visual effects then inserted second-unit footage actually shot in New Mexico to complete the illusion.[105]

The illusion of the proper setting has not always been this successfully created in *The X-Files*. Fans delight in spotting bloopers in the series. "Fresh Bones" is supposedly set on the coast of North Carolina—a totally flat area—but the mountains of British Columbia are clearly visible in the background in one shot in the episode.[106] Indeed, these mountains have a nasty habit of cropping up at the wrong moments in several *X-Files* episodes, as does the Vancouver skyline. But in general, *The X-Files* did a remarkable job of manufacturing its images of the United States during its production period in Canada. In a good illustration of the ability of television to ignore national boundaries and move with ease between the local and the global, the producers were able to operate out of Vancouver[107] and reproduce any part of the United States they wanted, or indeed any part of the world, given the technology at their disposal, especially new developments in computerized imaging. The product of new technologies itself, *The X-Files* has been well positioned to portray the impact of new technologies on the contemporary world.

Indeed, a fascination with new technologies has been basic to *The X-Files* from the start. Where would Mulder and Scully be without their cell phones? In general the show mirrors the information and communication revolution of the 1990s. Telephone answering machines, cellular phones, fax machines, personal computers, the Internet—all play important roles in one episode after another. One whole episode, "2SHY," is devoted to the perils of Internet dating.[108] The episode that records how Mulder first teamed up with the Lone Gunmen ("Unusual Suspects") features an electronic trade show, reminding us as "Anasazi" does of how much sophisticated equipment is now available to the ordinary consumer. As we have seen, this helps to even the odds in the struggle between the lone individual and the mighty state, but *The X-Files* is always ambivalent about technology and its effects. "Musings of a Cigarette-Smoking Man" begins with the sinister figure using an electronic device to overhear a conversation between Mulder and Scully and the Lone Gunmen. In a typically paranoid reaction—once again, as it happens, totally justified—one of the Gunmen, Frohike, will not continue until he can employ what he calls a "CSM-25 Countermeasure Filter." "CSM" may in fact refer to the Cigarette-Smoking Man, but he proves equal to the task. His surveillance is briefly interrupted, but all he has to do is flip one switch and he is back in the espionage business. This moment provides a disturbing comment on the question of who can stay ahead in the technology race, the government or private individuals, and leaves us with an Orwellian shudder that Big Brother will always be watching and listening. Yet by the very proliferation of new information and communication technologies *The X-Files* portrays, it offers hope that any government stranglehold on society can be broken. At the very least, the series shows how much more difficult it becomes for the nation-state to maintain its surveillance and control over its citizens as more and more techniques of transmission and encryption become available to them.

◆

One of the most interesting *X-Files* episodes linking the problem of technology with the problem of the nation-state came early in the sixth season. "Drive" opens with a "we interrupt this program for an important bulletin" gimmick that goes all the way back to Orson Welles's 1938 radio broadcast of *War of the Worlds*. We seem to be plunged into one of the reality-based police shows such as *Cops* and find ourselves following a high-speed car chase, reminiscent of the famous scenes of O. J. Simpson in his Bronco being pursued by the LAPD.[109] We learn that the car is being driven by a working-class man named Patrick Crump. When the police stop it, his wife's head explodes, a grotesque turn of events that draws Mulder and Scully to the case from another assignment. Taken into custody, Crump soon develops the same symptoms as his wife and is forced to commandeer Mulder to be his driver and help him escape from the police.

But Crump is seeking something more than a mere escape vehicle. As he has learned from the sad fate of his wife, he has developed a strange condition in which he must keep moving or he will die, and the faster he goes, the better he feels. Moreover he must keep moving west. As the producers of the show have admitted, this episode is based on the 1994 hit movie *Speed*; as Mulder begins to understand the situation, he self-consciously says: "I think I saw this movie."[110] Only in this case it is not the vehicle itself that threatens to explode if it slows down but the passenger's inner ear. This is one instance in which *The X-Files* unquestionably improves upon the movie it is imitating. *Speed* was a mere action film and made nothing interesting out of the unusual situation it portrays, but "Drive" develops the symbolism of its premise brilliantly. Like the lottery in "Hell Money," Crump's peculiar condition seems to be an allegory of America and represents what the country does to its citizens, especially the less fortunate. America is a country where everyone must keep on the move and indeed go faster and faster to keep up with the increasingly dizzying pace of modern society. Crump's fate is a literalization and an extreme case of what America demands of all its citizens. In the view of *The X-Files*, America has become a rat race in which only the perfectly mobile can survive. The episode thus fits the standard *X-Files* pattern of contrasting the rootedness of traditional society with the radical uprootedness of modern America. The dead giveaway in the allegory is the fact that Crump must keep heading west. He thus acts out the great imperative of American development, its famous Manifest Destiny, summed up in Horace Greeley's oft-quoted injunction: "Go west, young man." For Patrick Crump, the American dream of westward expansion turns into a nightmare of senseless mobility, of motion for pure motion's sake.

It is thus symbolically apt that Crump and his wife turn out to have lived in a trailer park. The profoundly American idea of the mobile home is another reflection of everything *The X-Files* is trying to say about the United States. Moreover, culturally speaking, the Crumps are what is vulgarly known as trailer trash. Crump is one more in a long line of *X-Files* portraits of the American underclass, and in many ways he is presented unsympathetically. He is narrow-minded and a bigot. Like the hate merchant in "Kaddish," he is anti-Semitic and, thinking that Mulder is Jewish, addresses him as "you and the rest of your Jew FBI."[111] Crump's anti-Semitism does not endear him to Mulder, who in a bigoted way himself refers to Crump as a "peanut pickin' bastard" and tells him sarcastically: "On behalf of the International Jewish Conspiracy, I need to inform you that we're almost out of gas." *The X-Files* is generally less sympathetic to the American underclass than it is to immigrants, even though, as we have seen, it often links the two groups as having similar problems fitting into the American mainstream. We see here the reason for the disparity in treatment, at least when the show is dealing with the white underclass (especially of southern origin). *The X-Files* tends to view this group as racially prejudiced and thus seems to hold it partially responsible for the troubles ethnic immigrants experience.

Moreover, Crump is a classic paranoiac, convinced that the government is responsible for all his troubles. Almost his first words to Mulder are: "You people put me here," and under questioning he elaborates: "Vicky and I were just some kinda government guinea pigs." Challenged by Mulder to substantiate his claims, Crump turns to the only authority his class knows: "You see it every day on the TV: They're droppin' Agent Orange, they're putting radiation in little retarded kids' gonads." As we have seen, *The X-Files* is suspicious of people whose view of reality is completely shaped by television.[112] And yet, given Crump's comments about government crimes, he might just as well have been citing *The X-Files* itself. For all the negative aspects of Crump's portrayal, the episode is ultimately sympathetic to him, allowing him to triumph over his bigotry and apologize, though somewhat halfheartedly, to Mulder: "The Jew stuff—no offense—a man can't help who he's born to." In a poignant moment, Crump says that his situation is "no way to treat a man—take away his dignity," thus reminding us that whatever he is, America has made him that way. Indeed, as the title and the central symbolism of the episode keep reminding us, Crump has been *driven* to his fate; he is a victim of the modern nation-state and the premium it puts on speed and motion. The technological rationality of a modern economy demands a mobile and migratory society. In a sense, it imposes a regime of domestic immigration on its citizens. Crump is forced to keep traveling, just as the unemployed seeking work must stay on the move, and his need to go west, shades of John Steinbeck, seems to mirror the Depression-era Okies in their pilgrimage to California.

The perfect symbol of the mobile character of American society in the episode is of course the cellular phone. Under the circumstances, Mulder and Scully need their favorite toy more than ever to keep in touch. But as if in retaliation against the technological regime that is tormenting him, Crump tosses Mulder's cell phone out the car window early in the episode. No greater deprivation could be imagined for our hero, and later in the episode, a California highway patrolman performs a risky maneuver to put Mulder electronically back in contact with Scully. His first comment when she anxiously asks him if he is okay is: "Yeah. Aside from terminal cell phone withdrawal." In his own way, Mulder is evidently as addicted to mobility as Crump. And in a wonderful example of the parallels between the actual production of *The X-Files* and its story lines, the staff reports:

> The shot where Crump throws his cell phone out of a moving car was accomplished by . . . throwing a cell phone out of a moving car. (Although,

reports second-unit production manager Harry Bring, it might have been
nice if they'd remembered to use the rubber dummy cell phone brought
for that purpose rather than mistakenly destroy one of their only links to
the production office.)[113]

Apparently the *X-Files* production crew are as dependent on their cell
phones as Scully and Mulder. They themselves became a victim of the
complexity of the modern technological world when someone mis-
took a real cell phone for its simulacrum.

These are humorous moments, but technology appears in a more
sinister light in this episode. Like most of the paranoiacs in *The X-Files*,
Crump turns out to be right—the federal government *is* the cause of
his troubles. As Scully investigates the case, she traces the problem to
a top secret navy program called "Project Seafarer," a way of commu-
nicating with Trident submarines by means of ELF (extremely low frequency) transmissions. A power surge in an underground antenna
bordering Crump's trailer park triggered a potentially fatal inner ear
problem in everyone in the area, except one deaf lady. "Project Seafarer," based on actual navy programs for long-distance communication such as Project HAARP ("High Frequency Active Auroral Research Program"), is one more *X-Files* symbol for the negative aspects
of the globalization brought about by the military-industrial complex.[114] Blanketing the earth with low-frequency waves may keep the
navy in touch with its premier weapons systems around the globe, but
it threatens U.S. citizens closer to home. The foreign interests of the nation-state, in particular its desire to project its power abroad, blind it
to domestic concerns.

Thus, as distasteful a character as Crump in many respects is, *The
X-Files* validates his paranoia and suggests that he has every reason to
be suspicious of the federal government. This creates a disturbing link
between his story and the frame tale of the episode. As it opens, Mulder and Scully are on an assignment investigating domestic terrorism
in Idaho, one of the prime areas for antigovernment militias in the
United States, and in particular the site of the Ruby Ridge incident.
The fact that they are specifically checking out a man who recently
bought five thousand pounds of fertilizer chemicals calls to mind the
Oklahoma City bombing incident (which involved a fertilizer bomb).
The X-Files seems particularly concerned about this actual confrontation between the federal government and its domestic opponents. The
image of a federal government building being blown up haunts the
opening sequence of the *X-Files* movie.[115] Perhaps *The X-Files* is trying

to come to terms with the way some people might respond to the antigovernment message it broadcasts in one episode after another. *The X-Files* is largely left-wing in its biases, but the extreme left and the extreme right have a way of meeting, and the Oklahoma City bomber probably had just as conspiratorial a view of the federal government as Mulder and *The X-Files* do. At the beginning of "Drive," Mulder and Scully interrogate a gruff figure named Virgil Nokes, who claims he had a perfectly good reason for ordering all that ammonium nitrate: "I grow sugar beets. Figger I got better things to do with my fertilizer than go around blowin' gummint buildings sky high." Virgil Nokes and Patrick Crump are essentially the same character, the sort of marginalized underclass figure who can either lead a harmless existence minding his own business or one day just "explode" under daily pressure from the government, turning into the kind of domestic terrorist Mulder and Scully are assigned to uncover. *The X-Files* never quite knows what to do with such characters. On the one hand, it presents them as something to be feared, the root of dangerous violence in America. On the other hand, it treats these figures sympathetically, understanding their alienation from American society and justifying their distrust of the federal government. Thus we must look carefully at how "Drive" resolves the story of Patrick Crump.

And indeed it turns out that "Drive" has one last twist on its central theme. As Mulder gradually comes to understand Crump and his plight, he becomes willing to help him, doing everything he can to keep him moving and hence alive. As they continue driving into the night, Mulder tries to reassure Crump: "We'll figure this out." But Crump ominously replies: "Better figure quick. We're runnin' out of west," and at that moment the camera pans to a road sign: "Welcome to California: Gateway to the Pacific." "We're runnin' out of west" becomes the ultimate theme of the episode, and once again it is a tagline that might serve as a motto for the whole series. The line brilliantly encapsulates the famous Frederick Jackson Turner thesis about the American frontier. America was in good shape as long as it had a real frontier, as long as it could keep expanding toward its natural geographic border on the Pacific Ocean. An expanding country relieves the pressure on underclass figures such as Patrick Crump (symbolized here by westward movement relieving the pressure on his inner ear). If their energies are bottled up in settled society, they can move on to the unsettled frontier and give their impulses free rein. In short, "Drive" embodies a profound understanding of everything that "California" has meant in the American imagination, especially California as the embodiment of the American dream and hence the great safety valve for American ambitions—the destination for immigrants and underclass figures alike—all hoping to better their lives on the West Coast. Accordingly, "Drive" comes to an end on the shores of the Pacific. Scully has devised a medical plan to save Crump's life, but unfortunately Mulder gets him to the coast just minutes too late, and his head has already exploded when Scully reaches him. For Crump, the dream destination of millions of Americans over the years turns out to be a dead end, both literally and figuratively.

◆

Crump "runs out of west" in his own life, but his fate seems to have a larger symbolic resonance. America's problem is that it is running out of west and one might generalize even further and suggest that the episode is showing that the whole West is running out of west. In American terms, "to run out of west" is "to run out of Indians," which is to say, "to run out of enemies" against which a civilization can define itself. In the American imagination, the western frontier was the point at which civilization supposedly intersected with barbarism—where the American nation met the Indian tribes, where a modern western culture confronted a people it viewed as tradition-bound savages. Americans thought that they could fulfill their national destiny, prove their heroism, and establish the superiority of their way of life by conquering and displacing the native inhabitants of the West. America thus made its history in the West. For America to run out of west is thus an ominous development: to be faced with running out of history. The successful westward expansion of the nation—known as the taming of the West—resulted in the domestication of the continent, thus closing off the outlet for the restlessness of its people and threatening the nation with an implosion of its energies. To run out of west is to experience Alexander the Great's problem of having no more worlds to conquer and hence no national purpose anymore. "Drive" may be the image *The X-Files* offers of what is called the end of history. History as traditionally understood ends when the nation runs out of new frontiers and reaches the state known as "California" (perhaps the perfect image of the end of history).[116]

"Drive" and *The X-Files* in general thus explore the impasse reached by the nation-state at the end of the twentieth century. The nineteenth century was the great era of imperialist expansion for the Western nation-states, as countries such as Britain and

France gradually and implacably extended their influence over all the continents of the globe. But there was only just so much "west" to go around for the West. Latecomers to imperialism among the modernized nation-states, such as Germany and (in the East) Japan, found their expansionist impulses blocked by the frontiers of existing European empires. The result was the world wars of the twentieth century, which when one cuts through all the bewildering historical and ideological details, threaten to reduce to a case of too many nation-states chasing too little territory. For *The X-Files*, the notion of "running out of west/running out of Indians" is fundamental to the logic of the nation-state. Expanding its territory has been the nation-state's program from the beginning, but these imperialist tendencies bring one nation-state into conflict with others. The result is to divide the world into armed camps, which further increases the power of individual nation-states over their citizens. In the name of national security, they impose all sorts of restrictions on their citizens and moreover frighten them into submission by raising the specter of foreign enemies. In *The X-Files* the nation-state fundamentally manifests itself in the form of military or paramilitary power, or more generally in the coercive force it exerts upon its citizens. In the view of *The X-Files*, the legitimacy of the nation-state fundamentally rests upon its claim to protect its citizens from "aliens."

We can thus see how the extraterrestrial mythology of *The X-Files* links up with its geopolitical concerns. By the middle of the twentieth century, the series of world wars and other global conflicts had made it abundantly clear that the West had run out of west. Allowing for some minor adjustments of borders, nation-states had basically reached their limits. One nation could not extend its borders or sphere of influence without running into other nations. The result was to impose an uneasy and unstable peace upon the world in the second half of the twentieth century, which went under the name of the Cold War. It was marked by sporadic outbreaks of conflict at various flashpoints around the earth, often engaging the geopolitical interests of the United States and the Soviet Union, but stopping short of involving the global superpowers directly in all-out war. By the 1990s, with the collapse of the Soviet Union, the West proclaimed victory in the Cold War and the resulting situation came to be described as the end of history. But as promising as this situation seems to be in many respects, it has ominous implications for the future of the nation-state. If the nation-state defines itself largely in terms of its military function and draws its power over its citizens from its claim to protect them from their enemies, what is the nation-state to do when it "runs out of west" and consequently "runs out of Indians," or, more generally, "runs out of aliens" as *The X-Files* conceives them?

Like *The Simpsons*, *The X-Files* is a distinctly post–Cold War phenomenon, as becomes clear when we compare them to TV shows from the 1960s. As we have seen, *Star Trek* and even *Gilligan's Island* grew out of a Cold War atmosphere, and *Star Trek* takes the U.S.-U.S.S.R. confrontation very seriously. It thus buys into the ideology of the nation-state. The *Enterprise* is essentially a ship of state, and a rather military state at that. For all the hostility to militarism and police states in *Star Trek*, it holds up a surprisingly autocratic ideal of order, as anybody who tries to contradict Captain Kirk on the bridge soon finds out. The *Enterprise* may stand up for democracy, but the ship itself is not run democratically. Thus the series inadvertently reveals the illiberal side of 1960s liberalism in America. American liberals may have wanted to give everyone the right to choose their government, but they also wanted that government to expand its role in running people's lives, from the proverbial cradle to the grave. *Star Trek* clearly reflects the heritage bequeathed to science fiction by its founder, the socialist H. G. Wells—the world should be run by a scientific elite, who will be better at ordering its affairs than ordinary human beings left to their own devices. In particular *Star Trek* reflects the political vision of the Kennedy administration, which set out to bring "the best and the brightest" to Washington in order to administer the country according to the latest scientific principles. As Robert McNamara's tenure as secretary of defense showed, the Kennedy administration thought that even war could be run according to management principles developed by the Harvard Business School. More generally, Mr. Spock seems to stand for all JFK's brainy advisors from Harvard—a sort of McGeorge Bundy with pointy ears.

Star Trek continually suggests that science has all the answers to human problems. Whether it is Dr. McCoy diagnosing a disease with his tricorder, or Engineer Scott figuring out how to get more power out of the *Enterprise* engines, or Mr. Spock analyzing an alien civilization's political structure at a glance, scientific expertise rules everywhere in *Star Trek*, or at least it *should* rule. Unfortunately, people are not always willing to take advice from scientists. *Star Trek* repeatedly suggests that the problem throughout the galaxy is that supposedly rational beings are too mired in tradition, superstition, and myth to listen to what the scientific elite has to tell them. That of course is where Captain

Kirk comes in. He is the executive arm of the scientific elite, the man of muscle who sees to it that the vision of Spock's brain gets carried out. In that sense, politics appears to be subordinate to science in *Star Trek*, but in fact just the opposite is the case. It is *Captain* Kirk and *Mr.* Spock. Although Kirk listens carefully to Spock's advice, it is always Kirk who in the end is responsible for decisions aboard the *Enterprise*.

Ultimately, in the vision of *Star Trek*, order has to be imposed upon the world from above—by a captain who always must be in charge. That is why, as we have seen, democracy is time and again undemocratically imposed on whole planets in the series. It takes the political order of the nation-state as its fundamental model of order, and in particular a 1960s liberal model of an activist state. Kirk and his crew are JFK and his Harvard brain trust. Wise men such as Spock come up with the solutions to problems and Kirk sees to it that they are imposed, even on extremely recalcitrant populations. Again, for all its democratic rhetoric, *Star Trek* does not assume that people can solve their problems on their own. In particular the show takes a dim view of free market activity and generally portrays businessmen in a negative light. Oddly enough, the original plans for the series suggested that one of the chief roles of the *Enterprise* was going to be facilitating galactic commerce.[117] But as the series developed, the role of the *Enterprise* turned out to be much more political than economic, and the show clearly subordinates economics to politics. The heroes of the show are generally scientists, diplomats, and of course military leaders such as Kirk, but not businessmen or entrepreneurs. In one early episode, "Mudd's Women," galactic commerce turns out to be nothing more than white slavery—interplanetary traffic in women of pleasure. The most common image of economic activity in *Star Trek* is mining, which is viewed as doubly exploitative—it rapes the environment and it takes advantage of the hapless miners.[118] One of the most famous episodes, "The Trouble with Tribbles," views commerce as a joke—it is just trafficking in worthless articles, which people unaccountably want and which therefore endlessly proliferate, threatening to crowd out the truly necessary and important things in life. Watching *Star Trek*, an impressionable youngster might want to grow up to be a scientist like Spock or a military leader like Kirk, but surely not a merchant like Harry Mudd. In a world in which evil empires such as the Klingon and the Romulan threaten peace, business activity seems trivial and the lowly businessman must take a backseat to the heroic military figure.[119] Command of a starship is clearly the apex of achievement in *Star Trek*, and the *Enterprise* cruising through the galaxy becomes a potent image of the nation-state on the prowl for problems to solve. However people anywhere in the universe may choose to order their lives, Kirk knows better and is prepared to straighten them out. One could have no clearer symbol of the self-confidence and indeed the arrogance of the interventionist nation-state in the 1960s.

All this is reversed in the 1990s in *The Simpsons*, which in a post–Cold War atmosphere effectively subordinates politics to economics.[120] Traditional political and military roles are downgraded in the series. They may have been important in the past, but a youngster such as Bart no longer looks up to presidents or generals as his heroes.[121] In *The Simpsons* the military, with no real foreign enemies anymore, is generally reduced to dealing with domestic problems, such as disciplining Bart (which may prove more difficult than subduing the Soviet Union). As "The Secret War of Lisa Simpson" (#4F21, 5/18/97) shows, the series is more interested in the place of women in the military than it is in the place of the military in world affairs. Generally *The Simpsons* shows the people of Springfield going about their private lives, with less and less regard for the concerns the nation-state has traditionally viewed as central to its citizens. Thus commerce comes to dominate their lives. It is not that *The Simpsons* takes a particularly positive view of business activity. On the contrary, in the typical left-wing spirit of Hollywood, the show tends to portray businessmen as corrupt, if not outright criminals—especially in the case of Montgomery Burns, the colossally evil owner of the Springfield nuclear power plant. *The Simpsons* continually shows businessmen preying upon the gullibility of the public and loves to expose the duplicity of TV advertising. The show is particularly hostile to conglomerates, big corporations that try to run people's lives from afar, and especially to media conglomerates (despite the fact that the show is of course broadcast by a media conglomerate itself).[122]

But as hostile as *The Simpsons* is to big business, the show is surprisingly sympathetic to small business. In its own quirky way, it celebrates the entrepreneurial spirit that was reawakened in the 1980s and 1990s and came to dominate the American scene. Apu is of course the entrepreneurial hero par excellence, and, as the operator of an all-night convenience store, he has the bullet wounds to prove it. *The Simpsons* may make fun of the prices Apu charges, but it grudgingly admits that he performs a service to the community and shows respect for his willingness to work hard to earn a living. But the entrepreneurial spirit is not confined to Apu in *The Simpsons*. In "When Flanders Failed" (#7F23, 10/3/91), Homer's neighbor Ned sees a business opportunity and seizes it, opening the Leftorium, a boutique catering to left-handed people. In "The Twisted World of Marge Simpson" (#4F08, 1/19/97), a group of female entrepreneurs in Springfield, the Investorettes, expels Marge from its ranks. She responds by starting up a pretzel franchise (with, it turns out, a little help from the local mob). Even Homer gets into the entrepreneurial act. He goes into the snowplow business in one episode, manages a country and western singer in another, tries to peddle his inventions in another, and in general invests in one get-rich-quick scheme after another.[123] To be sure, *The Simpsons* does not portray Homer as a successful entrepreneur. Indeed, like Marge and Ned, he is shown to be more likely to fail in his business ventures. Nevertheless, the series ends up presenting the entrepreneurial spirit as all-pervasive in Springfield and more responsible for the character of people's lives than the government. A number of episodes connect the small business ethos with the high-tech developments that have reshaped America. In one episode, Homer even sets up his own web site and becomes the chief source of news in Springfield, challenging the monopoly of the local TV station, to the point where reporter Kent Brockman must go on the air to reassert his authority.[124] In the January 7, 2001, episode about a "smart" Homer, his troubles actually begin when he gets excited about a new high-tech process called Animotion. To invest in the company, all Homer has to do is go down to his local mall and see a broker at IPO Friday's. The episode clearly makes fun of Homer's gullibility as an investor, but at the same time it suggests how the average American now feels in touch with the cutting edge of high-tech developments. In its ongoing celebration of "smallness," *The Simpsons* links small business to the small town, implicitly rejecting the symbiosis between big business and big government that was at the heart of 1960s liberalism.

Indeed, like most science fiction since Wells, *Star Trek* automatically assumed that the future would be in the hands of "bigness." Putting its faith in scientific elites and large-scale government projects, the series clearly believed that central planning would be the wave of the future. As it turned out, several of the high-tech innovations the show projected a century into the future were brought about within just over a decade, precisely because they were developed in the private, not the public, sector. It was not staffs of government scientists but computer entrepreneurs such as Steve Jobs and Steve Wozniak, the founders of Apple, who brought computers into the hands of the common man. *The Simpsons* of course has the benefit of hindsight in recognizing the importance of the entrepreneurial spirit in contemporary

America, but that is just the point. Released from the mesmerizing spectacle of the Cold War, the series was freer than *Star Trek* to see that national governments may not play the most important role in people's lives and that small businesses might have a greater impact on their existence than the massive, centrally planned projects that nation-states all over the world took to promoting in the 1960s, from urban renewal to hydroelectric dam construction.[125]

◆

The X-Files shares with *The Simpsons* this sense that, with the Cold War over, politics in general and the nation-state in particular have lost their centrality in people's lives. Both shows display skepticism toward the claims of scientific and intellectual elites to be able to run people's lives better than they themselves can. They raise doubts about the 1960s liberal vision of government intervention throughout society. To be sure, *The X-Files* is even more negative about business than *The Simpsons*. It tends to portray corporations as sinister, showing them taking over people's lives, sometimes poisoning them or otherwise experimenting on them in dangerous ways, and in general exploiting the public. A good example of this tendency is an episode called "Brand X" devoted to the evils of the tobacco industry.[126] But however *The X-Files* may evaluate corporations, it shows them playing a role in the world equal to that of national governments, and perhaps even greater. The international conspiracy that dominated the series for several seasons in many ways felt more like a multinational corporation than the United Nations (though both forces seemed at various times to be involved). *Star Trek* does not pay much attention to the power of corporations.[127] It is so taken with the centrality of nation-states that the real "business" in *Star Trek* is transacted between governments and especially their diplomatic representatives. There are of course still nation-states in the world of *The X-Files*, and they do have dealings with each other. But characteristically the series tends to show nations not dealing with each other through formal diplomatic channels. The deals in *The X-Files* take place in the shadows, and it is seldom clear if a given player is representing his or her nation-state or not.

In its emphasis on interplanetary diplomacy, *Star Trek* reflected the ideological clarity of the Cold War era. One side represents one principle and the other side represents a different principle, and episode after episode works to bring the two sides to the bargaining table as representatives of their planetary interests. The series was evidently taken with the defining event on the international scene in the 1960s— the summit meeting. In many ways the 1960s summit meeting constituted the apogee of the nation-state's hold on the world's imagination. The image was that representatives of the two most powerful nations on Earth (the United States and the Soviet Union) would sit down together and settle the fate of the planet. The very notion of the summit meeting embodied the ideology of the nation-state at its most absolute. All the power of a people could be centralized in a single figure, who would speak and deal for the nation as a whole. Notice that this conception cuts across ideological lines. Whether the summiteer comes from a democratic or a totalitarian regime, he still centralizes its power. The interplanetary summit meetings of *Star Trek* mirrored the 1960s sense that the fate of people lies completely in the hands of their national governments and their representatives.

The X-Files breaks with this Cold War image of power centralized in and radiating from national governments. Its image of power is a web, not a center.[128] What is most uncanny about the series is that we never know who is making the decisions that determine the fate of the world. As we have seen, the show demotes the traditional representatives of national power, such as presidents and congressmen. Instead, it suggests that the fate of the world may rest in the hands of some obscure figure, such as a chess-playing child prodigy or a woman who turns out to be the first successful alien-human hybrid.[129] Moreover, the threats to the world may come from any direction in *The X-Files*.[130] Something that happens in a remote research station in the Arctic or on the tundra of Siberia may have the potential to destroy life on Earth as we know it.[131] During the Cold War, people thought that they could easily tell where the threats in their world were coming from. For Americans, the real danger emanated from the communist nations. The world of *The X-Files* has lost this comforting sense of clear polarities. As Chris Carter himself describes the situation: "With the Berlin Wall down, with the global nuclear threat gone, with Russia trying to be a market economy, there is a growing paranoia because . . . there are no easy villains anymore."[132]

This statement may seem counterintuitive. One would think that with the end of Cold War hostilities, the whole world could breathe a collective sigh of relief. But Carter makes a valid point. In a sense, it is easier to deal with threats that can be clearly identified and located. What is hardest to deal with is a threat that may suddenly materialize out of nowhere. *The X-Files* portrays a kind of free-floating geopolitical anxiety that follows upon the collapse of the clear-cut ideological divisions of the Cold War. The world used to be divided into sharply demarcated armed camps, which was in its own way a frightening prospect, but one people learned to live with. *The X-Files* presents a post–Cold War world that, far from being polarized in terms of nation-states anymore, is interconnected in all sorts of clandestine and sinister ways that cut across national borders. That any point on the globe may be connected with any other point is of course a paranoiac's fantasy—or rather nightmare.[133] The central image of threat during the Cold War was a nuclear explosion—destruction that starts at a clear central point and spreads outward. The central image of threat in *The X-Files* is infection—a plague that may begin at any point on the globe and spread to any other—thanks to international air travel and all the other globalizing forces at work today.

The image of power as a web is of course appropriate for a series that continually features the Internet and hence the aptly named World Wide Web. As we have seen, *The X-Files* presents the Internet as its primary example of how power has been decentralized and diffused in the world of the wired generation.[134] Put computers in the hands of ordinary people and they suddenly have the resources to resist the efforts of big government to run their lives. For the creators of *Star Trek*, given the state of technology at the time, computers did not seem capable of playing this role. Before the silicon chip era, when computers had to be large, only big governments and big corporations could own them. Thus *Star Trek* tends to present the computer as necessarily a centralizing force in society, a way for a powerful center to control all points on the periphery. Several episodes deal with societies run tyrannically by a computer, and Kirk has to break its grip, usually by confusing the computer and getting it to destroy itself.[135] Kirk may be a science fiction hero, but he comes across as a raging cybernetic Luddite, leaving a trail of trashed computers behind him in the galaxy. But that is as it should be according to *Star Trek*, which in general presents the computer as the great enemy of human freedom. The series embodies the Orwellian view of technology as the greatest prop of the totalitarian state. As we have seen, *The X-Files* often adopts this Orwellian perspective, but it also recognizes how dramatic new developments in technology—above all, the miniaturization of computers—have altered the balance of power between the government and the individual. The show celebrates the newfound power of the hacker to penetrate any computer fortress the government may erect, but it goes further. The one kind of businessman likely to be presented in a positive light in *The X-Files* is the computer entrepreneur.

In several episodes, the show makes heroes out of computer geniuses, precisely because they are portrayed as rebels against the system. A first-season episode, "Ghost in the Machine," deals with Brad
Wilczek, the founder of a high-tech company named Eurisko, who
goes off on his own after a dispute with its CEO. Wilczek is the inven-
tor of an artificial intelligence that has gotten out of control and is
killing off anyone who tries to interfere with its operation. He helps
Mulder and Scully destroy the AI, rather than let it fall into the hands
of the government, which will, he is sure, misuse its power. A similar
episode called "Kill Switch" in the fifth season deals with a "Silicon
Valley software pioneer" named Donald Gelman. In what may have
been a jab at Al Gore, Mulder says of Gelman: "He invented the Internet." When Scully seems skeptical, Mulder corrects himself: "All right,
he didn't quite invent it. But he's a Silicon Valley folk hero. He was
writing Internet software even before there was an Internet." The Lone
Gunmen are even more in awe of Gelman than Mulder: "Jobs and
Wozniak at Apple. Gates and Allen writing BASIC. The Homebrew
Computer Club's first meetings—Gelman was there. Now they're
power brokers and billionaires. Back then they were all just inspired
nerds." Though *Star Trek* celebrates individual inventors, it never presents them as businessmen, as *The X-Files* does here. To be sure, given
its basic anticapitalist bias, the series is careful to distinguish Gelman
from the run-of-the-mill businessman; as one of the Gunmen says:
"Gelman was a visionary, not a capitalist. A subversive." And to show
his subversiveness, the episode portrays Mulder and Scully destroying another murderous artificial intelligence with help provided by
Gelman (who has been killed by his own software program). The businessman can be a hero in *The X-Files* only if he fights the system and
helps to reduce the control that technology exerts over people's lives.
Typically, the series shows computer geniuses forced to destroy their
own creations. (By contrast, *Star Trek* typically shows Kirk destroying
somebody else's computer invention.) The *X-Files* computer episodes
reflect the ambivalence toward technology we have seen throughout
the series. But however it may evaluate the individual achievements
of computer entrepreneurs, it shows them playing an extremely important role in the contemporary world, a role that makes them equal
to national government figures in shaping people's lives and perhaps
even superior.

Thus, like *The Simpsons*, *The X-Files* does not show economics subordinate to politics, the way *Star Trek* did in the 1960s. And also like
The Simpsons, it relates this shift in hierarchy to the end of the Cold

War. In fact, *The X-Files* shows more clearly than *The Simpsons* what a blow the end of the Cold War was to the power of nation-states—it removed one of the chief props by which they maintained the allegiance of their citizens. In "Musings of a Cigarette-Smoking Man," the chief representative of government conspiracy in the show greets the news "Gorbachev has just resigned" with alarm: "There's no more enemies." *The X-Files* portrays national governments at a loss once they no longer can frighten their citizens into submission with the bugbear of foreign threats. In "Dreamworld II," a comic episode from the sixth season, *The X-Files* satirically suggests the lengths to which governments will go to fill the ideological vacuum left by the end of the Cold War.[136] The comic bad guy of the episode, Morris Fletcher, is a kind of PR man for secret government projects at the notorious Area 51. In a meeting with the Lone Gunmen, he makes fun of their paranoia, and in particular their obsession with the danger posed by Saddam Hussein. Contemptuously holding up their newsletter and its headline: "Saddam Tests Mandroid Army in Iraq Desert," Fletcher decides to reveal a profound government secret: "There's no Saddam Hussein. This guy's name is John Gilnitz. We found him doing dinner theater in Tulsa. Did a mean *King and I*. Plays good ethnics." To the amazed Lone Gunmen, Fletcher goes on: "I'm saying I *invented* the guy! We set him up in '79. He rattles his saber every time we need a good distraction." This episode is obviously a comedy, and the exposure of Saddam as an invention of the American government is meant to be part of the fun. But the line between the comic and the serious in *The X-Files* is always thin, and the joking revelations about Saddam link up with claims made in all earnestness elsewhere in the series—which add up to the idea that governments use the specter of foreign enemies to keep their own citizens in line.

Thus *The X-Files* does not just show that the Cold War is over—it strongly suggests that it never happened. That is, the show completely reinterprets the conflict, developing the idea that the hostility between the United States and the Soviet Union was largely an illusion, fostered by both governments to maintain their power domestically. *The X-Files* effectively rewrites history from the 1940s to the 1990s. As we have seen, *Star Trek* more or less accepts the "official" American version of events since World War II. The show looks back upon World War II as a "good" war, in which the United States clearly represented the side of right. The show also views Americans as standing for justice vis-à-vis the Soviets in the Cold War. *Star Trek* starts to become revisionist only when it gets to the Vietnam War. It questions whether

188 ◆ Gilligan Unbound

Americans were justified in intervening in what it presents as internal affairs in Southeast Asia. But insofar as *Star Trek* suggests that America was in error in Vietnam, it presents the intervention as an aberration. The United States betrayed its basic principles (the Prime Directive) and for once strayed from the just path in the international arena. *The X-Files* portrays the Vietnam War even more negatively than *Star Trek* did, dealing with the issue of U.S. military atrocities against civilians, but even more importantly, the later series chooses not to isolate Vietnam as an aberration in U.S. foreign policy.[137] On the contrary, *The X-Files* views U.S. involvement in Vietnam as entirely consistent with what it regards as the nation's militaristic behavior on the international scene since World War II. The show is not quite willing to attack the notion that World War II was a just war.[138] As we have seen, *The X-Files* repeatedly evokes the stereotype of the evil Nazi and implies that it was good that the United States triumphed over its Axis enemies in World War II. But in the Anasazi trilogy and elsewhere, the show suggests that something went wrong with U.S. policy immediately after the war, as America compromised itself by making deals with German and Japanese scientists. And *The X-Files* is extremely cynical about every American military involvement since World War II, whether the Vietnam War, the Gulf War, or the Cold War itself. The show suggests that all these military enterprises were undertaken to promote not the cause of democracy but rather the interests of the military-industrial complex. In effect, *The X-Files* uses its alien mythology to write a secret history of the Cold War. In the terms of the series, what ties together all the U.S. military adventures in the second half of the twentieth century is the theme of alien invasion. For example, it suggests that UFOs have been shot down in both Vietnam and the Persian Gulf.[139] In that sense, the very improbability of stories of UFOs and alien invasions serves the deeper political agenda of *The X-Files*. What better way to suggest the fictionality of the Cold War than to link it up with fantastic stories of space aliens and their plot to conquer the Earth?

◆

Thus, in the mythological terms of *The X-Files*, the problem of "running out of west/running out of Indians" takes the form of "running out of aliens." For its first few seasons, the show tantalized its audience with the question of whether extraterrestrial beings really exist. At times the aliens seemed to be fabrications of the U.S. government, part of a plan, for example, to conceal sinister military experiments behind cover stories of alien flying saucers. Finally, in the fifth season, in an episode called "Redux," *The X-Files* hit its viewers with the startling revelation that the whole alien conspiracy story was a giant hoax put over on Mulder. A Defense Department official named Kritschgau takes Mulder into his confidence and explains to him the truth about the extraterrestrials he has been searching for. Appropriately, Kritschgau's revelation takes the form of a rewriting of the Cold War:

> This is the hoax into which you have been drawn. The roots go back fifty years, to the end of World War II. Playing on a virulent national appetite for bogus revelation and a public newly fearful of something called the atom bomb, the U.S. military command began to fan the flames of what were being called "flying saucer stories." There are truths which can kill a nation, Agent Mulder, and the military needed something to deflect attention away from its arms strategy: global domination through the capability of total enemy annihilation.

Kritschgau develops the idea that the financial interests of the military-industrial complex fueled the creation of the Cold War: "When the Russians developed the bomb, the fear in the military was not for safety at home, but for armistice and treaties. The business of America isn't business, Agent Mulder. It's war. Since Antietam, nothing has driven the economy faster."[140]

Thus Kritschgau presents the Cold War as an illusion, staged for the benefit of a gullible American public:

> We need a reason to keep spending money, and when there wasn't a war to justify it, we called it war anyway. The Cold War was essentially a fifty-year public relations battle. A pitched game of chicken against an enemy we did not much more than call names. The Communists called us a few names, too. "We will bury you," Khrushchev said, and the public believed it. After what McCarthy had done to the country, they ate it with a big spoon. We squared off a few times, in Korea and Vietnam. But nobody dropped the bomb. Nobody dared.

Here *The X-Files* develops explicitly the theme of the moral equivalency of the United States and the Soviet Union that we saw *Star Trek* merely flirting with.[141] Finally, Kritschgau claims that stories of UFOs played right into the hands of the U.S. military-industrial complex:

> The military saw a good thing in '47 when the Roswell story broke. The more we denied it, the more people believed it was true. Aliens had landed—a made-to-order cover story for generals looking to develop the national war chest. . . . I can't tell you how fortuitous the timing of it all

was. Do you know when the first supersonic flight was, Agent Mulder? 1947. Soon every experimental aircraft being flown was a UFO sighting.

With Kritschgau's revelation, *The X-Files* seems to be putting Mulder and itself out of business, debunking its own basic premise. But of course his story turned out to be a hoax itself, just another attempt to deceive Mulder and divert him from his investigation into the authentic alien conspiracy.

And yet one cannot simply dismiss "Redux" and the story Kritschgau tells. The producers would hardly have had him go on at such length and in such analytic detail if they did not regard the ideas he voices as important. Though specific details of his account may have been false in the terms of the series, his overall view of how the Cold War functioned in the American imagination is close to the truth as *The X-Files* wishes to present it. In the deepest sense, from the series' viewpoint, it does not really matter if aliens truly exist or not, because the series has always tried to show that the business of the nation-state is to manufacture aliens. To begin with, the state has an alienating effect. In its attempt to impose economic and bureaucratic rationality on its citizens, it alienates them from their ethnic heritage, their regional ties, their communal traditions, and above all their myths—which the nation-state views as an archaic source of irrationality that must be eliminated for the sake of progress. As *The X-Files* repeatedly shows, the underclass of a nation-state feels alienated from its mainstream, never fully integrated into its economic and social life. This problem is compounded for immigrants, who are always made to feel alien by the mainstream, unless they are willing to abandon completely the culture of their homelands. In short, the wide range of monsters in *The X-Files* is generated by the alienating logic of the modern nation-state.

But the connection between the nation-state and the monstrous alien goes deeper than this in *The X-Files*. The nation-state does not merely produce aliens as a by-product of the modernization process that in many respects is its reason for existing. The nation-state needs aliens—so much so that one can truly say that if they did not exist, it would have to invent them. The nation-state thrives on nationalism, and nationalism rests on a feeling of "us" versus "them." The nation-state in fact defines its identity against a background of aliens, generating its citizens' sense of what is native to them by generating a contrasting sense of what is foreign. Moreover, by playing off one group of alienated people against another—for example, the underclass against the immigrants—the nation-state prevents its citizens from uniting against it. That is why the end of history is an ominous development for the nation-state. If it runs out of enemies, it seems to lose its fundamental reason for existence.[142]

Thus it is apt in the terms of *The X-Files* that the first sightings of flying saucers began shortly after the end of World War II and the whole phenomenon of belief in extraterrestrial beings is historically bound up with the Cold War.[143] Just as the possibility of global conflict among nation-states was being foreclosed, people turned to outer space to find a new source of enemy aliens. Whether nation-states actually encouraged this development I would not presume to say, but *The X-Files* suggests that it was in their self-interest to do so. At the very least it is remarkable how closely the issue of outer space became bound up with Cold War issues in the decades after World War II. We have seen this link in every show we have looked at—*Gilligan's Island, Star Trek*, and *The Simpsons*—and it is also present in a number of *X-Files* episodes.[144] The space race became a focal point of U.S.-U.S.S.R. rivalry, and nationalist sentiments were powerfully engaged in the process. Time and again the conquest of space was offered as the new alternative to traditional forms of armed conquest here on Earth. H. G. Wells may have been the first to spell out this logic. As early as 1898, in *The War of the Worlds*, he was suggesting that someday humanity might have to unite against a foe from another planet, a theme picked up in countless science fiction stories ever since. In the film Wells made with the Korda brothers, *Things to Come* (1936), humanity, exhausted by decades of world war, turns to peaceful technological progress, culminating in an effort to send a rocket to the moon. In the American Apollo missions, life imitated art and indeed in the 1960s the nation-state sought a new justification for itself under the banner of space exploration. The imperialist ring of all the talk of conquering space was unmistakable. Forbidden by a newly emergent international legal framework and more importantly by geopolitical realities from conquering each other, the nations of the world—at least the richer ones—turned to outer space as a new realm for their expansion. The fact that no actual aliens have responded to the various space missions since the 1960s does not lessen the imperialist impulse behind these activities, which have in fact drawn upon exactly the sort of nationalist tendencies that engage people in terrestrial warfare. And of course in books, movies, television, and now videogames, science fiction has supplied all the enemy aliens the human imagination can handle.

But the specter of extraterrestrial beings has not been confined to the fantasy plane. Actual federal government agencies such as NASA

192 ◆ Gilligan Unbound

have played a game that comes perilously close at times to science fiction and the "invention" of aliens. Faced with dwindling interest in space on the part of the American public and, what is worse, the threat of dwindling budgets, NASA has searched for threats from outer space to justify its claim on the pockets of U.S. taxpayers. NASA has not gone as far as to raise the specter of little green men, but it has trumpeted the slightest evidence for life on other planets—speaking of course only of the existence of mere microbes, but knowing full well that when NASA speaks of "life on Mars," the American public thinks it is hearing "intelligent life on Mars"—which is to say . . . little green men. A spate of movies and television documentaries about killer comets and doomsday asteroids is one more reflection of the need to find new threats that can be countered only by the massive efforts of the nation-state.[145] If U.S. missiles and other advanced weaponry are no longer needed to combat enemies on Earth, perhaps they will someday be the only defense against marauding meteors from outer space. NASA and its supporters have seriously invoked the need to develop countermeasures against large extraterrestrial objects on a collision course with Earth as a justification for spending more federal tax money on space research and development. There may well be genuine scientific evidence in the geological past for earthly catastrophes with extraterrestrial causes, but one cannot help thinking that NASA scientists are very much living in the present and in effect promoting such stories in a way that serves their self-interest in a federal agency.

Just as we saw *The Simpsons* do in "Deep Space Homer" (#1F13, 2/24/94), in an episode called "Space" *The X-Files* shows NASA obsessively concerned with its budget and its image on television. The agency is prepared to send astronauts off on a mission that may have problems rather than risk a delay that would be a public relations embarrassment. For *The X-Files*, like *The Simpsons*, the sheen is off the U.S. space program.[146] Rather than celebrating its importance, as *Star Trek* did, *The X-Files* views NASA as just one more government agency somehow implicated in the worldwide alien conspiracy. In "Space," Mulder becomes progressively disillusioned with a former astronaut who was his childhood hero. Eventually he learns that the man, who is now controlling the space launch, has been possessed by some kind of alien spirit. This plot twist becomes the way *The X-Files* raises doubts about the motives of the space program, suggesting that it is serving something other than the interest of the American public. In general, *The X-Files* seems to be rooted in an awareness of how science fiction—

especially stories of alien threats—can serve the ideological interests of the state rather than of the people. Increasingly unable to offer itself as protection against the Red Menace from Russia, the U.S. government must set itself up as the only thing standing between its citizens and the Menace from the Red Planet. *The X-Files* began with the seemingly absurd claim that there is a connection between the power of the U.S. federal government and stories of UFO crashes in places such as Roswell, New Mexico. Whatever one may think of the narrative the show has developed to link these phenomena, it has succeeded in establishing an ideological connection—that the governments of nation-states somehow generate their power by creating "aliens"—of all kinds, domestic, foreign, and, if need be, extraterrestrial.

◆

The X-Files has developed its extraterrestrial aliens into an extraordinarily complex symbol over the years, embodying the many ambiguities of the nation-state. The aliens are emblems at one and the same time of the nation-state, its victims, and the threats to its existence. As an advanced technological civilization seeking to conquer the Earth, the aliens serve as a nightmare image of the nation-state and its drive to universal modernization and domination (domination *through* modernization). With their endless alien "probes," their ruthless experimentation on human beings, and their maintaining files on every U.S. citizen through their proxies in the Syndicate, the extraterrestrials represent bureaucratic rationality at its worst. The idea of the aliens symbolizing the nation-state is reinforced by linking them to government officials in countries all around the globe, who by aiding and participating in their schemes reveal how familiar in fact these seemingly alien activities are—indeed nothing more nor less than the daily functioning of government bureaucracies already established on Earth.

But for all their sinister technological power, when the aliens actually surface in *The X-Files*, they tend to appear more as victims than as oppressors.[147] We hear of Deep Throat and the Cigarette-Smoking Man executing aliens gangland-style in order to hide their existence from the American public. As we have seen, the Anasazi trilogy hints at some form of horrible holocaust of alien-human hybrids carried out by the U.S. government, with the results appropriately buried on Indian land (where other U.S. atrocities lie covered up). In the few glimpses we get of the extraterrestrials on the show, they appear to be physically frail, a point underlined by the fact that the scurrying aliens are played by children.[148] *The X-Files* links the aliens to traditional victims of the nation-state, such as ethnic minorities or supposedly inferior races—they are, after all, "aliens." Like Jews, they have evidently been subject to the heartless experiments of Nazi scientists. The U.S. government has apparently been studying them for years, and when we see them, they tend to be stuffed into test tubes, beakers, or other laboratory apparatus that symbolize the power of science to imprison humanity. In *The X-Files* the aliens are just as likely to be the victims of modern science as its masters.

Thus, in the fate of the aliens in *The X-Files*, we see the power of modern science turning in upon itself and in effect becoming self-destructive. Like the imperialist nation-state, technological science recognizes no boundaries to its power and seeks to universalize its sway. No one and no thing is exempt from its scrutiny or immune to its power. Thus the weapons the aliens use—especially their medical probes—can be turned against them. The term "alien autopsy" is profoundly ambiguous in *The X-Files*; it can mean aliens performing autopsies on abducted humans or aliens having autopsies performed upon them by government scientists.[149] The way science can backfire and the technological regime recoil upon itself is stressed in the fate of the Syndicate. Just as the aliens are destroying each other as the result of a mysterious split in their ranks, the conspiracy gradually kills off its own members as conflicts develop over how their plans are proceeding. Finally, in an episode called "One Son," as the Syndicate gathers to meet the long-anticipated alien act of colonization, they are wiped out en masse by the extraterrestrial rebels. As the mirror image of the mass murders the conspirators have been responsible for in the past, their holocaust seems like just retribution, but it again suggests the way technological power is indiscriminate and can easily turn back upon its masters. Recurrent images of genocide haunt *The X-Files*—the extermination of American Indians, Nazi death-camps, massacres of civilians in Vietnam. The series links these horrors to the nationalism and imperialism of the nation-state, and suggests, as evidenced by much twentieth-century history, that the only true mass murderer is the state. But at the same time the show suggests that the murderous power of the state can be turned against it, and he who lives by the holocaust may well die by the holocaust. In that sense, the aliens, while symbolizing both the masters and the victims of the state, also represent the greatest threat to its continued existence—the fact that the state's power—and especially technology—can eventually be used against it.

The central paradox of the nation-state in *The X-Files* is the ambiguity of power. The show repeatedly asks: Who really has the power, the state or some other force? And when it comes to technology more specifically, *The X-Files* asks: Does it give the state total control over its citizens or give them a new way of fighting back? These uncertainties are mirrored in the ambiguous status of the aliens. At times they appear to be all-powerful, able to take over and rule the Earth at a moment's notice. But at other times, their plans can be thwarted by a few human beings such as Mulder and Scully, and as individuals, they appear to be almost pitifully vulnerable and threatened with the extinction of their race themselves. The same may be said of the conspiracy with which *The X-Files* links the aliens. At times the Cigarette-Smoking Man seems to have unlimited power, capable of ordering anyone in the federal government to do his bidding (and even fixing the Super Bowl, according to the "Musings" episode).[150] But we then learn that even he has his superiors and acts on orders, and as the plot of the series unfolded, he became an increasingly vulnerable figure (though not necessarily more sympathetic). The Cigarette-Smoking Man has come to embody the dialectic of power that is at the heart of *The X-Files*—he who rules is somehow enslaved, and he who threatens is himself threatened by the very forces he seems to command.

All these patterns may be read as an allegory of the ambiguous status of the nation at the end of the twentieth century. From one point of view, the state appears to be omnipotent, or at least stronger than it has ever been in history. Whether under totalitarian or democratic regimes, the nation-state vastly expanded its strength during the twentieth century, largely as a result of its newfound military might and all the technological advances that entailed, which placed unprecedented powers, especially of destruction, in the hands of government officials. For example, the ability of the state to spy upon its own citizens reached an unparalleled degree of sophistication in the twentieth century and this unfortunately seems to be just as true of democratic as of totalitarian nations. Increasingly, it has become impossible for ordinary citizens to escape the scrutiny of their national governments in the most intimate aspects of their daily lives. But even as the nation-state began to look all-powerful from certain angles, chinks began to develop in its armor and it started to look impotent from others. As business globalizes, nation-states are losing control over what used to be relatively isolatable as their domestic economies. With the freer flow of international capital, national governments have become less free to set their own tax, monetary, interest rate, and trade policies. The very technologies that governments have used to maintain control over their citizens have been turned against them. The computer revolution has made possible new methods of offshore banking, tax havens, money laundering, and other means of avoiding government intrusion in economic life. As we enter the twenty-first century, the power of free markets is poised against the regulatory power of national governments on all sorts of fronts, and no one can yet tell which force will prevail.[151]

In short, the power of the nation-state seemed to reach its apogee in the twentieth century, and indeed by the end of the century, the one remaining superpower, the United States, seemed capable of projecting its military might all over the globe with remarkable speed and effectiveness. And yet at just this moment, a variety of theorists, approaching the issue from different angles, have begun to speak of the decline and perhaps the fall of the nation-state.[152] I hesitate to add the voice of *The X-Files* to this serious and complicated debate, and yet I think that the show has been addressing precisely these issues and has something valuable to say about them. Despite—or precisely because of—its bizarre conspiracy theories and convoluted plotlines, *The X-Files* has in effect portrayed the dialectic of omnipotence and impotence of the contemporary nation-state. Compared to its predecessors among forms of community, the nation-state appears all-powerful. Tribes, ethnic groups, religious sects, regional loyalties, cultural backwaters—all seem unable to resist the relentless march of the nation-state to incorporate every aspect of society and every individual under its rule. Above all, the nation-state seems to have progress on its side and to be the wave of the future. It claims to be the very engine of progress, especially in its role as champion of science, technology, and economic rationality. For the sake of modernity—in particular free trade and the division of labor—people had to give up their local interests and participate in the larger community of the nation. For all its use of the big stick, the nation-state had many carrots to dangle in front of its citizens, and it is doubtful that it could have developed and maintained their loyalty if it had not in some ways improved their lives, especially in economic terms. Let us not forget that, whatever else may be said about the nation-state, its historical role was to put an end to feudalism and many of the worst abuses of the old regime.

As the engine of modernization, the state was able to draw people out of their local communities, interests, and allegiances and into the larger life of the nation, but its victories may ultimately prove to be Pyrrhic. The very logic of modernization leaves no reason for the process to cease at the national level. The nation-state looks all-powerful compared to the communities that preceded it, but what of new forms of organization that may succeed it? Do they perhaps demand the dissolution of the nation-state, or at least a substantial weakening of its power? For example, in purely economic terms, the nation-state emerged in order to facilitate free trade among its citizens, but why should free trade stop at national borders? The logic of free trade—and the division of labor it reflects—demands the internationalization of free trade and the division of labor.[153] This is exactly what happened in the economic globalization that dominated the last decades of the twentieth century, which, with periodic setbacks, appears to be continuing and broadening. In the face of global economic forces, individual nation-states are increasingly compelled to allow markets to dictate their policies, rather than dictating policies to markets, as they attempted to do in the heyday of various forms of socialism in the twentieth century or the Keynesianism that was the equivalent of central planning in the supposedly free economies of the West. As economic organization progressively takes the form of globalized free markets, nation-states begin to lose much of their reason for existence and also find the scope of their authority greatly reduced.[154] In short, progressive in comparison to smaller and simpler forms of community, the nation-state may turn out to be reactionary in comparison to the larger and more sophisticated forms of organization that are emerging in the globalized markets of today. Far from marking the end of history, the triumph of the nation-state in the twentieth century may eventually appear to be equivocal from the point of view of later historians. Someday they may look back at the nation-state as the way station between the purely local markets of the medieval world and the fully globalized markets of the third millennium.[155]

I do not for a moment offer this as the view of history *The X-Files* takes. The show is too left-wing to be this sympathetic to the development of free markets, and it generally views capitalism as part—if not the heart—of the problem of the nation-state, and surely not the solution. The show seems to view globalization not as an alternative to nationalization, but as its extension and hence an even more sinister process. But I offer this view of globalization as another way of conceptualizing the process *The X-Files* is portraying in its mythological terms. In the logic of rationalized modernity, the nation-state unleashes forces that it cannot control and that then work to undermine its power. The very science and technology the nation-state employs to master its citizens may in the end prove to be its undoing. However the producers themselves interpret the process, *The X-Files* portrays the nation-state caught between the past and the future, between the traditional forms of community that it worked to displace and new forms of organization that are working to dissolve the integrity of its borders. Poised between more local and more global conceptions of community, the state can offer no cogent reason for settling for the halfway measure of national borders. Some will argue for the globalization of government and turn to international organizations such as the UN to move beyond the nation-state. Others who think that the problem with nation-states is not the limitation of their power but its extent will turn to the spontaneous order of free markets as the wave of the future. In any case, *The X-Files* suggests that the nation-state, far from gloriously presiding over the end of history, is in a very precarious position, challenged from below and above.[156] As the show repeatedly suggests, the nation-state has not fully succeeded in annihilating and transcending earlier forms of community. Its unassimilated underclass and immigrants are testimony to the resilience of the atavistic forces of myth and tradition in resisting the seemingly relentless march of modernity. At the same time, the increasing globalization of the world weakens the nation-state's ability to police its borders and define its separate identity. What the ultimate outcome will be of the contradictory pressures working on the nation-state at this moment of history *The X-Files* cannot show, and it would indeed be presumptuous of anyone to attempt to be prophetic in such a complex matter. But one thing is clear in *The X-Files*—at the end of the twentieth century, the nation-state is in trouble. In running out of west, it may be running out of time.

Conclusion:
"There's No Place Like Home"

In the episode that began the sixth season of *The X-Files*—aptly called "The Beginning"—a scene set at the Rolling Hills Nuclear Power Plant features a dozing control-room operator abruptly awakened by a co-worker in the following exchange: "Wake up, Homer." "I was awake—I was thinkin'." "Yeah. That'd be a first." The show thereby paid tribute to its sister series on Fox, returning on November 8, 1998, a compliment that *The Simpsons* had already paid *The X-Files* on January 12, 1997, with its "Springfield Files" episode. It seems only appropriate that the two shows that made the Fox Network's reputation should have acknowledged each other's existence with these cross-references. But we are now in a position to see that the connections between *The Simpsons* and *The X-Files* go deeper than an occasional nod or two in each other's direction.[1] In terms of the themes they deal with, the two shows are remarkably similar, though one treats its material comically and the other tragically.

As we have seen, both *The Simpsons* and *The X-Files* grow out of a thoroughgoing disillusionment with and cynicism about American politics, and especially politics at the national level. Both reflect a decline in the importance of the nation-state in the lives of Americans, in part because both reflect a distinctly post–Cold War atmosphere, in which the American government no longer seems as necessary to protect its citizens from foreign enemies. *The Simpsons* and *The X-Files* also show Americans as having become media savvy and thus aware of how the government and other forces try to manipulate and control public perception of domestic and international affairs. The two shows portray Americans developing an increasing sense that the center of their existence—if it has a center anymore—is somewhere other than Washington, D.C. In particular, *The Simpsons* and *The X-Files* trace the impact of globalization on their characters. They explore how life in any locale in America, no matter how seemingly isolated, may at a moment's notice be transformed by the impact of events happening halfway across the earth, whether it be Homer's image appearing in a Japanese TV commercial or radioactive sewage from Chernobyl producing a mutant monster in New Jersey (in "The Host" episode of *The X-Files*).

As the contrast between these particular episodes suggests, *The X-Files* tends to dwell on the sinister aspects of globalization, while *The Simpsons* tends to present the process as benign if not positively benevolent. That is one reason the two shows are so sharply contrasted in tonality. Though *The X-Files* has had its share of humorous moments, it is basically one of the darkest shows ever to appear on American television, whereas *The Simpsons*, for all the serious issues it raises, is lighthearted and comic in spirit. *The X-Files* concentrates on the way the globalization of America poses a threat to its citizens, chipping away at their confidence that their lives are within their own control and leaving them with a diminished sense of possibility. By contrast, *The Simpsons*, though it occasionally looks at the dark side of globalization, generally emphasizes the wide range of new options it is opening up for the American people. Despite a patriotic gesture now and then, the show does not look back with nostalgia to the days when Americans still had more or less unquestioning faith in their national government. On the contrary, the show stresses the liberating effects of political cynicism. Thrown back on their own resources, the citizens of Springfield do quite well for themselves, finding all sorts of avenues for fulfillment within their local community, without reference to the nation-state. For one thing, as we have seen, they can turn to religion, a force that can add meaning to their lives independently of the state. Above all, they can turn to the nuclear family, which, as we have seen, is shown to be strengthened in the show as the power of the nation-state weakens. I have argued that localization is ultimately more important than globalization in *The Simpsons*; in either case, the decline in the importance of the nation-state seems to lead to a richer life for the citizens of Springfield.

By contrast, *The X-Files* presents the loss of a national center in American life as a disturbing and problematic development. Unlike *The Simpsons*, it concentrates on the unnerving and disorienting aspects of globalization, which explains why the show images it in the sinister form of an international conspiracy and an alien invasion. I wish I had time to explore more fully the *inner* drama of *The X-Files*, the way it explores the transformation of the American psyche at the end of the twentieth century, but that would require another whole book. I will have to confine myself to a brief look at two related issues in the series: religion and the family. One of the surprising parallels between *The Simpsons* and *The X-Files* is the way both shows portray Americans turning to religion in the wake of the decline of the nation-state. *The X-Files* continually dwells upon the heartlessness and sterility of global modernity, and presents the remaining national allegiances in the world as purely a matter of rational calculation and hence soulless. In this spiritual vacuum, religion acquires a new power in the lives of Americans, or rather regains an old one. As we have seen in the immigrant episodes, *The X-Files* repeatedly pits the scientific rationality of the nation-state and its bureaucratic apparatus against various forms of prenational and subnational spirituality—from voodoo cults to Native American shamanism. In its very conception, *The X-Files* is open to the idea that paranormal, mythic, and even supernatural forces have a genuine role to play in human life and that rational science cannot provide us with all the answers to our fundamental questions. In contrast to the relentlessly secular 1960s *Star Trek*, *The X-Files* still sees room for the gods in the universe.

And yet, for all its embrace of archaic myth as an alternative to modern rationality, *The X-Files* seems incapable of picturing the mythic as anything other than *monstrous*, thus raising doubts about the forces it seems to want to champion. *The Simpsons* generally presents religion as a benign power. Though the show frequently finds something fanatical and unbalanced in religious belief, it also portrays a kind of flattening out of religious differences as part of the whole process of globalization. Even the very Protestant Reverend Lovejoy says of religions: "They're all pretty much the same," and as we have seen, in a pinch he is willing to perform a Hindu wedding ceremony. In *The Simpsons* religion is not a particularly divisive force, and indeed, the ready availability of all the world's religions in Springfield—recall Homer in his avatar as Ganesh—seems ultimately to be just one more example of the globalized consumer culture the show chronicles and in effect celebrates. The people of Springfield seem to choose a religion the way they would a car, open to any of the myriad possibilities the whole world now offers the informed consumer. In general, *The Simpsons* presents religion not as a counterforce to globalization, but as part of the process.

By contrast, in *The X-Files* religion still seems to represent a genuine alternative to the rationalist worldview, and as such, it offers a principle of cultural differentiation in the increasingly homogenized world of global modernity. But precisely because religion stands for something truly different in *The X-Files*, it often takes on a sinister and threatening aspect, or at least proves to be a profoundly disruptive force. Whereas in *The Simpsons* religious belief tends to make a character part of a larger community, in *The X-Files* it tends to separate people from the mainstream. This is even, and perhaps especially, true in the *X-Files* episodes that treat religion as a domestic phenomenon in the United States. A number of episodes deal with the resurgence of Scully's religious faith, episodes that are particularly significant because she originally represented the pole of scientific rationality in the series.[2] Scully is pointedly presented as a Catholic, and hence not part of the Protestant mainstream in the United States. *The X-Files* has even hinted at parallels between Scully's Catholicism and the archaic and exotic religious beliefs the show tends to associate with immigrant populations. And, as positively as Scully's faith may be portrayed, *The X-Files* also shows something profoundly disturbing about her religious experiences; they certainly work to unsettle her life and her role on the X-Files team.

Thus, although *The X-Files* is clearly trying to find a place for religious experience in modern life, it has a hard time integrating that experience into the modern world. Even when the show presents religion as an American rather than a foreign phenomenon, it tends to present religious believers as outside the American mainstream. Faith healers, charlatans, doomsday prophets, charismatic preachers, evangelical missionaries—they all repeatedly appear in *The X-Files* as profoundly disruptive of the American community.[3] A seventh-season episode called "Theef" presents a hillbilly from Appalachia practicing what coauthor Frank Spotnitz calls "a sort of homegrown voodoo or American voodoo" to gain his revenge on a California doctor he thinks was responsible for his wife's death.[4] The episode is remarkably similar in conception to the immigrant episodes we examined, as it pits the supernatural power of folk magic against the scientific power of modern medicine. "Theef" is a good example of the way we have seen *The X-Files* link immigrant experience with that of the American underclass. Like Patrick Crump in "Drive," the villain Peattie in "Theef" represents the dispossessed and disadvantaged in the United States—scorned by the American establishment (embodied in the person of a well-respected, upper-middle-class physician, who hardly knows he exists). "Theef" reminds us of how difficult it is to distinguish the immigrant from the "true" American. When Mulder refers to Peattie's magic as "Celtic" or "Scots-Irish," he points to the fact that the inhabitants of Appalachia are descended from immigrant stock themselves, and the episode implies that, like the Chinese Americans, African Americans, and Mexican Americans we discussed, they have never fully assimilated into the United States mainstream. "Theef" thus might be regarded as another "immigrant" episode in *The X-Files*, and indeed it displays the same ambiguity we saw in episodes such as "Teliko" and "El Mundo Gira." The show would like to be sympathetic to cultural difference and is profoundly suspicious of cultural homogeneity, and yet at the same time it tends to portray cultural difference as monstrous and hence threatening.

In short, *The X-Files* never seems to be able to take an unequivocal stand either for or against the American mainstream, in religion or in any other area. Another religious episode in the seventh season, "Signs and Wonders," deals with a phenomenon far outside the American mainstream: snake handlers—believers who prove the strength of their faith by their ability to touch poisonous snakes unharmed. But although for much of the episode we are led to believe that an overzealous Pentecostal preacher is responsible for the crime in a small Tennessee community, eventually we learn that the really sinister figure in town is the liberal, mainline Protestant minister—indeed, at the end he appears to be the devil himself. The ambivalent treatment of religion in *The X-Files*—the fact that religion is constantly presented as both a form of salvation and a form of threat—reflects the larger ambiguity about the globalization of modernity in the show as a whole.

Indeed, in contrast to *The Simpsons*, *The X-Files* presents the processes of globalization and localization as in tension with each other. Despite some sense that globalization might create problems for Springfield, particularly in the episode about Apu as an illegal alien, *The Simpsons* tends to portray the new global and local interests of the Springfielders as fundamentally in harmony. The Simpsons as well as other characters in the show have an easy time assimilating the global into the local, basically because globalization chiefly takes the form of a globalized marketplace in the series and markets have a way of getting people to minimize their differences and to learn to deal with each other. For all its local prejudices, Springfield is a remarkably inclusive community—which is another way of saying that *The Simpsons* is fundamentally comic in spirit, showing people working out their differences, rather than fighting to the death over them. I hesitate to dignify *The X-Files* by calling it "tragic" in conception—the show is after all *not*

Shakespeare—but it does repeatedly show globalization leading to the kinds of conflicts of irreconcilable differences that Hegel labeled "tragic." In *The X-Files* globalization creates clashes between people representing principles that are fundamentally opposed, for example, the principle of scientific rationality and the principle of religious faith—hence principles that cannot easily be reconciled and that often do lead to a fight to the death. To the extent that *The X-Files* is tragic, it deals with tragedies of nonassimilation, of people (or creatures) who feel that they would have to sacrifice their identities, especially their cultural identities, in order to fit into a community at heart alien to them. Like tragic heroes, they would in fact rather die than abandon and betray the ways in which they differ from the ordinary people around them. Time and again in *The X-Files*, the monstrous alien must be destroyed, and in particular be prevented from reproducing, or it might penetrate and overwhelm the mainstream community. The show tends to portray the community as fundamentally exclusive, unwilling to assimilate the alien into its ranks. The characters in *The Simpsons* continually learn to split their differences—that is why the show is fundamentally comic. The characters in *The X-Files* are instead continually split by their differences—that is why the show is fundamentally tragic.

One can see this contrast between the two shows in their treatment of one specific theme—the family. Perhaps the most remarkable parallel between *The Simpsons* and *The X-Files* is the fact that at the center of both shows stands a dysfunctional nuclear family. This is obvious in the case of *The Simpsons*, but in the case of *The X-Files*, one must for the moment block out the horror and science-fiction elements, and recall that over the years the series has obsessively kept returning to a domestic drama—the story of the Mulder family, Bill Mulder and his wife, and their children Fox and Samantha. And despite the fact that the well-educated and upper-middle-class Mulders appear at first sight to be far more respectable than the Simpsons, in the end the central family in *The X-Files* turns out to be more dysfunctional than their cartoon counterparts. As we have seen, the "dysfunctional" Simpsons actually function quite well as a family, largely because they always stick together and resist attempts by outside forces, including the state, to interfere in their lives. This is precisely what the Mulders fail to do. *The X-Files* presents them as martyrs to the process of globalization. Bill Mulder's involvement as a U.S. State Department official in national and international affairs proves to have disastrous consequences for his family. The worldwide conspiracy concerning the alien invasion has the effect of breaking up and destroying the Mulders as a family unit. Forced by the Syndicate to offer up one of his children as a hostage to ensure his silence about their scheme, Bill Mulder chooses Samantha rather than Fox and thereby permanently alienates his wife (from whom he is eventually divorced). In psychological terms, the heart of *The X-Files* is Fox Mulder's quest to find his lost sister and thus to reunite and re-create his nuclear family. Unfortunately for him, his search has exactly the opposite effect—the more he learns about his family history and its dark secrets, the more he discovers that his "happy family" was a sham, artificially held together by guilt rather than love. In a sense, globalization and the nuclear family are the two poles between which both *The Simpsons* and *The X-Files* move, but the former shows them comically compatible and the latter tragically at odds. In *The Simpsons* the nuclear family is presented as the bedrock of life, the one thing on which people may unconditionally rely. In its tragic counterpoint to the comic *Simpsons*, *The X-Files* revolves around an absent nuclear family—one that no longer exists and maybe never really did. Whereas the nuclear family is a source of fullness in *The Simpsons*, in *The X-Files* it is presented as hollow at the core.

To be sure, the second central family in *The X-Files*—the Scullys—is much happier than the Mulders and in its own way tightly knit. And yet, Dana ends up being indirectly responsible for the death of her sister Melissa, and her commitment to the FBI creates many tensions in her family. In general the show portrays domestic values threatened by forces outside the family. (This is especially true in the third main family in the series, the Spenders—the Cigarette-Smoking Man, his wife, and his son.) As FBI agents, both Mulder and Scully put work ahead of family, and their devotion to duty seems to be standing in the way of either one having a family of his or her own. (The tension between Scully's FBI career and her aspirations to motherhood is an ongoing theme in the series.) Being able to reconcile family and nondomestic obligations seems to be part of the comic vision of *The Simpsons*, and accordingly the Simpson family takes globalization in stride. By contrast, in *The X-Files* the forces that draw people out of the family and lead them beyond its limits threaten to poison the happiness of the family and perhaps even to destroy it. In *The Simpsons* it seems possible to have your global cake and eat it locally, too. But *The X-Files* continually presents tragic choices, and in particular the achievement of globalization seems to require the sacrifice of all local interests and concerns. Global modernity is built upon the subversion and destruction of all smaller communities, including the nation-state.

That is why *The X-Files* tends to present globalization as a sinister force, something that undermines the values of religion and the family. At times *The X-Files* seems to be suggesting that the minute you step outside of the safety and comfort of the nuclear family, you are doomed to a life of permanent alienation.

And yet even on the issue of the nuclear family, *The X-Files* maintains its characteristic ambivalence. In a way, the most serious charge the show makes against globalizing modernity is that it undermines the nuclear family, as epitomized by the effect the worldwide conspiracy has on the Mulders. But in an episode coyly entitled "Home," *The X-Files* delivered the most devastating critique of the nuclear family as a unit of human organization since Greek tragedy was in its heyday and works such as Aeschylus's *Oresteia* or Sophocles' *Oedipus tyrannos* were being staged. First broadcast on October 11, 1996, "Home" may not be the best *X-Files* episode, but it surely is the most remarkable, and perhaps the most remarkable hour of television ever to make it onto the airwaves in America. Like a Greek tragedy, "Home" tells a grim story of incest and infanticide. It chronicles the existence of the Peacock clan—three virtually subhuman brothers, one of whom, it turns out, sired the other two on their deformed and crippled mother. The product of generations of inbreeding, the Peacocks have developed every genetic defect humanity is subject to, and as the episode opens they are burying alive the latest fruit of their incestuous behavior. The discovery of the corpse of this mutant baby draws Mulder and Scully to the town of Home to investigate the case. Even they, who, like Macbeth, have supped full with horrors, are shocked by what they discover.

The X-Files usually is devoted to criticizing modernity, but in "Home," it pauses to consider the alternative, and for once ask: What would the world be like if modernization and globalization had never taken place, if people had simply remained within the confines of the family unit? The answer is the Peacocks, brutal savages, who mercilessly kill to protect their lair from outsiders. Mulder aptly describes them: "What we're witnessing, Scully, is undiluted animal behavior. Mankind, absent its own creations of civilization, technology, and information, regressed to an almost prehistoric state, obeying only the often savage laws of nature." As we have seen, *The X-Files* often questions the values of "civilization, technology, and information," but here it suggests that they are essential to our humanity. If man had not moved beyond the nuclear family, he would have remained an animal. "Home" exposes the pitfalls of clinging to the past and especially of romanticizing the past, and above all any kind of primitive past. In the town of Home, the episode conjures up an image straight out of America's past, a kind of Norman Rockwell vision of the virtues of American small-town life. After its horrific opening sequence, "Home" seems to turn sentimental, serving up the most nostalgic of all American images—kids playing sandlot baseball. But their home plate conceals a gruesome secret—that is where the Peacocks have buried the grotesquely deformed baby, and its tiny hand projecting out of the dirt soon brings the American national pastime to a halt.

Even Mulder gets caught up in the mood of small-town nostalgia with which the episode begins. Paying no attention to Scully's investigative inquiries, he launches into an evocative fantasy of his boyhood days, significantly linked to his ongoing obsession with Samantha:

> God, this brings back a lot of memories of my sister. All-day pick-up games out on the Vineyard. Ride our bikes down to the beach. Eat baloney sandwiches. Only place you had to be on time was home for dinner. Never had to lock your doors. No modems, no faxes, no cell phones.

We see here how Mulder's clinging to his memories of his sister embodies whatever resistance to modernity he still harbors. Scully notes the irony of his nostalgia: "Mulder, if you had to do without a cell phone for two minutes, you'd lapse into catatonic schizophrenia." As usual in *The X-Files*, "Home" contrasts a simpler past with the complexities of the modern technological world, but from the beginning it raises the question whether we really want to do without the technology that admittedly complicates our life, but may enrich it as well.

The Peacocks somehow manage to survive without modern technology. As the local sheriff explains, they live in an old farmhouse (built during the Civil War). The Peacocks have resisted not just globalization but any forces that would lead them out of the self-sufficiency of the family unit. As the sheriff points out, "They grow their own food. Raise their own pigs. Breed their own cows." But unfortunately this seemingly admirable independence passes over easily into their horrifying incestuous way of life, as the sheriff goes on to hint: "Raise and breed their own stock—if you get my meaning."[5] It soon emerges that the Peacocks have only carried to an extreme a tendency endemic to all the citizens of Home—the urge to shut out the external world and try to remain true to their indigenous ways. The sheriff is himself a partisan of Home:

> Look, this town is my home. It's peaceful. I don't even wear a gun. I've seen and heard some of the sick and horrible things that go on outside

my home. At the same time, I knew we couldn't stay hidden forever. That one day the modern world would find us and my hometown would change forever.

"Home" thus presents a typical *X-Files* dilemma—the town avoids many of the negative aspects of modern life, but the price it pays for its peacefulness is its utter lack of progress. The sheriff realizes that when he calls in the FBI to investigate the infanticide, he risks losing his traditional way of life, but he still hopes that it may be preserved: "I'd like it if the way things are around here didn't have to change." But even the tradition-bound sheriff ought to be open to change. Ironically the fact that he does not carry a gun makes him easy prey for the Peacocks when they come to kill him and in fact brutally club him and his wife to death.

The sheriff's name is Andy Taylor—the same name as the sheriff played by Andy Griffith in his 1960s sitcom about life in a rural North Carolina small town. And the sheriff's deputy is named Barney—just like Barney Fife in *The Andy Griffith Show*. Mulder cannot resist drawing the parallel when Scully uncovers evidence that the buried baby was murdered: "There's something rotten in Mayberry." In "Home" *The X-Files* found a brilliant way of criticizing American nostalgia for the past—the show presents it as specifically *television* nostalgia, a fantasy return to the image of the small town created in a 1960s sitcom. As we have seen, *The Simpsons* self-consciously evokes the ideal of the American small town made popular in 1950s and 1960s sitcoms, and (with some twists) chooses to reaffirm it. *The X-Files* is more suspicious of the television past and seems to suggest that we must move beyond it—that perhaps its idyllic images covered over buried horrors. As the oblique comment of a 1990s TV show on a show from the 1960s, "Home" sums up everything we have been examining in this book. It hints that, however attractive an image of America 1960s TV created, it was hiding something—it was not telling the whole truth about the United States.[6]

As so often happens in *The X-Files*, television itself becomes one of the central symbols in "Home." Forced to stay in a dilapidated motel, Mulder finds himself struggling with a relic of the technological past—a black-and-white TV that seems incapable of showing anything but old-fashioned nature documentaries. To make matters worse for Mulder, he has to fiddle with an antiquated antenna just to get any image on the screen at all. Whatever the attraction of Home may be, it does not include the greatest of modern inventions in Mulder's eyes—

cable TV. When Scully sarcastically harks back to his initial nostalgia for the small town—"You still planning on making a home here?"—Mulder replies: "Not if I can't get the Knicks game." Evidently globalization has its positive aspects even for Fox Mulder, the sworn enemy of the worldwide conspiracy. Even with the prospect of living in a town where, as the sheriff explains, "everybody knows everybody, pretty much" and no one has to lock his door, Mulder is not prepared to sacrifice his precious legacy from modernity—the ability to follow his home team's fortunes anywhere around the globe.

"Home" offers a nightmare image of a world utterly without globalization, a world in which the first steps out of the confines of the nuclear family have never even been taken. The Peacock household is frozen in time, filled with objects out of the past—fading photographs of the family and old newspapers (one with the headline "Elvis Presley Dead at 42"). The family remains mired in past history, still talking about the Civil War (which Mama Peacock pointedly refers to as "the War of Northern Aggression"). In a skirmish with Mulder and Scully, two of the Peacock boys are killed, but the eldest, Edmund, escapes with his mother. When Scully says: "In time, we'll catch them," Mulder adds: "I think time already caught them." And yet, when we last see the Peacocks, even they seem to have adapted to the changing world, as the mother proclaims: "But now we have to move on. Start a new family—one we'll be proud of. And find a new place to call ours. A new home. A brand-new home." Our final glimpse of the Peacocks is a quintessentially American scene, already familiar to us from other *X-Files* episodes—they have in fact hit the road, as Edmund drives the family Cadillac off into the night, with his mother safely stowed in the trunk. Perhaps their first purchase will be a cell phone, or, even better, a mobile home. The Peacocks seem to be entering the world of American trailer trash, a realm we have already seen *The X-Files* explore in episodes such as "Drive," and indeed the Peacocks seem to have much in common with the Crumps, or the Peatties for that matter. For all its sympathy with the American underclass, *The X-Files* seems to take a dim view of its southern branch, whether it gets caught up in its ancestral roots or becomes uprooted and pursues the life of the road. "Home" starkly and unforgettably embodies the two poles between which *The X-Files* continually moves—the Home and the Road, the world of pure fixity and the world of pure mobility. One either stays at home and risks the dangers of stasis and stagnation, or one ventures forth into the larger world to confront the equally perilous challenge of change.

I end with "Home," not because I think it is the definitive *X-Files* episode and provides us with all the answers to the questions the series raises, but because, in counterpoint to other episodes, it suggests the show's genuine complexity, especially when it comes to the issue of globalization. I do not want to give the impression that this one episode is offering a simple lesson to the *X-Files* audience: "Globalize, or you'll end up like the Peacocks—and, besides, even they learned to move on." "Home" is in fact unusual among *X-Files* episodes in its dark portrayal of the nuclear family. The series is more likely to portray globalization as the sinister force, and precisely insofar as it undermines the family. Nevertheless, "Home" has an important place in *The X-Files* as a whole for the way it suggests that the nuclear family, left to itself, is not the simple answer to the human problem. For all its doubts about globalizing technology, for once the show poses the question: What would the world be like without cell phones, modems, fax machines, and all the other paraphernalia of mobile modernity? Would it really be a better place? The answer at least of this episode seems to be "Not necessarily."

"Home" thus raises serious doubts about the great counterforce to globalization—the human propensity to remain content with any particular stage of development and to resist any attempts to go beyond it. The episode reminds us that at some point in the dim past the human race essentially had to be dragged kicking and screaming out of the warm embrace of the nuclear family. Our greatest memorial to this primeval moment is Greek tragedy, which shows that no less than the power of the divine had to be brought to bear to break the stranglehold of the family on human life. In a work such as Aeschylus's *Oresteia*, we see humanity struggling to move beyond the family as a principle of organization—to attain the rule of civic institutions in the Greek polis. But once constituted, the city proved resistant to the further development of human organization into nation-states. We are perhaps witnessing a similar moment of transition today, as the nation-state is yielding grudgingly and hesitantly to more advanced modes of organization (whatever they may turn out to be). As always happens in history, people have become used to the nation-state and in effect feel comfortable with it—indeed, most people now think of it as their "home." Hence they have a hard time seeing beyond the nation-state and are inclined to view it as the culminating point of human organizational development, and thus proclaim its seeming worldwide triumph as the end of history. But if one goes back to the not-so-remote past, one realizes that the nation-state has its own history, and if it had a beginning in time, it may yet have an end. As *Star Trek* suggests, perhaps someday a successfully globalized humanity will balk at its next step—the move beyond the planet Earth into the depths of interstellar space. Ultimately, what I read out of "Home" is the lesson that once humanity takes its first tentative steps out of the clutches of the nuclear family, there may be no stopping point in the restless expansion of its liberated energies, despite the perennial and powerful nostalgic urge to look back to "simpler" and "happier" days. The episode suggests that, however attractive the principle of self-sufficiency or autarchy may be, in the end it offers a blueprint for stagnation and a dangerous turning inward of the human spirit.[7]

But, once again, I do not mean to offer "Home" as the last word *The X-Files* has to say on the subject of globalization. It is only one of many *X-Files* episodes, and as we have seen, the show raises at least as many doubts about globalization as it does about the alternative. For that matter, I do not mean to offer even *The X-Files* as a whole as the last word on globalization. I do not believe that there is a last word on globalization, especially while the process is so obviously still going on. My purpose in this book has been to set up a dialogue in American popular culture on the subject of globalization, to which I hope each series I have discussed—even *Gilligan's Island*—has contributed. It was never my expectation that I would be able to come up with a definitive answer to the question of whether globalization is good or bad. As I said at the beginning, my own inclination is to say that, as the ultimate extension of the principle of the division of labor, globalization is on the whole a positive development for humanity. But I see sufficient crosscurrents and cross-purposes at work in globalization today to remain skeptical about the outcome, and my doubts are only deepened by the complexities I see revealed in the way globalization is portrayed in popular culture. This is one area where I think popular culture has much to teach us. Television is itself the product of many of the economic and social forces driving globalization and has in turn accelerated and broadened the process. It is not surprising, therefore, that globalization has emerged as a theme in some of the most interesting and important TV programs of the past few decades. I realize that discussing only four of those shows comes nowhere near exhausting the subject, but if I have succeeded in opening up the question of globalization with my commentary on *Gilligan's Island*, *Star Trek*, *The Simpsons*, and *The X-Files*, then in my view this book will have accomplished its goal.

Notes

INTRODUCTION

1. I have in fact rewritten all of the essays for the purpose of this volume and they differ significantly from the earlier published versions. However, at the risk of some repetition, I have tried to preserve something of their original self-contained character so that readers should be able to begin at any point that particularly interests them.

2. Or one might argue, for example, that the popularity of *Hogan's Heroes* (1965–71)—a sitcom grotesquely set in a German prisoner-of-war camp in the 1940s—suggests an emotional distance from World War II already in the 1960s not evident in either *Gilligan's Island* or *Star Trek*.

3. For a good overview of the topic of globalization, I would recommend—in addition to a number of books cited in my *X-Files* chapter—John Tomlinson, *Globalization and Culture* (Chicago: University of Chicago Press, 1999). The September 23, 2000, issue of *The Economist* (Vol. 356, No. 8189) is devoted to the subject of globalization and contains many useful articles on the subject.

4. See Kenichi Ohmae, *The End of the Nation State: The Rise of Regional Economies* (New York: Free Press, 1995) and Jean-Marie Guéhenno, *The End of the Nation-State*, trans. Victoria Elliott (Minneapolis: University of Minnesota Press, 1995).

5. For an excellent treatment of globalization in modern literature, see Michael Valdez Moses, *The Novel and the Globalization of Culture* (New York: Oxford University Press, 1995).

NOTES ON METHOD

1. Unless otherwise indicated, all books and essays referred to in this section are cited in full at appropriate points in subsequent chapters.

2. Paul A. Cantor, "Jurassic Marx: Cultural Studies Discovers the Dinosaur," *Weekly Standard* 4, No. 1 (25 January 1999): 35–39.

3. Champions of Cultural Studies are sometimes sensitive to this charge. Stuart Hood and Thalia Tabary-Peterssen, in their well-known book *On Television*

214 ◆ Gilligan Unbound

(London: Pluto Press, 1997), become defensive on this issue: "The view that comedy shows cannot be dismissed as 'only entertainment', and that to invite audiences to laugh at certain jokes is to ask them to collude in sexism and racism, invokes the charge of being a tiresome, humourless, niggling espouser of political correctness (itself an easy and common target for ridicule)" (25). But despite their acknowledgment of this standard concern about Cultural Studies, Hood and Tabary-Petterssen do very little to allay it in the course of their book. Indeed, later in the same paragraph, they show their underlying hostility to humor by stating baldly "that comedy is probably always unfair" (25). What is astounding—and also, alas, fairly typical—about this book as an example of Cultural Studies is that Hood and Tabary-Petterssen purport to write a history of British television without showing any interest in its artistic achievements—for example, such pathbreaking series as *The Prisoner* and *The Avengers*. Indeed, Hood and Tabary-Petterssen display little if any sympathy for television as an entertainment medium. For them television is basically a tool in the class struggle; as they themselves write: "The authors make no apology for considering these and other related matters from the Left of the political spectrum" (ix). Hence they are interested in television chiefly as a medium for news broadcasts, talk shows, and social documentaries. That anyone might *enjoy* television seems to strike them as a violation of its fundamental reason for existing. *On Television* is an excellent example of Cultural Studies as the New Puritanism.

4. Thomas S. Hibbs, *Shows about Nothing: Nihilism in Popular Culture from* The Exorcist *to* Seinfeld (Dallas, Tex.: Spence, 1999). I reviewed this book under the title "The Owl of Minerva and the NBC Peacock," in *American Enterprise* 11, No. 6 (September 2001): 57–58.

5. Paul A. Cantor, "Pro Wrestling and the End of History," *Weekly Standard* 5, No. 3 (4 October 1999): 17–22.

6. For the origin of the name, see Russell Johnson (with Steve Cox), *Here on Gilligan's Isle* (New York: HarperCollins, 1993), 90–91. Minow made his "vast wasteland" comment in a speech to the National Association of Broadcasters in 1961. Schwartz actually blames this speech for the fact that the three networks acquired control over TV programming in the 1960s: "Until his speech, the networks were conduits and they had no control of programming. Sponsors had more power, and the creative people who created the shows had more authority. Minow gave networks authority and placed the power of programming in the hands of three network heads, who, for a long time, controlled everything coming into your living room. They eventually became the de facto producers of all prime-time programs by having creative control over writing, casting, and directing" (91). As the producer of *Gilligan's Island* and later *The Brady Bunch* (1969–74), Schwartz probably knows as much about the TV business as anyone, and thus his view that FCC actions helped centralize power in the hands of the national networks must be taken into account in any understanding of the history of American television. For more on this subject, see Schwartz's own book, *Inside Gilligan's Island* (New York: St. Martin's, 1994), xv–xvi, 264–70.

7. There are of course further complexities to interpreting television series. One can legitimately raise the question of whether a given series does not just display minor inconsistencies but may in fact have fundamentally altered its character over time. For example, some critics have argued that *The Simpsons* has become

more mainstream over the years; they feel that the show was "edgier" in its early seasons and in effect moderated its satirical force in order to gain wider acceptance with the public. I briefly go into this issue in one of the notes in my *Simpsons* chapter. Similar questions have been raised about whether *The X-Files* went "mainstream" after its first season. TV series often end up in a "damned if you do, damned if you don't" situation—if they do not change over the years, critics complain that they have stagnated and gone stale; if they do change, critics complain that they have betrayed their original vision. On the whole, I believe that *The Simpsons* and *The X-Files* have over the years struck a good balance between a commitment to their original vision and a willingness to explore new possibilities.

There are special problems in discussing a TV series while it is still in progress. Some critics writing about *The X-Files* after its first season went out on a limb and stated categorically that one of the great virtues of the show is that it takes itself seriously and predicted that it would never resort to comedy. One critic (I do not wish to embarrass him by naming him) even said that what he liked about *The X-Files* is its determination to avoid the pitfalls of precious postmodernism. Of course, in later years *The X-Files* has become about as postmodern as television gets, and in its fifth season even entitled one episode "The Post-Modern Prometheus." As early as the second season, as soon as Darin Morgan began writing for the show (in "Humbug"), it started to offer some of the funniest moments ever seen on television, and David Duchovny in particular revealed that he is a brilliant comic actor. I confess that I feel particularly awkward writing about *The X-Files* during its eighth season, when the show has been struggling to do without the services of Duchovny. The quality of episodes has dropped, and what is worse, the show appears to have lost its creative momentum (some would say that this process of decline began earlier). Most of my career I have been writing about authors who have been safely dead for sometimes hundreds of years, thus giving us plenty of time to have sorted out their achievement. I am acutely aware of the difficulties in dealing with an artistic achievement that is still unfolding and that can literally change from week to week. But if one is going to come to terms with contemporary popular culture, one has to be willing to run certain risks.

8. Here is an example of the ongoing role of the creator of a television series—Mike Scully (head writer of *The Simpsons* and executive producer for several seasons) praises Matt Groening: "[He] cares as much about the show as he did in Season 1. *The Simpsons* is famous for its subversive humor, but there's always been a big underlying heart to the show that's as, if not more, important. And Matt is good at keeping the writers honest. If he thinks Homer is becoming too insane, he'll pull us back." See *TV Guide* 49, No. 6 (10 February 2001): 28. Of course, the creators of television shows tend to garner this kind of praise from the people who work for them, but there does seem to be at least some truth to this kind of comment, which one consistently hears about figures such as Groening and Carter.

9. The best discussion I know of the role of contingency in literary creation is Gary Saul Morson, *Narrative and Freedom: The Shadows of Time* (New Haven, Conn.: Yale University Press, 1994).

10. Among Foucault's many works, perhaps the most important for developing what has come to be known as the subversion/containment theory is *Discipline & Punish: The Birth of the Prison*, trans. Alan Sheridan (New York: Vintage, 1977). For good expositions of the Cultural Materialist position, see Jonathan Dollimore and

Alan Sinfield, eds., *Political Shakespeare: New Essays in Cultural Materialism* (Ithaca, N.Y.: Cornell University Press, 1985) and Jonathan Dollimore, *Radical Tragedy: Religion, Ideology and Power in the Drama of Shakespeare and His Contemporaries* (Chicago: University of Chicago Press, 1984). For the New Historicist position, see Stephen Greenblatt, *Renaissance Self-Fashioning: From More to Shakespeare* (Chicago: University of Chicago Press, 1980). I analyze the New Historicist position in detail and in particular criticize the subversion/containment theory in my essay "Stephen Greenblatt's New Historicist Vision," *Academic Questions* 6, No. 4 (Fall 1993): 21–36.

11. In a call for papers about *The Simpsons* issued in 1998 by John Alberti of the Department of Literature and Language at Northern Kentucky University, he sought treatments of "the possibilities of oppositional culture" in the show. (I do not know what became of this project.) Here are some of the questions he posed at the time: "How have cartoons and animation in general and *The Simpsons* in particular functioned as oppositional culture? How has the status of *The Simpsons* as 'cartoon show' given it greater satirical license and/or mitigated its satirical impact?" "What is the role of *The Simpsons* in fostering the appearance of an 'alternative' animation genre on television, from *Beavis & Butthead* to *South Park*? To what extent do these shows represent a dissemination of subversion or the co-optation of dissent, and can we tell the difference anymore?" Here we see the subversion/containment theory being applied to *The Simpsons*.

CHAPTER I

1. These reviews are cited with admirable honesty by Sherwood Schwartz, the creator/producer of *Gilligan's Island*, in his book about the series, *Inside Gilligan's Island* (New York: St. Martin's, 1994), 161. To be fair to Schwartz, he also cites several positive reviews of the show on 162–63.

2. Schwartz discusses the ratings of the show on 164–65. It was often in the top ten overall and consistently won its time slot.

3. I have taken information about the dates of television shows, here and elsewhere in this book, from Tim Brooks and Earle Marsh, *The Complete Directory to Prime Time Network and Cable TV Shows 1946–Present*, 6th ed. (New York: Ballantine, 1995), 398. *Gilligan's Island* consists of 98 episodes, produced over three seasons and originally aired on CBS from September 26, 1964, to September 4, 1967. I cite all episodes by title and number as listed in Joey Green, *The Unofficial Gilligan's Island Handbook* (New York: Warner, 1988) and Russell Johnson with Steve Cox, *Here on Gilligan's Isle* (New York: HarperCollins, 1993). I want to thank Hampden-Sydney College, and especially James Pontuso, for giving me my first opportunity to develop my thoughts on *Gilligan's Island* in a public lecture in 1989. I presented an earlier version of this paper at a panel on popular culture at the American Political Science Association Annual Meeting in Atlanta in September 1999.

4. One advertisement with Wells was for Western Union. One without any of the cast members but featuring Gilligan's image was part of the BBDO ad agency's "Hungry? Why Wait?" campaign for Snickers candy bars and centered on Gilligan's long-suffering and long-waiting fiancée. On this advertisement, see *TV Guide*, 1 May 1999, 9.

5. See *TV Guide*, 24 July 1999, 10.

6. The May 27, 2000, *TV Guide* offers a chart comparing the two shows in terms of such categories as "Accommodations" and "Sex" (24). The July 1, 2000, issue quotes an unnamed university professor saying that in the year 3000 "we're going to be watching *Gilligan's Island*—we're not going to be watching *Survivor*" (10).

7. For more on *Gilligan's Island* in popular culture, see Green, *Handbook*, 15.

8. See "'V' for Vitamins" (episode #66) and "Lovey's Secret Admirer" (episode #87).

9. For a brief overview of politics in the show, see Green, *Handbook*, 91–93; for the cast members' comments on "What kind of government is on the island?" see 96. Russell Johnson points out in his tell-all book about the show that its star Bob Denver "has a degree in political science from Loyola University" (*Isle*, 42).

10. As difficult as it may be to believe that any thought at all went into *Gilligan's Island*, its creator, Sherwood Schwartz, said: "There's a great deal of sociological implication in *Gilligan's Island*. It takes a group of very carefully selected people who represent many different parts of our society and shows how in a circumstance—being shipwrecked together—they have to learn how to get along with each other." See Green, *Handbook*, 3–4. In his own book about the show, Schwartz criticizes scholars who find meanings in *Gilligan's Island* but assume that they were not intended by its creator. He writes: "I know about the social content of my show, and that the seven characters were carefully chosen after a great deal of thought" (*Inside*, 167). Reading Schwartz's account, which contains references to Aristophantic Old Comedy and *commedia dell'arte* (*Inside*, 256), one is forced to reconsider how truly "mindless" *Gilligan's Island* was.

11. The name *Gilligan*, on the other hand, *is* a sort of accident; Schwartz admits to having picked it out of a phonebook (*Inside*, 16).

12. See "How to Be a Hero" (episode #23). Incidentally the Professor is not a professor but a high school science teacher, though he does have several advanced degrees, including an M.A. from SMU and a Ph.D. from TCU. See Green, *Handbook*, 51.

13. Schwartz says of this episode: "it dealt with the female Castaway's right to have an equal voice with the men. Male and female opinions were equally important" (*Inside*, 194). Schwartz denies that there was anything sexist about the show.

14. In the Miss Castaway episode Ginger does a Monroe-like performance of "Let Me Entertain You," and she clearly impersonates Monroe in "The Producer" (episode #72). On the association between the Ginger character and Monroe, see Schwartz, *Inside*, 141, and Johnson, *Isle*, 30, 60.

15. See "So Sorry, My Island Now," episode #15. Schwartz himself cites the parallel with the Kurosawa movie (*Inside*, 289).

16. As was episode #41, "The Sweepstakes," in which Gilligan again gets to play the part of a marshall.

17. The conventionality and indeed the worthlessness of money are stressed particularly in "The Big Gold Strike" (episode #9), "Three Million Dollars More or Less" (episode #13), "Plant You Now, Dig You Later" (episode #16), "The Sweepstakes" (episode #41), and "Agonized Labor" (episode #44).

18. When asked "Who was the island's leader?" the cast members did not agree that it was Gilligan; in fact each one gave a different answer and they ended up naming every castaway except Mary Ann. See Green, *Handbook*, 90.

19. This is Sherwood Schwartz's favorite episode; see Green, *Handbook*, 102. In his own book, Schwartz states the episode's theme as follows: "Democracy and freedom are precious, and one must fight, if necessary, to preserve them" (*Inside*, 291; see also 193).

20. In episode #83, "Gilligan Goes Gung Ho," the castaways elect Gilligan sheriff and he does let his new position of authority go to his head. Schwartz writes that this episode "illustrated the abuse of power in a democracy when the person in command is unaware of the responsibilities of office. . . . Gilligan almost wrecked the entire community because he didn't know how to interpret or administer the 'official rules' he was given. He became completely dictatorial as he exercised the power of office" (*Inside*, 192–93).

21. See Green's comment about the series: "Despotism results only from foreign invasion" (*Handbook*, 93).

22. For a diametrically opposed view of Gilligan's role, see Will Miller, *Why We Watch: Killing the Gilligan Within* (New York: Simon & Schuster, 1996), especially 64–66. Miller argues: "*Gilligan's Island* is about the repressed rage we feel at those inept, self-defeating fools around us. . . . Whenever you make a mistake that impedes another person . . . your 'Inner Gilligan' has risen up. Like Gilligan who . . . unintentionally destroyed the lives of six other innocent people, we all have been the cause of another's missed opportunities." This view is obviously true to the surface of *Gilligan's Island*, but it neglects what is going on beneath the surface. If all we felt toward Gilligan was rage, the show would never have achieved its popularity.

23. See "Three to Get Ready" (episode #29).

24. In fact, Schwartz reports that Kennedy was assassinated while the pilot for the series was being shot in Hawaii (*Inside*, 78–79).

25. See "The Sound of Quacking" (episode #7), "'V' for Vitamins" (episode #66), and "Pass the Vegetables Please" (episode #71).

26. For a fuller discussion of this point, see my *Creature and Creator: Myth-Making and English Romanticism* (Cambridge, U.K.: Cambridge University Press, 1984), 9, 14–17.

27. Jean-Jacques Rousseau, *The First and Second Discourses*, trans. Roger and Judith Masters (New York: St. Martin's, 1964), 150–51.

28. Rousseau, *Second Discourse*, 151.

29. The song was written by Sherwood Schwartz and George Wyle and was sung by the Wellingtons.

30. In one of the few "awards" ever won by *Gilligan's Island*, "The Producer" was chosen one of the 100 greatest television episodes of all time by *TV Guide*. For a brief discussion of this episode in light of the long tradition of *Hamlet* parodies, see my *Shakespeare: Hamlet* (Cambridge, U.K.: Cambridge University Press, 1989), 92. For an elaborate analysis of this episode, see Richard Burt, *Unspeakable ShaXXXpeares: Queer Theory & American Kiddie Culture* (New York: St. Martin's, 1998), 170–71, 181–89. This episode offers Ginger a good reminder of how repellant Hollywood can be. Hecuba behaves so obnoxiously that he provokes the normally even-tempered Mary Ann into an outburst: "Why should we be a servant to a self-centered, abusive, overbearing human being?" Drawing upon her Hollywood experience, Ginger sagely replies: "Mary Ann, that's the way producers are."

31. Schwartz states that the show focuses on "the problems of modern man dealing with primitive life" (*Inside*, 13).

32. See "Our Vines Have Tender Apes," episode #88.

33. See "Little Island, Big Gun" (episode #17) and "The Kidnapper" (episode #80).

34. See "Not Guilty" (episode #52), "And Then There Were None" (episode #81), and "Court-Martial" (episode #85).

35. See "Will the Real Mr. Howell Please Stand Up?" (episode #62), "Gilligan vs. Gilligan" (episode #70), and "All About Eva" (episode #82).

36. This was Schwartz's own conception of *Gilligan's Island*: "The various characters learning to live together because they *had* to live together was the core of the series" (*Inside*, 5). In his account, he has his wife Mildred reinforce this principle: "You said it's important to show that all sorts of people can learn to live together. . . . Because it applies to nations as well as to the Castaways. You said it was comedy on top and allegory underneath" (*Inside*, 9).

37. Schwartz offers a more cosmopolitan interpretation of the show: "It's not only a social microcosm, it's an international microcosm where eventually the Irish and the English have to learn to live together, where the Arabs and the Jews have to learn to live together, where the United States and Russia have to learn to live together—because we're all on the same island." See Green, *Handbook*, 10. Green begs to differ with Schwartz and points to the homogeneity of the castaways: "They still share major similarities: a common race, religion, ethnic origin, and nationality"—in short "seven WASPs stranded on an island" (*Handbook*, 10–11). Schwartz clings to his internationalist vision of the show in his own book: "The world, in a very real sense, is an island, where Americans and Russians, Arabs and Jews, Turks and Armenians, Irish and English, Afrikaners [sic] and Blacks, all must somehow learn to live together if they are to remain alive at all. Rich nations, poor nations, religious nations, godless nations, big nations, small nations, modern nations, backward nations, all exist on this same island we call Earth" (*Inside*, 13–14). Here Schwartz approaches the rhetoric of *Star Trek*. I have no doubt that Schwartz sincerely believes these principles, but the question remains: Where are they embodied in *Gilligan's Island*? Where, for example, are Arabs shown learning to live together with Jews? The series did not even show the castaways learning how to coexist peacefully with the natives on the island.

38. In addition to "The Producer," see "Angel on the Island" (episode #11) and "Erika Tiffany Smith to the Rescue" (episode #51).

39. For other episodes dealing with military technology, see "Gilligan's Living Doll" (episode #57) and "It's a Bird, It's a Plane, It's Gilligan" (episode #95).

40. "Don't Bug the Mosquitoes" (episode #48).

41. The fact that *Blair Witch Project* grossed over $140 million at the box office makes it the highest moneymaking independent film ever. For its use of the Internet in marketing, see John Horn, "The Blair Witch Myth: Why movie studios still don't get the Web," *Premiere* 4, No. 2 (October 2000): 67.

CHAPTER 2

1. I was first given the opportunity to reflect on these matters by the Political Science Department of Hampden-Sydney College, where I gave a lecture entitled

"Shakespeare Was a Klingon: *Star Trek* and the End of History" on February 18, 1991. I wish to thank James Pontuso in particular for this invitation. An earlier version of this chapter was published in *Perspectives in Political Science* 29, No. 3 (Summer 2000): 158–66.

2. See Ron Magid, "Directing the Last Hurrah," *Cinefantastique* 22, No. 5 (April 1992): 47. This issue of *Cinefantastique* is largely devoted to *Star Trek VI*, and contains much useful background information on the movie. On the relation of the movie to the end of the Cold War, see also 28, 46. For further Cold War parallels, see Mark Houlahan, "Cosmic Hamlets? Contesting Shakespeare in Federation Space," *Extrapolation* 36, No. 1 (Summer 1995): 30–31.

3. See Francis Fukuyama, "The End of History?" *The National Interest*, No. 16 (Summer 1989): 3–18, and *The End of History and the Last Man* (New York: Free Press, 1992).

4. See especially Alexandre Kojève, *Introduction to the Reading of Hegel*, trans. James H. Nichols Jr. (New York: Basic, 1969).

5. On the end of history in Hegel, see especially Kojève, *Hegel*, 160–61, and Fukuyama, "End of History," 64. Hegel's philosophy of history is obviously a very complicated matter, especially given the fact that his view of the French Revolution changed over the years. Moreover, Kojève's interpretation of Hegel is highly controversial. But my argument about *Star Trek* does not depend on the accuracy of any particular interpretation of Hegel. For analyzing the impact of the idea of the end of history on contemporary culture, what matters is not what Hegel meant by the notion but what it has come to mean in the discourse of writers such as Fukuyama. I doubt that anyone involved in *Star Trek VI* read Fukuyama; I am certain that no one involved read Hegel; but it is clear that the film was affected by the "end of history" debate, if only on the level of *Time* magazine reporting.

6. For a sampling of reactions to Fukuyama, see the responses that were published along with his original article in the Summer 1989 issue of *National Interest*. More responses were published in the Fall 1989 issue, and Fukuyama replied to his critics in the Winter 1989/1990 issue. See also Timothy Burns, ed., *After History? Francis Fukuyama and His Critics* (Lanham, Md.: Rowman & Littlefield, 1994) for a collection of essays responding to Fukuyama, as well as another reply from him. For the two senses of *end* in Fukuyama, see in this volume Gregory Bruce Smith, "The 'End of History' or a Portal to the Future: Does Anything Lie Beyond Late Modernity?" 14. For another collection of essays dealing broadly with the issues raised by Fukuyama, see *History and the Idea of Progress*, ed. Arthur Melzer, Jerry Weinberger, and Richard Zinman (Ithaca, N.Y.: Cornell University Press, 1995); this volume contains an essay by Fukuyama, "On the Possibility of Writing a Universal History" (13–34), that provides an excellent summary of his "end of history" thesis.

7. See Smith, "Late Modernity," 17 (note 11): "Many of those who attacked Fukuyama had been operating upon their own furtive, usually suppressed, End of History theses."

8. In the last years of the communist regime in the Soviet Union, it was fascinating to watch how the facade of representative political institutions gradually changed into a reality.

9. On this point, see Smith, "Late Modernity," 15–16 (note 3) and 21 (note 27).

10. As reported in *New York Times*, 24 September 1991, A14.

11. On this point, see Fukuyama, "Reflections on *The End of History*, Five Years Later," in Burns, *After History?* 239–40.

12. That this article of the Constitution was originally controversial is evident from the fact that no less a patriot than Patrick Henry attacked it at the Virginia Ratifying Convention on June 9, 1788: "Tell me not of checks on paper; but tell me of checks founded on self-love. The English Government is founded on self-love. This powerful irresistible stimulus of self-love has saved that Government. It has interposed that hereditary nobility between the King and Commons. . . . Here is a consideration which prevails, in my mind, to pronounce the British Government, superior in this respect to any Government that ever was in any country. . . . Have you a resting place like the British Government? . . . Where are your checks? You have no hereditary Nobility—An order of men, to whom human eyes can be cast up for relief: For, says the Constitution, there is no title of nobility to be granted." Quoted in Thomas L. Pangle, *The Ennobling of Democracy: The Challenge of the Postmodern Age* (Baltimore: Johns Hopkins University Press, 1992), 95.

13. The same point is made about the tribal people in "A Private Little War"—"Left alone they undoubtedly will develop a remarkably advanced and peaceful culture."

14. On this point, see my essay "Romanticism and Technology: Satanic Verses and Satanic Mills," in *Technology in the Western Political Tradition*, ed. Arthur Melzer, Jerry Weinberger, and Richard Zinman (Ithaca, N.Y.: Cornell University Press, 1993), 127.

15. Herbert F. Solow and Robert H. Justman, *Inside Star Trek: The Real Story* (New York: Pocket, 1996), report that this episode "was roundly criticized by some for being a heavy-handed attempt to preach" (400).

16. "The Devil in the Dark" is probably the best example of such episodes, but others include "Balance of Terror," "Arena," and "Is There in Truth No Beauty?"

17. Allan Asherman, *The Star Trek Compendium* (New York: Pocket, 1989), 120.

18. I am not suggesting that *Star Trek* was actually modeled on *Gilligan's Island*; I am just comparing the shows structurally to highlight their ideological differences.

19. Asherman details the parallels (*Compendium*, 40).

20. Fascist elements are also evident in the parallel universe episode, "Mirror, Mirror," which portrays a kind of anti-*Enterprise*, run like a police state.

21. Asherman points out that this episode incorporates film footage provided by NASA (*Compendium*, 101).

22. See "Balance of Terror" and "The Enterprise Incident."

23. "Spectre of the Gun" actually transports the *Enterprise* crew to the American Wild West, where they are forced to replay the gunfight at the O.K. Corral. In "The Paradise Syndrome," Kirk becomes a god to a tribe of primitive people who closely resemble American Indians.

24. See, for example, "A Taste of Armageddon," "Errand of Mercy," "The Day of the Dove," and "The Savage Curtain."

25. See, for example, "The Doomsday Machine," "The Changeling," "The Ultimate Computer," and "Assignment: Earth."

26. Asherman, *Compendium*, 90.

27. Asherman, *Compendium*, 90. Solow and Justman report on the ability of different viewers to decode the antiwar message of the episode: "Surprisingly, Stan

Robertson [the NBC Program Manager for *Star Trek*] never seemed to realize that the story was supposed to be an allegory about the growing 'police action' in Vietnam. In fact, no one at NBC made the connection and took us to task. But the audience did; we got letters. Lots of them" (*Inside Star Trek*, 356).

28. See Asherman, *Compendium*, 100.

29. A good example in 1960s popular culture of equating the United States and the Soviet Union is the Lennon/McCartney song "Back in the USSR" on the Beatles' *White Album*. This parody of the Beach Boys' "California Girls" features the line "Back in the U.S. Back in the U.S. Back in the U.S.S.R.," as if the two nations were indistinguishable.

30. The original plans for *Star Trek* included a South American named José Ortegas on the bridge. See Asherman, *Compendium*, 9.

31. Chekov was not part of the original *Enterprise* crew; he was added in the second season, in the fall of 1967. An NBC press release claimed that the part of Chekov was created in response to an article in the Soviet newspaper *Pravda* complaining about the lack of a Russian in what was supposed to be an internationalized crew. Although this story sounds suspiciously like a press agent's invention, it is confirmed in Asherman, *Compendium*, 69, and in Solow and Justman, *Inside Star Trek*, 343–44, who even print a copy of an October 10, 1967, letter explaining the addition of Chekov from the creator of *Star Trek*, Gene Roddenberry, to the editor of *Pravda*, Mikhail Zinyanin.

32. On the importance of this moment, see Houlahan, "Cosmic Hamlets," 30.

33. In terms of the central globalization metaphor of the film, this would be like asking if the United Nations is really run for the benefit of Americans only.

34. In *End of History* (82), Fukuyama notes this paradox about science fiction: it offers "a curious mixture of old social forms and modern technology, as when emperors and dukes fly between solar systems in space ships." Both the novel *Dune* and the *Star Wars* movies follow this pattern; it was quite prominent in the old *Flash Gordon* serials as well.

35. Ron Magid, "Designing the Final Frontier," *Cinefantastique* 22, No. 5 (April 1992): 55.

36. The nostalgia for an aristocratic past is clearest in "Space Seed," in which the *Enterprise* crew revive a tyrant literally out of Earth's past (from the 1990s!). They compare this would-be superman, Khan Noonian Singh, to earlier avatars of heroic greatness, such as Alexander and Napoleon. Khan himself says that if he had been given his way on Earth, "one man would have ruled eventually, as Rome under Caesar." Kirk and the others of course eventually turn against Khan, but they at first seem fascinated by his aristocratic charisma. Mr. Scott says: "I must confess, gentlemen, I've always held a sneaking admiration for this one." Even Kirk admits: "He was the best of tyrants." Spock is puzzled by "this romanticism about a ruthless dictator," but Kirk explains to the Vulcan: "Spock, we humans have a streak of barbarism in us—appalling, but true nevertheless." Thus "Space Seed" ends up stamping aristocratic pretensions as barbaric. Kirk formulates his ambivalence about Khan: "we can be against him and admire him, all the same." This comment provokes one of Spock's standard replies: "Illogical," but it actually goes right to the heart of the political logic of *Star Trek*. The show at times looks back nostalgically to the nondemocratic and heroic past, but it always reaffirms

the democratic and egalitarian future. In fact, this episode shows that the one most threatened by Khan's personal magnetism is a female historian assigned to the case; Dr. McCoy worries that Khan "could overpower McGivers, with her preoccupation with the past." Preoccupation with the past is dangerous in *Star Trek*, because the past is aristocratic. Psychologically, the most interesting aspect of this episode is that Khan is really a mirror image of Kirk, simply a heightened version of his aggressiveness and ambition (as well as his womanizing tendencies).

37. Hegel's writings on tragedy have been conveniently assembled (in English translation) in *Hegel on Tragedy*, ed. Anne and Henry Paolucci (New York: Harper & Row, 1962).

38. One image of the end of history for a particular species is provided by the television episode "The Gamesters of Triskelion." Kirk, Uhuru, and Chekov are whisked off the *Enterprise* to a planet on which they are trained for gladiatorial combat. The planet turns out to be ruled by three detached brains, beings who have evolved beyond their bodies. These creatures have developed mental superiority, once again taking the form of psychokinetic powers. The problem for these creatures is that with their advanced evolution, they have reached the end of history and have nothing to struggle for anymore. As Kojève predicts, the Triskelions have turned to pure gambling at the end of history—all they can do is risk money on gladiators chosen from what they regard as inferior species. As they say: "We have found athletic competitions our only challenge, the only thing which furnishes us with purpose." Kirk comes up with his typical criticism: "[that is an] unproductive purpose, unworthy of your intellect." Faced yet again with what he regards as an unproductive aristocracy, Kirk can only seek to undo this static world and return it to history. When the Triskelion brains tell Kirk that they use "only inferior species" in their games, he tells them: "We have found that all life forms in the galaxy are capable of superior development; perhaps you're not as evolved as you think." Kirk sets up a real wager with the Triskelions—if he defeats their gladiators, they must free all their slaves. Naturally, he wins, and thereby allows the slaves to develop what he calls "a normal self-governing culture." Committing the Triskelions to educating their former slaves, Kirk consoles them: "I think you'll find it a much more exciting game than the one you've been playing." By forcibly dragging the Triskelions back into history, and thus reinaugurating a kind of Hegelian dialectic of masters and slaves, this episode suggests that the end of history is inherently boring; all excitement disappears when the real struggle is over. This episode thus has ominous implications for the end of *Star Trek VI*.

39. See Kojève, *Hegel*, 162.

40. The Spring 1995 issue of *Extrapolation* (Volume 36) is devoted to the question of uses of Shakespeare in *Star Trek* in general and especially in *Star Trek VI*. It includes the essays by Prendergast, Buhler, and Houlahan cited elsewhere in these notes. For an intriguing analysis of how the use of Shakespeare in *Star Trek VI* relates to the issue of American imperialism, see Richard Burt, *Unspeakable ShaXXXspeares: Queer Theory & American Kiddie Culture* (New York: St. Martin's, 1998), 127–58.

41. III.ii.155–56. I quote Shakespeare from the Riverside edition, ed. G. Blakemore Evans (Boston: Houghton Mifflin, 1974). It is interesting that the film omits

the preliminary "For God's sake" from this speech by Richard. The film also mis-quotes Falstaff's line as: "Have we not heard the chimes at midnight?" The Fal-staff line is from *Henry IV, Part II*, III.ii.214; the Prospero line is from *The Tempest*, IV.i.148.

42. Allan Bloom, *Shakespeare's Politics* (New York: Basic, 1964), 23.

43. Or consider the problem pointed out by John Prendergast: "The Klingons do bleed, just like humans, but not the same blood." See his "A Nation of Ham-lets: Shakespeare and Cultural Politics," *Extrapolation* 36, No. 1 (Spring 1995): 16 (note 4).

44. On this subject, see my essay "Religion and the Limits of Community in *The Merchant of Venice*," *Soundings* 70, Nos. 1–2 (Spring/Summer 1987): 239–58, and also my essay "*Othello*: The Erring Barbarian Among the Supersubtle Venetians," *Southwest Review* 75, No. 3 (Summer 1990): 296–319.

45. See Burt, *Unspeakable ShaXXXspeares*, 136, 144.

46. Magid, "Directing," 48. Christopher Plummer is well known as a Shake-spearean actor (he once played Iago to James Earl Jones's Othello, for example). It is less well known that William Shatner, who played Captain Kirk, began his ca-reer as a serious stage actor; in fact, Magid reports ("Directing," 48) that Shatner once understudied to Plummer in a production of *Henry V* in Canada. The strange interweaving of Shakespeare and *Star Trek* of course continues in the "Next Gen-eration" series, in which the *Enterprise* is captained by the superb Shakespearean actor Patrick Stewart. One wonders whether Shatner had any thoughts of his "re-placement," Stewart, when in *Star Trek VI* he got to blast a pompous, Shakespeare-spouting actor out of the sky. On the relation between Plummer's character in *Star Trek VI* and Stewart's in the "Next Generation," see Houlahan, "Cosmic Hamlets," 32, and Stephen M. Buhler, "'Who Calls Me Villain?' Blank Verse and the Black Hat," *Extrapolation* 36, No. 1 (Spring 1995): 19. Incidentally, the fact that Shatner is Canadian (and Jewish) gives a certain irony to his successful portrayal of the all-American WASP hero, Kirk.

47. Ron Magid, "ILM's Effects Final Frontier," *Cinefantastique* 22, No. 5 (April 1992): 51. This concern for cultural literacy appears again in *First Contact* (1996), the first of the *Star Trek* movies devoted exclusively to the "Next Generation" crew. In this time travel story, a woman from the twenty-first century is trying to con-vince Captain Picard (who is from the twenty-fourth century) to abandon his ob-sessive efforts to save his beloved starship *Enterprise*. When all other means of curbing Picard's Kirk-like determination fail, the woman reproaches him with be-having like the mad Captain Ahab in *Moby-Dick*. "You still do have books in the twenty-fourth century, don't you?" she asks Picard. This shock tactic works, restoring the uncharacteristically macho Picard to his normal scholarly tempera-ment and in fact provoking him into reciting from memory a passage from Melville's novel. But the puzzled look on the woman's face suggests that they may still have the book *Moby-Dick* in the twenty-first century, but nobody actually reads it anymore.

48. On this subject, see my essay "*Waiting for Godot* and the End of History: Postmodernism as a Democratic Aesthetic," in *Democracy and the Arts*, ed. Arthur Melzer, Jerry Weinberger, and Richard Zinman (Ithaca, N.Y.: Cornell University Press, 1999), 172–92, 201–6. In this essay, I discuss at length the relation between postmodern art and the end of history.

CHAPTER 3

1. As reported in Ed Henry's "Heard on the Hill" column in *Roll Call* 44, No. 81 (13 May 1999). His source was the *Albany Times-Union*. The *Simpsons* episode in question is called "The Cartridge Family," episode #5F01, and originally aired on November 11, 1997. I cite *Simpsons* episodes by title, number, and original broadcast date, using the information supplied in the invaluable reference work *The Simpsons: A Complete Guide to Our Favorite Family*, ed. Richmond and Antonia Coffman (New York: HarperCollins, 1997) and its supplement, *The Simpsons Forever*, ed. Scott M. Gimple (New York: HarperCollins, 1999). I will cite episodes that aired subsequent to the publication of these books simply by broadcast date. I first developed the argument of this chapter in an address entitled *"The Simpsons*: Nuclear Family," at a symposium on the family at Hampden-Sydney College on October 2, 1997. For the invitation to this event, I wish to thank James Pontuso. I developed the argument further at a panel on popular culture at the Annual Meeting of the American Political Science Association in Boston in September 1998. An essay based on that presentation and entitled *"The Simpsons*: Atomistic Politics and the Nuclear Family" was published in *Political Theory* 27, No. 6 (December 1999): 734–49. The essay has been reprinted in *The Simpsons and Philosophy: The D'oh! of Homer*, ed. William Irwin, Mark T. Conrad, and Aeon J. Skoble (Chicago: Open Court, 2001). This valuable collection of essays on *The Simpsons* reached me too late to be incorporated into my discussion.

2. The identification is made complete when Quimby says: *"Ich bin ein Springfielder"* in "Burns Verkaufen der Kraftwerk," #8F09, 12/5/91.

3. "Two Bad Neighbors," #3F09, 1/14/96. The animus of *The Simpsons* against Bush may have been triggered by the fact that in his 1992 State of the Union address he urged Americans to be more like the Waltons than the Simpsons. In a January 30, 1992, rebroadcast of "Stark Raving Dad" (#7F24, aired originally 9/19/91), *The Simpsons* showed a clip of Bush making his comment and Bart shot back: "Hey, we're like the Waltons. We're praying for the end of the depression, too." Clear proof, if any were needed, that *The Simpsons* has better gag writers than the White House.

4. For the reluctance to go after Clinton, see the rather tame satire of the 1996 presidential campaign in the "Citizen Kang" segment of the Halloween episode, "Treehouse of Horror VII" (#4F02, 10/27/96). Finally in the 1998–99 season, faced with the mounting scandals in the Clinton administration, the creators of *The Simpsons* decided to take off the kid gloves in their treatment of the president, especially in "Homer to the Max," #AABF09, 2/7/99. Marge, hustled by Clinton at a party in this episode, is forced to ask: "Are you sure it's a federal law that I have to dance with you?" Reassuring Marge that she is good enough for a man of his stature, Clinton tells her: "Hell, I've done it with pigs—real no foolin' pigs." A number of Bart's trademark appearances at the blackboard at the opening of episodes turned into barbs directed against Clinton. In "D'Oh-in' in the Wind" (#AABF02, 11/15/98), Bart writes on the blackboard: "No one cares what my definition of 'is' is" and in "Mayored to the Mob" (#AABF05, 12/20/98), he writes "'The President Did It' is not an excuse." Despite this seeming turn against Clinton, *The Simpsons* revealed its underlying pro-Democrat bias in its 250th episode, broadcast on November 5, 2000, that is, two days before the presidential election. Bart seems to be

writing on the blackboard: "I will not plant subliminal messages," but closer inspection reveals that he has really written: "I WILL NOT PLANT SUBLIMINAL MESSAGORES"—with the letters I have italicized actually standing out in green.

5. "The Front," #9F16, 4/15/93.

6. An amusing debate developed in the *Wall Street Journal* over the politics of *The Simpsons*. It began with an Op-Ed piece by Benjamin Stein entitled "TV Land: From Mao to Dow" (5 February 1997), in which he argued that the show has no politics. This piece was answered by a letter from John McGrew given the title "The Simpsons Bash Familiar Values" (19 March 1997), in which he argued that the show is political and consistently left-wing. On March 12, 1997, letters by Deroy Murdock and H. B. Johnson Jr. argued that the show attacks left-wing targets as well and often supports traditional values. Johnson's conclusion that the show is "politically ambiguous" and thus appeals "to conservatives as well as to liberals" is supported by the evidence of this debate itself.

7. For Elton John, see "I'm with Cupid," #AABF11, 2/14/99; for Paul and Linda McCartney, see "Lisa the Vegetarian," #3F03, 10/15/95.

8. There seems to be confusion in discussions of *The Simpsons* over whether Apu comes from India or Pakistan. The preponderance of evidence suggests that he is from India, and of course the fact that he is a Hindu makes India more plausible as his country of origin.

9. Groening explains the origins of the family names in an article by Susan G. Hauser, "Mr. Groening's Neighborhood," *Wall Street Journal*, 7 October 1999, A28. Only the name of Bart is made up. The figure of 2.3 children comes from "Homer's Phobia," #4F11, 2/16/97.

10. Perhaps the most famous example is the creation of *Green Acres* (1965–71) by inverting *The Beverly Hillbillies* (1962–71)—if a family of hicks moving from the country to the city was funny, television executives concluded that a couple of sophisticates moving from the city to the country would be a hit too. And it was.

11. For a good analysis of this trend by a true expert on sitcoms, see Sherwood Schwartz, *Inside Gilligan's Island* (New York: St. Martin's, 1994), 260–63.

12. *TV Guide*, 29 April 2000, 46.

13. On the self-reflexive character of *The Simpsons*, see my essay "The Greatest TV Show Ever," *American Enterprise* 8, No. 5 (September/October 1997): 34–37.

14. On the relation of *The Simpsons* to television tradition, see Robert Pinsky, "Creating the 'Real,' in Bright Yellow and Blue," *New York Times*, 5 November 2000, 12.

15. Typically, television is now repaying the favor, as sitcoms become imitations of *The Simpsons*. In its preview issue for the 1999–2000 season, *TV Guide* described Fox's upcoming family sitcom *Malcolm in the Middle* as "a live-action *Simpsons*" (14).

16. Alexis de Tocqueville, *Democracy in America*, trans. Harvey C. Mansfield and Delba Winthrop (Chicago: University of Chicago Press, 2000), 558.

17. Tocqueville, *Democracy*, 560.

18. For references to Dennis the Menace in *The Simpsons*, see the episodes that aired on October 30, 1999, and November 28, 1999.

19. "Marge on the Lam," #1F03, 11/4/93. The feminist tendencies of *The Simpsons* were strikingly evident in the episode that retells a number of stories from the Bible (broadcast April 4, 1999). In the retelling of the Garden of Eden story, it is Homer as Adam who first eats of the Forbidden Fruit, and, in sharp contrast to the original account in the Bible, Marge as Eve is completely blameless.

20. "Make Room for Lisa," #AABF12, 2/28/99.

21. "The Devil and Homer Simpson" in "Treehouse of Horror IV," #1F04, 10/30/93.

22. "Lisa the Greek," #8F12, 1/23/92.

23. In an Associated Press story dated January 11, 2000, Seth Sutel quotes Mike Scully, the executive producer of *The Simpsons*, as saying: "We'll get complaints once in a while about Homer's drinking, but he isn't presented as a role model. He's an idiot. . . . People don't look up to him for drinking too much or being lazy, but they look up to him for loving his family."

24. "Lisa's Pony," #8F06, 11/7/91. On the issue of Homer's devotion to his family, *The Simpsons* has undergone significant changes over the years. The earlier episodes tend to be edgier and the later ones more sentimental. For example, in "The Crepes of Wrath" in the first season (#7G13, 4/15/90), Lisa gets very upset with her father's willingness to contemplate the deportation of his children and even says to Homer: "Your paper-thin commitment to your children sends shivers down my spine." By contrast, in a much later episode in the tenth season, "Make Room for Lisa," she comes to realize how much her father puts up with in catering to her cultivated tastes. By the end of the episode she is even willing to go with Homer to a demolition derby. Of course, it takes several hours in a sensory deprivation tank to force Lisa to this realization.

25. An episode that illustrates how much Homer can help Bart and Lisa is "Lisa's Substitute" (#7F19, 4/25/91). Homer actually ends up paying too much attention to his children in "Grampa vs. Sexual Inadequacy" (2F07, 12/4/94). Good examples of Homer rescuing his son are "Radio Bart" (#8F11, 1/9/92) and "Boy Scoutz N the Hood" (#1F06, 11/18/93). Homer strives bravely to save the whole family in the "Dial 'Z' for Zombies" segment of "Treehouse of Horror III" (#9F04, 10/29/92).

26. In naming Homer Simpson #14 among its "TV's Fifty Greatest Characters Ever," *TV Guide* (16 October 1999, 44) aptly summed him up: "[He] does hold down a job (calling it *steady* might be stretching the point), brings home work with him (with a half-life of 40 million years) and despite being a coarse, oafish, self-involved, oblivious, overgrown child, he's a devoted husband and a role model to his youngsters (if you're not too picky about which role, and you loosely define 'model')."

27. "Home Sweet Homediddly-Dum-Doodily," #3F01, 10/1/95.

28. *The Simpsons* repeatedly makes fun of various contemporary notions of psychotherapy. See, for example, "There's No Disgrace Like Home" (#7G04, 1/28/90) and "Bart's Inner Child" (#1F05, 11/11/93).

29. Other episodes that explore the possibility of substitute parents for the Simpson children teach a similar lesson. See, for example, "Brother from the Same Planet" (#9F12, 2/4/93) and "Burns' Heir" (1F16, 4/14/94).

30. For an insightful and comprehensive treatment of religion in *The Simpsons*, see Gerry Bowler's "God and *The Simpsons*: The Religious Life of an Animated Sitcom." I found the essay on the Internet at <http://www.cadvision.com/Home_Pages/ accounts/cnaz/Simpsons.html> (30 March 2000). The paper was originally delivered at a symposium on "The Media and Family Values" held at Canadian Nazarene College, Calgary, in October 1996 and, according to the web site, was published in the 1997 volume of *North American Religion*. My attention was called to this essay after the

first publication of my essay on *The Simpsons* in 1999. Thus Bowler and I arrived at very similar conclusions about the show independently.

31. "Homer the Heretic," #9F01, 10/8/92.

32. "Bart's Girlfriend," #2F04, 11/6/94.

33. The difficulties the producers of *The X-Files* had with the Fox Network over their episode "Miracle Man" illustrate this point well. Dealing with a charismatic faith healer, this episode actually provoked network censorship, as its director, Michael Lange, explains: "Some of the things I put in were actually pulled back by the network when they saw it. . . . I had this one image that I shot, which was the silhouette of [the faith healer] against the wall with the bars, and he actually had taken a crucifix pose, and that of course went bye-bye. Even the bold Fox network couldn't handle that one." Quoted in Ted Edwards, *X-Files Confidential: The Unauthorized X-Philes Companion* (Boston: Little, Brown, 1996), 68.

34. A particularly bizarre manifestation of this trend involved *Star Trek*. As reported in Herbert F. Solow and Robert H. Justman, *Inside Star Trek: The Real Story* (New York: Pocket, 1996): "in 1965, the NBC Sales Department was concerned. It was as if they believed that, after Satan had been cast out of the Garden of Eden, he was reincarnated as actor Leonard Nimoy and cast into *Star Trek* as Science Officer Spock, a pointed-eared, arched-eyebrowed 'satanic' Vulcan alien. Though it was well before the rise of the 1970s Christian fundamentalism, NBC feared its advertisers and local stations would be targets of a religious backlash protesting this 'devil incarnate'" (231).

35. The attitude of the television community toward conventional religion is well illustrated by a comment Glen Morgan, one of the producers of *The X-Files*, made about the "Miracle Man" episode: "I think it's kind of easy to pick on religion, especially one of the fundamentalist backgrounds. It's easy to portray them as Bible thumpers. To tell you the truth, there are a lot of people for whom it's their faith, and I would like to have had a little more respect towards that. Overall, my personal belief is that some of the phoniness needs to be exposed; however, it's just kind of easy to say this is all that it is. I think there is more to it. There are good people who have Christian faith in their background. They're not just on bad cable. It's a tough challenge because, really, on network TV they don't want you to deal with religion" (Edwards, *X-Files Confidential*, 68). Morgan is trying very hard to be sympathetic to believing Christians here, but one senses all too clearly what a struggle it is for him to make the admission "There are good people who have Christian faith in their background." I would guess that for him the foreground is simply out of the question.

36. I would like to comment on this show, but it is scheduled at the same time as *The Simpsons* and I have never seen it.

37. Consider, for example, the minister played by Tom Skerritt in Robert Redford's film of Norman Maclean's *A River Runs through It* (1992).

38. A good example of this stereotyping can be found in the film *Contact* (1997), with its contrasting religious figures played by Matthew McConaughey (good) and Jake Busey (evil).

39. "In Marge We Trust," #4F18, 4/27/97.

40. "My Sister, My Sitter," #4F13, 3/2/97.

41. "The Last Temptation of Homer," #1F07, 12/9/93.

42. "Dancin' Homer," #7F05, 11/8/90.

43. For another comment on wasteful federal government spending, see "Make Room for Lisa," where a representative of a cell-phone company explains why it has bought many of the Smithsonian Institution's treasures: "Uncle Sam needs to spend our tax dollars on the essentials: anti-tobacco programs, pro-tobacco programs, killing wild donkeys, and Israel."

44. Homer gets in trouble with the IRS again in the May 21, 2000, episode—a fictionalized biography of the Simpsons called "Behind the Laughter." In this parody of the standard plot of the rise and fall of celebrities, a poorly disguised Apu turns informer on Homer with the IRS and nearly destroys his life.

45. More evidence of the libertarian impulses of *The Simpsons* can be found in the episode that makes fun of Prohibition, "Homer vs. the Eighteenth Amendment" (#4F15, 3/16/97), which includes a send-up of the Eliot Ness figure from *The Untouchables*. "The Canine Mutiny" (#4F16, 4/13/97) treats smoking marijuana with a degree of sympathy surprising for American television.

46. The various manifestations of the Nuclear Regulatory Commission in *The Simpsons*—see, for example, "Homer Goes to College" (#1F02, 10/14/93)—might seem to present the federal government performing a useful and important function, especially given the deplorable conditions at Burns's power plant under Homer's reign as safety inspector. But the fact that the plant is not shut down permanently hints at the incompetence if not the outright corruption of federal regulatory agencies.

47. "Bart's Comet," #2F11, 2/5/95.

48. For an analogous shift in another area of popular culture, see my essay "Pro Wrestling and the End of History," *Weekly Standard* 5, No. 3 (4 October 1999): 17–22.

49. "Mr. Lisa Goes to Washington," #8F01, 9/26/91.

50. In "The Day the Violence Died" (#3F15, 3/16/96), *The Simpsons* satirizes the kind of cartoon civics lesson often inflicted on children, as Bart and Lisa are forced to watch a short entitled "Amendment To Be," charting the course of a constitutional amendment to make flag-burning a crime. It is a clever parody of the sort of "How a Bill Becomes a Law" short that once was popular. *The Simpsons* returned to the subject of the Jimmy Stewart movie *Mr. Smith Goes to Washington* (1939) in the opening episode of its eleventh season, broadcast on September 26, 1999, and featuring the voice of Mel Gibson. Gibson plays himself, in Springfield to preview his remake of the Stewart film and sample the average American's reaction to it. If Homer is a good example, the average American now finds a film dealing with national politics intolerably boring. Homer wants Gibson to remake the movie as an action flick, concluding with a scene in which he guns down all his opponents in Congress. The only person in town who gets genuinely worked up over Gibson's performance in the first version of the remake is the quintessentially political man, Mayor Quimby, who comments: "That man knows how to filibuster." Marge defends Gibson's film against Homer's criticism: "It's not boring—he's passionate about government." But Marge's praise for Gibson's passion for government seems to be fueled by her own passion for him and not by genuine patriotism.

51. William Shawcross, *Murdoch: The Making of a Media Empire* (New York: Simon & Schuster, 1997), 281. In his January 11, 2000, AP story, Sutel reports that Sandy Grushow, chairman of the Fox TV Entertainment Group, said: "The bottom line is that 'The Simpsons' is this network's flagship show. It's largely responsible

for putting this network on the map." Sutel adds that "he said 'The Simpsons' and 'The X-Files' are the two most profitable series Fox ever made."

52. "The Secret War of Lisa Simpson," #4F21, 5/18/97. The February 25, 2001, episode of *The Simpsons* portrays the U.S. military so desperate to recapture the interest of America's youth that the navy implants subliminal recruiting messages in the music of a new boy band featuring Bart.

53. "Raging Abe Simpson and His Grumbling Grandson in 'The Curse of the Flying Hellfish,'" #3F19, 4/28/96.

54. "The Principal and the Pauper," #4F23, 9/28/97. Skinner's most pointed reflection on his experience in Vietnam occurs during the episode about his school being closed down by a blizzard, broadcast on December 17, 2000. In a flashback to his internment in a Vietnamese prison camp, Skinner recalls one of his comrades saying: "Let's make a break for it while the guards are partying with Jane Fonda."

55. "One Fish, Two Fish, Blowfish, Blue Fish," #7F11, 1/24/91.

56. "The Homega Man" in "Treehouse of Horror VIII," #5F02, 10/26/97.

57. "Lost Our Lisa," #5F17, 5/10/98.

58. Jonathan Kay, "Caste of Characters," *Saturday Night*, 9 September 2000, 16.

59. In an article in *TV Guide* (21 October 2000), Matt Groening admitted about Apu: "We were worried he might be considered an offensive stereotype," but as the magazine points out: "The writers made Apu a Pakistani [sic] of great dignity and industry" (20).

60. "The Two Mrs. Nahasapeemapetilons," #5F04, 11/16/97.

61. *The Simpsons* occasionally seems to reflect anxieties about the impact of foreign competition on American economic interests, though it usually satirizes those anxieties and shows its global perspective by portraying the foreign interests positively. In a flashback in "Last Exit to Springfield" (#9F15, 3/11/93), a disgruntled worker at a plant owned by Burns's grandfather makes the ominous (and accurate) prediction: "One day we'll form a union and get the fair and equitable treatment we deserve! Then we'll go too far, and get corrupt and shiftless, and the Japanese will eat us alive!" In "Burns Verkaufen der Kraftwerk," Lisa's characterization of the Germans taking over the plant sounds a warning to America: "They're efficient and punctual with a strong work ethic."

62. The superficiality of globalization in *The Simpsons* is underlined in "The Springfield Files" when Moe turns Homer's favorite local brew, Duff beer, into a premium Swedish import by simply adding an umlaut to its name.

63. In this regard, it is instructive to look at how *The Simpsons* is received in other countries. The show was attacked in an angry letter by Renais Nisbett of Ontario in the August 12, 2000, issue of the Canadian *TV Times*: "The show that makes me sick to my stomach is *The Simpsons*. The reason why I hate this show is because of its insulting story lines. In my opinion, the show sends a message that Americans are better than everyone else in the world. We all know that isn't true." Many Americans complain that *The Simpsons* runs down their country, but evidently some foreigners think that the show is offensively pro-American.

64. "30 Minutes over Tokyo," #AABF20, 5/16/99.

65. "Itchy & Scratchy & Marge," #7F09, 12/20/90. For a fuller discussion of *Itchy & Scratchy* and the concept of the "cartoon within a cartoon," see my "Greatest TV Show Ever."

66. The episode called "Radioactive Man" (#2517, 9/24/95) provides an amusing reversal of the usual relationship between the big-time media and small-town life. A Hollywood film company comes to Springfield to make a movie featuring the comic book hero Radioactive Man. The Springfield locals take advantage of the naive moviemakers, raising prices all over town and imposing all sorts of new taxes on the film crew. Forced to return to California penniless, the moviemakers are greeted as small-town heroes by their caring neighbors in the tight-knit Hollywood community.

67. In his review of *The Simpsons: A Complete Guide to Our Favorite Family*, Michael Dirda aptly characterizes the show as "a wickedly funny yet oddly affectionate satire of American life at the end of the 20th century. Imagine the unholy offspring of *Mad* magazine, Mel Brooks's movies, and 'Our Town.'" See *Washington Post*, "Book World," 11 January 1998, 5.

68. As we will see, this theme is also at the heart of *The X-Files*.

69. Sutel's AP story, January 11, 2000. In the episode broadcast January 7, 2001, *The Simpsons* finally explores what would happen if Homer were smart. It turns out that his stupidity can be traced to a crayon stuck up his nose and into his brain. With the crayon surgically removed, Homer is a new man—he walks around humming Bach's *Brandenburg Concerto #3*, calls Moe the bartender a "pusillanimous Pilsner pusher," comes up with an irrefutable proof that God does not exist (which Ned Flanders tries to destroy), and is even able to correct fellow moviegoers who have confused Bill Paxton with Bill Pullman. But Homer's newfound intelligence proves to be a curse. His increased vigilance as safety inspector leads to the closing down of the nuclear power plant and puts much of Springfield out of work. This turns Homer's friends against him, to the point where he says at Moe's: "I'm detecting a distinct strain of anti-intellectualism in this tavern." Finally, Homer turns to Lisa: "Why didn't you warn me? Being a brain has alienated me from all my friends." Though Homer's increased IQ has brought him closer to Lisa than ever before, he regretfully has the crayon surgically put back and returns to the good-natured stupidity that basically makes everyone want to hug him (including Lisa at the end).

70. See *Die fröhliche Wissenschaft*, sect. 193 (my translation) in Friedrich Nietzsche, *Sämtliche Werke: Kritische Studienausgabe*, ed. Giorgio Colli and Mazzino Montinari (Berlin: de Gruyter, 1967–77), Vol. 3, 504.

CHAPTER 4

1. Of course the success of *The X-Files* cannot simply be attributed to its ideological content. Efforts to duplicate the dark mood and conspiratorial atmosphere of the show in other series have generally failed. What other shows have not been able to duplicate is the *quality* of *The X-Files* as a television program. Few series in the history of television have equaled *The X-Files* in sheer production values. The producers try to achieve feature film quality in each episode in all aspects of the show—the writing, the directing, the casting, the acting, the editing, the music, the lighting, the special effects, and so on—and they usually succeed. The show's popularity is thus no fluke, a simple case of being at the ideological right place at

the historically right time. And we must not underestimate the star power of David Duchovny and Gillian Anderson in the lead roles as a factor in the show's popularity. Many factors obviously go into the success of any television program. All I am claiming is that the controversial view of American politics The X-Files embodies has been one factor in its success, and therefore the show can serve as a measure of a change in political perceptions in the United States in the 1990s. I presented an earlier version of this chapter at a panel on popular culture at the Annual Meeting of the American Political Science Association in Washington, D.C., in September 2000.

2. Brian Lowry, The Truth Is Out There: The Official Guide to The X-Files (New York: HarperCollins, 1995), 27. The series of "official guides" to The X-Files has been very helpful to me; the volumes contain useful background information and, after the first two seasons, the synopses of individual episodes are detailed and filled with extensive quotations from the scripts.

3. Chris Carter comments: "The show's original spirit has become kind of the spirit of the country—if not the world. . . . On their own, people are starting to say things like 'Trust No One.' 'The Truth Is Out There.' That the world is run by selfish people whose motives are selfish." Quoted in Andy Meisler, I Want to Believe: The Official Guide to The X-Files (New York: HarperCollins, 1998), 9.

4. According to Meisler, from its first episode, The X-Files has dealt with subjects that "most authoritative observers (including network programming executives) consider the lunatic fringe" (I Want to Believe, 8).

5. In her essay "'Are You Now or Have You Ever Been?' Conspiracy Theory and The X-Files," in "Deny All Knowledge": Reading the X-Files, ed. David Lavery, Angela Hague, and Marla Cartwright (Syracuse, N.Y.: Syracuse University Press, 1996), Allison Graham does an excellent job of showing how ideas (particularly about the Kennedy assassination) that originally got comedian Mort Sahl labeled a "bona fide paranoiac" have become routinely embodied in The X-Files (52–53). One of the producers of The X-Files, Glen Morgan, understands the show's genealogy but not the issue of mainstreaming paranoia: "The X-Files almost seems like the kind of show that would have gone over during the Reagan years. Films like JFK and Silence of the Lambs—Scully, especially in the beginning, was very much like the Jodie Foster character—and older films like Parallax View, The Conversation, Three Days of the Condor, and Klute are all conspiracy-oriented, weird, paranoid movies that I think Chris [Carter] tapped in to." Quoted in Ted Edwards, X-Files Confidential: The Unauthorized X-Philes Compendium (Boston: Little, Brown, 1996), 88. Morgan confuses the way movies function in popular culture with the way television does. This is a complicated issue, but to simplify it, the fact that the public is ready to accept a view of the world in a movie does not automatically mean that it is ready to accept it in a television series. One always "goes out" to a movie, but television is something one invites into one's home and on a weekly basis. In general, then, the embodiment of a worldview in a television series is a better indication of its having entered the cultural mainstream. We will never know whether, as Morgan suggests, The X-Files might have succeeded on television during the Reagan years, but I think it actually took another decade of political scandals, as well as the cultural effect of the very films Morgan mentions (and others like them), to prepare the American public to accept The X-Files into their homes on a reg-

ular basis. Again, these are complicated matters, but cultural historians may eventually conclude that *The X-Files* was profoundly linked to the Clinton, not the Reagan, years.

6. See Andy Meisler, *Resist or Serve: The Official Guide to* The X-Files (New York: HarperCollins, 1999), 211. "Travelers" concentrates on what it presents as the anticommunist paranoia of the Cold War in America, associating Hoover closely with Senator Joseph McCarthy and his aide, Roy Cohn. Meisler points out that the speech I quoted "was taken almost verbatim from a speech by Senator McCarthy" (211). Meisler reveals that the coauthors of the episode, John Shiban and Frank Spotnitz, were students at the American Film Institute of a screenwriter named Howard Dimsdale—a victim of Hollywood anticommunist blacklisting in the 1950s who wrote screenplays under the pseudonym Arthur Dales (the name given to an FBI agent in this episode). Shiban and Spotnitz (two of the most important figures in the creation of *The X-Files* over the years) conceived of this episode as a tribute to Dimsdale (who died in 1991).

7. Edwards, *X-Files Confidential*, 79, 81.

8. In Mulder's famous characterization of himself in the first episode, he says: "Nobody down here but the FBI's most unwanted." On this point, see Elizabeth Kubek, "'You Only Expose Your Father': The Imaginary, Voyeurism, and the Symbolic Order in *The X-Files*," in Lavery, Hague, and Cartwright, *"Deny All Knowledge,"* 172.

9. For a brief but very helpful survey of the representation of the FBI in movies and television, see Michele Malach, "'I Want to Believe . . . in the FBI': The Special Agent and *The X-Files*," in Lavery, Hague, and Cartwright, *"Deny All Knowledge,"* 63–76. For a systematic discussion of the subject, see Richard Gid Powers, *G-Men: Hoover's FBI in American Popular Culture* (Carbondale: Southern Illinois University Press, 1983).

10. According to the film's director, Mervyn LeRoy, Hoover "and his men controlled the movie. . . . Everybody on that picture, from the carpenters and electricians right to the top, everybody, had to be okayed by the F.B.I. . . . I had two F.B.I. men with me all the time, for research purposes, so that we did things right." Quoted in Powers, *G-Men*, 242. In general, Powers's book shows the remarkable degree of control Hoover exerted over Hollywood representations of the FBI.

11. For an excellent discussion of the turn against the FBI in popular culture in the 1970s, see Malach, "'I Want to Believe . . . in the FBI,'" 67–68.

12. In his *Little Man: Meyer Lansky and the Gangster Life* (Boston: Little, Brown, 1991), Robert Lacey makes the interesting observation that our sense of how organized "organized crime" is may be colored by the lens through which we view it. Since it is federal bureaucracies that generally supply us with information about the Mafia, the crime syndicate may end up looking more bureaucratic than it really is: "The FBI and other law enforcement agencies . . . [set] out their criminal intelligence data on huge organization charts. . . . These charts had the virtue of demonstrating, in graphic and human terms, the pool of criminal activity in any major city. But they reflected the bureaucratic and semimilitary cast of thought prevailing in the average police office. Everybody had a rank, and they did little justice to the confused, fluid, and essentially entrepreneurial character of most criminal activity" (293).

13. On the role of the FBI in defining boundaries, see Malach, "'I Want to Believe . . . in the FBI,'" 70.

14. For example, doubles of Mulder appear in "Small Potatoes" and the "Dreamland" episodes, though in these cases the doubling is played largely for comic effect. In "The Pine Bluff Variant," we will see that Scully has serious reasons for becoming suspicious of Mulder's behavior, and in "Wetwired," Mulder has serious reasons for becoming suspicious of Scully's.

15. The political bent of *The X-Files* is a complicated and much debated subject, to which this chapter is meant to make a contribution by showing that the sympathy for left-wing causes in the show does not tell the whole story. Lowry reports: "A conservative newsletter published by the Media Research Center not long ago put *The X-Files* on its top 10 list of programs with a perceived liberal bias, citing its 'proffered conspiracy theories alleging outrageous government atrocities'" (*The Truth Is Out There*, 27). But in the 1990s "outrageous government atrocities" became a theme of the right as well as the left (Waco, Ruby Ridge, and so on). Lowry goes on to say of the Media Research Center claim: "Carter is amused by that charge, pointing to what some feel is an inherently conservative bent to the slogan (and Mulder's computer log-on) 'TrustNo1,' which is really saying in effect to be wary of government. 'It's really more libertarian,' he says. 'Conservatives say, 'Trust us.' This is really saying, 'Don't trust anyone.' That summarizes my political views in a nutshell." As Carter's remarks suggest, in general the issue of the end of the nation-state cuts across normal left-right political distinctions.

16. Meisler quotes Shiban with regard to this episode: "It always seemed fit to me—putting Mulder in a situation where he has to lie; so that they don't know his allegiance and eventually we don't know his allegiance" (*Resist or Serve*, 253).

17. See Malach's summary of the attitude toward the FBI in *The X-Files*: "The FBI, and the larger federal intelligence community, are portrayed in *The X-Files* as a kind of shadow government, operating outside the boundaries of legality and acceptability, willing and able to do anything to achieve their own obscure ends. They have no concern for the rights of individuals, freedom of information, or the 'truth.' [*The X-Files* draws] on the perception of the federal government that was popularized in the 1970s by the far left and co-opted by the right-wing populist movement" ("'I Want to Believe . . . in the FBI,'" 73).

18. A similar moment occurs in "Humbug," when a character says to Mulder: "I've taken in your all-American features, your dour demeanor, your unimaginative necktie design, and concluded that you work for the government . . . an FBI agent." "Humbug" was written by Darin Morgan, the same man who wrote "Jose Chung's *From Outer Space*." He also wrote "Clyde Bruckman's Final Repose" and "War of the Coprophages." These happen to be my four favorite *X-Files* episodes, and I was amazed to discover that they were all scripted by the same author. This circumstance raises the question of "pockets" within the *X-Files* universe— whether certain of the regular writers have developed their own distinctive takes on the show. This is a fascinating question, but I do not have time to go into it. I do think that some writers, Darin Morgan above all, have put their personal stamp on *The X-Files*, but still within parameters largely established by Chris Carter.

19. Though I have tried to develop a comprehensive view of *The X-Files* in this chapter, I make no claims to have exhausted the subject. There are many interesting and important aspects of the series that I have only touched upon or neglected entirely. Since I am interested chiefly in the political implications of *The X-Files*, I

have not attempted to go into many of the psychological and mythological issues the show raises, which are equally worthy of analysis and which have been profitably discussed by others. The Lavery, Hague, and Cartwright volume, *"Deny All Knowledge,"* with its excellent essays on a wide range of subjects in *The X-Files*, gives a good idea of what a rich mine the show offers for future research and scholarship.

20. On Carter's role in producing *The X-Files*, see Lowry, *The Truth Is Out There*, 36, 39; Meisler, *I Want to Believe*, 15; and Brian Lowry, *Trust No One: The Official Third Season Guide to* The X-Files (New York: HarperCollins, 1996), xiii, 227–29, 236. According to these accounts, in the first three seasons, for example, Carter wrote or cowrote eighteen of the fifty-four episodes.

21. *The X-Files* is by no means alone in exploiting this pun, which is implicit in many stories about extraterrestrials. It is, for example, at the center of the films *Men in Black* (1997) and *Alien Nation* (1988—spun off into a television series with the same name on Fox in 1989). This is also the name of one of the most controversial books on the problem of immigration: Peter Brimelow, *Alien Nation: Common Sense about America's Immigration Disaster* (New York: HarperCollins, 1996). Whatever one may say about the policy recommendations of this book, it gives as dark a picture of the situation of immigrants as *The X-Files* does.

22. Carter says of an episode called "The Beginning": "we wanted to suggest that there was a blurred line between what is terrestrial and extraterrestrial." Quoted in Andy Meisler, *The End and the Beginning: The Official Guide to* The X-Files (New York: HarperCollins, 2000), 18.

23. On the effort to get the Cantonese dialect right in "Hell Money," see Lowry, *Trust No One*, 191. On a comparable effort to get the Hebrew dialogue right in "Kaddish," see Meisler, *I Want to Believe*, 132.

24. That some fans resent untranslated foreign dialogue is evident in James Hatfield and George Burt, *The Unauthorized X-Files* (New York: MJF, 1996). In the section they call "nitpicking," they write of "Hell Money": "One major drawback of this entire episode is the extensive foreign dialogue. And if subtitles are to be used, then it's only fair to translate *all* of the dialogue. There are several scenes in which vital information is withheld from the audience by simply not subtitling" (246). As we have seen, *The Simpsons* shares with *The X-Files* this willingness to risk alienating fans by using foreign languages extensively.

25. Only by stressing the thematic importance of immigrant experience in "Hell Money" and *The X-Files* in general can one understand the place of this episode in the series as a whole. Many fans have felt that "Hell Money" is not really an *X-Files* episode because of its lack of "authentic" supernatural or paranormal elements. See Hatfield and Burt, *Unauthorized X-Files*, 248, and Edwards, *X-Files Confidential*, 173–74.

26. On the theme of sinister biotechnology in *The X-Files*, see Linda Badley, "The Rebirth of the Clinic: The Body as Alien in *The X-Files*" in Lavery, Hague, and Cartwright, *"Deny All Knowledge,"* especially 151, 153–54.

27. The complementarity of Mulder and Scully is commented on throughout the literature on *The X-Files*. See, for example, Edwards, *X-Files Confidential*, 4, for Chris Carter's own comment: "Mulder and Scully are equal parts of my nature. . . . I'm a natural skeptic, so I have much of the Scully character in me, yet I'm willing to take leaps of faith, to go out on a limb. I love writing both those characters,

because their voices are very clear in my head." For a thorough treatment of the Mulder-Scully pairing, see Rhonda Wilcox and J. P. Williams, "'What Do You Think?': *The X-Files*, Liminality, and Gender Pleasure," in Lavery, Hague, and Cartwright, *"Deny All Knowledge,"* 99–120.

28. For example, in discussing his plans for Mulder and Scully in the fifth season of the show, Carter says: "So one day I thought why not take everything away from him? Take away all his hopes, and give them back to him slowly? And at the same time play with Gillian's character, make Scully suddenly start to develop and confront new spiritual aspects of her life. And then watch those characters really change places and then come back to where they started." Quoted in Meisler, *Resist or Serve*, 9. For a good discussion of the Mulder-Scully role reversals in *The X-Files*, see Malach, "'I Want to Believe . . . in the FBI,'" 72–75. One way the show has coped with the reduced role of David Duchovny in the eighth season is to place Scully in the traditional Mulder role and have her new partner, John Doggett, play the skeptical role she used to represent.

29. On this subject, see Jean-Marie Guéhenno, "Globalization and Fragmentation," in *Globalization, Power, and Democracy*, ed. Marc F. Plattner and Aleksander Smolar (Baltimore: Johns Hopkins University Press, 2000), 18–19.

30. Badley's essay is especially good on this Foucauldian aspect of *The X-Files*—the world viewed as a giant clinic ("Rebirth of the Clinic," 150). She gives a more comprehensive list of the "institutions or outposts in which the production, reproduction, and manipulation of biological power are carried on: fertility clinics, abortion clinics, biochemistry labs, convalescent homes, leper colonies, psychiatric wards, prisons (infected with a deadly disease), reservations, refugee camps, military bases, military ships, zoos. The list sounds like it might have come from an index to the works of Foucault" (154).

31. An early episode that deals with this issue is the first-season "Eve." Mulder's sister, Samantha, becomes the focus of a plot involving cloning in the second-season "Colony" and "End-Game."

32. See Jean-Marie Guéhenno, *The End of the Nation-State*, trans. Victoria Elliott (Minneapolis: University of Minnesota Press, 1995), 44–45, who describes the way immigrants are "rejected, cast aside like imperfectly manufactured articles by 'quality control.'"

33. Chris Carter speaks of "Mulder's postmodern fanaticism" in his foreword to Anne Simon, *The Real Science behind* The X-Files (New York: Simon & Schuster, 1999), 12.

34. In another episode involving Native Americans, "Shapes," an Indian tells Mulder: "I sense you are different, FBI. You're more open to Native American beliefs than some Native Americans. You even have an Indian name—Fox."

35. This episode thus raises the same questions about Americanization we saw developed in *Star Trek VI*. It is a measure of the sophistication of *The X-Files* that it handles white-black symbolism more subtly than the *Star Trek* TV series did in "Let That Be Your Last Battlefield."

36. The fascination of *The X-Files* with this motif began with its third episode, "Squeeze," the story of the monstrous Eugene Tooms, a character so interesting that the series brought him back toward the end of the first season in "Tooms." The "squeeze" motif helps tie the immigrant episodes of *The X-Files* to its more conventional monster episodes.

37. Carter comments: "I think the writers on the show have hooked in to what really scares people." Quoted in Edwards, *X-Files Confidential*, 82.

38. See Carter's comment on the fourth-season episode "Tunguska": "We'd been wanting to expand the conspiracy globally, and we had done that as early as 'Talitha Cumi,' the finale of Season Three, when we'd brought in a sort of global perspective." Quoted in Meisler, *I Want to Believe*, 102.

39. See Guéhenno, "Globalization and Fragmentation," 25: "Territorial containment becomes meaningless in the world of globalization. Diseases, weapons, and people can move freely."

40. On the relevance of the Haitian situation, see Lowry, *The Truth Is Out There*, 197, and Edwards, *X-Files Confidential*, 114, where writer Howard Gordon explains: "The story came very much out of the newspaper."

41. In its satirical use of the Statue of Liberty, this *X-Files* episode offers a parallel to what we saw in the "Much Apu about Nothing" episode of *The Simpsons* and seems to embody a similar attitude toward restrictive immigration policies.

42. *The X-Files* makes fun of its lack of narrative closure at the end of "Jose Chung's *From Outer Space*" when Scully says of her own version of the story that it "probably doesn't have the sense of closure you want, but it has more than our other cases." The lack of closure in the episodes was originally a source of tension between Carter and the Fox Network. See Lowry, *The Truth Is Out There*, 3, 20.

43. On the Mexican soap opera elements in the episode, see Meisler, *I Want to Believe*, 122.

44. Writer John Shiban explains that the story grew out of his experience working in Ventura County in California: "I'd look out my window and see the long lines of migrant workers in the strawberry fields alongside the freeway. . . . It's a shame, but just about everybody, including myself, passed them every day on the way to work without noticing them at all." He adds that Chris Carter helped him develop "one of the central themes of the episode": "Chris actually pointed this out to me when I was pitching the story. He said to me, 'These people are invisible. We see them, but we don't see them. They move through our world—they clean our homes and tend our gardens and pick our food—but we just don't think of them as people like us'" (Meisler, *I Want to Believe*, 122).

45. This episode thus treats tragically the issues we saw treated comically in the episode of *The Simpsons* in which Bart, Lisa, and Maggie are handed over to the Flanders family on the orders of social workers.

46. "Isaac Luria" is actually the name of one of the great Kabbalists, a fact no doubt known to David Duchovny, from his studies at Yale with Harold Bloom, who has written extensively on Luria and the Kaballah.

47. The episode describes Williamsburg as "an area also known for its racial tension and hate crimes," but for once the show backed away from the reality it was portraying. Meisler explains how the writer, Howard Gordon, developed the episode: he "decided early on not to mirror the actual situation in Brooklyn, which involves tension, sometimes erupting into violence, between Orthodox Jews and their African-American neighbors. 'On my first stab at this I made the protagonists black,' he says, 'but then I realized that black anti-Semitism is a very subtle and difficult subject and not what I needed in my dramatic structure. I needed straw dogs—characters whose bigotry was unbridled and excuseless.

This was also what the network wanted, and I didn't put up much of a fight, because I think they were right'" (*I Want to Believe*, 131–32). This is a fascinating admission from one of the principal forces behind *The X-Files* and raises interesting questions about the show's political biases. Gordon all but says that there are excuses for black anti-Semitism; however, he sees nothing wrong in presenting caricatures of white men as pure bigots. It says something about *The X-Files* that it is willing to make the most outrageous claims about representatives of mainstream white American society (such as J. Edgar Hoover), but draws back from suggesting anything problematic about the behavior of extremists within the black community. It is perhaps even more significant that the Fox Network, which as we have seen had no problems with the show's treatment of Hoover and the FBI, insisted on the racial sanitizing of the "Kaddish" episode. James Hatfield and George Burt, in their *The Unauthorized X-Cyclopedia* (New York: MJF, 1997), give an account of this episode that is even less flattering to Fox: "As originally penned the victim was to have died at the hands of black teenagers; they were changed to white racist youths after Fox's race-sensitive Standards and Practices department rejected the initial script as 'unacceptable for broadcast standards'" (177).

48. This point is reinforced by having the Cigarette-Smoking Man, the central figure in the conspiracy, cast as a Nazi in several fantasy or dream sequences in *The X-Files*; see "The Field Where I Died" and "Triangle." The many references to Nazism in *The X-Files* are one measure of the left-wing bias of the show. In its terms, Nazism appears to be more of a threat than Soviet communism—*during the Cold War*. Given the way it links J. Edgar Hoover to McCarthyism, *The X-Files* tends to present anticommunism as mere red-baiting and portrays FBI officials trumping up charges of Communist treason against innocent Americans (this is especially true in the "Travelers" episode). Thus *The X-Files* manages to present the threat of Soviet communism as illusory, while insisting that the threat of Nazism is somehow real—as late as the 1990s. This is what I have in mind when I claim that *The X-Files* tends to portray all conspiracies as right-wing and tends to downplay or in fact ignore any threats from the left.

49. See especially the pair of episodes "Nisei" and "731."

50. See, for example, Ludwig von Mises, *Nation, State, and Economy: Contributions to the Politics and History of Our Time*, trans. Leland B. Yeager (New York: New York University Press, 1983), especially 9–27.

51. On this process, see Marshall McLuhan, *Understanding Media: The Extensions of Man* (New York: McGraw Hill, 1965), 14, 177, and Benedict Anderson, *Imagined Communities* (London: Verso, 1991), 44–45.

52. Analysts have particularly concentrated on the correlation between the railroad and the nation-state, showing how nation-states facilitated the building of railways and how rail systems in turn made it possible for nation-states to integrate their territories. See Robert Cooper, "Integration and Disintegration", in Plattner and Smolar, *Globalization*, 34, 37, and Martin van Creveld, *The Rise and Decline of the State* (Cambridge, U.K.: Cambridge University Press, 1999), 201–2, 251–53, 260–62, 287–88, 377–78.

53. For this correction of Orwell, see van Creveld, *Rise and Decline*, 392–93.

54. For a full account of this process, see Scott Shane, *Dismantling Utopia: How Information Ended the Soviet Union* (Chicago: Ivan R. Dee, 1994).

55. See, for example, "Kill Switch" and "First Person Shooter." Carter developed a whole series called *Harsh Realm* based on the idea of being trapped in virtual reality, but Fox canceled it after a few episodes.

56. Meisler reports the strategy of the episode's writer, Vince Gilligan: "The notion that one's boss is secretly a demon also resonates widely, he adds. In making the tormented protagonist a telemarketer, his intention was to funnel some of the torment generated by these intrusive, dinner-wrecking pitchmen." Meisler goes on to say that the actor who plays the protagonist "drew on a soul-draining experience, during his starving-actor period, of selling auto insurance over the phone" (*Resist or Serve*, 267).

57. In postmodern fashion, several *X-Files* episodes deal self-reflexively with television as a medium. The show has kept searching for ways to portray its own condition—what it is like to be trapped in a successful TV series, having to turn out one episode after another basically in the same mold. The best example of this kind of episode is "Monday," in which Mulder and Scully get caught in a strange time loop—they are condemned to live over the same disastrous day endlessly. As we watch scenes being repeated with only minor variations, we begin to share the frustration of the real actors in the series, doomed to a life of endless retakes. In two other sixth-season episodes, "How the Ghosts Stole Christmas" and "Field Trip," Mulder and Scully must in effect wake up to the fact that they are really actors, playing parts that exist only on the level of fantasy. In the first of these episodes, for example, the agents in essence find themselves imprisoned on a set—they must come to the realization that when they are "shot," it is not with real bullets, and as actors they need only stand up to be whole again and get on with their lives. The sense that these sixth-season episodes convey of being locked into an ongoing television series and especially of the actors feeling like prisoners of their roles seems to have reflected in particular David Duchovny's attitude toward *The X-Files*, which eventually led him to opt out of full-time participation in the show.

58. Mulder similarly tears up his apartment in an episode called "E.B.E." Graham notes the parallels with *The Conversation* ("Conspiracy Theory," 59).

59. Lowry reports that the episode's writer, Mat Beck, "drew his inspiration for the story not only from the debate about television violence but his desire to explore the effect television has on people" (*Trust No One*, 217).

60. The Kennedy assassination is one of several real events that has been worked into the mythology of *The X-Files*. Perhaps the best indication of its significance in the series is a speech by one of the Lone Gunmen, John Fitzgerald Byers, at the beginning of an episode called "Three of a Kind": "In my dream, the events of November 22, 1963, never happened. In it, my namesake was never assassinated. Other things are different, too, in my dream. My country is hopeful and innocent, young again. My fellow citizens trust their elected officials, never once having been betrayed by them. My government is truly of the people, by the people, for the people." But since Kennedy *was* assassinated, Byers becomes a prime candidate for political paranoia.

61. Lowry, in discussing Chris Carter's background, points out: "Though he was still a teenager at the time of the Watergate hearings, those events clearly left their mark on Carter, who admits that coverage of the scandal and President Nixon's subsequent resignation was 'the most formative event of my youth'" (*The Truth Is Out There*, 12). Graham ("Conspiracy Theory," 57–59) does an excellent job

of analyzing the importance of the Watergate affair for *The X-Files* as a whole. She points out that, according to the "Little Green Men" episode, the abduction of Mulder's sister occurred on the night of November 27, 1973, when television reported the news of the infamous eighteen-and-a-half-minute gap on the Nixon tapes. Tapes that have been tampered with feature prominently in several *X-Files* plots, and other allusions to Watergate can be found throughout the series. One of the sinister figures in the series, Agent Diana Fowley, turns out to live in the Watergate Apartments ("One Son"), and when Mulder goes to visit her there, he finds the Cigarette-Smoking Man instead.

62. Wilson Bryan Key, *Subliminal Seduction: Ad Media's Manipulation of a Not So Innocent America* (New York: New American Library, 1973).

63. This is of course McLuhan's famous claim that "the medium is the message"; see *Understanding Media*, 7, 9, 305.

64. In describing the genesis of the episode, Lowry explains: "Chris Carter had been wanting to do something that incorporated digital readouts. 'We had always tried to have regular things be scary,' [co-writer Glen] Morgan says, particularly objects like fax machines or cellular phones that are relatively new additions to the modern world" (*The Truth Is Out There*, 168).

65. Chris Carter himself says of "Anasazi": "This episode was the culmination of a lot of ideas. Generally, when we pitch stories to the staff everyone comments on them, and Darin Morgan called this the kitchen sink episode, because it had so much in it." Quoted in Edwards, *X-Files Confidential*, 126.

66. Kubek's Lacanian analysis of *The X-Files* offers an interesting view of the significance of Navajo in the Anasazi trilogy ("Imaginary, Voyeurism, Symbolic Order," 191–92).

67. As improbable as it sounds, *The X-Files* is not making this up. See, for example, Rose Houk, *Anasazi: Prehistoric Cultures of the Southwest* (Tucson: Southwest Parks and Monuments Association, 1992), 2: "*Anasazi* is a Navajo word that can mean 'enemy ancestors' or 'ancient people who are not us,' depending on pronunciation." One of the principal Anasazi ruins is at Bandelier National Monument, New Mexico, which is near the Los Alamos National Laboratory, where the atomic bomb was developed, as well as many other secret government projects. In a true *X-Files* experience, to get to the Anasazi ruins, one must drive by the LANL satellite uplink station. Fans of the series will be forgiven if they imagine that the Anasazi are still "linked" with extraterrestrial beings.

68. Kubek offers an interesting formulation of this contrast ("Imaginary, Voyeurism, Symbolic Order," 192).

69. See Lowry, *The Truth Is Out There*, 233–34, for the parallels to Nazi atrocities; he quotes Carter: "These are Nazi scientists. . . . Why wouldn't they behave as they behaved really?" See also Kubek, "Imaginary, Voyeurism, Symbolic Order," 193.

70. Max Horkheimer and Theodor W. Adorno, *Dialectic of Enlightenment*, trans. John Cumming (New York: Continuum, 1986).

71. Memory is a central theme throughout *The X-Files*, which for several seasons centered on Mulder's efforts to regain his memory of the night on which his sister was abducted. In many episodes, Mulder and/or Scully have their memories tampered with or wiped out by sinister forces. By the same token, several episodes deal with memory therapy and specifically regression hypnosis (which Scully, for example, undergoes in "The Blessing Way"). For the central importance

of memory in *The X-Files*, see Graham, "Conspiracy Theory," 57–58; she points out that "'recovered memory' is, of course, a central convention of [alien] abduction narratives."

72. For a different formulation of the opposition in this speech, see Kubek, "Imaginary, Voyeurism, Symbolic Order," 195.

73. See van Creveld, *Rise and Decline*, 135–36.

74. See Anderson, *Imagined Communities*, 62, 77, and also McLuhan, *Understanding Media*, 353.

75. See Anderson, *Imagined Communities*, 135: "the very idea of 'nation' is now nestled firmly in virtually all print-languages."

76. Mitch Pileggi, the actor who plays Skinner, says: "That will be one of my favorite lines forever" (Lowry, *Trust No One*, 84).

77. On the importance of oral tradition in the trilogy, see Leslie Jones, "'Last Week We Had an Omen': The Mythological *X-Files*," in Lavery, Hague, and Cartwright, *"Deny All Knowledge,"* 97–98.

78. Lowry reports that "Carter likes the notion of using something as low-tech as the Navajo oral tradition as a means to 'buy Mulder and Scully some insurance' and undermine the Cigarette-Smoking Man's high-tech government apparatus" (*The Truth Is Out There*, 238).

79. One could argue with this division of the history of "filing" into three stages. Like *The X-Files*, I am running together writing and print as if they were one and the same phenomenon. In fact, there are many important distinctions between the era of writing and the era of print, but for the purposes of analyzing the Anasazi trilogy, they can be ignored. The episodes fundamentally contrast orality with literacy and then view computer literacy as a third stage that synthesizes and transcends the earlier two.

80. To explain why the Syndicate is fixated on recovering the digital tape, Skinner reveals that he cannot print out the secret files because they are copy protected.

81. On the importance of statistics to the state, see van Creveld, *Rise and Decline*, 146–47, and see his characterization of the state as "an elaborate hierarchy of administrators, offices, filing cabinets, and finally computers" (170).

82. See McLuhan, *Understanding Media*, 27, 172, 301, 358. To see how close McLuhan comes to the "language" of *The X-Files*, consider this passage: "Literacy creates very much simpler kinds of people than those that develop in the complex web of ordinary tribal and oral societies. For the fragmented man creates the homogenized Western world, while oral societies are made up of people differentiated . . . by their unique emotional mixes. The oral man's inner world is a tangle of complex emotions and feelings that the Western practical man has long ago eroded or suppressed within himself in the interest of efficiency and practicality" (50).

83. On these developments and their significance, see Jimmie L. Reeves, Mark C. Rodgers, and Michael Epstein, "Rewriting Popularity: The Cult *Files*," in Lavery, Hague, and Cartwright, *"Deny All Knowledge,"* 22–35. Focusing on *The X-Files*, this essay offers a succinct and insightful characterization and comparison of the two eras of television I have been discussing in this book. What I call "national" and "global" television, they refer to as "TV 1" and "TV 2."

84. See Reeves, Rodgers, and Epstein, who speak of "the systematic fragmentation of television's mass audience into lifestyle sectors, psychographic segments, and niche markets" ("Rewriting Popularity," 29).

85. Reeves, Rodgers, and Epstein point out that "where once ABC, NBC, and CBS commanded over 90 percent of the audience, today the major network audience has decreased to about 60 percent" ("Rewriting Popularity," 30).

86. Reeves, Rodgers, and Epstein argue that *The X-Files* and similar shows reflect "a rewriting of popularity that expresses the deterritorializations and reterritorializations of the decline of television's consensus culture and the weakening of its unifying influences" ("Rewriting Popularity," 24). They regard this development as a problem and look forward at the end of their essay to a return to "consensus culture." They do not view the opening up and broadening of creative possibilities in television as a positive development.

87. On the importance of *Kolchak* to *The X-Files*, see Lowry, *The Truth Is Out There*, 9–10; Edwards, *X-Files Confidential*, ix–xiii, 3–7, 10, 30; and Ted Johnson and Tim Williams, "The Stalk Market," *TV Guide*, 4 November 2000, 23–25. In homage to the earlier series, *The X-Files* cast the actor who played Kolchak, Darren McGavin, as agent Arthur Dales in "Travelers" and "Agua Mala."

88. Probably the clearest allusion to *Twin Peaks* in *The X-Files* occurs in "Jose Chung's *From Outer Space*," where Mulder, imitating the earlier series' Agent Cooper, becomes obsessed with ordering pie in a diner. In an odd link between the two shows, David Duchovny actually had a recurring role in *Twin Peaks*, as a transvestite FBI agent named Dennis/Denise Bryson. On the links between the two shows, see Reeves, Rodgers, and Epstein, "Rewriting Popularity," 32–33, and Malach, "'I Want to Believe . . . in the FBI,'" 63–64, 69–70.

89. This is how Jeff Rice, the creator of *Kolchak*, explains why the earlier series failed and the later one succeeded: "If *The X-Files* has succeeded in terms of ratings and longevity, where *Kolchak* did not (at least in its single 1974–75 season as a series), it must be due in part to superior writing, in part to a willingness by Fox to stick by it, and in part due to a much more diverse and fragmented TV marketplace. There were only three networks when *Kolchak: The Night Stalker* was on the air and very little original dramatic programming being syndicated for 'local' TV stations. Today, thanks to the advent of cable broadcasting, there are so many TV venues that it is possible with much lower ratings—relative to all the shows extant—for a series to survive and even to thrive and become not only a cult classic but a genuine phenomenon" (Edwards, *X-Files Confidential*, xii). On the greater likelihood of *The X-Files* prospering on Fox as opposed to the old major networks, see also Lowry, *The Truth Is Out There*, 4; Lowry quotes Fox executive Sandy Grushow saying of *The X-Files*: "I remember thinking to myself that it was a distinctive type of show, that there wasn't anything else on the air quite like it" (14). In the era when the national networks dominated television, this perception might have been the kiss of death for *The X-Files*.

90. Murdoch personally screened the pilot of *The X-Files* and participated in the decision to air the show. See Lowry, *The Truth Is Out There*, 18. Murdoch became an American citizen in order to be legally entitled to purchase the Fox Network.

91. For a list of worldwide broadcast outlets for *The X-Files*, see Meisler, *The End and the Beginning*, 293. In *I Want to Believe*, Meisler says of the importance of *The X-Files* to Fox and its parent company, News Corp: "it is a prime ingredient in that company's plans to span the globe with direct-broadcast satellites and blanket the Earth with irresistible TV programming" (10).

92. See Meisler, *The Truth Is Out There*, 19.

93. Edwards quotes one of the producers of *The X-Files*, J. P. Finn: "We arrived at the same time as the Internet took off. We were probably the first show to be adopted by the Internet, and that drove the underground word of mouth. . . . Fox paid attention to it. It kept us going when the ratings weren't so great, and so we survived" (*X-Files Confidential*, 81–82). For an interesting essay on the role of the Internet in the success of *The X-Files*, and in particular a discussion of the way male and female fans react differently online, see Susan J. Clerc, "DDEB, GATB, MPPB, and Ratboy: *The X-Files'* Media Fandom, Online and Off," in Lavery, Hague, and Cartwright, "*Deny All Knowledge*," 36–51.

94. According to Lowry, "*The X-Files* launched its own World Wide Web site on June 12, 1995, but fans were becoming involved in the series well before that. Delphi, the on-line service, estimates that 25,000 people go in and out of sessions pertaining to the show on a monthly basis, more than all other Fox series available via the service combined" (*The Truth Is Out There*, 239). Lowry later reported of the Fox web site: "According to the studio, the show receives at least 1,000 visits and postings per day, more than any other television program" (*Trust No One*, 243).

95. On the way Carter and others involved in the production of *The X-Files* respond to the Internet, see Lowry, *The Truth Is Out There*, 242: Carter says of the Internet, "It's like an interactive tool for me"; Lowry, *Trust No One*, xviii, 238; and Clerc, "Media Fandom," 50. It is appropriate that perhaps the clearest impact that the Internet has had on *The X-Files* was in elevating the Lone Gunmen to regular characters. As Lowry reports: "the Lone Gunmen were initially thrown in for a laugh in this episode ["E.B.E."], and [writer Glen] Morgan wasn't happy with the result, feeling he and his partner had botched things a bit in terms of execution. 'We had kind of written them off,' he notes, until the producers started to hear about the response to the Gunmen along the Internet. That prompted a return appearance during the second season and eventually a recurring role on the series" (*The Truth Is Out There*, 140). On March 4, 2001, they finally got their own series on Fox, and they ultimately owe it all to the Internet.

96. The October 2000 issue of *Premiere* (Vol. 14, No. 2) is called "The Cyber Issue" and is devoted to the impact of the Internet on Hollywood. See especially the article with the *X-Files*-inspired title "The Websites Are Out There" (60–61).

97. On the merchandising of *The X-Files*, see Edwards, *X-Files Confidential*, 129, and also Reeves, Rodgers, and Epstein, "Rewriting Popularity," 22–23, 27–29 (who compare the series in this respect with *Star Trek*).

98. Lowry reports: "the first San Diego gathering was attended by roughly 2,500 people in June 1995. A total of 20 conventions have been scheduled through the end of calendar-year '95, with conservative estimates that 35,000 to 40,000 people will ultimately participate by the time the year's over" (*The Truth Is Out There*, 240). Meisler points out that "during the spring of 1998 more than 55,000 fans attended the official *X-Files* Expos" (*Resist or Serve*, 7).

99. Thus some fans have actually regretted the increased popularity of *The X-Files*; as Frank Spotnitz observes: "I think there's a nostalgia for the first season, when *The X-Files* was their own little discovery and there was a very small but intensely loyal audience for the show. Now I think a lot of people feel it's not just their private 'find' anymore. They are sharing it with a mass audience." Quoted in Edwards, *X-Files Confidential*, 131.

100. Reeves, Rodgers, and Epstein argue that for avid fans a favorite show becomes "a major source of self-definition, a kind of quasi-religious experience" ("Rewriting Popularity," 26).

101. Clerc observes that "to newcomers, this attitude reeks of elitism and snobbery, but for those in specialized groups sharing a competence level serves as a unifying factor" ("Media Fandom," 46).

102. On the economics and other details of shooting in Vancouver, see Lowry, *The Truth Is Out There*, 17, 32, 41, and Edwards, *X-Files Confidential*, 26.

103. On the casting of Canadians, see Lowry, *The Truth Is Out There*, 35. Among the Canadians in the regular cast of *The X-Files* have been Dean Haglund, Tom Braidwood, and Bruce Harwood (who play the Lone Gunmen), as well as Nicholas Lea (who plays Agent Krycek).

104. William B. Davis talks about having to be careful about his Canadian accent: "I have to watch my vowel sounds" (Lowry, *The Truth Is Out There*, 74). The producers were relieved when an episode was set in Maine ("Chinga")—"A Maine accent is quite similar to a Canadian accent, says Vancouver casting director Coreen Mayrs" (Meisler, *Resist or Serve*, 139).

105. Lowry, *Trust No One*, 79. The *X-Files* crew was not as lucky during the shooting of "El Mundo Gira," which is set in California though of course filmed in Vancouver. "Unfortunately, a freakish storm dumped several inches of snow onto the sun-baked 'San Joaquin Valley' the night before filming was to start. . . . Crew members scurried ahead of each camera setup, melting the snow with hot water and blow dryers" (Meisler, *I Want to Believe*, 123).

106. Director Rob Bowman saw it as a real challenge to "make an internment camp in Vancouver that looks anything like Virginia or the Carolinas" (Edwards, *X-Files Confidential*, 114).

107. *The X-Files* was actually "produced" in Los Angeles even while it was shot in Vancouver, thus complicating matters further; as Chris Carter said: "The drawback is that I'm sitting in Los Angeles right now while they're shooting up there and I can't walk over to the stage to make changes and tweaks" (Edwards, *X-Files Confidential*, 26).

108. The *X-Files* producers were actually worried about alienating part of their audience by seeming to raise doubts about the Internet; see Lowry, *Trust No One*, 108.

109. In the seventh season, *The X-Files* finally did its own version of *Cops*, appropriately called "X-Cops."

110. On the conscious use of *Speed* in this episode, see Meisler, *The End and the Beginning*, 27.

111. For what it is worth, Lowry reports: "In an interview David Duchovny once said that he would consider Mulder Jewish until told otherwise" (*The Truth Is Out There*, 142).

112. In "The Post-Modern Prometheus," Mulder criticizes this kind of obsession with television: "What we're seeing is an example of a culture for whom daytime talk shows and tabloid headlines have become a reality against which they measure their lives."

113. Meisler, *The End and the Beginning*, 29.

114. For details on these various military projects, see Meisler, *The End and the Beginning*, 29.

115. The movie contains references to both the Waco and the Ruby Ridge incidents, but characteristically does not explore them. In "The Field Where I Died," *The X-Files* had a perfect opportunity to examine the morality and legality of the federal government's actions against David Koresh and his followers at Waco—the episode deals with "an effort to prevent a mass suicide at a fanatical religious cult" (Meisler, *I Want to Believe*, 58). But in what seems like a failure of nerve, the episode drifts off into a strange story of reincarnation and the Civil War. With all its sympathies for cults, *The X-Files* shows very little sympathy for right-wing cults. Even in "The Pine Bluff Variant," the show does little to question federal government activities directed against right-wing figures outside the political mainstream.

116. We have seen that both *Gilligan's Island* and the original *Star Trek* TV series embodied a kind of frontier spirit and therefore a sense that America's history still lay ahead of it. The "running out of west" motif in *The X-Files* suggests, by contrast, a sense of belatedness—America's history now seems to lie behind it.

117. In *Inside Star Trek: The Real Story* (New York: Pocket, 1996), Herbert F. Solow and Robert H. Justman reprint the original NBC publicity material for *Star Trek* as a centerfold; on page 2, it says: "The *Enterprise's* mission includes scientific investigation and reconnaissance of previously unexplored worlds; providing aid and supplies for Earth colonies; diplomatic courtesy calls on alien civilizations; and the enforcement of laws regulating commerce with the Earth colonies." Even this original formulation has the ring of an activist government to it; evidently in a future Supreme Court decision, the Constitution's Commerce Clause was ruled as applying to interplanetary as well as interstate commerce.

118. See "The Devil in the Dark" and "The Cloudminders."

119. One way in which the later television versions of *Star Trek*, from "The Next Generation" on, have differed from the original series is that they have tended to present commerce as a more significant activity in space. They have not shown commerce in a particularly flattering light, as witness the portrayal of the Ferengis, but they have shown it as basic to the functioning of the cosmos. And even the Ferengis have had their moments and have earned a grudging respect over the years. I wish I had the space to analyze *Star Trek: The Next Generation* (which I personally prefer to the original series) and the later avatars of the show. Many of the points I have made about the differences between "national" and "global" television could be worked out in terms of the contrasts between the original *Star Trek* and the later versions.

120. On "the triumph of economics over politics" in the globalized world, see Cooper, "Integration and Disintegration," 38–39. One might say that *The Simpsons* answers *Star Trek's* "The Trouble with Tribbles" with its own "The Trouble with Trillions" (#5F14, 4/5/98), which, as we have seen, portrays government intervention in economic affairs negatively.

121. Lisa still aspires to be president in the series, but that seems to be specifically a feminist issue.

122. It is something of a mystery why Hollywood, which is so capitalist in practice, should be so anticapitalist in "theory." For thoughts on this subject, see Ludwig von Mises, *The Anti-Capitalistic Mentality* (Princeton, N.J.: Van Nostrand, 1956), especially 30–33, and Ben Stein, *The View from Sunset Boulevard: America as Brought to You by the People Who Make Television* (New York: Basic, 1979).

123. See "Mr. Plow" (#9F07, 11/19/92), "Colonel Homer" (#8F19, 3/26/92), and "The Wizard of Evergreen Terrace" (#5F21, 9/20/98).

124. This episode was broadcast on December 3, 2000. It contains a wonderful parody of, and hence a tribute to, the 1960s British TV series *The Prisoner* (broadcast 1967–68 in the U.K.; 1968–69 in the U.S.), which is one of the principal forerunners of *The X-Files*.

125. *The Simpsons* seems to comment negatively on such projects in "Marge vs. The Monorail" (#9F10, 1/14/93), which appropriately features Leonard Nimoy, the actor who portrayed Spock in *Star Trek*.

126. Once again offering a comic parallel to a serious *X-Files* episode, *The Simpsons* took on the tobacco industry in the November 7, 1999, episode in which Homer markets a product that blends tobacco and tomatoes, called tomacco.

127. Ridley Scott's *Blade Runner* (1982) is probably the most influential science fiction movie that develops the theme of corporate power.

128. I owe this observation to Michael Valdez Moses, who has explained a great deal about *The X-Files* to me over the years. In *The End of the Nation-State*, Guéhenno argues that in today's globalized world, the proper image for power is no longer a center but a network—"a world that is at once unified and without a center" (xii). He also calls this "the era of the diffusion of power—the era of power that cannot be located" (47). In a passage that particularly resonates with *The X-Files*, he says: "We are entering into the age of open systems, whether at the level of states or enterprises, and the criteria of success are diametrically different from those of the institutional age and its closed systems. The value of an organization is no longer measured by the equilibrium that it attempts to establish between its different parts, or by the clarity of its frontiers, but in the number of openings, of points of articulation that it can organize with everything external to it" (49). Consider also this passage: "The hierarchical, pyramidal structure, in which to be powerful was to control and command, is succeeded by a structure of diffusion of power, with multiple connections, in which to be powerful is to be in contact, in communication, and in which power is defined by influence and no longer by mastery" (62–63). See also 8–9, 56–57, 64, 98. In general, Guéhenno's book reads like a commentary on *The X-Files* and particularly its image of power as a network.

129. See "The End" and "Two Fathers." See also Guéhenno, *End of the Nation-State*: "The age of politics implicitly reproduces a mechanistic model of behavior, in conformity with a linear vision of power: in this model, we must have great causes to produce great effects, and great powers to conduct great policies. The age of the networks has no such ambition. In a century that has known two world wars, . . . it knows that strength is not a linear function of power and that, from small causes, can come great effects" (77).

130. See Guéhenno, *End of the Nation-State*: "In a system that is no longer governed by a pyramidal and centralized hierarchy, one can certainly hope that no breakdown, no sabotage is decisive; the circuits, the networks, recompose themselves around the affected zone, in an almost biological fashion. Nevertheless, the architecture of the networks, while it multiplies the possibilities for connection, also multiplies the possible points of attack" (120).

131. See "Ice" and "Tunguska"/"Terma."

132. Quoted in Meisler, *I Want to Believe*, 9. Guéhenno makes a similar comment on the fall of the Soviet Union: "This victory, still so recent, seems threatened, not

because the enemy is gathering strength—the threat of that would be more likely to rekindle the initial enthusiasm—but because we no longer know exactly who are the real enemies" (*End of the Nation-State*, 121).

133. See Guéhenno's formulation: "And the very volatility of the world in which all the elements are holding each other in place, and which a mere nothing can set in vibration, is at the heart of the modern angst" (*End of the Nation-State*, 83).

134. McLuhan was making this point long before the Internet: "Obsession with older patterns of mechanical, one-way expansion from centers to margins is no longer relevant to our electric world. Electricity does not centralize, but decentralizes. It is like the difference between a railway system and an electric grid system: the one requires railheads and big urban centers. Electric power, equally available in the farmhouse and the Executive Suite, permits any place to be a center" (*Understanding Media*, 36).

135. See especially "The Return of the Archons," "A Taste of Armageddon," and "The Apple." For other episodes that present computers in a negative light, see "The Changeling," "I, Mudd," and "The Ultimate Computer."

136. This and its companion episode feature a number of references to *Star Trek*, including a flashback scene of Mulder as a child wearing an outfit from the earlier series.

137. Graham discusses the importance of the Vietnam War in *The X-Files* ("Conspiracy Theory," 61). That the evil consequences of the Vietnam War are still haunting the United States is the subject of several *X-Files* episodes, including "Sleepless," "Avatar," and "Unrequited."

138. In a comic variation on this kind of serious debate, *The Simpsons* frequently distinguishes between "Veterans of Popular Wars" and "Veterans of Unpopular Wars."

139. See, for example, "E.B.E.," which begins with a UFO shot down over Iraq and ends with Deep Throat revealing that he once executed an alien shot down over Hanoi.

140. For a trenchant critique of this view of the relation of business and the military, see Mises, *Nation, State, and Economy*, 154–55.

141. "Redux" is one of the most anti-American of all *X-Files* episodes; Kritschgau goes on to suggest that the United States used biological weapons in the Gulf War.

142. See Guéhenno, "Globalization and Fragmentation," 14–15.

143. Graham does a wonderful job of showing how the year 1947 functions in the mythology of *The X-Files*: "That year—the beginning of the cold war, the year Nixon first took office in Congress as the coldest of warriors and the House Un-American Activities Commission [sic] (HUAC) began 'investigating' communist 'infiltration' in the media, and the year of the Roswell crash—was also the year (according to the series) when the Jersey Devil first appeared, when alien tissues were first collected by the government, and when the governments of the United States, the Soviet Union, China, both Germanies, Britain, and France secretly agreed to 'exterminate' any alien retrieved from a UFO crash" ("Conspiracy Theory," 58).

144. See, for example, "Deep Throat," "Space," and "Little Green Men."

145. A typical example is the *World of National Geographic* documentary, "Asteroids: Deadly Impact."

146. In "Bart's Comet" (#2F11, 2/15/95), *The Simpsons* specifically ridicules government efforts to use rockets to destroy threatening objects from space.

147. Badley observes: "As extraterrestrial-multinational conspiracy theories proliferate, in episodes set in railroad cars, mass graves, and conflagrations, the autopsied alien is increasingly identified with victims of covert medical, military, and government experiments. Reversing the alien invasion scenario, the alien body comes to stand metonymically for all marginalization and commodification of human bodies: the holocaust Japanese internment camps, a leper colony in North Carolina, Native American survivors, and implanted female abductees" ("Rebirth of the Clinic," 151).

148. See Lowry, *The Truth Is Out There*, 237–38, and Edwards, *X-Files Confidential*, 142.

149. On this point, see Badley, "Rebirth of the Clinic," 150–51, who argues: "The alien abduction and the alien autopsy are reverse mirror images proclaiming the same thing, that aliens R US."

150. I keep citing the bizarre "Musings" episode, even though I am aware that it is a fantasy, that is, it shows the Cigarette-Smoking Man the way he imagines himself to be, not the way he "really" is (or perhaps just the way Frohike imagines him to be). Hatfield and Burt report: "William Davis, who plays the enigmatic Cigarette-Smoking Man, asked Chris Carter if the episode was the actual backstory of his character, to which *The X-Files* creator firmly replied, 'No.'" (*X-Cyclopedia*, 237). Nevertheless, even the CSM's fantasies reveal something about his character.

151. The literature on this subject is vast, but three books I have found particularly helpful are Thomas L. Friedman, *The Lexus and the Olive Tree* (New York: Random House, 2000); Richard Rosecrance, *The Rise of the Virtual State: Wealth and Power in the Coming Century* (New York: Basic, 1999); and Daniel Yergin and Joseph Stanislaw, *The Commanding Heights: The Battle between Government and the Marketplace That Is Remaking the Modern World* (New York: Simon & Schuster, 1999).

152. Again, the literature on this subject is vast; two of the books I have found most helpful are Guéhenno's *The End of the Nation-State* and van Creveld's *The Rise and Decline of the State*; to those I would add Kenichi Ohmae, *The End of the Nation State: The Rise of Regional Economies* (New York: Free Press, 1995).

153. On this point, see Mises, *Nation, State, and Economy*, 64.

154. See Guéhenno, *End of the Nation-State*, 10–11, 15.

155. On the historicity and contingency of the nation-state, see Ohmae, *Regional Economies*, 99–100 and especially 141: "In the broad sweep of history, nation states have been a transitional form of organization for managing economic affairs." See also van Creveld, *Rise and Decline*, 415, and Guéhenno, *End of the Nation-State*, xii: "This political form, far more European than is the idea of empire, has imposed itself upon the world in the past two centuries, and we have taken for an inevitable ending point what is perhaps only the precarious result of a rare historical conjunction, closely linked to particular circumstances, and which could disappear with them." For another effort to define and delimit the nation-state as a historical phenomenon, see Walter C. Opello Jr. and Stephen J. Rosow, *The Nation-State and Global Order: A Historical Introduction to Contemporary Politics* (Boulder, Colo.: Lynne Rienner, 1999).

156. For a similar formulation of this challenge, see Philippe C. Schmitter, "Democracy, the EU, and the Question of Scale," in Plattner and Smolar, *Globalization*, 43.

In *The X-Files* challenges indeed tend to come from below and above—either monsters coming up out of the bowels of the earth or aliens descending from the skies.

CONCLUSION

1. For other references to *The Simpsons* in *The X-Files*, see "Anasazi," in which the Thinker uses an image of Homer as a screen-saver on his computer, and "Revelations," in which Mulder refers to one character as looking like "Homer Simpson's evil twin." See James Hatfield and George Burt, *The Unauthorized X-Cyclopedia* (New York: MJF, 1997), 309.

2. Among the many episodes that deal with Scully's faith, see, for example, "Miracle Man," "Revelations," "Gethsemane," "Christmas Carol," "Emily," "All Souls," and "All Things."

3. Among the many episodes that deal with religious figures, see, for example, "Miracle Man," "Revelations," "Millennium," and "Orison."

4. *The X-Files Official Magazine* 4, No. 3 (Fall 2000): 48.

5. This sequence gives a whole new twist to the American agrarian ideal we saw celebrated in *Gilligan's Island*.

6. As we have seen happen before in *The X-Files*, the buried issue in "Home" may well be race. The sheriff is black and the Peacocks are white; as a result, the most violent image in the episode is of three white men beating a black man and his wife to death. That the Peacocks are clearly associated in the episode with the cause of the South in the Civil War makes them prime candidates to represent racism. "Home" may be hinting at a connection between a small-town mentality and racism. The great irony in the nostalgia of the episode is of course that the sheriff of TV's Mayberry would never have been a black man—a comment on both small towns in the South and network television in the 1960s. The more one analyzes "Home," the more one realizes that it is merciless in its debunking of the tendency—especially the tendency of 1960s television—to idealize a small-town past in America that is largely a fiction. In a strange way, "Home" is really *The X-Files'* answer to *The Simpsons* and its celebration of both the nuclear family and the small town. The Peacocks are the ultimate dysfunctional nuclear family—and at the same time the most tightly knit. And they are nothing to laugh at.

7. I realize that there is a logical fallacy in suggesting that the only alternative to full-scale globalization is the nuclear family—it is called the Fallacy of the Excluded Middle. Even a show as dumb as *Gilligan's Island* is smart enough to know that happy mediums are sometimes possible. As we have seen, the show holds up an ideal halfway between utter primitivism and hypercivilization. Rousseau is a good example of a brilliant thinker who argued that there are ways for humanity to leave an animal-like state of nature and still stop short of an overly developed form of civilization that destroys its happiness. Thus I am open to arguments against globalization that suggest that smaller forms of community might preserve the real benefits of civilization, while avoiding some of its principal defects. Nevertheless, I also see the point of the argument that would say that once humanity leaves behind the autarchic ideal represented by the nuclear family, it is driven to expand its webs of interdependence, chiefly

economic, until they encompass the entire globe. And even if the nation-state turns out to be inferior to smaller communities as a form of organization, (as Rousseau was in effect arguing), the answer may not be to return to those smaller communities, but to try to advance beyond the nation-state to new forms of organization that can remedy its defects. These are immensely complicated issues that I cannot hope to settle in this book, but I am grateful to *X-Files* episodes such as "Home" for helping to open them up.

Index

About the Author

Paul A. Cantor received his B.A. and Ph.D. from Harvard University, where he taught as an assistant professor from 1971 to 1977. He is currently professor of English at the University of Virginia. From 1992 to 1999, he served on the National Council on the Humanities. He is the author of *Shakespeare's Rome, Creature and Creator,* and the *Hamlet* volume in the Cambridge Landmarks of World Literature Series. His essays on popular culture have appeared in *The Weekly Standard, The American Enterprise, Reason, The Free Market,* and other journals.